D0910577

Living and Working in
Germany

A Survival Handbook

Edited by
Pamela Wilson

SURVIVAL BOOKS • LONDON • ENGLAND

First published 2000
Second Edition 2003
Third Edition 2008

Survival Books Limited
26 York Street, London W1U 6PZ, United Kingdom
☎ +44 (0)20-7788 7644, 🖷 +44 (0)870-762 3212
✉ info@survivalbooks.net
🖥 www.survivalbooks.net

British Library Cataloguing in Publication Data.
A CIP record for this book is available
from the British Library.
ISBN-10: 1-905303-36-X
ISBN-13: 978-1-905303-36-6

Printed and bound in Finland by WS Bookwell Ltd.

ACKNOWLEDGEMENTS

My sincere thanks to all those who contributed to the successful publication of the third edition of this book, in particular Joe Laredo (proofreading) and Kerry Laredo (typesetting and layout). Also a special mention to the many people who assisted with the first edition – written by Nick Daws – including Bev Laflamme, Iva Pearlstein, Norman and Su Griffiths, Ralph Lohmann, Alf B. Meier and Roberta Beach Jacobson, and the second edition – edited by Dan Finlay – including Kathryn Dingle of Deutsche Bahn, Dr. Friedrich Lampe, Jürgen Ebert of the Postbank. I must also express thanks to the many people who took the trouble to read and comment on the draft versions, including Dave Thomas, Anita and Joerg Epple, and Karen Verheul. Also a special thank you to Jim Watson for the cover design, illustrations, cartoons and map.

TITLES BY SURVIVAL BOOKS

The Best Places To Buy A Home
France; Spain

Buying a Home
Australia; Bulgaria, Cyprus; France;
Greece; Italy; New Zealand;
Portugal; Spain;
Buying, Selling & Letting Property (UK)

Buying and Renting a Home
London; New York

Culture Wise
Australia; Canada; England; France;
New Zealand; Spain

**Foreigners Abroad: Triumphs
& Disasters**
France; Spain

Living and Working
America; Australia; Britain
Canada; France; Germany

The Gulf States & Saudi Arabia;
Ireland; Italy;
London; New Zealand;
Spain; Switzerland

Earning Money from Your Home
France; Spain

Making a Living
France; Spain

Retiring Abroad
France; Spain

Other Titles
Investing in Property Abroad;
Renovating & Maintaining
Your French Home;
Running Gîtes and B&Bs in France;
Rural Living in France;
Shooting Caterpillars in Spain;
Wild Thyme in Ibiza

WHAT READERS & REVIEWERS

When you buy a model plane for your child, a video recorder, or some new computer gizmo, you get with it a leaflet or booklet pleading 'Read Me First', or bearing large friendly letters or bold type saying 'IMPORTANT – follow the instructions carefully'. This book should be similarly supplied to all those entering France with anything more durable than a 5-day return ticket. It is worth reading even if you are just visiting briefly, or if you have lived here for years and feel totally knowledgeable and secure. But if you need to find out how France works then it is indispensable. Native French people probably have a less thorough understanding of how their country functions. – Where it is most essential, the book is most up to the minute.

LIVING FRANCE

Rarely has a 'survival guide' contained such useful advice. This book dispels doubts for first-time travellers, yet is also useful for seasoned globetrotters – In a word, if you're planning to move to the USA or go there for a long-term stay, then buy this book both for general reading and as a ready-reference.

AMERICAN CITIZENS ABROAD

It is everything you always wanted to ask but didn't for fear of the contemptuous put down – The best English-language guide – Its pages are stuffed with practical information on everyday subjects and are designed to complement the traditional guidebook.

SWISS NEWS

A complete revelation to me – I found it both enlightening and interesting, not to mention amusing.

CAROLE CLARK

Let's say it at once. David Hampshire's *Living and Working in France* is the best handbook ever produced for visitors and foreign residents in this country; indeed, my discussion with locals showed that it has much to teach even those born and bred in l'Hexagone. – It is Hampshire's meticulous detail which lifts his work way beyond the range of other books with similar titles. Often you think of a supplementary question and search for the answer in vain. With Hampshire this is rarely the case. – He writes with great clarity (and gives French equivalents of all key terms), a touch of humour and a ready eye for the odd (and often illuminating) fact. – This book is absolutely indispensable.

THE RIVIERA REPORTER

A mine of information – I may have avoided some embarrassments and frights if I had read it prior to my first Swiss encounters – Deserves an honoured place on any newcomer's bookshelf.

ENGLISH TEACHERS ASSOCIATION, SWITZERLAND

HAVE SAID ABOUT SURVIVAL BOOKS

What a great work, wealth of useful information, well-balanced wording and accuracy in details. My compliments!

THOMAS MÜLLER

This handbook has all the practical information one needs to set up home in the UK – The sheer volume of information is almost daunting – Highly recommended for anyone moving to the UK.

AMERICAN CITIZENS ABROAD

A very good book which has answered so many questions and even some I hadn't thought of – I would certainly recommend it.

BRIAN FAIRMAN

We would like to congratulate you on this work: it is really super! We hand it out to our expatriates and they read it with great interest and pleasure.

ICI (SWITZERLAND) AG

Covers just about all the things you want to know on the subject – In answer to the desert island question about the one how-to book on France, this book would be it – Almost 500 pages of solid accurate reading – This book is about enjoyment as much as survival.

THE RECORDER

It's so funny – I love it and definitely need a copy of my own – Thanks very much for having written such a humorous and helpful book.

HEIDI GUILIANI

A must for all foreigners coming to Switzerland.

ANTOINETTE O'DONOGHUE

A comprehensive guide to all things French, written in a highly readable and amusing style, for anyone planning to live, work or retire in France.

THE TIMES

A concise, thorough account of the DOs and DON'Ts for a foreigner in Switzerland – Crammed with useful information and lightened with humorous quips which make the facts more readable.

AMERICAN CITIZENS ABROAD

Covers every conceivable question that may be asked concerning everyday life – I know of no other book that could take the place of this one.

FRANCE IN PRINT

Hats off to *Living and Working in Switzerland*!

RONNIE ALMEIDA

THE EDITOR

Minnesota-born Pamela Wilson has lived in Germany for over ten years. After obtaining a Master's degree in Art History, she worked as an archaeologist in Egypt and in Germany, where she helped excavate a Roman military camp. Moving to Munich, she became an English teacher and subsequently a pedagogical supervisor for a language school. Pamela's writing experience includes writing a monthly travel guide about Munich and Bavaria, and researching and editing a safety guide for travellers to Germany. She met her husband at the Munich Oktoberfest and they now have a son. Pamela has recently written *Culture Wise Germany* for Survival Books, due to be published in 2008.

CONTENTS

11. MOTORING 209

12. HEALTH 253

16. SPORTS 333

17. SHOPPING 349

IMPORTANT NOTE

Germany is a diverse country with many faces, a variety of ethnic groups, religions and customs, as well as continuously changing rules, regulations (particularly regarding business, social security and taxes), interest rates and prices. A change of government in Germany can have far-reaching effects on many important aspects of life. **I cannot recommend too strongly that you check with an official and reliable source (not always the same) before making any major decisions, or taking an irreversible course of action. However, don't believe everything you're told or read – even, dare I say it, herein!**

Useful addresses and references to other sources of information have been included in all chapters and in **Appendices A to C** to help you obtain further information and verify details with official sources. Important points have been emphasised, **in bold print**, some of which it would be expensive, or even dangerous, to disregard. **Ignore them at your peril or cost.** Unless specifically stated, the reference to any company, organisation or product in this book doesn't constitute an endorsement or recommendation.

Editor's Notes

- Frequent references are made in this book to the European Union (EU), which comprises Austria, Belgium, Bulgaria, Cyprus, the Czech Republic, Denmark, Estonia, Finland, France, Germany, Greece, Hungary, Ireland, Italy, Latvia, Lithuania, Luxembourg, Malta, the Netherlands, Poland, Portugal, Romania, Slovak Republic, Slovenia, Spain, Sweden and the United Kingdom, and the European Economic Area (EEA), which includes the EU countries plus Iceland, Liechtenstein and Norway.

- The former East Germany or the German Democratic Republic (Deutsche Demokratische Republik or DDR) comprises the following federal states: Mecklenburg-Western Pomerania, Brandenburg, Saxony-Anhalt, Thuringia, Saxony and the eastern part of Berlin. The remaining 11 federal states (see **Appendix E**) belonged to the Federal Republic of Germany (FDR), which is now the name of the whole of Germany.

- Times are shown using am for before noon and pm for after noon (see also **Time Difference** on page 390).

- Prices should be taken as estimates only, though they were mostly correct at the time of publication. Unless otherwise stated, all prices quoted usually include VAT (*Mehrwertsteuer/MwSt* or *Umsatzsteuer/USt*) at 19 per cent.

- His/he/him also means her/she/her (please forgive me ladies). This is done to make life easier for both the reader and (in particular) the author, and isn't intended to be sexist.

- The German translation of many key words and phrases is shown in brackets in *italics*.

- All references to Frankfurt are to Frankfurt-am-Main and not Frankfurt-an-der-Oder.

- Warnings and important points are shown in **bold** type.

- The following symbols are used in this book: ☎ (telephone), ▤ (fax), 🖳 (internet) and ✉ (email).

- Lists of further information sources, further reading material and useful websites are contained in **Appendices A** to **C** respectively.

- For those unfamiliar with the metric system of weights and measures, imperial conversion tables are included in **Appendix D**.

- A map of Germany showing the states (*Länder*) is included in **Appendix E**.

INTRODUCTION

Whether you're already living or working in Germany or just thinking about it – this is **THE BOOK** for you. Forget about all those glossy guidebooks, excellent though they are for tourists; this amazing book was written particularly with you in mind and is worth its weight in frankfurters. *Living and Working in Germany* is designed to meet the needs of anyone wishing to know the essentials of German life, including immigrants, temporary workers, businessmen, students, retirees, long-stay tourists and holiday homeowners. However long your intended stay in Germany, you'll find the information in this book invaluable.

General information isn't difficult to find in Germany (provided you speak German) and a multitude of books are published on every conceivable subject. However, reliable and up-to-date information in English specifically intended for foreigners living and working in Germany isn't so easy to find, least of all in one volume. Our aim in publishing this book was to fill this void and provide the comprehensive, practical information necessary for a trouble-free life.

You may have visited Germany as a tourist, but living and working there is a different matter altogether. Adjusting to a different environment and culture and making a home in any foreign country can be a traumatic and stressful experience, and Germany is no exception. You need to adapt to new customs and traditions and discover the German way of doing things – from saying 'hello' to hanging out your washing. For most foreigners in Germany, overcoming the everyday obstacles of life has previously been a case of trial and error. **But no more!** With a copy of *Living and Working in Germany* to hand, you'll have a wealth of information at your fingertips – information derived from a variety of sources, both official and unofficial, not least the hard-won personal experiences of the editor and her family, friends, colleagues and acquaintances.

Living and Working in Germany is a comprehensive handbook on a wide range of everyday subjects and represents the most up-to-date source of general information available to foreigners in Germany. It isn't simply a monologue of dry facts and figures, but an entertaining and occasionally humorous look at life in Germany. It doesn't, however, contain all the answers (most of us don't even know the right questions to ask!). Adapting to life in a new country is a continuous process, but this book will help reduce your beginner's phase and minimise frustrations by enabling you to make informed decisions and calculated judgements, rather than uneducated guesses and costly mistakes. **Most importantly, it will help save you time, trouble and money, and repay your investment many times over.**

Although you may find some of the information a bit daunting, don't be discouraged. Most problems occur only once and fade into insignificance after a short time (as you face the next half a dozen!). The majority of foreigners in Germany would agree that, all things considered, they enjoy living there. A period spent in Germany is a wonderful way to enrich your life, broaden your horizons and hopefully please your bank manager. I trust that this book will help you avoid the pitfalls of life in Germany and smooth your way to a happy and rewarding future in your new home.

Viel Glück!   **Pamela Wilson**
                                                                 November 2007

1.

FINDING A JOB

German workers enjoy high salaries, with generous benefits and job protection mandated by the state, thanks to years of negotiation and co-operation between employers and national trade unions. Finding a job in Germany, however, is anything but plain sailing, as the high unemployment figures (currently 9.5 per cent) suggest. If you're well qualified and experienced, and have lots of perseverance and at least some luck, you'll find that openings in various sectors do exist. At the bottom end of the scale are jobs that most Germans aren't willing to do (being unemployed in Germany is often a considerably more comfortable proposition than being fully employed on a low wage), although the number of foreigners willing to do them has increased. If you're a national of a European Union (EU) country, you'll (at least theoretically) be on an equal footing with the locals in the job hunt. Americans and others without an automatic right to work in Germany must meet visa and work permit requirements (see **Chapter 3**) in order for a prospective employer to justify hiring them in preference to an EU national.

The Germans have for half a century taken great pride in their role as leaders of the European economy and champions of industrial productivity and engineering excellence. The title of engineer (*Ingenieur*) carries considerable prestige, and degrees and other qualifications are proudly displayed on business cards and letterheads. Education is highly prized in Germany and many engineers in industry have earned doctorates. (It's common for engineers to become company bosses.) German national apprenticeship and on-the-job training programmes are the envy of the world, and for good reason. German workers are renowned for their high levels of skill and efficiency.

In the '60s and '70s, the Federal Republic recruited large numbers of foreign workers, euphemistically called 'guest workers' (*Gastarbeiter*), mostly from Mediterranean countries, in response to labour shortages. Many guest workers stayed on as long-term residents, so that by the end of 1994 there were over 2m foreigners employed in western Germany, the largest national groups being (in diminishing order) those from Turkey, the states of the former Yugoslavia, Greece and Italy. The now defunct German Democratic Republic recruited a number of Vietnamese workers, several thousand of whom now live and work in what was formerly East Germany.

Nowadays, from the outside, the German labour market looks completely self-sufficient, with none of the shortages of unskilled labour of the type that made the *Gastarbeiter* necessary, and German companies involved in international markets don't have to look to foreigners for general language skills, as local schools turn out enough individuals fluent in English and other foreign languages.

EMPLOYMENT PROSPECTS

To find employment in Germany takes special qualifications or experience in a field or profession where demand matches or exceeds supply. Unless you're intending to seek out a job in the upper echelons of a multi-national organisation, one which has connections with an English-speaking country, certain scientific or academic areas in which English is the *lingua franca*, or in a sector such as IT in which demand greatly exceeds supply, it's essential to have at least a good working knowledge of German. Fluency is always highly desirable. Most Germans study English at school and, although only a small proportion are fluent, enough are sufficiently competent to make a native command of English less of an automatic advantage in the job market unless you have complementary skills or experience.

The free public education system is geared toward producing highly skilled workers through on-the-job training and apprenticeship programmes as well as a large academic elite. By the time a young German has earned his qualifications, he has considerable first-hand experience of the profession or trade he's entering. Surprisingly, however, there are still some areas where training programmes haven't kept up with demand and, if you have experience in one of these, your prospects of finding a job may be good, even with no German initially.

Information and communication technology (IT) is the principal area of demand, with around 20,000 available positions. Qualified professionals in IT and natural scientists (biologists, chemists, physicists) engineers and professors are eligible under the German Immigration Act, 2005 to receive permanent residence straightaway (one normally has to wait a minimum of five years) on condition that they have a firm job offer and request permission from the German Federal Labour Office. Other areas where there's currently a shortage of qualified staff, especially engineers, are the automobile, chemical, health and machine tool industries.

Although most opportunities are in western Germany, resolute job seekers with much-needed management and organisational skills, and the patience to effect lasting change, may find opportunities in eastern areas.

In order to find a job in Germany, it's important to have a positive reason for living and working there – being fed up with your boss or your job isn't the best motive for moving there. It helps if you can show that you have friends or family in the area, or the experience of living or working abroad. Having a genuine interest in German culture or specific aspects of German society can give you added credibility in the job search, as well as greatly enhancing your stay in the country.

UNEMPLOYMENT

Like much of the rest of Europe, Germany continues to struggle with a high rate of unemployment, although it's steadily declining. In April 2007, it stood at 9.5 per cent, a significant decrease from April 2006 (12 per cent). However, this figure masks a sharp disparity between the regions of the former Federal Republic ('West Germany') and those of the erstwhile German Democratic Republic

(*Deutsche Demokratische Republik/DDR*) or 'East Germany', now called the *neue Länder*, where the unemployment rate is over double that in the former West Germany: 15.9 per cent compared with 7.8. (The southern states Bavaria and Baden-Württemberg have the healthiest unemployment rate at around 5-6 per cent.) In the old *DDR*, everyone had the right to a job by constitutional decree, so most state-run companies (and virtually all companies were state run) were vastly overstaffed. Unemployment soared in the wake of the closure, reorganisation and privatisation of these companies, and the entire population had to be re-educated in free enterprise, market economics and competitive management techniques. Despite the strides made in the east since reunification, there's still a lingering sense of 'foreignness' between the *Ossies* (residents of the former East Germany) and the *Wessies* (those from the former West Germany), which is likely to persist for some time.

In both parts of Germany, massive 'over-production' of qualified people in many occupations adds to unemployment; there simply aren't enough new jobs created each year to absorb the influx of highly trained, highly skilled workers into the labour force. Official statistics show that more than half a million foreigners are in the ranks of the unemployed.

ECONOMY

Germany is one of the world's wealthiest countries, despite currently enduring its worst economic problems for almost half a century, with one of the highest per capita gross domestic products (GDPs) in the EU at $33,854. It's also the world's largest exporter, and its inflation rate (1.7 per cent in the 12 months to March 2007) is invariably among the lowest in industrialised countries.

Thanks in part to its generous social security system, along with the distaste of Germany's wealthy classes for conspicuous consumption and their tendency to understatement, extremes of wealth and poverty aren't apparent as in some other European countries. Cynics may claim that it's difficult to become rich in Germany because of the high tax rates, particularly on income from 'speculative' activity, and it's true that those who have made fortunes have almost invariably built them up through hard work over a long period and that people rarely become millionaires 'overnight' in Germany. This minimises social resentments. There's also somewhat less stigma attached to receiving social benefits than in many other countries, and the state benefits system provides a reasonable, if not exactly luxurious, standard of living for those who have fallen on hard times (although more people fall through its safety net than casual observers notice).

The Germans are justifiably proud of their successes in what they refer to as a 'social market economy'. Less *dirigiste* than their French counterparts, German governments have fostered competition in the marketplace and encouraged enterprise among individuals and businesses. However, the government exercises considerable control over business, both by direct regulation and through high taxes on income and capital; its purpose is to protect economic equilibrium by promoting price stability, high employment, balanced imports and exports, and continuous growth.

A good deal of Germany's success over the last 50 years has been due to the rise of middle-size companies – family-owned and operated industries often started after the Second World War. Many of these companies made excellent use of German engineering skills to produce high quality industrial products known and sold around the world. At the start of the new millennium, however, many of these highly successful companies are facing a crisis of transition, as the founders reach retirement age and must decide whether to keep the business in the family, sell it or merge with larger companies or corporations. In many cases, their children aren't interested in carrying on the family business or face considerable difficulties in changing the company culture and image to reflect their own management ideas.

The reunification of Germany in 1991 carried an enormous price tag, particularly given the government's decision to integrate the two radically different economies as quickly as possible. Much of the infrastructure of the former East Germany had to be rebuilt, with concepts of efficiency and profitability introduced into what for the previous 50 years had been a centrally planned economy. The one-for-one exchange rate agreed for the Ostmark and the Deutschmark meant that the East lost its considerable export markets and competitive edge in eastern Europe, while any incentive to invest in eastern Germany was lost because there was no economic advantage to it.

Among the many unpleasant surprises to hit western Germans on reunification was the damage done to the environment in the east. Pollution of the air, water and land was much worse than many had expected, and the cost of the clean-up operation, combined with the creation (almost overnight) of an elaborate benefit structure in the former *DDR*, have meant that taxes in Germany, on business and personal income as well as capital, are now among the highest in Europe. This further restricts the ability of businesses to create and sustain employment.

This lack of foresight as to the financial implications of reunification coupled with the constraints imposed by the euro left the German government in a difficult situation, which led to heavy borrowing and a huge national deficit that exceeded the EU borrowing limit of 3 per cent. German companies were forced to put expansion on hold, transfer parts of their operations to cheaper countries, contract out, or in some cases go bust. The present administration (elected at the end of 2005) has implemented strict reforms to reduce the deficit and boost economic growth including reductions in subsidies, the closing of tax loopholes and increased taxes. Value added tax (*Mehwertsteuer/MWST*) has gone up a whopping three per cent to 19 per cent, which has decreased consumer purchasing, while healthcare costs have increased proportionately. To offset this, business taxes have been decreased moderately. Although these changes slightly reduced growth at the outset, they're expected to boost growth by the end of 2007 by around 2 per cent. The deficit fell to a healthier 1.3 per cent of GDP in 2006 (well below the 3 per cent EU limit) and it's steadily declining. Unemployment is still high, at 9.5 per cent, but is also gradually decreasing.

Despite its economic difficulties, Germany remains the leading exporter in the world, with over €894bn in exports in 2006 – more than half of which goes to other EU countries (73 per cent to Europe as a whole), 9 per cent to the US, and some 2.4 per cent to Japan – and the second-largest importer. In 2005, Germany's trade surplus was an incredible €160bn. German products are world renowned for their quality, reliability and state-of-the-art engineering. They rarely compete on price, but provide good value given the standards they exemplify.

Manufacturing and service industries predominate, and Germany is the third-largest producer of cars in the world (including Audi, BMW, Mercedes, Opel, Porsche and Volkswagen). In 2006 4.2m cars were exported, primarily to the US, the UK and Italy. Other major sectors include chemicals, iron and steel, transport equipment, electrical machinery, generators, machine tools, communications equipment, food and drink. Agriculture, forestry and fishing form a relatively small part of the economy, employing 2.4 per cent of the workforce and contributing just 1.2 per cent of gross national product (GNP), yet Germany is still almost 90 per cent self-sufficient in food. Service industries, on the other hand, account for over 60 per cent of all jobs.

INDUSTRIAL RELATIONS

Strikes in Germany are fairly rare, although much more frequent than they used to be. Like many other aspects of German society, they're strictly controlled by laws and regulations. Civil servants (*Beamte*) aren't permitted to strike at all.

Germany has a number of large, powerful national unions, which negotiate regional contracts with employers' groups representing specific industries. A regional contract is binding on all companies within that industry and region, whether they're part of the employers' group or not, although it has recently been proposed that firms be allowed to negotiate wage rises according to their financial situation.

In the last 50 years, relations between the unions and employers' organisations have tended to be cordial and constructive, both sides willing to compromise in the interest of saving or creating jobs. The more stressful economic climate of recent years is, however, threatening to erode this consensual approach.

All businesses with more than a few employees may establish an elected works council (*Betriebsrat*), made up of worker representatives, who have an advisory role in management affairs. The works council must be consulted on all significant management decisions, including the hiring and firing of key executives, lay-offs and plant closures, and must be regularly informed about the state of a business. Individuals serving on a works council enjoy privileges and guaranteed job protection under labour law; in larger companies representatives of the works council are guaranteed a certain number of seats on the board of directors. They may work closely with local unions but aren't required to be members themselves. Works council decisions can override even those of regionally organised trade unions under certain circumstances.

WORK ATTITUDES

Traditional German companies – particularly small and medium-size enterprises, whose owner-managers comprise a recognised social class, called the *Mittelstand* – often have a strict hierarchical structure with formalised relations between management and workers. Jobs and job titles are often strictly defined by regional industry contracts, with legal distinctions between workers and management. Neither group is keen to take on responsibilities outside their defined duties. Experience, maturity and loyalty are highly valued and the frequent changing of jobs as a way of increasing your salary or promotion prospects is rare. However, this is beginning to change, particularly in high-tech industries and multi-national companies.

It's expensive to hire and fire employees in Germany, and the works council (*Betriebsrat*) often has the right to review candidates and offer suggestions regarding personnel decisions, even where upper management positions are involved. The process of hiring new employees (particularly managers and executives) and making business decisions is slower in Germany than in many other developed countries. This is due more to the various levels of review and approval required than to indecision.

On the other hand, snap decision making is considered suspect, and German managers generally prefer to rely on careful planning and a rational, considered approach to solving problems. As a result, many foreigners, particularly Americans, find that they must adjust to a more deliberate pace of working life in Germany.

German managers and executives rarely take work home, and they never work at weekends, which are sacrosanct. Many businesses close for two or three weeks during the summer, and employees are generally expected to take the bulk of their annual leave during this period. Many union contracts stipulate the closing dates each year to coincide with the region's school holiday calendar.

Time spent in the office or on the job is generally highly productive, with little or no time wasted on socialising or idle chatter, except during official (and short) break periods. Socialising with colleagues is usually done primarily in formal settings such as the annual company outing, holiday gatherings and other events.

WORKING WOMEN

Women in Germany comprise around 45 per cent of the workforce and generally enjoy legal protection from discrimination in the hiring process. However around a third of the female workforce works only part time, compared with just 3 per cent of men. There are a number of laws designed to protect women (*Frauenarbeitsschutz*) from dangerous jobs, excessive overtime or late working. Maternity leave is generous and time off for family duties (including caring for sick children) is a basic legal right. This can work against women, as many employers are reluctant to hire women of child-bearing age for jobs involving lifting, for example, which would have to be modified during pregnancy (and the law requires a female employee to notify her employer as soon as she knows she's pregnant). Other employers may fear losing a key supervisor or manager to extended maternity leave at a crucial point in the business cycle.

Women don't have professional and salary equality with men. There are still few top-level women managers and executives, women are paid on average 29 per cent less for the same work and women continue to hold the majority of part-time and lower paid jobs, as in other countries. On the other hand, women are well represented in the political sphere in Germany (i.e. Angela Merkel) and there's an active women's movement. Women enter the German university system in roughly equal numbers to men, but far fewer complete the rigorous business and engineering programmes required for managerial and executive level jobs. Women in management fields may have some difficulty establishing credibility with older, more 'traditional' bosses or colleagues.

Young women eager for high-paying employment in Germany have been tempted by organised criminal gangs promising jobs, only to find themselves part of prostitution or 'white slavery' rings.

GERMANY & THE EUROPEAN UNION

Germany was one of the six founder members of the European Community (now the European Union or EU) in 1957, along with Belgium, France, Italy, Luxembourg and the Netherlands. The German government has been a driving force behind the extension of EU membership to poorer countries in eastern and southern Europe, including its neighbours the Czech Republic and Poland, who joined in 2004 along with Cyprus, Estonia, Hungary, Latvia, Lithuania, Malta, the Slovak Republic, and Slovenia. The latest additions to the EU were Romania and Bulgaria in 2007.

Nationals of 'old' EU states (pre-2004) have the right to work in Germany or any other member state without a work permit, provided they have a valid passport or national identity card and comply with the member state's laws and regulations on employment. Nationals of new EU states must apply for a work permit, but after one year may be eligible for a unrestricted work permit. All EU nationals are entitled to the same treatment as German citizens in matters of pay, working conditions, access to housing, vocational training, social security and trade union rights, and their families and dependants are entitled to join them and enjoy the same rights.

There are, however, still barriers to full freedom of movement and the right to work within the EU. For example, certain jobs in various member countries require job applicants to have specific skills or vocational qualifications. The EU has developed a general system for the recognition of professional and trade qualifications and guidelines for mutual recognition of qualifications (see below). Nevertheless, there are restrictions on employment in the civil service, where the right to work may be limited in individual cases on grounds of public policy, national security or public health. Differences persist among the various German states regarding the civil service status of some occupations, particularly teachers and health professionals.

QUALIFICATIONS

A remarkable number of jobs are regulated, at least to the extent of requiring a formal qualification. Most qualifications involve a training programme lasting at least two years, with or without supervised on-the-job experience or a formal apprenticeship. Germany has a world-renowned apprenticeship system and offers its young people a dizzying array of training programmes when they finish their school careers. (The system of job-related qualifications is so pervasive that you may hear Germans making jokes about how even jobs such as toilet attendant or road sweeper require a two-year training programme these days.) Qualifications can be highly specific, making it difficult to change jobs unless you've taken a supplementary training programme meeting the particular requirements of the new job. Employers are required by law to provide continuing training for employees, and a company's annual educational plan must be approved by its works council.

Germany abides by the EU's general system for recognition of diplomas and qualifications, which means that, if your field of work is regulated in Germany, you must have your home country's qualification formally recognised before you'll be allowed to work in that field. This obviously applies to professionals such as doctors, nurses and teachers, but recognised qualifications are required to work in many other fields as well: as an electrician or computer technician or in building trades, for example.

Generally speaking, to have your home country qualifications formally recognised in Germany, you must contact the competent authority (usually a guild, trade association or professional society) for your trade or profession. They will provide you with their requirements, which usually involve the submission of your diploma, certificate or other documentation confirming your training or work experience. You must be able to show that the qualification from your home country is equivalent to the German one, in terms of both duration and subject matter. If there are significant differences in the practice of your profession between the two countries, you may be asked for evidence of mastery of specific areas considered significantly different in your home country.

This can take the form of job experience, an aptitude test or additional training. Under German law, the competent authority has four months to respond positively to your application; no response after this period is legally equivalent to a refusal, but you're entitled to know the reasons for any negative decision.

All EU member states issue occupation information sheets containing a common job description with a table of qualifications. These cover a large number of professions and trades and are intended to help someone with the relevant qualifications look for a job in another EU country. You can obtain a direct comparison between any EU qualification and those recognised in Germany from the *Zentralstelle für Ausländisches Bildungswesen*, Nassestrasse 8, 53113 Bonn (☎ 0228-5010). In the UK, information can be obtained from the Department for Education and Skills, Comparability Co-ordinator, Room 3b, Moorfoot, Sheffield S1 4PQ (☎ 0114-259 1045). A series of fact sheets called *Citizens' First Guides* can be downloaded from the EU website (🖳 http://citizens.eu.int); these provide detailed information on the European and German procedures for recognition of experience and qualifications.

GOVERNMENT EMPLOYMENT SERVICE

The German Federal Labour Office (Bundesagentur für Arbeit, also known as the BA, Arbeitsagentur or, colloquially, the Arbeitsamt) provides a wide range of employment-related services through 178 agencies and around 660 offices in Germany. The Arbeitsagentur publishes lists of jobs available throughout Germany and abroad, and provides vocational training, assessment and re-integration services for disabled people, and vocational guidance for students and others. It also administers various benefit programmes related to employment, compiles labour statistics and conducts market and labour research.

The Arbeitsagentur provides its services free to both job seekers and employers. If you're already in Germany, you can pick up a copy of its weekly magazine, *Markt und Chance*, at any of its offices. This publication includes job vacancies and a 'jobs wanted' section, where job seekers can place adverts. You can find similar information on the Arbeitsagentur website (🖳 www.arbeits agentur.de). The Arbeitsagentur has a department for foreign applicants seeking work in Germany, called the Zentralstelle für Arbeitsvermittlung (ZAV), which also handles placements for Germans abroad. The main office of the Arbeitsagentur is at Regensburger Strasse 104, 90478 Nuremberg (☎ 0911-1790). The ZAV is located at Villemombler Strasse 76, 53123 Bonn (☎ 0228-7130).

There's also a European Employment Service (EURES) network, members of which include all EU countries plus Norway and Iceland. Members exchange information regularly on job vacancies, and local EURES offices have access to extensive information on how to apply for a job and living and working conditions in each country. The international department of your home country's employment service can put you in touch with a Euroadviser, who can provide advice on finding work in Germany. Euroadvisers can also arrange to have your personal details forwarded to the Arbeitsagentur. The Citizens First website (🖥 http://citizens.eu.int) contains information about EURES and EURES-related agencies in many European countries.

Given the high level of unemployment in Germany, EURES is rarely the fastest or the most efficient way of finding a job there, especially from abroad. As can be expected, national employment services give priority to their own nationals and jobs aren't generally referred to EURES or other national agencies until after all prospective local candidates have been considered.

RECRUITMENT AGENCIES

In addition to the Arbeitsagentur, many intermediaries post vacancies in German newspapers as 'employment consultants', mostly for management level jobs. In larger cities there are branches of many of the major international executive recruitment firms or 'head-hunters' (*Kopfjäger*). Michael Page, Korn/Ferry and Heidrick & Struggles all maintain offices in Germany, although they don't normally accept CVs unless in response to a specific vacancy.

There's a variety of small to medium-size recruitment agencies in the US and UK which specialise in international placements. Agents advertise in daily and weekly newspapers and trade magazines but don't mention the client's name, not least to prevent applicants from approaching the company directly, therefore depriving the agency of its fat fee!

In a few instances, agencies advertise directly in international publications to assemble a stable of potential job candidates. International companies may list management positions in Germany with recruitment agencies in the UK, particularly if they're seeking multi-lingual, highly experienced or mobile executives.

Most legitimate recruitment services charge the employer a fee based on the annual salary negotiated for the candidate. Fees can run to as much as 40 or 50 per cent of a year's salary, which the head-hunter may have to refund if employees don't survive the initial probationary period (anywhere from one to six months). **Be extremely wary of recruiters that demand a fee up front from job applicants or expect you to reimburse them for postage, telephone costs or other charges incurred during the course of the job hunt.**

Temporary Agencies

In addition to recruitment agencies for permanent positions, there are temporary private employment agencies in Germany, such as Manpower and Adecco, handling either all types of jobs or jobs in specific industries or fields only. To be employed by a temporary agency (*Zeitarbeitsfirma*), you must be eligible to work in Germany and be registered with social security (see page 270). You must usually register with temporary agencies (you can register with any number of agencies), which entails completing a form and providing a CV and references. **Always ensure that you know exactly how much, when and how you'll be paid.** Deductions for income tax and social security will be made from your gross salary.

Because of the long annual holidays in Germany and generous maternity leave, companies often require temporary staff, and a temporary job can frequently be used as a stepping stone to a permanent position. On the other hand, companies may also use temporary agencies as a way of avoiding unlimited contracts, which are difficult and expensive to get out of due to strict German labour laws (see **Employment Contracts** on page 48). To find a temporary agency, look in the yellow pages under *Zeitarbeit*, *Personalvermittlung* or *Personalberatung*.

Online Agencies

The rapid development of the internet has led to a big increase in the number of online recruitment agencies and 'job search' sites. Some sites charge a subscription fee to access their vacancy lists, but many permit job seekers to view and respond to vacancies free of charge. It's also possible to post your CV online (again, usually free), but it's wise to consider the security implications of this move; by posting your home address or phone number in public view, you could be laying yourself open to nuisance phone calls or worse.

A number of internet sites that regularly list vacancies in Germany are:

- www.craigslist.com;
- www.jobnet.de;
- www.job-office.com or www.job-office.de;
- www.jobs.com or http://jobs.de;
- www.monster.de;
- www.overseasjobs.com;
- www.stepstone.de.

Note that German sites (those ending .de) don't usually include an English-language version unless a major organisation is involved. However, if your German skills are still rudimentary, you can obtain a rough-and-ready translation using the (free) Babel Fish translator provided by the search engine company Alta Vista. Enter 'http://babelfish.altavista.digital.com' in your browser, then enter the address of the website that you wish to visit in the Babel Fish dialogue box that appears; you'll then be presented with an instant translation of the web page in question – though you shouldn't expect it to be idiomatic or even accurate!

Casual Work

Temporary or casual work (*befristete Arbeit*) is usually for a fixed period, ranging from a few days to a few months (or work may be intermittent). Casual workers are often employed on a daily, first-come-first-served basis. Anyone looking for casual unskilled work in Germany must usually compete with newly arrived Turks and eastern Europeans, who are often prepared to work for less money than anyone else. Many employers illegally pay temporary staff in cash without making deductions for social security, insurances and taxes (see **Working Illegally** on page 44), although casual work earnings are subject to the same taxes and other deductions as full-time employment.

Temporary and casual work includes the following:

- Office work – well paid if you're qualified and generally the easiest work to find due to the large number of temporary secretarial and office staff agencies;

- Work in the building trade – this can be found by applying directly at building sites and through industrial recruitment agencies such as Manpower;

- Jobs in shops over Christmas and during sales periods;

- Gardening jobs in private gardens, public parks and garden centres, particularly in spring and summer;

- Peddling ice cream, cold drinks and fast food, e.g. in tourist areas or at trade shows and fairs;

- Work as a security guard (long hours for low pay);

- Nursing and auxiliary nursing in hospitals, clinics and nursing homes (temps are often employed through nursing agencies to replace permanent staff at short notice);

- Newspaper, magazine and leaflet distribution;

- Courier work (own transport required – motorcycle, car or van);

- Driving jobs, including coach and truck driving, and ferrying cars for manufacturers and car hire companies;

- Office cleaning, babysitting, labouring and other jobs – these can be obtained through a number of agencies specialising in temporary work.

Temporary jobs are also advertised in Arbeitsagentur offices (see page 28), on notice boards in expatriate clubs, churches and organisations, and in expatriate newsletters and newspapers.

Mini-jobs

Recent labour law reforms have led to the 'mini-job', which is poorly paid, exists in a deregulated sphere largely outside the traditional framework, and is without trade union involvement. It's supposed to be for people in transition or who are waiting to get a 'proper' job, but some would say that its advent is principally designed to reduce the unemployment numbers to save politicians' blushes.

SEASONAL JOBS

Seasonal jobs are available throughout the year in Germany, the vast majority in the tourist industry. Many seasonal jobs last for the duration of the summer or winter tourist seasons – May to September and December to April respectively – although some are simply casual or temporary jobs for a number of weeks. Some fluency in German is necessary for all but the most menial (and worst paid) jobs. Additional languages can be a big advantage, particularly in the tourist industry, as Germany hosts visitors from around the world.

Seasonal jobs include most trades in hotels and restaurants, couriers and representatives, a variety of jobs in theme parks and holiday camps, sports instructors, service staff in bars and clubs, fruit and grape picking and other agricultural jobs. The main job opportunities are described below.

If you aren't an EU national, you should make sure that you're eligible to work in Germany by checking with the German embassy or consulate in your home country before you start looking for a seasonal job. The Arbeitsagentur has been gradually reducing the number of seasonal work permits it issues to non-EU nationals in an attempt to encourage the hiring of Germans and other EU nationals, and non-EU nationals may find it difficult or impossible to secure seasonal work. There are, however, a number of international summer and holiday work programmes that offer work permits and placement assistance, particularly for students (see **Training & Work Experience** on page 34).

Foreign students in Germany can usually obtain a temporary permit for part-time work during the summer holiday period and between school terms.

Grape & Fruit Picking

As in many wine-producing countries, grape-picking is a popular late summer job in Germany, despite being boring, badly paid and back-breaking. The major vineyards are on the banks of the Rhine and Moselle rivers, where the harvest usually starts in mid- to late September, depending on the climate each year. Other fruits that need to be picked by hand include apples and pears, mostly in the south (e.g. Baden-Württemberg and Bavaria). Traditionally, farmers have hired fruit pickers from southern and eastern Europe on a 'cash in hand' basis, but in these days of high unemployment the Arbeitsagentur is trying to crack down on the use of illegal foreign labour, so in theory at least it ought to be easier to obtain a bona fide fruit-picking job.

Holiday Camps & Theme Parks

German holiday camps offer a number of summer job opportunities, ranging from camp counsellors and sports instructors to administrative and catering posts. The school summer holidays aren't as long in Germany as in some other European countries, so the season is correspondingly shorter. There are a number of internet sites devoted to holiday camps, such as 💻 www.summer camps.de, which lists job openings for the coming season.

Germany boasts a dozen or so theme parks (*Freizeitpark*), which rely to a large extent on seasonal staff. The larger parks may provide on-site accommodation for employees (the cost is deducted from your wages). Positions range from maintenance and catering to performing in shows and pageants. Check local newspapers from January or February for job advertisements for the coming summer season. April is a popular month for parks to hold auditions for performing roles. Most theme parks have websites containing employment information. The better-known parks are listed below.

● Europa Park Rust, Europa-Park-Strasse 2, 77977 Rust/Baden (☎07822-770, 💻 www.europapark.de);

● Hansapark, 23730 Siersdorf (☎ 04563-7051, 💻 www.hansapark.de);

● Legoland, Legoland Allee, 89312 Günzburg (☎ 08221-700 700, 💻 www.legoland.de);

● Moviepark, Warner Allee 1, 46244 Bottrop-Kichhellen (☎ 02045-899899, 💻 www.movieparkgermany.de).

● Phantasialand, Bergeiststr. 31–41, 50321 Brühl b. Köln (☎ 02232-36200, 💻 www.phantasialand.de);

● Tripsdrill, 74389 Cleebronn/Tripsdrill (☎ 07135-9999, 💻 www.tripsdrill.de).

Ski Resorts

While Germany isn't as well known for ski resorts and winter sports in general as its neighbours France, Switzerland, Austria and Italy, it boasts many winter resorts. Cross-country skiing (*Langlauf*) is particularly popular in the Black Forest and parts of Bavaria, and there are many small inns and tourist centres catering to winter sports enthusiasts.

One of the best ways to find jobs in ski resorts is via the internet, where the following sites might prove useful:

- www.coolworks.com;
- www.equity.co.uk;
- www.jobs-in-the-alps.com;
- www.natives.co.uk;
- www.skijobs.net.

TRAINING & WORK EXPERIENCE

A number of organisations run trainee and work exchange programmes for students and recent graduates. For most programmes you must be under 30. Some arrange job placements, while others offer work permits for up to 18 months to applicants who find their own placement and meet qualification criteria. Principal programmes include the following:

- Technical and commercial students wishing to gain experience by working in Germany during their holidays can apply to the International Association for the Exchange of Students for Technical Experience (IAESTE) in over 60 countries (www.iaeste.org). Applicants must possess a working knowledge of German and be enrolled at an educational institution as a full-time student of engineering, science, agriculture, architecture or a related field of study, or be undergraduates in their penultimate year of study and aged between 19 and 30. In the UK, applicants should apply to IAESTE UK, c/o Education Section, British Council, 10 Spring Gardens, London SW1A 2BN (☎ 020-7389 4771, www.iaeste.org.uk).

- The Association for International Practical Training (AIPT) provides a career development programme for university graduates and a student exchange programme for US nationals. Both programmes require applicants to find their own internships or job placements but provide them with work permits for up to 18 months. For further information contact the Association for International Practical Training, 10400 Little Patuxent Parkway, Suite 250, Columbia, MD 21044-3519, USA (☎ 410-997-2200, www.aipt.org).

- For students and those within a term of graduation, the Council on International Educational Exchange (CIEE) provides short-term work permits and job search support for over 30 countries, including Germany. CIEE programmes also include study and volunteer programmes. Contact the CIEE, 3 Copley Place, 2nd floor, Boston, MA 02116, USA (🖳 www.ciee.org) for information.

● AIESEC is a student-run, non-profit organisation that provides paid internships in business and technical fields in over 87 countries and territories, including Germany. You can contact the AIESEC chapter at your university for details of qualifications and application procedures. In the UK, contact AIESEC UK, 29-31 Cowper Street, 2nd Floor, London, EC2A 4AT, UK (☎ 020-7549 1800, 🖳 www.aiesec.co.uk); the website contains contact information for other countries.

● For those with an interest in politics, the Bundestag provides an internship programme, which combines work and study in Berlin. Students and teachers interested in exchange opportunities should contact the Deutscher Akademischer Austauschdienst (DAAD, 🖳 www.daad.de). The address of the UK service is 34 Belgrave Square, London SW1X 8QB.

● *Transitions Abroad* magazine, aimed at Americans, is a good source of information about a wide range of educational and exchange programmes. Its website (🖳 www.transitionsabroad.com) contains country-by-country listings of programmes for studying, working, internships and volunteering, all in searchable form.

● The EU and EURES have a number of programmes for young people interested in training and work experience outside their home country. Contact your country's national employment services agency or the national trade association for the industry in which you wish to train, who may be able to put you in contact with a suitable German employer. Information on EURES is available on 🖳 http://europa.eu.int (see also page 28).

VOLUNTARY WORK

Voluntary work provides a means for students and young people to visit Germany for a few weeks or months to learn about the country and its people at first hand. The minimum age limit for volunteers is usually between 16 and 18 and they must usually be under 30, although some organisations have no upper age limit. Qualification requirements vary with the organisation and the nature of the work. Voluntary work is unpaid (of course) and you must usually pay a registration fee plus your transport costs to and from the work site. Although meals and accommodation are normally provided, you may be expected to contribute towards the cost of board and lodging. The usual visa regulations apply to voluntary workers (see **Chapter 3**) and you'll be informed when applying whether you need one.

Many of the organisations that arrange training and work experience programmes, such as CIEE (see **Training & Work Experience** on page 34), also host volunteer programmes for students and young people. For those willing to pay their own way, the Earthwatch Institute (international headquarters at 3 Clock Tower Place, Suite 100, Box 75, Maynard, MA 01754, USA, ☎ 617-926 8200, 🖳 www.earthwatch.org; European HQ at Earthwatch Europe, 267 Banbury Road, Oxford OX2 7HT, UK, ☎ 01865-311600, ✉ info@earthwatch.org.uk) provides a variety of volunteer opportunities, mostly in support of environmental and cultural research projects.

The Belgian-based Association of Voluntary Service Organisations (AVSO, rue Joseph II 174, 1000 Brussels, Belgium, ☎ 02-230 6813, 🖳 www.avso.org), which is an international non-government organisation, maintains a directory of volunteer opportunities throughout the world, and the group Action Without Borders, a non-profit-making organisation aiming to increase political, social and environmental awareness, has a website (🖳 www. idealist.org) providing links to other voluntary work organisations.

There are a number of books providing information about voluntary work, including *Doing Voluntary Work Abroad: A Practical Guide to Opportunities Worldwide* (HowTo Books) and the *International Directory of Voluntary Work* (Vacation Work), a guide to 400 agencies and sources of information on short to long-term voluntary work worldwide.

JOB HUNTING

There are numerous places to look for jobs in Germany, whether you're already in the country or not. Some of the more effective resources are detailed below. As in any other country, the more job applications you make, the better your chance of finding the right job.

● **Newspapers & magazines** – Obtain copies of German newspapers, most of which contain job advertisements (*Stellenangebote*), often concentrated in weekend editions. The *Frankfurter Allgemeine Zeitung* (*FAZ*) runs the largest and best-known job advertising section in its Saturday edition, available at international news-stands throughout the world. The *Süddeutschezeitung* (🖳 www.sueddeutsche.de) is also an excellent source for job seekers. German business publications and trade journals often have job vacancy notices, particularly for positions requiring specific qualifications. International newspapers and magazines that sometimes contain advertising for positions in Germany include the *Financial Times* and the *Wall Street Journal* (for business managers), the *Economist* (economic research and university teaching and administrative positions), the *International Herald Tribune*, and occasionally the English Sunday newspapers.

● **Recruitment agencies** –Apply to international recruitment agencies acting for multi-national or German companies. These companies recruit primarily executives and key personnel, and many have offices worldwide. British and American companies often use recruitment agents in the UK to locate managers. Applying to so-called blind ads (i.e. those with only a brief, general job description and no indication of the employer's identity) can lead to valuable contacts with freelance recruiters, but be careful if you want to avoid having your employer find out that you're looking elsewhere.

● **Employment offices** – The Arbeitsagentur (see page 28) publishes a weekly list of job opportunities, which is available at any Arbeitsagentur office in Germany and also on its website (🖥 www.arbeitsagentur.de), where you can sign up for an automatic job notification service to inform you when a position in your field becomes available. Free use of computers and telephones is also provided in Arbeitsagentur offices. If you're an EU national, you can check with your home country's EURES network office (see page 28).

● **Current employer** – One frequently overlooked source of overseas jobs is your current employer, though this will apply mainly if you work for an international company or at least an organisation with one or more offices in Germany. It's far easier for your current employer to justify the transfer of someone to the German office or factory who's already familiar with the company policies and procedures than for him to hire a foreigner in Germany. This can be a particularly useful avenue if you require a work permit. Make sure that your personnel department knows of your interest in working in Germany, particularly if you already speak and read the language. Mention your interest to any German contacts you have within your own company, who may be willing to mention your name to fill a local vacancy that you wouldn't otherwise hear about.

● **Internet** – Most of the above resources can be accessed to some degree via the internet. German newspapers, in particular, are nearly all available online, with search facilities that enable you to quickly identify vacancies in specific occupational and geographic areas. Several large recruitment agencies are also online (see page 29). There are even websites devoted exclusively to job hunting, such as 🖥 http://jobs.de and www.monster.de, where you can post your CV free of charge and search the available listings.

Many executive recruitment agencies list their website addresses in their advertisements and it's worth checking these sites regularly for new postings that may never make it into print. If there's a particular company that interests you, particularly in the information technology field, don't forget to check their website for job listings by location. Many companies are now using their websites to advertise vacancies, thereby saving themselves advertising and recruitment fees, and several multi-national companies now claim to do most of their hiring via their own websites.

- **Unsolicited job applications** – Apply to American, British and other multi-national companies with offices or subsidiaries in Germany. If you're writing to German businesses in English, don't forget to mention your level of German fluency; otherwise, it's likely to be assumed that you don't speak or understand the language at all.

  Making unsolicited job applications to targeted companies is naturally a hit-and-miss affair. It can, however, sometimes work to your advantage when, for example, your application arrives just as a position comes available. Make sure, however, to specify the kind of job that you're interested in and qualified for. There's no point in stating that you will 'consider any job' and offering no hint of the skills or experience that may be of use to the company concerned. If you're writing to a manufacturer, for example, be sure to indicate whether you're interested in working in the factory or are looking for office work as a clerk or manager.

CURRICULUM VITAE

The basic job-hunting package (*Bewerbung*) consists of a curriculum vitae or resume (*Lebenslauf*) plus a covering letter explaining your interest in the job or company and stating where you saw the advertisement (if you're replying to one) and highlighting any relevant skills or experience you have to offer.

Whether you use a German curriculum vitae (CV) and covering letter depends on your fluency in the language and the type of job you're applying for. It's generally acceptable to use an English CV when applying to multi-national companies, particularly if English is the company's *lingua franca* or the job advertisement appears in English or mentions the need for excellent English-language skills. You'll need a German CV and covering letter for applications to smaller companies (especially those run by members of the *Mittelstand* – see page 25) and for jobs involving public contact.

A German CV contains much the same information as a standard CV but is in a slightly different format from that of a British or American CV, as follows:

- It should include detailed personal information, including your date of birth and age, nationality, marital status, number of children and, in the case of men, whether you're required to undertake military service, which could interrupt your work. Although this is no longer required, most companies still expect it.

- A good-quality photograph should be attached. Failure to include a photo may be taken by more traditional employers as an attempt to hide something – such as your real age or the fact that you have a bone through your nose. A photograph taken in an automatic photo booth is generally considered inadequate and may eliminate you from the running faster than no photo at all. Instead, you should go to a good portrait photographer, who can produce a professional-looking picture.

- Your educational background should include training courses completed, including employer-sponsored programmes, although you should limit these to training courses relevant to the job you're seeking. You may include copies of certificates of completion for each programme (including university diplomas), but Americans should resist the temptation to include grade transcripts; this information is considered personal and inappropriate, particularly if you didn't complete a certificate or degree.

- Your work experience should be listed in chronological order (i.e. earliest first) rather than starting with the most recent. Each job should be listed with your exact job title and dates of employment. Only the briefest description of job responsibilities should be given or none at all if the duties are obvious from the job title. The American style of 'self-marketing' by listing personal achievements or quantifying cost savings you've implemented may be seen as bragging, particularly in the more traditional family-owned companies.

- Many German job candidates submit copies of their termination review or last annual job appraisal but, due to the many legal restrictions on employee evaluations in Germany, such information is generally given little weight by employers.

- It's important to state your earliest available start date (though this could be included in your covering letter). German job contracts often specify quite long notice periods for quitting a job, from a minimum of a month to three months for management-level employees; your ability to start a new job on the date the employer needs the job filled can therefore give you a significant advantage over local candidates. On the other hand, saying you're immediately available can be taken as an indication that you're currently unemployed, although this isn't necessarily regarded as a negative point, particularly by larger employers.

You should of course take care to ensure that any information in your covering letter is consistent with your CV and may wish to enclose your application in a binder, which will be returned to you even if you're unsuccessful – in fact as an indication that you've been unsuccessful. (Even if you decide to use a standard British CV or American resume, don't be surprised to receive your application back in the post.) If you've applied through a head-hunter or other employment agency, you may receive a letter asking for permission to keep a copy of your application on file for reference. This is obviously a good sign, indicating that the agency believes that it may be able to match you with a future job vacancy.

INTERVIEW

For all but the most menial or short-term jobs, most employers will insist on interviewing short-listed candidates in person and on site. This is where foreign job candidates may be at a serious disadvantage, irrespective of their background, education or fluency in German or other languages, as employers are expected to reimburse all travel costs to their interviewees. For local candidates, this involves either a per kilometre allowance for motoring expenses or a round-trip train ticket, possibly with a single night's hotel bill and a meal or two. Few, if any, employers are willing to consider flying a job candidate in from London, New York or Sydney for a first-round interview for any but the most rarefied management positions.

If you're serious about job-hunting in Germany, you may wish to consider making yourself available for interview at your own expense, perhaps as part of a holiday. Mention this in your covering letter, even if your plans are vague ('I'll be in Frankfurt in the near future...' or 'As I am planning to spend my summer holidays in Germany this year, I will be available to meet you between...'). This tactic, while admittedly expensive, demonstrates the seriousness of your interest in the job and in making an international relocation. Assuming you're well qualified for the job in question, you may be able to overcome an employer's unwillingness to consider a foreign candidate simply by being available for a meeting. However, if you go down this route, you should ask your prospective employer what support he would be prepared to give you for your move and resettlement, should you get the job (see **Relocation Expenses** on page 52).

SALARY

It can be difficult to determine the level of salary you should receive in Germany, as salaries aren't often quoted in job advertisements and are kept strictly confidential. However, Germans are among the best paid workers in Europe, receiving both a '13th month', year-end bonus and a holiday bonus (generally an additional half month's salary or more) during the summer (see **Salary & Bonuses** on page 49). If you're quoted an annual salary, you should therefore divide it by 13.5 (not 12) to determine what your monthly pay will be. On the other hand, the cost of living is high in Germany, as are taxes and the various social insurances deducted from pay packets (see **Cost of Living** on page 309, **Social Security** on page 270 and **Income Tax** on page 298).

Usually only starting salaries are negotiable and it's up to you to ensure that you receive the level of salary and benefits commensurate with your qualifications and experience. If you have friends or acquaintances living in Germany or who have lived there, ask them what an average or good salary is for your trade or profession. Minimum salaries exist in many industries for factory or entry-level workers and the industry agreement for the region may govern pay rises and cover extras that must be paid for certain experience or qualifications, unsociable hours, overtime, weekend work or home work, and dangerous or unpleasant working conditions. You don't need to be a union member to be subject to the local industry agreement.

For many employees, particularly executives and senior managers, remuneration includes much more than monthly pay. Some companies provide benefits such as a company car, interest-free home or other loans, and membership of local clubs or sporting organisations. These benefits are usually taxable, however, and you should take this into account when calculating your take-home pay or comparing job offers.

An overview of salary levels is provided by the current digest (*Datenreport 2006*) of the Federal Office for Statistics (Statistisches Bundesamt), although the figures quoted should be taken as a guide only. Manufacturing workers in western Germany earned an average of €2,669 per month in 2006, while their white-collar colleagues received €3,595, excluding bonuses and overtime (the salary of the average male was €3,889 and for women €2,785, although generally for lower level jobs). Comparable workers in the east earned some 74 per cent of western pay levels. The complete digest is available online from the Statistisches Bundesamt website (💻 www.destatis.de).

SELF-EMPLOYMENT

If you want to be self-employed (*Selbstständiger*) or start a freelance business in Germany, you must meet certain legal requirements, including: establishing residence, applying for a work permit (see **Work Permits** on page 75), tax number and trade licence (*Gewerbeschein*) and registering with the appropriate organisation, which is usually a trade or craft guild (*Handwerkskammer*). If you're starting a business (as a foreigner) you must prove that you can afford the investment and will create at least ten jobs. Of course, you must have the appropriate qualification, recognised by the proper authority in Germany, to legally establish yourself as self-employed (see **Qualifications** on page 27). However, those with a record of practical experience supported by a recognised certificate in another country are able to set up in self-employment in certain fields, e.g. crafts, retailing (from a shop or mobile unit), catering and hotel-keeping, food and drink production, insurance broking, transport services, wholesale and hairdressing. Britons should contact the Certificate of Experience Unit of the Department of Trade and Industry, European Policy Directorate, Bay 211/212, Kingsgate House, 66–74 Victoria Street, London SW1E 6SW (☎ 020-7215 5000) to check whether they're eligible for a certificate.

In the building trades, the government is cracking down on unqualified and inexperienced foreign labourers, who are seen to be 'taking jobs away' from Germans. The law requires self-employed construction workers to hold a qualification at least equivalent to that of a German master craftsman (*Meister*) and to have a contract for a specifically defined segment of a building project – down to defining exactly which wall or room they've been commissioned to construct. **Many people who have been lured by the prospect of high wages for short-term construction jobs in Germany have encountered hostility on the job.**

AU PAIRS

People between the ages of 17 and 30 are eligible to work as au pairs for a German family. Technically speaking, this isn't a job at all but a 'cultural exchange experience' for both the au pair and the family involved. The au pair system in Germany is strictly regulated and generally conforms to the terms of the European Council decree on au pairs, although Germany has never officially ratified this decree.

In Germany, as in most of Europe, an au pair is a live-in part-time child minder who may also be expected to perform light housekeeping duties, in exchange for which he or she receives board, lodging and pocket money. The great majority of au pairs in Germany, as is the case elsewhere, are young women, but male au pairs are generally accepted, particularly in families with boys. (On the whole, the Germans are rather less anxious about men working in positions such as this than the Americans or British.)

Au pairs must be allowed adequate free time to attend language classes and cultural events and to pursue other activities and interests. The official brochure on au pair work from the Arbeitsagentur stresses that an au pair should be considered more of a family member than an employee. There are many cases of successful placements where families maintain contact with their former au pairs for many years afterwards. Unfortunately, there are also regular horror stories of au pairs burdened with long hours of strenuous work, driven to distraction by spoiled, unruly children, or even preyed upon by unscrupulous family members.

While it's possible (if you're an EU national) to arrange for an au pair position directly with a family, it's usually better to use a reliable agency. **Prospective au pairs from outside the EU must be placed by an agency licensed by the local office of the Arbeitsagentur.** This ensures that the proper immigration documents have been obtained and that the terms of the contract are in accordance with the applicable laws. It also provides you with someone to turn to should problems arise during your stay (see below) and the family with a replacement if you need to return home unexpectedly. Most agencies provide au pairs with a list of other au pairs living in the area, and they may even arrange small social gatherings or excursions to encourage interaction.

You can contact an au pair agency in your home country or contact a German agency directly. Many au pair agencies can be contacted via their websites, although you should check carefully that they're bona fide agencies. Check for affiliation with both the German Arbeitsagentur and one or more of the various international au pair associations that monitor practices. Two of the main German agencies are:

- Agentur Grenz, Friedrich-Weich Strasse 20, 76189 Karlsruhe (☎ 721-986 36 82, ✉ vgrenz@t-online.de);

- MAX AuPair International, Rehhagenhof 42, 33619 Bielefeld (☎ 521-16 00 50, ✉ maxaupair@aol.com).

Websites of interest to those considering an au pair position in Germany include:

💻 http://au-pairs.de;

💻 www.iapa.org (International Au Pair Association);

💻 www.uapa.com (Universal Au Pair Association).

Agencies will ask you to complete an application form. This will request considerable background information about you – hobbies, interests, training, experience of living and working with young children, education, etc. – in order to match you with a suitable host family. You'll be required to provide references (sometimes in German) and evidence of good health. Most au pair agencies expect you to have some knowledge of German, even if it's basic. Applicants from outside the EU (except those from the US, Norway and Iceland) must apply for a visa at a German embassy or a consulate in their home country (see page 70). You should allow at least two months for processing and must have the visa **before** you arrive in Germany.

When an agency has matched you with a family, you should receive a written 'invitation' which serves both as an introduction to your host family and as a form of contract for the au pair position. Au pairs are generally contracted to work for 10 to 12 months. You'll be expected to spend up to five hours a day (an average of 30 hours a week) childminding and performing light household chores. Typical duties include dressing and bathing children, taking them to school and picking them up, preparing light meals or snacks for them, and playing with them or supervising their play. Housekeeping may include cleaning up after yourself and the children, helping with laundry or ironing, and running errands for the family as required. You shouldn't be expected to undertake heavy house cleaning, redecoration of the home or other caretaker-type duties, but you're free to help if you wish. In fact, your stay is likely to be much more enjoyable if you pitch in with family chores and activities.

The host family must provide you with health and accident insurance during your stay, as well as room and board. They must also give you pocket money (*Taschengeld*), currently a minimum of €260 per month, which isn't considered a salary but an 'allowance'. In addition, you're entitled to have your own room in the family home, at least one full day free each week and adequate free time to take language classes, pursue cultural and other activities, and attend religious services if applicable. You're also entitled to four weeks' holiday during a 12-month contract (somewhat less for a shorter term), when you may return to your home country or travel independently of your host family.

Working as an au pair can be a wonderful opportunity to meet people and experience German family life, or it can be a nightmare, depending on the individuals involved. If serious problems arise between you and your host family, you should contact the agency that placed you. They will attempt to sort out the problems and, if necessary, find you an alternative family. You should never remain with a family if you're unhappy with the way you're treated. Most agencies, however, will hesitate to intervene during your first few weeks in Germany, on the assumption that in the early days of your contract a certain amount of homesickness or culture shock is natural for a young person living away from home for the first time.

WORKING ILLEGALLY

Working illegally isn't nearly as easy or as lucrative an option in Germany as it is in some other European countries and is more dangerous than in most. Germans tend to be law-abiding people, who are knowledgeable about regulations that apply to the workforce. Until some years ago, even the holding of a second job was considered a form of working in the 'black economy' (*Schwartzarbeit*) and was officially illegal. Industrial workers are also well aware of the threat of cheap foreign labour in a country with a high standard of living and low unemployment. Foreign labourers on building sites have been subjected to harassment, even when operating within the law.

Unscrupulous employers use illegal labour in order to pay low wages and avoid mandatory social insurances, particularly for foreigners who are unable to obtain residence visas. Foreigners caught working illegally are subject to deportation and fines. The employer can also be fined and may be required to reimburse the state for any costs incurred in deporting illegal employees. Even if you aren't caught, if you work illegally, you have no entitlement to social security benefits, such as healthcare, unemployment pay or pension contributions. Without the proper paperwork, you'll be unable to open a bank account, seek medical treatment or rent an apartment.

LANGUAGE

Although English is Germany's unofficial second language (it's taught in state schools from an early age, so that a considerable number of Germans have a reasonable knowledge of English) and many jobs require good English skills, for most positions you must have at least a grasp of basic conversational German. Besides, outside the major cities and tourist areas, it may be difficult to find information or help unless you speak German, particularly in the eastern states.

German belongs to the Indo-European language group and is the mother tongue of over 100m people worldwide. The standard form of German, which is the form generally taught abroad, is referred to as High German (*Hochdeutsch*), and is widely spoken in northern Germany. It's also the language spoken between Germans from different regions, many of whom have strong accents or dialects. There are several regional dialects, including *Bayerisch* (spoken in Bavaria), *Hessisch* (Hesse), *Schwäbisch* (the south-west, in and around the Black Forest) and *Sächsisch* (parts of Saxony), and the inhabitants of Berlin and Cologne have distinctive accents. These can be difficult to understand at first if you've learned *Hochdeutsch*. There are also officially recognised minority languages (as distinct from dialects), e.g. that of the *Sorb* community in eastern Germany, and *Plattdeutsch* and *Frisian* in northern Germany, which those living in these parts will need to be able to cope with.

The good news is that Germans are generally fairly easy-going about their language. If your pronunciation is less than perfect or you use the wrong gender (which is likely, as there are three) or adjective or noun ending (there are five of the former and eight of the latter), it's very unlikely that you'll be corrected – at least not in public. Germans recognise that their language can be difficult for foreigners to learn on account of its grammatical complexity.

Particular confusion is caused by the 'alternative' spelling *ss* or *ß*. An attempt was made in the mid-'90s to simplify and 'modernise' some spellings – for example, eliminating the *scharfe S* (*ß*) character. Unfortunately, these changes are being phased in over several years, rather than being imposed instantly, and you can expect to see both old and new forms in use for some time to come, especially as a number of (mainly older) Germans reject such changes as a 'dumbing down' of the language. In fact, the new spelling has been described as madness and has created chaos.

The German language has adopted many English words and terms, particularly from the worlds of business, computer technology and marketing; for example, 'manager', 'marketing', 'computer', 'online' and many other familiar English words are in common use, both in conversation and in print. Needless to say, they're pronounced like German and not like English.

For information about learning German, see **Learning German** on page 182.

START STOP

2.

EMPLOYMENT CONDITIONS

Employment conditions in Germany are governed by German labour law (*Arbeitsgesetze*), collective agreements (*Tarifverträge*), and the terms of an employee's employment contract (*Arbeitsvertrag* – see below). Collective agreements are negotiated between unions and employers' associations in many industries, and generally apply to employers and employees, irrespective of whether they're union members. Agreements specify minimum wage levels for each position in the main employment categories for the industry, as well as controlling the permissible working hours and often even holiday periods. Different rules apply to different categories of employee, e.g. directors, managers and shop-floor workers. Foreigners are employed under the same conditions as German citizens, and part-time employees generally receive the same rights and benefits as full-time employees on a pro rata basis.

German employees enjoy excellent employment conditions and social security benefits, and extensive rights under labour laws, collective agreements and local custom. Labour laws (and there are many) detail the minimum conditions of employment, including working hours, overtime payments, holidays, trial and notice periods, dismissal conditions, health and safety regulations, and trade union rights.

An employer's general rules and regulations or terms (*Arbeitsbedingungen*) regarding working conditions and benefits applicable to all employees are usually contained in a booklet provided to employees. When negotiating your conditions of employment for a job in Germany, you may find the checklists at the end of this chapter useful.

As in many other European countries, all business establishments with more than a handful of workers must have a works council (*Betriebsrat*) – see **Unions & Works Councils** on page 58.

The severity of the unemployment situation combined with the high costs and onerous responsibilities of hiring people has prompted the government recently to introduce significant labour market reforms, which essentially create a subsidiary realm of work where different rules apply: the 'mini-job'. These offer no protection against dismissal, no permanent contract and no union involvement, and are poorly paid – around 20 per cent less than the standard for the industry concerned – but are considered to be 'better than no job at all'. Surprisingly, Germany's powerful unions have accepted the concept. Mini-job employees who earn up to €400 per month don't have to pay any income tax or social security contributions and their employers pay a flat rate of 25 per cent to cover the latter. Those earning between €400 and €800 pay lower tax and social security than those with 'proper' jobs.

EMPLOYMENT CONTRACTS

Under German law, a contract exists as soon as you undertake a job for which you expect to be paid, although employees have the right to demand a written contract (*Arbeitsvertrag*) formalising the work relationship (*Arbeitsverhältnis*). This relationship is regulated by various labour laws (*Arbeitsgesetze*), which contain specific requirements for virtually every aspect of employment.

The standard employment contract is referred to as an 'unlimited' contract (*unbefristete Vertrag*), meaning that it's for an indefinite period. It usually includes a probationary period of one to six months, depending on the job or industry, before the contract becomes legal and binding on both parties.

A 'limited' employment contract (*befristete Vertrag*) is a contract for a fixed term, usually 6 to 18 months. Normally the job ends on the expiration date, which must be stated in the contract, but under certain conditions the work relationship may be extended to up to two years. If an employee continues to work after the end of a limited contract, he automatically falls under the rules for an unlimited contract and is considered a permanent employee of the company, whether or not a written contract exists. Limited contracts are officially used when a company needs a temporary substitute, e.g. when a key employee is on maternity leave, or to complete a specific project, and unofficially when a company wishes to circumvent the strict labour laws by hiring staff for what amounts to an extended probationary period.

All employment contracts are subject to German labour law and references may be made to other regulations such as collective agreements. Anything in contracts contrary to statutory provisions and unfavourable to an employee may be challenged in a labour court (*Arbeitsgericht*), but in principle you're allowed to strike an agreement with an employer that waives some or all of your rights under the law or the collective agreement – at your own risk.

As with all contracts, you should know exactly what an employment contract contains before signing it. If your German isn't fluent, you should obtain an English translation or at least have it translated verbally so that you don't receive any nasty surprises later.

Employment contracts usually contain a paragraph stating the date from which they take effect and to whom they apply. Other terms and conditions which may be covered by a contract or by an employer's general rules and regulations are outlined below.

SALARY & BONUSES

Your salary (*Lohn/Gehalt*) is stated in your employment contract, and details of salary reviews, planned increases and cost of living rises may also be included (or these may come under general terms). Contracts normally state the (monthly) gross income (*Bruttoeinkommen*), i.e. before all deductions and withholdings for benefits, taxes and social security. Salaries are generally paid monthly, although they may be quoted in contracts on an hourly, monthly or annual basis, depending on the type of job you're being offered. If a bonus is paid, such as a 13th month's salary or the so-called 'holiday bonus' in the summer, this is stated in your employment contract (see below). If you're quoted an annual salary in your contract, you should divide this by either 13, 13.5 or 14 as appropriate to arrive at your monthly gross pay.

General points, such as the payment of your salary into a bank or post office account and the date of such payments, are usually included in general terms. You'll receive a pay 'slip' (usually an A4 document) that itemises your salary, bonuses and any commissions or special pay rates, and shows tax and other deductions (both your share and your employer's).

Salaries in Germany are generally reviewed once a year, in around November/December, with pay rises taking effect from 1st January of the following year. Annual increases are determined to a large extent by the regional or industry collective agreements that apply to your German employer. Small 'merit' increases above the general negotiated pay rise may be granted to individual employees, but the total amounts available for such increases are subject to scrutiny by works councils.

13th Month's Salary & Bonuses

Most employers pay their employees' annual salary in 13 (or sometimes 14) instalments and not 12. If your employment contract mentions a 'holiday' bonus, this usually means that a '13th month' is paid – half in the summer (usually July) and half at the year end. In some companies, a full extra month's salary is paid both in July and at the end of the year, either in December or early in January, amounting to 14 months' salary. In both cases, the annual salary quoted in your contract is the total you'll receive in a year. Divide this by either 13 or 14 to determine what your 'regular' monthly salary will be. In your first and last year of employment, your 13th month salary or holiday bonus is paid pro rata if you don't work a full calendar year.

Some employers offer an additional annual bonus (*Gratifikation*) scheme, based on an employee's individual performance or the company's profits. If you're employed for a fixed period, you may also be paid an end-of-contract bonus depending on the terms of your contract.

Expenses

Expenses (*Spesen*) paid by an employer are usually listed in your employment conditions. These may include travel costs from your home to your place of work, usually consisting of a second class rail season ticket or the equivalent cost, paid monthly with your salary. Companies without an employee restaurant or canteen may pay a lunch allowance or provide luncheon vouchers. Expenses paid for travel on company business or for training and education may be detailed in your contract or in general terms or listed in a separate document. See also **Relocation Expenses** below.

WORKING HOURS & OVERTIME

Working hours (*Arbeitsstunden*) in Germany vary according to your employer, your position, the industry in which you're employed and the regional or industry collective agreement. The average is just under 40 hours per week; in most companies it's 38.5. Some companies are formally on a 35-hour or even four-day working week in order to try to preserve as many jobs as possible.

In manufacturing industries and factories, work may start as early as 7 or 7.30am with leaving time at 3.30 or 4pm, depending on the length of the official lunch break. Most business premises are open from around 6.30 or 7am until 6 or 7pm. Companies with a 35- or 37-hour working week may close completely on Friday afternoons.

Coffee or tea breaks (*Pausezeit*) are strictly scheduled in Germany, where the right to break time (like everything else, it seems) is enshrined in both the law and most union contracts. Breaks usually last 15 or 20 minutes and are strictly monitored. Lunch breaks may be only 30 minutes, although 45 minutes to an hour for lunch is usual in most offices. Eating at your desk is generally frowned upon unless you have urgent work to complete. And don't forget to wish your co-workers '*Mahlzeit*' as they leave for their lunch break. (The word literally means 'mealtime' and it can be debated whether it's a wish that they have a pleasant lunch or just confirmation that you've noted the time they started their lunch break!)

If you work more than the standard number of hours in a week, you must usually be paid overtime at a premium of at least 25 per cent (i.e. 125 per cent of your regular hourly rate). The overtime premium often depends on the time of day when the overtime is worked, with overtime after 9 or 10pm subject to higher premiums than overtime worked during 'regular' working hours. Work on Saturdays, Sundays or public holidays is usually paid at premium rates, from 150 per cent ('time and a half') to 200 per cent ('double time'). Employers can offer time off to compensate for weekend or holiday work and this must be at the appropriate premium rate (e.g. double time off for a Sunday worked, time and a half for a Saturday).

Salaried employees, particularly executives and managers, aren't generally paid overtime, although this depends on their employment contracts and their legal classification within the company. Salaried employees may, however, receive compensating time off if their presence was required outside their normal work schedule.

It may come as a nasty surprise to discover that many German employers (including some large companies) require all employees to clock in and out of work. If you're caught fiddling the clock, you're liable for instant dismissal.

Flexi-time

Many German companies operate flexi-time (*Gleitzeit*) working hours. A flexi-time system requires all employees to be present between certain hours, known as the core time (*Kernzeit*), e.g. from 8.30 to 11.30am and from 1.30 to 4pm. Core time can start at 7.30 or 8am, which isn't early by German standards. Employees may make up their required working hours by starting earlier than the required time, reducing their lunch break or working later. Smaller companies may allow employees to work as late as they wish, provided they don't exceed the maximum permitted daily working hours. Because flexi-time rules are often quite complicated, they may be contained in a separate set of regulations.

RELOCATION EXPENSES

Relocation expenses in Germany depend on your agreement with your employer and are usually included in your employment contract or general terms. If you're hired from outside Germany, your air ticket and other travel costs are often booked and paid for by your employer or his representative. You can usually also claim any incidental travel costs, e.g. for transport to and from airports. If you travel by car to Germany, you can usually claim a mileage rate (actually a kilometre rate) or the cost of an equivalent flight.

An employer may pay a fixed relocation allowance based on your salary, position and family size, or he may pay the total cost of removal. Most German employers pay your relocation costs up to a specified amount, although you may be required to sign a contract which stipulates that if you resign before a certain period elapses (e.g. five years), you must repay a percentage of your removal costs, depending on your length of service. An allowance should be sufficient to move the contents of an average house (castles aren't usually catered for) and you must normally pay any excess costs yourself. If you don't want to ship your furniture to Germany or have only a few belongings to ship, it may be possible to purchase furniture locally up to the limit of your allowance. For international relocations, it's common to receive an extra month's salary to cover incidentals, such as electrical equipment you must replace. Check with your employer. When the company is liable for the total cost, you may be asked to obtain two or three removal estimates.

Generally you're required to organise and pay for the removal in advance. Your employer usually reimburses the equivalent amount in euros after you've paid the bill, although it may be possible to get him to pay the bill directly or make a cash advance. If you change jobs within Germany, your new employer may pay your relocation expenses when it's necessary for you to move house. Don't forget to ask, as he may not offer to pay (it may depend on how desperate he is to employ you).

INSURANCE & PENSIONS

All German employees, foreign employees working for German companies and the self-employed must enrol in the German social security (*Sozialversicherung*) system. Social security includes disability, health, long-term care and unemployment benefits, work accident insurance and pensions. Contributions are usually calculated as a percentage of your gross income and are deducted 'at source' by your employer.

The cost of social security contributions is split 50-50 between you and your employer. Social security contributions are high (to cover the comprehensive and generous benefits available) and can easily total 40 per cent or more of gross pay, i.e. your share will be around 20 per cent. For details see **Social Security** on page 270.

Health Insurance

Health insurance is mandatory for all workers in Germany and is considered part of the social security system. Employees can choose from a number of state-run health insurance providers for cover for themselves and their families. Above certain salary levels, employees may choose to have private health insurance. For further information see page 278.

Unemployment Insurance

Unemployment insurance is compulsory for all employees of German companies and is covered by social security contributions. For details see **Unemployment Insurance** on page 274.

Salary Insurance

Salary insurance for sickness and accidents is included under social security, usually as part of your health or work accident cover. For information see **Health Insurance** on page 272 and **Work Accident Insurance** on page 276.

Company Pension Fund

Due to the comprehensive German state retirement plan (see page 276), private or company pensions haven't been considered necessary and many companies don't offer a private pension scheme. This is starting to change, particularly as the state has been forced to scale back its benefits. If you're working for a large international company, you may have the option to continue contributing to a pension plan taken out in another country while you're working in Germany. For further information about private pension plans in Germany (usually through banks or life insurance companies), see **Supplementary Pensions** on page 279.

HOLIDAYS & LEAVE

Annual Holidays

Your annual holiday entitlement (*Urlaubsanspruch*) depends on your employer, and the collective agreement (*Tarifvertrag*) under which he operates. Under German labour law, all employees working a five-day week must receive a minimum holiday allowance of 20 working days (i.e. four weeks) per year. In fact, in most industries, 25 days (or five weeks) is standard and the average is nearly 30 days. Part-time employees receive a pro rata holiday allowance based on the number of days they work per week. For example, if you normally work three days a week, your annual holiday allowance will be 15 days (five weeks at three days a week). Employers cannot count official German public holidays (see below) as annual holiday.

Some collective agreements provide for longer annual holidays or grant extra days to employees based on their age or long service. In some industries, the collective agreement may call for a summer shut-down, when all employees are required to take the same two or three weeks' holiday while a factory or business is closed. An individual employer may also declare a holiday shut-down, but this must be announced in advance and be approved by the works council. Many businesses close between Christmas and New Year, sometimes requiring employees to use part of their holiday allowance.

Be sure to ask about the process for requesting holiday dates, particularly if the bulk of your holiday time is already committed to business closure periods. There's usually a formal process for submitting holiday requests, often surprisingly early in the year. Senior employees are given priority over more junior workers under contract rules or other regulations, but only if they make their preferences known according to the rules. Employees with children have priority on taking holidays during local school breaks, and married people are often allowed to schedule their holidays at the same times as those of their spouse, whether they work for the same company or not.

Under German law, new employees are entitled to take holiday only after six months' work (the usual probationary period), but some employers permit you to take holiday before you've completed your probationary period (anything from one to six months). Before starting a new job, check that your new employer will approve any planned holidays, particularly if they fall within your probationary period.

Public Holidays

Public holidays (*Feiertage*) vary from state to state (*Land*) and sometimes from community to community within a given *Land*, depending on whether the predominant local religion is Catholic or Protestant. The following days are public holidays in all German states (the nine days prefixed by an asterisk are compulsory but Christmas Eve and New Year's Eve are normally also observed, but are often only half-day holidays) or certain states as noted:

Date	Holiday
1st January	*New Year's Day (*Neujahr*)
6th January	Epiphany (*Heilige Drei Könige*) – only in Baden-Württemberg, Bavaria and Saxony-Anhalt
March or April	*Good Friday (*Karfreitag*), *Easter Sunday (*Ostern*) & *Easter Monday (*Ostermontag*)
1st May	*May Day or Labour Day (*Maifeiertag* or *Tag der Arbeit*)
May or June	*Ascension Day (*Himmelfahrt*)
	*Pentecost or Whitsun (*Pfingsten/Pfingstmontag*)
	Corpus Christi (*Fronleichnam*) – only in Baden-Württemberg, Bavaria, Hessen, North Rhine-Westphalia, Rhineland-Palatinate and Saarland
August	Assumption Day (*Mariä Himmelfahrt*) – only in Bavaria and Saarland
3rd October	*Day of German Unity (*Tag der Deutschen Einheit*)
31st October	Reformation Day (*Reformationstag*) – Protestant areas only
1st November	All Saints Day (*Allerheiligen*) – Catholic areas only
November	Day of Repentance (*Buß und Bettag*) – Saxony only
24th December	Christmas Eve (*Heilige Abend*)
25th December	*Christmas Day (*Weihnacht*)
26th December	*Boxing Day
31st December	New Year's Eve (*Sylvester*)

In predominantly Catholic areas, there may be semi-official holidays for Mardi Gras (*Karneval*) in February, such as *Weiberfastnacht* in Cologne and Düsseldorf, *Fasching* in Bavaria and Baden-Württemberg, or *Rosenmontag* in Bonn, Cologne and Düsseldorf. Baden-Württemberg and Bavaria are well known as the states with the most public holidays each year, usually 12 or 13.

If a public holiday falls on a weekend, there's no substitute weekday holiday. If a holiday falls on a Tuesday or a Thursday, many workers (particularly civil servants) are also allowed to take the preceding Monday or following Friday off, known as a 'window day' (*Fenstertag*). Many German companies close during Christmas and New Year, e.g. from midday on 24th December until 2nd January, all employees being required to take part of their annual holiday allowance on the days that aren't public holidays.

Sick Leave

Employees are entitled to six weeks' paid sick leave (except in the case of pregnancy – see **Parental Leave** below), although the period is generally unlimited provided your doctor gives you a sick note (*Arbeitsunfähigkeits bescheinigung* or, more commonly, *Krankmeldung*) stating that you're unable to work. To those from countries with less liberal workplace cultures, it may initially appear that their German colleagues are abusing a generous system, although they would be wise to keep such views to themselves; they will soon discover that coming to work with a cold can make them unpopular – the German attitude is 'keep your germs to yourself'.

Special Leave

Most German companies provide additional days off for moving house, your own and a family marriage, the birth of a child, the death of a close relative, and other major life events. Grounds for compassionate leave (*Sonderurlaub*) are usually defined in collective agreements.

Parental Leave

Under German law, mothers and mothers-to-be are entitled to a wide range of physical and financial protection in the workplace. The extremely low birth rate has caused the government to frequently review the Mother Protection Law (*Mutterschutzgesetz*, abbreviated to *MuSchG*) in order to make parenthood more financially attractive in addition to protecting the mother from discrimination and bodily harm in the workplace.

A woman must notify her employer as soon as she's sure that she's pregnant by submitting a notification form from her doctor to the personnel or human resources department. This notification activates the provisions of the Mother Protection Law, which include not only her right to time off when the baby is born, but also restrictions on the type of work she may do during her pregnancy (see below), additional rest periods and other benefits. While pregnant or on maternity leave, an employee cannot be fired for any reason, provided the employer has been properly informed of the pregnancy. Maternity protection is the same for all women, irrespective of their length of employment or marital status.

Pregnant employees may not work in jobs requiring them to bend or stretch, or to lift or carry heavy loads. Neither are they allowed to work at night, on Sundays or holidays, or in any job that exposes them to chemical solvents or any other increased risk of illness or accident. After the start of the fifth month, pregnant employees cannot be required to stand for long periods. They must be permitted adequate time off to attend doctors' appointments and for tests related to the pregnancy.

Maternity leave normally starts six weeks before the projected birth date and continues for eight weeks after a baby is born, although this can be extended on doctor's orders. This is regarded as normal sick leave (see above), during which the employee receives her regular salary, although part or all of it may actually be paid by her health insurance provider.

Either parent has the right to (unpaid) child-rearing leave (*Elternzeit*) of up to three years, two of which must be taken before a child reaches its third birthday. During this leave either parent is eligible for state parent benefit (*Elterngeld*) for a period. *Elterngeld* is paid at 67 per cent of your average net salary for the last 12 months, subject to a minimum of €300 and a maximum €1,800, and is available to a parent going on leave or working up to 30 hours per week. If the mother stays at home, she's entitled to 12 months' *Elterngeld*; if the father does so, he may take 14 months – a rule designed to counter discrimination in the workplace against young women and to encourage fathers to take leave. The agency which officially gives advice on *Elterngeld* varies from state to state.

During child-rearing leave, you continue to earn credit in the state pension plan as if you were working. Provided you comply with the notification procedures and don't extend your leave beyond the permitted period, your employer must allow you to return to the same job at the same or a higher salary, taking into account general increases in wages.

EDUCATION & TRAINING

Employee training is taken seriously in Germany, whether it's conducted in your own office or in some exotic location. Training may include management seminars, technical courses, language lessons or any other form of continuing education. If you need to learn or improve your language proficiency in order to perform your job, the cost of study may be paid by your employer.

Most employers in Germany are required by law to allocate a set proportion of their gross payroll for employee education and training, and must develop a formal training plan covering all employees. The works council (*Betriebsrat*) must review and approve the training plan and ensure that the amounts spent are appropriately distributed to benefit workers at all levels in the company. A portion of the training budget is usually available to members of the works council to attend courses covering labour law, management, finance and other areas related to their responsibilities.

It's in your interest to investigate courses of study, seminars and lectures that you feel will be of benefit to you and your employer. Most employers give reasonable consideration to a request to attend a course during working hours, provided you don't make it a full-time occupation. If you decide to pursue a formal degree or certification programme requiring several months or years to complete, some companies may agree to pay for the programme (including books, examinations and other costs), but only if you sign an agreement to reimburse them should you leave the company within a certain number of years (generally no more than five) after you complete the course. If you leave one German company for another, it's likely that your new employer will reimburse you for any fees you've had to repay in this manner, assuming that he will benefit from your training.

UNIONS & WORKS COUNCILS

Trade unions in Germany are highly organised and play an important role in the 'social market economy'. By far the largest and most powerful union organisation is the Deutsche Gewerkschaftsbund (DGB), which is an umbrella group for the eight industrial unions that operate throughout Germany. The DGB unions represent all workers in specific industries, irrespective of their job titles or professions, and has around 8.6m members in total. For example, the well known and powerful IG (Industriegewerkschaft) Metall negotiates for all workers in the metalworking and information technology industries, including factory workers, janitorial crews, office workers and management, whether or not they're members of the union.

Normally, unions negotiate directly with the industry employer organisations and agreements are concluded which establish terms and working conditions for an entire industry, rather than individual companies or categories of employee.

In addition to the DGB unions, there's an employees' union (Deutsche Angestellten-Gewerkschaft/DAG), with some 500,000 members. There's also a union for German civil servants (i.e. government employees), the Deutsche Beamtenbund (DBB), which is the main employee organisation for civil servants, with over a million members.

Under German law, unions are allowed to organise on company premises but 'closed shops' are banned. Civil servants aren't permitted to strike in Germany, although they may be members of unions. Most private employees have the right to strike, but due to the system of strict co-operation between works councils and management, strikes are rare and usually of short duration (an hour or so – just long enough to hold a march and make a point). Employees in the private sector (including management employees) cannot be dismissed for striking, although, as usual in Germany, there are rules and regulations governing exactly how and when strikes must be announced and carried out.

Works Councils

All businesses with more than five employees must elect a works council (*Betriebsrat*). The delegates to this council or committee are elected from among the employees and serve as an advisory board to management, with their duties and responsibilities spelled out in German labour law.

A works council must have regular access to all important financial information and be kept informed of a company's major operating and marketing strategies. It must be consulted before any significant decisions are made that affect the workforce, including redundancies, relocation, or changes in working conditions or schedules.

The works council is consulted on the need for overtime or reduced hours and many day-to-day administrative matters, including the hiring and firing of employees, including executive managers. If the survival of the company is threatened, the council can make an agreement with the employer to suspend benefits granted in a collective agreement for a certain period. The works council also handles individual grievances and brings issues affecting the workforce to management's attention.

In large companies with multiple locations, there's usually a works council in each, and there may also be an all-company works council, whose representatives are guaranteed a certain number of seats on the company's board of directors.

All council delegates enjoy special protection from dismissal. They're allowed to use work time for council business, attend meetings and take training classes relating to their position. The industry-wide unions work closely with works councils and with management, often providing training programmes and general legal advice on key issues.

OTHER TERMS

Probationary & Notice Periods

For most jobs there's a probationary period (*Probezeit*), ranging from one to six months, depending on the type of work, the position and the employer. The duration of the probationary period is limited by law, according to the pay level and legal classification of the employee, and normally isn't renewable or extendable. The probationary period is usually stated as part of the employment contract or collective agreement. During the probationary period, either party may terminate the employment contract without stating a reason, unless otherwise stated in the contract. If you work even for a few hours after the end of the official probationary period, you're deemed to have been hired permanently, irrespective of whether an employment contract exists.

Your notice period depends on your employer, profession and length of service, and is usually stated in your employment contract and general employment conditions. If it isn't stated, the legal notice period applies (both to the employee and the employer). The legal notice period varies from one month (which must end on either the 15th or the last day of a calendar month) to seven months, for employees with over 20 years' service.

It isn't unusual for managers or executives to have contracts requiring them to work to the end of the calendar quarter (i.e. March 30th, June 30th, September 30th or December 31st) following the three months' notice period. This means that, if you submit your notice on 3rd April, for example, you may be expected to work until the end of September. The notice period may rise to six months or even a year after a few years in the job, which, if applicable, will be noted in your employment contract.

It's possible for part or all of the notice period to be waived if both sides agree, although this normally requires that the departing employee give up his right to a redundancy payment, which can amount to several months' salary and is partly tax-free.

If an employer goes bankrupt and cannot pay you, you can terminate your employment without notice. Other valid reasons for not giving notice are assault or abuse of you or a colleague by your employer or other gross violations of the terms of your employment contract.

Part-time Job Restrictions

Restrictions on part-time employment (*Nebenarbeit*) are usually detailed in your employment conditions. Most German companies don't allow full-time employees to work part-time (i.e. moonlight) for another employer, particularly one in the same line of business. You may, however, be permitted to take an additional part-time teaching job or similar part-time employment (or you can write a book!).

Changing Jobs & Confidentiality

Companies in a high-tech or highly confidential business may have restrictions on employees moving to a competitor in Germany or within Europe. You should be aware of these restrictions, as they're enforceable under German law, although it's a complex subject and disputes must often be resolved by a court of law. German laws regarding industrial secrets and general employer confidentiality are strict but, like most German labour laws, include considerable protection for the employee. If you breach this confidentiality, you'll be dismissed and may be unable to find further employment in Germany.

Acceptance of Gifts

The acceptance of gifts (*Geschenkannahme*) of more than a token value from customers or suppliers is normally forbidden. Many suppliers give bottles of wine or small gifts at Christmas that don't breach this rule.

Retirement

Your employment conditions may be valid only until the official German retirement age (*Ruhestand*) – 65 or 67, depending on your date of birth and sometimes your profession (see page 277). If you wish to continue working after you've reached retirement age, you may be required to negotiate a new employment contract.

Dismissal

The rules governing dismissal and redundancy (severance) pay are complicated and generally depend on an employee's length of service, the reason for the dismissal (e.g. misconduct or redundancy) and whether the employee has a protected status, such as that enjoyed by works council (*Betriebsrat*) members, who can be dismissed only for 'serious misconduct'.

After your probationary period, you can be dismissed only for a valid (and stated) reason, and the proposed dismissal must be reviewed and approved by the works council before notice is given. The works council can oppose the dismissal of an employee if they feel that the grounds are unfair or lacking in substance. In the event of an 'economic' lay-off involving a number of employees, an employer is obliged to submit a written plan to the works council, detailing the reasons for the action, the method for selecting the employees to be made redundant and the redundancy package being offered. The council then has to be given time to review the plan and all the supporting documentation, comment and offer suggestions or alternatives for minimising the number of redundancies.

Irrespective of the reason for the dismissal, a strict procedure must be followed. This involves the formal notification of the employee (or each employee in the case of mass redundancies) by letter to his or her home address. The letter must include the official reason for the termination, make reference to any previous disciplinary actions or warnings (if applicable), and indicate the effective employment termination date in accordance with the legal or contractual notice terms. You're normally expected to work up to your termination date, even though that date may be three months or more away. If you're being fired for a serious offence (e.g. stealing from the company or assaulting a co-worker), you may be barred from returning to work; however, the employer must usually still pay your salary for the full notice period.

A dismissed employee is entitled to accrued holiday pay and may receive a redundancy payment, which is determined according to his normal pay rate, years of service, family situation and any extenuating or unusual circumstances. There's no legally prescribed minimum, but each region and industry has guidelines for what's 'fair' under various circumstances, usually calculated as a number of months' salary.

If any of the procedural details of the dismissal have been overlooked or poorly carried out (particularly involving the notice period) or if the stated reasons are deemed deficient, you can go to a labour law court (*Arbeitsgericht*) and demand to be reinstated in your old job (at which point, the employer will restart the dismissal process, being particularly careful not to miss any of the details this time). A labour law judge can also require an employer to increase the redundancy payment to comply with local standards or to compensate for other injustices committed during the dismissal process. In the case of mass dismissal, the works council may insist on negotiating a redundancy package (*Sozialplan*).

CHECKLISTS

When negotiating your terms of employment for a job in Germany, the following checklists will prove useful. The points listed under **General Positions** (below) apply to most jobs, while those listed under **Executive Positions** (see page 65) usually apply to executive and managerial appointments only.

General Positions

Salary

- Is the total salary (including expenses) paid in euros or will it be paid in another country (in a different currency) with expenses for living in Germany?

- Is the total adequate, taking into account the high cost of living in Germany? Is the salary index-linked?

- When and how often is the salary reviewed?

- Does the salary include a 13th month's salary and annual or end-of-contract bonus?

- Is overtime paid or time off given in lieu of extra hours worked?

Relocation Expenses

- Are removal expenses or a relocation allowance paid?

- Does the allowance include travelling expenses for all family members?

- Is there a limit and is it adequate?

- Are you required to repay relocation expenses (or a percentage) if you resign before a certain period has elapsed?

- Are you required to pay for your relocation in advance? This can run into many thousands of euros for normal house contents.

- If your employer fires you before a certain period has elapsed, under what conditions will your repatriation expenses be paid or reimbursed?

- If employment is for a limited period, will your relocation costs be paid by the employer when you leave Germany?

- If you aren't shipping household goods and furniture to Germany, is there an allowance for buying furnishings locally?

- Do relocation expenses include the legal and estate agent's fees incurred when moving home?

- Does the employer use the services of a relocation consultant?

Accommodation

- Will the employer pay for a hotel (or pay a lodging allowance) until you find permanent accommodation?

- Is subsidised or free (temporary or permanent) accommodation provided? If so, is it furnished or unfurnished?

- Must you pay for utilities, such as electricity, gas and water?

- If accommodation isn't provided by the employer, is assistance provided to find accommodation? What does it consist of?

- What will accommodation cost?

- Are your expenses paid while looking for accommodation?

Working Hours

- What are the weekly working hours?

- Does the employer operate a flexi-time system? If so, what are the fixed working hours? How early must you start? Can you carry forward extra hours worked and take time off at a later date or carry forward a deficit and make it up later?

- Are you required to clock in and out of work?

Holidays & Leave

- What is the annual leave entitlement? Does it increase with age?

- What are the paid public holidays? Is Monday or Friday a free day when a public holiday falls on a Tuesday or Thursday respectively?

- Is free air travel to your home country or elsewhere provided for you and your family and, if so, how often?

Insurance

- Is extra insurance cover provided besides obligatory insurance?

- Is free life insurance provided?

- Is health insurance provided for you and your family? What does it include?

- For how long will your salary be paid if you're ill or have an accident?

Company Pension

- What percentage of your salary must you pay?

- Are you able to pay a lump sum into the pension fund in order to receive a full or higher pension?

- Is the pension transportable to another employer or to another location with the same employer?

Other Terms

- Are free or subsidised German-language lessons provided for you and your spouse?

- Is a travelling allowance paid from your German residence to your place of work?

- Is free or subsidised parking provided at your place of work?

- Is a free or subsidised company restaurant provided? If not, is a lunch allowance paid? Some German companies provide excellent staff restaurants, which save you both money and time.

- Will the employer provide or pay for any professional training or education required, if necessary abroad? Will he pay for part or the total cost of non-essential education, e.g. a computer or language course?

- Are free work clothes or overalls provided? Does the employer pay for the cleaning of work clothes (including office clothes)?

- Does the employer provide any fringe benefits, such as subsidised in-house banking services, low interest loans, inexpensive petrol, employees' shop or product discounts, sports and social facilities, and subsidised tickets, e.g. for local theatres or sports events?

- Do you have a written list of your job responsibilities?

- Have your employment conditions been confirmed in writing?

- If a dispute arises over your salary or working conditions, under the law of which country will your employment contract be interpreted?

Employer

- What are the employer's prospects?

- Is his profitability and growth rate favourable?

- Does he have a good reputation as an employer?

- Does he have a high staff turnover? If so, why?

Executive Positions

- Is private schooling for your children paid for or subsidised? Will the employer pay for a boarding school in Germany or abroad?

- Is the salary index-linked or protected against devaluation and cost of living increases? This is particularly important if you're paid in a foreign currency that fluctuates wildly or could be devalued against the euro. Are you paid an allowance for working in Germany?

- Is there a non-contributory pension fund besides the compulsory state scheme? Is it transferable and, if so, what are the conditions?

- Are the costs incurred by a move to Germany (e.g. the cost of selling your home, employing an agent to let it for you or storing household effects) reimbursed?

- Will the employer pay for domestic help or make a contribution towards the cost of a servant or cook?

- Is a car provided? With a chauffeur?

- Are you entitled to any miscellaneous benefits such as membership of a club or free credit cards?

- Is there an entertainment allowance?

- Is there a clothing allowance? For example, if you arrive in Germany in the winter from the tropics, you'll probably need to buy winter clothes.

- Is compensation paid if you're made redundant or fired? Redundancy payments are compulsory for all employees in Germany (subject to length of service), but executives often receive a generous 'golden handshake' if they're made redundant, e.g. after a take-over.

3.

PERMITS & VISAS

If you plan to live or work in Germany and, in some cases, even if you're only visiting, you may require a visa and/or a work permit. If you're a non-EU national who wishes to remain in Germany for longer than three months, you require a residence permit, irrespective of your country of origin or the purpose of your stay.

VISAS

The requirement to obtain a visa before entering Germany changes periodically according to the German Foreign Office's assessment of the risk of illegal immigration (according to the outbreak of wars, civil unrest, economic collapse and other global disruptions). It's a very rough rule of thumb that the poorer the country you're coming from the higher the probability that you'll need a visa for even a short visit, although in most cases visas are required only for stays of more than three months. The regulations outlined below were current in mid-2007.

- EEA nationals plus those of Switzerland don't require a visa to visit Germany for any purpose. After three months in the country, however, citizens of Iceland, Norway, Liechtenstein and Switzerland must apply for a residence permit and EU nationals must register their residence in Germany at the *Einwohnermeldeamt* (see **Council Registration** on page 83).

- Nationals of American Samoa, Andorra, Argentina, Australia, Bermuda, Bolivia, Brazil, Brunei, Canada, Chile, Cook Islands, Costa Rica, Croatia, El Salvador, Guam, Guatemala, Honduras, Hong Kong (HK-SAR only), Israel, Japan, Korea (South), Macoa (RAE only), Malaysia, Mexico, Monaco, Nicaragua, Niue, New Caledonia, New Zealand, Panama, Paraguay, San Marino, Singapore, the US, Uruguay, Vatican City, Venezuela and the US Virgin Islands don't require a visa for stays of up to three months, provided they don't intend to do any paid or self-employed work. Nationals of all the above countries except Australia, Canada, Israel, Japan, New Zealand, South Korea, and the US may not enter Germany as a tourist and change their status to that of an employee, student or resident but must return to their country of residence and apply for a visa.

- Nationals of former Soviet Union countries, most African and Asian countries and some South American countries require a visa to enter Germany for any purpose.

Holders of diplomatic passports from certain countries may be exempt from visa requirements.

Visa application forms and full details can be downloaded from German embassy websites (e.g. 🖥 www.german-embassy.org.uk in the UK or 🖥 www.

germany.info in the US). Visas may be valid for a single entry only or for multiple entries within a limited period. A visa is stamped in your passport, which must be valid for at least four months at the time of entry into Germany.

Transit Visas

Nationals of certain countries changing planes in Germany require a transit visa. These include Afghanistan, Angola, Bangladesh, Columbia, Cuba, Democratic Rep. of Congo, Eritrea, Ethiopia, Gambia, Ghana, India, Iraq, Iran, Jordan, Lebanon, Nigeria, Pakistan, Somalia, Sri Lanka, Sudan, Syria, and Turkey. Exceptions are:

● those that have 'leave to remain in the UK for an indefinite period' or a 'certificate of entitlement to the right of abode in the UK';

● those that have a valid visa or residence permit for any EEA country or Canada, Switzerland or the US;

● some diplomatic passport holders.

If a stopover requires accommodation in Germany, full visa regulations apply (see above).

Au Pairs

Au pairs who are EEA or US nationals don't require visas. Others are required to apply for a visa at the German embassy or a consulate in their home country. You should allow at least two months for the application to be processed and be aware that you must obtain the visa before you can enter Germany to take up a position. For further information about au pairs, see page 42.

RESIDENCE PERMITS

All foreigners are permitted to stay in Germany for up to three months without a residence permit (*Aufenthaltserlaubnis*), although some require a visa (see above). After this time, all non-EU nationals must have a residence permit. EU nationals need only register at their local council (see page 83. **No one has an automatic right to a residence permit. If you have a criminal record or a serious contagious disease or have previously violated German law, you're likely to be denied a permit.**

Non-EU nationals of the EEA and nationals of Australia, Canada, Israel, Japan, New Zealand, South Korea and the US can apply for a permit during their first three months in Germany – if you know from the outset that your stay in Germany will be longer than three months, it's wise to start the process immediately after your arrival – or can apply in advance at a German consulate in their home country if this is likely to be more convenient or if you require a work permit (see page 75). All other nationals must apply in their country of domicile for a residence permit, which cannot be sent to them in Germany.

When applying in Germany, you must first register your residence at the local registration office (*Einwohnermeldeamt* – see page 83). If there are no problems, the official at the registration office will give you a confirmation form (*Anmeldebestätigung*) as proof of your registration and a tax card (*Lohnsteuerkarte*). You obtain the application forms for a residence permit at the foreigners' office (*Auslandsbehörde*), which is often in the same building. Once you've completed the forms, you must compile the necessary supporting documentation, which includes some or all of the following:

- two completed forms;

- two passport photographs, showing a full and unobstructed frontal view of your face, which must measure between 32 and 36mm from the bottom of the chin to the hairline, and printed at 600 dots per inch (dpi) on high-quality paper;

- a valid passport and one copy of the relevant pages;

- proof of health insurance;

- proof that you have a place to live, e.g. a signed statement or lease (*Mietvertrag*) from your landlord;

- proof of means of support (usually a letter from your employer). If you're married to a German citizen this isn't usually necessary.

- a 'certificate of health for a residence permit' (*Gesundheitszeugnis für Aufenthaltserlaubnis*), which can be obtained from any registered German doctor or local health office (*Gesundheitsamt*) and costs between around €100 and €150 from a doctor or around half as much from a health office. In some states, blood must be tested for HIV.

- a 'certificate of good conduct', which can be obtained from your home country's embassy or your local police station or consulate in Germany.

Exact requirements depend on the state (*Land*) and your marital status – for example, the last two items aren't required everywhere – check with your local aliens department, which can be found in the yellow pages under *Ausländerbehörde* or *Kreisverwaltungsreferat*. Being married to a German citizen makes the process simpler and also means that you're exempt from the fee, which is normally around €50.

You must then take your completed application forms and required documents to your local *Ausländerbehörde*. (It's sometimes possible to hand everything in at the *Einwohnermeldeamt*, but this will involve giving up your passport for up to a month.) Check the business hours of the *Ausländerbehörde* – most are closed in the afternoons and many are open for just a few days a week. There's usually a long queue for non-EEA nationals and you should plan to arrive at least an hour before closing time. In larger towns and cities, there's usually a queue ticket system in the waiting room, such as you might find at a supermarket delicatessen. If you aren't sure or don't understand the instructions posted in German, ask the receptionist. If you're an EEA national, you may not have to queue as long (in large cities, there's usually a dedicated counter or service centre for EEA nationals).

Eventually you'll be called for an interview, which usually takes around ten minutes, provided everything is in order. (First the official will go through a checklist to confirm that you've brought all the necessary documents; if anything is missing, you'll be given a sheet indicating what you need and be sent away!) Assuming your paperwork is in order, you'll be asked about your job and planned stay. Obviously the preferred language is German, but many officials can speak enough English to manage the interview. Even so, you may want to arrange for someone to come with you to translate. Officials aren't particularly concerned with how well you speak the language, but whether you have a place to live and a job that will adequately support you and your dependants. If you can demonstrate to them that you'll be a responsible, law-abiding, tax-paying resident, you'll normally be granted a permit.

At the end of this process, and having paid your fee (if applicable), you receive a residence permit for a period of between six months and five years (*befristete Aufenthaltserlaubnis*) – the duration depending largely on your country of origin. For example, EEA nationals are entitled to a five-year residence permit immediately, although you must specifically apply for one and you must have either a job in Germany or evidence of means of support in order to qualify. Non-EEA nationals are normally issued with a one-year permit, renewable annually at the *Ausländerbehörde* for a fee of €20; you must apply for a new permit before your existing permit expires.

After five years, EEA citizens are entitled to an open-ended or 'permanent' residence permit (*unbefristete Aufenthaltserlaubnis* or *Niederlassungs erlaubnis*), provided they still meet the necessary criteria for residence. Non-EEA nationals can apply for a *Niederlassungserlaubnis* after five years (three years if they have a German spouse), provided they've worked (not freelance) and paid into the system for that amount of time. To obtain an open-ended permit, you're required to be able to speak at least basic German as well as to have proof of employment or means of support. If you're unable to speak German, you must take an integration course (*Integrationskurs*).

Your residence permit must be attached to a current passport in order to be valid. This means that, if your passport expires while you're in Germany, you must go through the process of applying for a residence permit again once you receive a new passport. Therefore, if your passport is due to expire in the near future, it may pay you to renew it in advance to avoid the hassle (and expense) of having to apply for a new residence permit.

Your children must also have residence permits, which are entered individually in their passports, and they must attend the interview with you to be registered. If you have a baby during your stay in Germany, you should obtain a passport for the baby from your consulate before going to the *Ausländer behörde*. If your baby doesn't have German citizenship, he or she will be given a residence permit for eight years initially, which you should have no problem renewing should you wish to remain in Germany indefinitely. Babies must also be registered with the *Einwohnermeldeamt*, but this is usually done by the hospital where the baby is delivered. You should check with the hospital for the documentation required to register a baby (see also **Registration** on page 264). Apply for a birth certificate at the register office, which can be found under *Standesamt* in the yellow pages or on the internet.

Students

In order to remain in Germany for longer than three months, all students from non-EU countries must have a residence permit. The application procedure is the same as for other EU nationals (see above). The documentation required for students is, however, different and includes:

- two passport photographs;

- a valid identification card or passport;

- proof of health insurance;

- a rental contract;

- proof of adequate financial resources – the minimum amount required varies with the area but is generally around €700 per month;

- certificates of school or university examination results;

- certificates proving your ability to speak German or confirmation of enrolment in a German course (*Deutschkurs*);

- a certificate of matriculation (*Immatrikulationsbescheinigung*), which is also necessary to obtain health insurance and student discounts such as for public transport.

The requirement regarding proof of financial resources is strict. It isn't sufficient to say that you plan to work, even if you've obtained a work permit. If you cannot provide the required proof, one possible solution is to obtain a formal statement from a third party that he will assume responsibility for your living expenses, accompanied by evidence that he has sufficient financial resources. Alternatively, you can open a bank account with the required sum for one year.

Students from Honduras, Iceland, Liechtenstein, Monaco, Norway, San Marino, Switzerland and the US can wait until after their arrival in Germany before starting the visa application process. It's best to start it immediately upon arrival, however, as the procedure can take from up to ten weeks. Other nationals must begin the application process at a German consulate or embassy in their home country and obtain a permit before arriving in Germany.

WORK PERMITS

There are stiff fines for employers who hire people without residence and work permits, so most will demand that you have both (if applicable) before starting work.

EU Nationals

Citizens of countries that joined the EU before 2004 don't require permits to work in Germany. Citizens of countries that became EU members in 2004 and 2007 (and probably future members) must apply for a work permit (*Arbeitserlaubnis*) at the relevant Labour Office (*Arbeitsagentur*), which can be found in the yellow pages or on the internet under *Arbeitsagentur*.

Nationals of new EU countries must register at the local council (see page 83) and then take their registration certificate (*Anmeldung*) to the local employment office (*Arbeitsagentur*) and apply for a work permit. This can take eight weeks to obtain, so you may apply for a work permit before arriving in Germany. After working for a year, you're eligible for an unlimited work permit (*Arbeitsberechtigung*).

Non-EU Nationals

Non-EU nationals (including those from the US and Canada), must also obtain a work permit, but the application is combined with that for a residence permit, and the work permit is likewise stamped in your passport. German law prohibits employers from hiring non-EU nationals unless they're unable to find an EU national who is qualified and available to fill a position. As a non-EU national applying for a work permit, you therefore require evidence from a prospective employer that he wishes (and is permitted) to hire you. This is typically a copy of an employment contract (*Arbeitsvertrag*), but it can be a letter or written statement offering you a job. You must also provide a detailed job description provided by your employer along with a statement explaining why you, a non-EU national, are uniquely qualified for the position. You may also be asked to provide copies of your educational, professional and trade qualifications. Americans and Australians are generally given 'privileged' treatment and receive a work permit without question (but don't bank on it), whereas other non-EU nationals may find their applications obstructed by over-zealous officials interviewing dozens of unemployed Germans in an effort to find one suitable for the job! After the work permit application forms and supporting documents have been filed at the *Ausländerbehörde,* they're forwarded to the *Arbeitsagentur* for approval and then you're notified when to return for your work permit or if more documentation is needed. This process normally takes between one and three months.

If you're a non-EU national married to a German citizen, the procedure is simplified: it isn't necessary to find a job before applying; your work permit will apply to any job, including self-employment, although restrictions apply to the setting-up of certain businesses (e.g. restaurants and other catering establishments), for which you may need a licence; no time limit applies to your permit provided your residence permit remains valid; and processing is much quicker and simpler – a permit may be issued on the day you apply. In addition to your passport and residence permit, you must present your marriage certificate and your spouse's passport, but your spouse doesn't need to accompany you (although you may wish to have him along for linguistic or moral support).

Spouses of non-EU employees who are on assignment in Germany normally have no trouble obtaining a work permit and usually have a number of options for obtaining employment in Germany. For example, in most cities there's a demand for native speakers who can teach English and for British or American citizens there's the possibility of finding employment at a US or British military installation.

Self-employed & Freelance Workers

Non-EU nationals may work freelance, which (in Germany) means that you have three or more employers but no fixed contract (with social security, benefits etc.), but you must have received a letter from the prospective employers to receive a freelance work permit. To receive a permit to open your own business you must make an investment of at least €1m, convince the authorities that your business idea is viable and that it will create at least ten jobs, prove that you have suitable business experience and register with the relevant trade associations and authorities. These restrictions also apply to non-EU spouses of German nationals – usually for the first three years of residence. Any limitations will be stated on your residence permit, and the official issuing the permit will tell you exactly what's permitted and what isn't. **If you plan to work freelance make sure to inform the official before he issues your residence permit/work**

permit. Restrictions are lifted when an open-ended residence permit (*Niederlassungserlaubnis*) is issued (see **Residence Permits** above).

If you own your own business, you must apply for a trade licence (*Gewerbeschein*) at the local tax office (*Finanzamt*). The same form will also set you up with a tax number (*Steuernummer* – see page 299), which isn't the same as a tax card (see page 299). If you're freelance you need only a *Steuernummer*, but to get one you fill out the same form as for a *Gewerbeschein*. The two most important things on the form are your projected earnings – which you should grossly underestimate in order to avoid paying a hefty pre-tax payment – and whether you earn VAT (*Mehrwertsteuer*) on your services or not. If you invoice your customers you'll have to include VAT charges of 19 per cent, which you must later pay the *Finanzamt*. If you work freelance for a language school on an hourly wage basis, you don't have to pay VAT.

Students

All students except those from the 'old' EU countries must be authorised by the *Ausländerbehörde* to work in Germany. Generally you may work with a permit for either 90 full days or 180 half-days per year. Exceptions may be made if there's a close connection between your studies and a desired job (typically a job on the university campus or one organised by the university), in which case you may work during terms without a permit. If you wish to work before commencing or after completing your studies in Germany, you must obtain a work permit. Otherwise, holding a wage-earning job while a student is illegal and can be grounds for expulsion from the country, even if you have time remaining after completing your studies.

There are, however, programmes that allow for the reciprocal exchange of students seeking short-term, paid employment in Germany. The biggest and best known of these programmes is administered by the Council on International Educational Exchange (🖳 www.ciee.org). You must apply for and receive a work permit before leaving your home country. There's a fixed fee and opportunities exist for three or, in some cases, six months' employment.

At the conclusion of your studies, you're permitted to remain in Germany with a student visa for up to a year while seeking a job. An employer may be able to expedite the work/residence permit process.

4.

ARRIVAL

On arrival in Germany, your first task will be to negotiate immigration and customs. Fortunately this presents few problems for most people, particularly citizens of a country that's a member of the European Economic Area (EEA see page 15). However, non-EEA nationals coming to Germany for any purpose other than as visitors usually require a visa (see page 70).

Germany is a signatory to the Schengen agreement (named after a Luxembourg village on the Moselle River where the agreement was signed in 1995), which introduced an open-border policy between member countries. Other Schengen members are Austria, Belgium, Denmark, Finland, France, Greece, Iceland, Italy, Luxembourg, the Netherlands, Norway, Portugal, Spain and Sweden. Under the agreement, immigration checks and passport controls take place when you first arrive in a member country, after which you may travel freely between member countries.

If you're travelling to Germany by road from a non-Schengen country, you should bear in mind that not all border posts are open 24 hours a day, so if you plan to enter the country via a minor border post you should check the opening times in advance.

In addition to information about immigration and customs, this chapter contains a list of tasks that must be completed before (or soon after) your arrival, and includes suggestions for finding local help and information. **Note that you should always carry an identity card, passport or residence permit in Germany.**

IMMIGRATION

When you arrive in Germany from another EU country, there are usually no immigration checks or passport controls. If you're a non-EU national and arrive in Germany by air or sea from outside the EU, you must go through immigration for non-EU citizens. Unless you require a visa to enter Germany, however, the official will usually do little more than look at your passport to see that you vaguely resemble the photograph, although at major border posts they may feed your details into a computer to check whether you're wanted for a crime in Germany. Residence and work permits are handled by the local authorities at your final destination, rather than on entry to the country.

All non-EU foreigners residing in Germany for longer than 90 days must obtain a residence permit (see page 71). Failure to apply for a residence permit before three months have expired is an offence and may result in a fine or theoretically even expulsion from Germany.

Most EU nationals who visit Germany with the intention of finding employment (or starting a business) have no restrictions and need only register their presence (see **Council Registration** below). Nationals from new EU member countries, however, must apply for a work permit at the labour office (see **Work Permits** on page 75).

CUSTOMS

The Single European Act, which came into effect on 1st January 1994, created a single trading market and changed the rules regarding customs (*Zoll*) for EU nationals. The shipment of personal (household) effects to Germany from another EU country is no longer subject to customs formalities, although it might be useful to have an inventory of the items you're bringing with you. For more information contact the Customs Information Centre at Frankfurt (☎ 069-4699 7600, 🖳 www.zoll-d.de).

Visitors

Imported belongings aren't subject to duty or valued added tax (VAT) if you're visiting Germany for less than 90 days, provided their nature and quantity doesn't imply a commercial aim. This applies to private cars, camping vehicles (including trailers or caravans), motorcycles, aircraft, boats and personal effects, but all means of transport and personal effects imported duty free mustn't be sold or given away in Germany and must be exported before the end of the 90-day period.

If you cross into Germany by road you may drive through the border without stopping. However, any goods (and pets) that you're carrying must fall within the exempted categories and mustn't be the subject of any prohibition or restriction. Customs officials can stop anyone for a spot check, e.g. to search for drugs or illegal immigrants.

Non-EU Residents

If you're a non-EU resident planning to take up permanent or temporary residence in Germany, you're permitted to import your furniture and personal effects free of duty. These include vehicles, mobile homes, pleasure boats and aircraft. However, to qualify for duty-free import, articles must have been owned and used for at least six months. VAT must be paid on all items owned for less than six months purchased outside the EU, as well as on those purchased in the EU if a VAT receipt cannot be produced.

To import personal effects as a non-EU national, you must contact the local customs office (*Zollamt*) in the area where you'll be resident and provide documentation showing that:

● you've been living outside Germany for at least 12 consecutive months prior to your entry. This requirement may be waived if there are unusual circumstances, such as when you're transferred abroad and back to Germany by the same employer.

- you've given up your residence outside Germany, i.e. documents showing the termination of your lease or employment, the sale of your home or a statement from your employer stating that you've been transferred to Germany;

- you're establishing residence in Germany, i.e. a lease agreement, a statement from your German employer or your registration receipt (*Anmeldung*) from the local authorities in the area where you'll be living.

To import a vehicle into Germany duty-free, it must have been registered in your name for at least six months prior to its importation. You may be required to have it inspected to check that it meets German standards and, if you're coming from another EU country, that VAT was paid at the time of purchase. For more information see page 210.

All items must normally be imported within a year of the date of your change of residence, either in one or in a number of consignments. If you cannot bring in all your goods within your first year, you can apply for an exception to this requirement. In this case your remaining goods must be imported as soon as possible after the initial consignment and no later than three years after your move.

If you use a removal company (see page 94) to transport your belongings to Germany, it will usually provide all the necessary forms and take care of the paperwork. On the arrival of your shipment, the removal company will ask you to send copies of the clearance documents (see above) so that it can attend to the formalities with the local customs office before delivering your goods. Always keep a copy of all forms and communications with customs officials, with officials both in Germany and in your previous or permanent country of residence. You should have an official record of the export of valuables (e.g. jewellery, works of art and antiques) from any country, in case you wish to (re-)import them later.

Germany has no currency restrictions but may require your bank to report on large transfers of funds into or out of the country. On the other hand, there are detailed and strict regulations regarding the importation of guns, rifles or ammunition into the country, and certain kinds of pets and plants require prior approval and health certificates. You're permitted to bring in personal medication, but it's advisable to obtain a doctor's prescription (if applicable). Prescription medicines (including some vitamins and herbal preparations) cannot be sent by post to a personal address in Germany. If you need prescription items that aren't available in Germany, you should arrange for them to be sent to a local pharmacy (*Apotheke*), where they can then be dispensed to you.

Further information regarding German customs regulations is available from customs offices. If you enquire at your local German consulate abroad, they can give you the address and telephone number of the appropriate office to contact. German embassies and consulates cannot offer authoritative information on customs practices and should refer you to the German customs service. For details of embassies and consulates in Germany see **Appendix A**.

COUNCIL REGISTRATION

Everyone in Germany, including German citizens, must register with the local residents' registration office (*Einwohnermeldeamt*), and there are fines for those who fail to comply with this rule. Registration (*Anmeldung*), which simply involves reporting your address, must be done within a week of taking up residence in a private dwelling in Germany (including accommodation with friends), or within two months of taking up residence continuously in the same hotel. Hotels usually provide a registration service for long-term guests, whereby you may not be required to attend the registration office in person. Otherwise, look in the phone book under *Stadtverwaltung* to find out in which of the local council's offices the registration office is located. (The *Stadtverwaltung* shouldn't be confused with the *Rathaus*, both of which are often translated as 'town hall'; the latter is usually an imposing edifice and has a representative function, whereas the former is a local administration centre, often functional in appearance and not necessarily near the *Rathaus*.)

There are set times in the week for registering, usually before midday, and you should phone to check or look on the notice detailing '*Sprechstunden*', which is usually located in the main entrance area of the *Stadtverwaltung*. On arrival take a number slip from the inevitable machine and wait until your number is called.

When dealing with officials, remember that they embody the state rather than just work for it, as is the case in the UK or US. In the former DDR, some officials have been performing the same function since before the fall of Communism. Insulting officials (*Beamtenbeleidigung*) is a specific crime in German law and punishment can be severe.

If you move to a different state within Germany, you must de-register before you leave, although when you register in some states, the town where you were previously registered will be notified. De-registration is also required when you leave the country. Fortunately this process is straightforward and the forms can be returned by post.

Church Tax

One item on the registration form to pay careful attention to is the question asking you to state your religion. **If you list a Christian religion or Judaism, you'll automatically be registered to pay church tax.** This is calculated as 8 or 9 per cent (depending on the *Land*) of your income tax (*Einkommensteuer*). No one cares whether you actually practise the religion or attend services, so if you wish to avoid this tax, you must answer the question with the word *'keine'* (none) – no justification for your answer is required. Muslims, Hindus, Sikhs and members of other religions can, at present, register their beliefs without being taxed, although there is some discussion about implementing a Muslim tax in the future.

If, due to ignorance of the tax implications, you previously indicated a (taxable) faith, your decision can be rescinded, but not without some effort and inconvenience on your part – and, of course, there's a fee.

Income Tax Card

When you register as a resident, you should ask for an income tax card (*Lohnsteuerkarte*), even if you haven't started work. This will be required for your income tax calculations. When registering your tax class (*Steuerklasse*), you must show evidence of your marital, family and employment status. The tax card must be given to your employer when you start work and will be returned to you at the end of the year with a summary of your annual income; it must be included when you file your income tax return (*Einkommensteuererklärung*). Provided you haven't moved to another district during the year, a new *Lohnsteuerkarte* will be posted to you the following January. For more information, see page 299.

Tax Number

A tax number (*Steuernummer*) is required if you wish to work freelance or to be self-employed. You apply for it at the tax office (*Finanzamt*). For more information see page 299.

EMBASSY REGISTRATION

Nationals of some countries are required to register with their local embassy or consulate as soon as possible after arrival in Germany, and most embassies like to keep a record of their country's nationals resident in Germany. Embassies and consulates (see **Appendix A**) are usually an excellent source of information and if you have a problem with German bureaucracy they can be contacted for help and advice.

FINDING HELP

One of the main difficulties facing new arrivals in Germany is how and where to obtain help with day-to-day problems, e.g. finding a home, enrolling your children in school and obtaining insurance. This book was written in response to this need. However, in addition to the comprehensive information it contains, you'll require detailed local information. How successful you are in finding it depends on your employer, the town or area where you live (Frankfurt's residents are better served than, for example, Baden-Baden's), your nationality and your language proficiency.

As you'd expect, there's a wealth of general local information available in German, although it isn't usually designed for foreigners and their particular needs, but little in English and other foreign languages. You may find that friends and colleagues can help, as they're often able to proffer advice based on their own experiences and mistakes – though this may be inappropriate or irrelevant to your situation.

Your local council is usually an excellent source of reliable information, but you must speak German to benefit from it. Similarly public libraries often have lots of free government publications (in German) about many different subjects, usually located near the entrance. Some companies may have a department or staff whose job is to help new arrivals settle in, or they may contract this task out to a relocation company. Unfortunately, however, many employers in Germany seem totally unaware of (or uninterested in) the problems and difficulties faced by their foreign employees.

A good source of information and help is the American Women's Clubs (AWC) located in Berlin, Cologne, Dusseldorf, Hamburg and the Taunus region around Frankfurt. AWC clubs provide comprehensive information in English about both local matters and topics of more general interest, and many provide data sheets, booklets and orientation programmes for newcomers to the area. Membership is generally limited to Americans or those with active links to the US, e.g. through study, work or a spouse who works for a US company or the US government, but most publications and orientation programmes are available to others for a small fee. AWC clubs are part of the Federation of American Women's Clubs Overseas (FAWCO), which can be contacted through its website (🖥 www.fawco.org). In Munich the English-speaking International Women's Club (IWC), which fulfils much the same functions as the AWC, is open to women of all nationalities (🖥 www.internationalwomensclub.org).

In addition to the above, there are many social clubs and other organisations for foreigners in Germany, including Anglo-German 'friendship' clubs and other English-speaking organisations, whose members can help you find your way around. They may be difficult to locate, as small clubs run by volunteers often operate out of the president's house and they rarely bother to advertise or take out a phone listing, so you should ask among neighbours or colleagues. Many embassies and consulates (see **Appendix A**) provide information, particularly regarding clubs for their nationals, and many businesses (particularly large multinational companies) produce booklets and leaflets containing useful information about clubs or activities in the area.

Bookshops may have some interesting publications about the local region and tourist and information offices are also good sources. Finally, don't forget to check the internet, where you can find the websites of expatriate groups as well as local newspapers, government offices, clubs and organisations.

CHECKLISTS

Before Arrival

The following checklist contains a summary of the tasks that should (if possible) be completed before your arrival in Germany:

- Obtain a visa, if necessary, for you and all your family members (see **Chapter 3**). Obviously this **must** be done before your arrival in Germany.

- If possible, visit Germany to compare communities and schools, and arrange schooling for your children (see **Chapter 9**).

- Find temporary or permanent accommodation (see **Chapter 5**) and buy a car if you'll need one. If you purchase a car in Germany, you must register it and arrange insurance (see **Chapter 11**).

- Arrange the shipment of your personal effects (see **Chapter 6**) to Germany.

- Arrange health insurance (see **Chapter 13**) for yourself and your family. This is essential if you aren't already covered by a private insurance policy and won't be covered automatically through your employer.

- Obtain an international driving permit, if necessary.

- Open a bank account in Germany and transfer funds (see **Chapter 14**) – you can open an account with some German banks from abroad or even via the internet. It's best to obtain some euros before your arrival, which will save you having to change money immediately on arrival.

- Collect and update your personal records, including medical, dental, schools, insurance (e.g. car insurance), professional and employment (including job and bank references).

- Obtain an international credit or charge card, which will prove invaluable during your first few months in Germany.

Don't forget to bring all your family's official documents, including birth certificates, driving licences, marriage certificate, divorce papers or death certificate (if a widow or widower), educational diplomas and professional certificates, employment references, school records and student identity cards, medical and dental records, bank account and credit card details, insurance policies and receipts for any valuables.

You'll also need the documents necessary to obtain a residence or work permit (if applicable) plus certified copies, official translations and numerous passport-size photographs (students should take at least a dozen).

After Arrival

The following checklist contains a summary of tasks to be completed after arrival in Germany (if not done before arrival):

- On arrival at a German airport, port or land border, have your visa cancelled and passport stamped, as applicable.

- If you don't own a car, you may wish to hire one for a week or two until you buy one. **Note that it's difficult to get around in rural areas without a car.**

- Register with your local council within one week of arrival (see page 83).

- Register with your local embassy or consulate (see page 84).

- Open a post office or bank account and give the details to your employer.

- Arrange schooling for your children (see **Chapter 9**).

- Arrange whatever insurance is necessary (see **Chapter 13**).

5.

ACCOMMODATION

Finding reasonably priced accommodation can be particularly difficult in Germany due to an enduring housing shortage. Government programmes intended to remedy the situation resulted in a building boom during the '90s (in 1993 alone, a total of 455,503 new housing units were completed – an all-time record for the country) but due to the various incentives available, most were in the west rather than in the former East Germany, where in some areas even now the shortage is still obvious, even if nothing like as acute as before. Although housing is generally no longer as difficult to find as it once was, you must be able to pay the frequently high rents and deposits charged. Many developers took advantage of state aid to build luxury accommodation with rents to match, so that the government still finds it necessary to provide housing subsidies for many citizens. Expect to pay around a quarter to a third of your net income for housing in most areas of Germany.

Home ownership is far less common in Germany – around 42.2 per cent – than in most of the rest of Europe. Nearly 60 per cent of the population rent their homes, the proportion being as high as 70 per cent in former East Germany. And as the law provides tenants with considerable protection, landlords are often particular when choosing new ones and most would rather leave an apartment vacant than rent it to someone who might cause problems or disappear owing several months' rent.

TEMPORARY ACCOMMODATION

On arrival in Germany, you may find it necessary to stay in temporary accommodation for a few weeks or months, perhaps while waiting for your furniture to arrive or for a property to become vacant. Some employers provide rooms, self-contained apartments or holiday houses (*Ferienwohnungen*) for transferred employees and their families as part of their moving and relocation costs, but usually for a limited period.

Many hotels and bed-and-breakfast establishments cater for long-term guests and offer reduced weekly or monthly rates. Serviced apartments (or apartment hotels) are available in most large cities, comprising furnished apartments with their own bathrooms and kitchens, which are cheaper than a hotel and more convenient for families. In more rural areas, particularly in the south of Germany, you can often rent self-catering holiday accommodation by the week or month, although this can be prohibitively expensive or impossible to arrange at short notice during the main summer holiday season.

GERMAN HOMES

Most Germans live in various forms of multi-family housing – apartments, duplexes, 'triplexes' and semi-detached properties – particularly if they live in or near a major city. Detached, single-family houses (*Einfamiliehäuser*) are normally available only in rural areas, although housing estates are beginning to spring up on the edges of cities and towns. Most of the available housing has been built since 1950; a property described as *Altbau* may date from before 1914, as there was little building in Germany between the wars, and will generally command a high price, whether for sale or rent, despite its age and (sometimes) lack of modern conveniences, due largely to Germans' romantic attachment to older styles. Timber and mortar buildings (*Fachwerk*) are particularly popular and can command top prices, even when in poor condition. Note, however, that the term *Altbau* may simply refer to an existing house or building, as opposed to a new one.

Exacting building standards and the German liking for modern conveniences ensures that new buildings (*Neubau*) are solidly built. Nearly all building in Germany nowadays is in stone or reinforced concrete, and wooden or wood-frame buildings are rare. All modern homes have central heating, usually oil or gas. Air-conditioning is rarely provided, nor is it often required, given Germany's moderate summer climate.

Germans take great pride in their homes and spend considerable effort keeping them and their gardens attractive and tidy. Unless you do likewise, you may be frowned upon by your neighbours.

Area

When it comes to housing in Germany, size really does matter! The price of a home, whether to buy or to rent, is determined by its floor space, measured in square metres (*Quadratmeter*, abbreviated as *qm* or m^2). Furthermore, as with many things in Germany, there's a strictly regulated method – stipulated by the German Standards Institute (Deutsches Institut für Normung/DIN) – for determining the official size of an apartment or house. The following areas are included in the calculation of habitable living space:

● living rooms and bedrooms;

● kitchen, bathroom and toilet;

● entrance halls, hallways and cloakrooms;

● cupboards and stairways inside the dwelling;

● enclosed porch or balcony areas that can be heated for winter use.

The following areas **aren't** included in the calculation of habitable living space:

● storage areas outside the main living area, for example in a cellar or garage;

● lofts;

- utility or machine rooms;

- any space where the ceiling height is less than 1m.

The following areas are calculated at 50 per cent of actual floor space:

- any space where the ceiling height is greater than 1m but less than 2m;

- open balconies, porches and roof gardens and uncovered decks or terraces;

- enclosed porch or balcony areas that cannot be adequately heated during winter.

When comparing the prices of properties, it's important to bear in mind the above. For example, a 60m² apartment may have only 55m² of indoor living space because there's a 10m² balcony, while a rooftop unit (*Dachwohnung*) with the same official size of 60m² could yield only 45 or 50m² of usable living area if it has a massive roof garden.

In 2002, the average home in western Germany was 89m² and the average in the east 76m². In university towns such as Freiburg or Leipzig, you can sometimes find 'apartments' with just 12m² of living space, although even this doesn't guarantee a low rent. Generally, a 70 to 80m² property is considered the normal size for a small family, a couple or a well off single person. Larger apartments, particularly those over 100m², are considered up-market if not luxury dwellings. Larger properties are generally harder to find and are more likely to be listed with estate agents than standard-size properties.

Number of Rooms

The number of rooms is also important in determining whether a given house or apartment fits your needs. Any advertisement or information sheet will include not only the size of a property but also the number of rooms. The way rooms are counted is, oddly enough, not subject to DIN standards, but certain conventions do apply. Normally only the bedrooms, living room and dining room are included. A half-room indicates that there's a dining area off the main living room that isn't separated by a door which can be closed (doors are very important in German homes) or a bedroom under 10m². Kitchens and bathrooms or toilets aren't included in the room count. Thus, an apartment advertised as 3.5 rooms probably has two bedrooms with a living room and dining area. A four-room dwelling usually has three bedrooms and a living room but could have two bedrooms, a dining room and a living room. Separate dining rooms are rare in new properties, although you could of course use a spare bedroom as a dining room. Bathrooms, showers and toilets are usually listed separately in advertisements.

Kitchens

One of the biggest shocks for many newcomers to Germany is that you aren't just expected to supply your own light fittings, but must literally provide the kitchen sink (plus cupboards and other fittings) as well. If you view an apartment or house before the previous tenants have vacated it, you may offer to buy the fittings from them – if you like what you see and the outgoing tenants agree to leave them in place. If you don't include fixtures and fittings in the purchase contract, however, the chances are they will be gone when you move in. The advantage of this arrangement is that you don't have to limit your house-hunting to apartments with dishwashers or a certain kind of cooker, if that's what you want. However, you must allow extra in your budget to cover the cost of fitting out a kitchen. Sometimes landlords will provide a kitchen and charge you a separate rent for its use. Otherwise you must provide your own kitchen cupboards and appliances even in rented accommodation.

Kitchen fittings in Germany come in standard-size units, so mixing and matching appliances with cupboards isn't difficult. For those tiny student apartments, there are even compact, all-in-one units consisting of a sink, a small refrigerator and a cooker in a single, stainless-steel box. The Germans like modern conveniences and sturdy, well engineered products, and you'll have no problem finding state-of-the-art appliances when shopping for new ones. Ceramic hobs are popular, as are ovens equipped to handle a variety of cooking methods: forced hot air, baking, grilling or microwaving, all at the flick of a switch or sometimes programmable in sequence. Most Germans still prefer rather small refrigerators – generally the type that fit under kitchen worktops – but larger upright fridge-freezer combinations are becoming more popular and it's even possible to find full-size, American-style fridge-freezers in appliance shops, complete with water and ice dispensers in the door. While these may be tempting (particularly to Americans), you should ensure that you can fit such a large item into your kitchen along with all the other appliances, worktops and cupboards you may want. Connecting the water supply may involve running pipes along the walls in full view unless you can place your refrigerator next to the sink – and those automatic ice-makers and self-defrosting features may run up your electricity bill more than you realise.

As you may imagine, there's an active market in used kitchen fittings. Most furniture stores and do-it-yourself (DIY) shops sell new cupboards and appliances and can arrange for installation if you don't feel up to the task. Keep an eye out for offers – often a display unit will be sold for an attractive price, particularly when new models are introduced. Bear in mind that most shops must order a kitchen, unless you're buying a display model or other special unit, delivery normally taking 3 to 12 weeks.

By law you must have the plumbing and electrical connections for a cooker made by a qualified tradesman. If you hire someone to install your kitchen or have the store where you purchased it do the installation, they will usually organise a plumber and electrician for you. Some independent kitchen installers are certified in all the necessary trades and can handle the entire job.

Garages & Parking Space

Public transport in most cities and towns in Germany is frequent and convenient. As a result, it's possible to live and work in many areas without owning a car. If you own a car, you'll probably have to rent a garage or parking space for it, as on-street parking is difficult to find in most residential areas. Most modern apartment blocks have parking spaces or garage space available for an added monthly fee. You may have the option of buying or renting a garage or parking space in the building itself or within its grounds, and this may belong to someone other than the owner of the apartment. If you're lucky enough to find an apartment with a garage or parking space, the cost of it will be itemised separately on the lease or purchase documents.

If there are no available parking spaces in or around your building, you may be able to rent a space in a nearby covered car park or garage or even in another apartment building. Parking spaces for rent are advertised in local newspapers and in apartment building entrance halls.

The cost of a parking space varies according to its size, type (e.g. covered garage or open-air parking space), location and other factors, such as security. Generally, you should be able to find adequate parking for around €30 to €70 per month.

MOVING HOUSE

Once you've found a home in Germany, it usually takes only a few weeks to have your belongings shipped from within continental Europe. From anywhere else it varies considerably, e.g. four weeks from the east coast of America, six weeks from the west coast of America and the Far East, and around eight weeks or longer from Australasia. Customs clearance is no longer necessary when shipping your household effects from one EU country to another. **When shipping your effects from a non-EU country to Germany, you should enquire about customs formalities in advance, or you can encounter numerous problems and delays and may be charged duty or even fined.** Removal companies usually take care of the administration and ensure that the right documents are provided and correctly completed. If you plan to transport your belongings to Germany yourself, check the customs requirements of all the countries you must pass through.

For international removals, you should use a company that's a member of the International Federation of Furniture Removers (FIDI, 🖥 www.fidi.org) or the Overseas Moving Network International (OMNI, 🖥 www.omnimoving.com), with experience in Germany. Members of FIDI and OMNI usually subscribe to an advance payment scheme providing a guarantee. If a member company fails to fulfil its commitments to a customer, the removal is completed at the agreed cost by another company or your money is refunded. Some removal companies have subsidiaries or affiliates in Germany, which may be more convenient if you encounter problems or must make an insurance claim. Obtain at least three written quotations before choosing a company, and, if you're moving from overseas, give careful thought to how you plan on shipping your belongings. Most employer-sponsored overseas moves allow for a limited air freight shipment of around 250kg (550lbs), which should arrive at your new home within a week or two. **Make sure you include the items that you'll need most.**

It's sensible to fully insure your belongings during removal with a well established insurance company. Insurance premiums are usually 1 to 2 per cent of the declared value of your goods, depending on the type of cover chosen, and most insurance policies cover for 'all risks' on a replacement value basis. Some insurance companies require separate cover (riders) for valuable artwork or jewellery, and most insurers won't cover fragile or breakable items unless they've been packed by the removal company. You should make a list of all the items you're shipping and insuring, along with the price you paid for each item, purchase dates and the replacement values. This may be required for the insurance company to issue the cover and will be needed if you file a claim. The same list may be required by the removal company to clear your goods through German customs if you're coming from outside the EU.

Unless your move is simple, it isn't advisable to try to do it yourself. It's no fun heaving beds and wardrobes up stairs and trying to squeeze cupboards or sofas through narrow doorways. German removal companies have an array of specialised equipment designed to hoist large pieces of furniture into rooftop apartments or transport boxes on a sort of conveyor belt through a convenient window or balcony door.

Bear in mind that moving house rarely goes smoothly and it's a chaotic and stressful time for all involved. You're entitled to a day off from work to move house under German law and you should plan on taking it, if only to enjoy a moment of peace and quiet once the removal van has left!

Relocation Consultants

If you're fortunate enough to have your move to Germany paid for by your employer, he may arrange for a relocation consultant to handle the details. If you have special needs or requirements and enough money to pay for his services, you may wish to consider engaging a relocation consultant on your own behalf – although you shouldn't be surprised to find that many of the larger agencies work exclusively with corporations.

The main service provided by relocation consultants is finding accommodation (for rent or purchase), arranging viewing and assisting with the negotiations, particularly if you aren't fluent in German. Other services include handling the details of your move; arranging for temporary housing; advising on local schools, health, transport and recreational facilities; and assisting you with various regulations, including immigration requirements. Some consultants offer or can refer you to seminars on living and working in Germany, multicultural living and even language training. If you're interested in finding this kind of help for your relocation, it pays to contact local expatriate clubs. Members can recommend agencies or individuals, very often club members, who offer relocation services and know the area well. In other cases, local expatriate groups hold 'Welcome to Germany' programmes for newcomers. These may include presentations by local relocation consultants, removal companies and other professional services.

ESTATE AGENTS

The quickest and easiest way to find a property, whether to rent or buy, is to contact an estate agent (*Immobilienmakler, Wohnungsmakler* or, more often, just *Makler*). If your employer is paying your relocation costs, the agent's fees (for a rental property at least) will usually be covered without question, particularly if your employer is keen to have you settle in and start work quickly. If not, however, you should be aware that this approach will cost you dearly. If you rent an apartment or house through an agent, you must pay a finder's fee (*Provision*), which generally runs to two to three months' rent plus VAT at 19 per cent. Therefore, if you find an apartment for €500 per month through an agent, it will cost you a minimum of €1,190 before you pay the first month's rent or the rental deposit! The agent involved in the purchase of a home may charge you anywhere from 2 to 7 per cent of the purchase price (plus VAT). On average, an agent's fee for a purchase is around 3 per cent **and it's the buyer who pays**, so on a purchase price of €300,000 you should reckon on paying around €9,000 plus VAT at 19 per cent.

What agents do to earn these hefty fees varies considerably. Perhaps surprisingly, the profession isn't stringently regulated in Germany and almost anyone can set himself up as an estate agent after taking a three-day training course (mostly dealing with business registration and taxes) and paid a local licensing fee. All an agent is obliged to provide is a referral (*Nachweis*) or some form of mediation (*Vermittlung*) in the transaction. In some cases, the agent may do nothing more than provide a list of properties meeting your requirements, along with (possibly) the name and phone number of the current tenant, so that you can arrange a viewing of the property. Others will set up an appointment for you but may not be present when you view a property. However, most reputable agents, particularly those used to dealing with foreigners, will handle all aspects of a transaction, including scheduling visits, accompanying you to properties and assisting in negotiations with the landlord or vendor. Officially, an agent is a mediator between the parties and isn't a representative of one side or the other.

His fee, however, is determined by the selling price or monthly rental, so he obviously wants to get the highest price or rent possible.

It's possible to find your own accommodation in Germany without using an agent, but it takes time and organisation. Many Germans spend weeks, months or even years conducting house-hunting searches, whether to rent or to buy. An agent can help you make the most efficient use of a short house-hunting trip and may reduce the time (and therefore money) you spend in temporary accommodation on your arrival. Some agents speak English and other languages.

To find a reputable agent, the best approach is to ask around. Your employer and co-workers will be able to advise you on those they've used and can recommend – or which you should avoid! Most banks have a property (*Immobilien*) department handling both rental and purchase properties. Doing business with a bank's estate agent can be an advantage in that the bank has an interest in protecting its reputation by exercising control over its property (real estate) agents. When dealing with a bank's property department, you may be hard pressed to arrange financing or insurance through the bank, but this can work in your favour if you let it be known that you also require banking services.

You can contact as many agents as you wish, but be careful to keep track of which one referred you to which property. If a second agent shows you a listing sheet for a property you've already seen, you must notify the second agent of the duplication in writing and return any listing sheets or other information you received about the property. If you don't, you may find yourself liable for two agents' fees, although this is more likely when you're buying than renting.

RENTED ACCOMMODATION

Renting is common in Germany, where some 60 per cent of the population rent rather than own their homes. One reason is that the property market is fairly stagnant and most Germans don't consider owning their own home to be an investment, but rather a form of insurance for retirement. Most tax benefits go to property owners who let to others. Tenants have considerable security of tenure in Germany and rental costs and practices are strictly controlled by law.

Most rental properties in Germany are let unfurnished. Furnished properties (*möbeliert*, abbreviated to *möbl.* in advertisements) are difficult to find, other than for short-term lets or student accommodation. Unfurnished properties consist of floors, ceilings, windows, doors and walls, and not much more. The bathroom and toilet will have permanently installed fixtures – sinks, baths, showers and toilets – but you must supply everything else. Expect to provide your own lighting fixtures, curtain rods and even kitchen fittings, unless you can do a deal with the previous tenants to buy theirs (see **Kitchens** on page 93).

Check whether a garage or parking space is included in the rent – particularly if you don't have a car!

Finding a Rental Property

All German local newspapers contain rental advertisements, usually concentrated towards the end of the week in Thursday, Friday and Saturday editions. Advertisements may be placed by property owners seeking to let properties or by vacating tenants looking for someone to take over their lease before the notice period expires (see **Contract Termination** on page 101). Look out for a notice headed '*Nachmieter gesucht*' in the case of the latter. If you don't want to pay a hefty *Makler*'s fee (see **Estate Agents** above), avoid responding to advertisements placed by letting agencies. It's also fairly common in Germany for apartment seekers to place advertisements in local papers. This isn't as desperate a ploy as you may think. A 'for rent' advert can easily attract 50 to 100 phone calls in the day or two after it appears, particularly in areas where housing is in short supply. Therefore landlords usually check the advertisements of would-be tenants before subjecting themselves to this onslaught. Placing an advertisement to find a property to rent is particularly worthwhile if you have particular requirements – such as a large apartment (over 100m^2), one that accepts large pets, or when you require a ground floor (*Erdgeschoss*) apartment or wish to be near a particular school or other facility. German landlords appreciate stability, so if you're a professional being transferred by a large company or are in some other 'prestige' occupation (professors, doctors, lawyers, etc. are particularly prized), mention this in your advert.

Be sure to ask among colleagues, friends and acquaintances, as rented accommodation can often be found by this method. Many businesses maintain a bulletin board (*schwarzes Brett*) for the use of employees, which is usually a good way of finding rentals as well as furnishings (e.g. kitchen units) for sale. If your German is up to it, you can also find accommodation via the internet (e.g. on 🖳 www.immowelt.de and 🖳 www.immobilienscout24.de). You can also check the classified sections of local newspapers on the internet.

Some abbreviations used in rental advertisements are shown below:

Abbreviation	Full Term	Meaning
2MMK	2 Monate Miet Kaution	2 months' rent as security deposit
EBK	Einbauküche	Built-in kitchen
KM or WM	Kaltmiete/Warmmiete	Heating excluded/included
Nfl.	Nutzfläche	Usable space
Stpl.	Stellplatz	Parking space
TG	Tiefgarage	Underground garage
Wfl.	Wohnfläche	Living space
Zi	Zimmer	Rooms

Rental Costs

Rental costs vary considerably across Germany but are generally related to the size of a property, measured in square metres (m^2), rather than the number of rooms or bedrooms (see **Area** on page 91). Your local council office (*Stadtverwaltung*) can tell you the typical rent per square metre for a particular town or district (known as the *Mietspiegel*); some estate agents also have this information. Some towns impose upper limits on rental charges, although enforcement may be lax. The national average rent for a 65m^2 flat (excluding heating costs) in 2006 was €371, but the average in the south (the most expensive part of Germany) was €437 and in the east €330. But as Germans generally prefer not to commute, rents are higher in city centres and areas with good public transport. In Dusseldorf and Munich, for example, rents are from around €6.50 to over €10 per m^2 – meaning that the lowest monthly rent on a 'standard' 80m^2 apartment is around €520.

Rents are normally quoted 'cold' (*kalt* or *Kaltmiete*), which means without heating or other costs. Incidental charges (*Nebenkosten* – see page 104) are added to the base rent each month for such things as heating, water, taxes, rubbish disposal and other utilities, and maintenance costs for the building and grounds. If the rent is quoted as *warm* or *Warmmiete*, heating costs are included.

You're also expected to pay a security and cleaning deposit (*Kaution*), which is usually equal to two or three months' base rent. The deposit must be paid into a separate bank account in your name and the passbook given to your landlord for safe keeping during the term of your lease. The landlord is required to provide proof that the account still holds your deposit in the form of annual statements from the bank (including interest payments). It's sometimes possible to negotiate the payment of the security deposit in two or three instalments at the beginning of your lease.

Rental Contracts

A rental contract (*Mietvertrag*) is usually a standard document and can be long. Most rental contracts run to seven or more pages of small print. Like many contracts in Germany, housing rental contracts are often open ended, although some landlords specify a minimum term of a year, particularly for a new tenant. Even a contract with a defined term, however, will automatically be renewed unless you follow the prescribed notice procedure (*Kündigung*). You should read a contract carefully before signing it; if you have doubts or questions about any of the terms, have them translated or explained to you. Many standard contracts include marginal marks, such as exclamation marks or asterisks, flagging paragraphs and provisions considered particularly important or most likely to cause problems (for the landlord, that is!).

The contract will first identify the property that you're renting: not only the address and number or location of the property, but also the official size of the property (in square metres) and what other areas, facilities or privileges are included in the rent. You should ensure that any garage space or parking space you were counting on is listed, as well as cellar storage areas, balconies, garden space, and the right to access laundry or drying rooms in a building. If your landlord is providing a built-in kitchen, this must also be listed. The contract should include or refer to a list of the keys you're given for the property and its common areas (see **Security & Keys** on page 109).

The contract must list the base rent, the monthly allocation for incidental charges (see page 104) and any other costs, such as a parking space or garage, to arrive at your total monthly payment (*Gesamtmiete*). You'll be given a detailed list of items covered by the incidental charges, such as a caretaker (*Hausmeister* or *Hausdienst*) and grounds and building maintenance (e.g. lift, hallway lighting and TV aerials). Planned rent increases should be noted in the contract, particularly if you're renting a new property, or (at the very least) the method used to calculate and notify you of increases.

Most landlords expect you to pay your rent by automatic bank transfer or standing order (*Lastschrifteneinzugsverfahren*) and this is usually stipulated in the contract, along with the day of the month on which rent is due and the penalty for late payment. **Make sure that your wages are paid into your account in time to cover your rent payment, as fines for late payment are steep and it can take a long time to recover your good standing in the eyes of a landlord once he starts suspecting that you're a liability.**

If you have a pet or intend to get one, you must ensure that permission is written into the contract. While it generally isn't too difficult to find landlords sympathetic to pet ownership, most standard contracts require specific permission (and occasionally a small additional deposit) for a pet to be kept legally.

In general, tenants are expected to maintain everything inside their home, which means that it's up to you to deal with plumbers, carpenters or electricians should anything go wrong in your apartment. Normally you're free to decorate your home as you wish, e.g. paint the walls, hang wallpaper, put up shelves or hang pictures. However, when you move out you must return it to the same condition as it was in when you moved in. Most contracts also specify that the tenant must replace the carpeting, repaint walls and complete other renovation at specific intervals during the lease term, e.g. every three years or so. If you move out before major renovation is due, you may still be liable for a pro rata share of the estimated cost, which will be withheld from your deposit unless you make other arrangements. These terms must all be detailed in the rental contract.

Some landlords require evidence that you have adequate insurance to cover them and adjoining properties in the event of damage to the property. Policies covering personal effects (*Hausratversicherung*) and personal liability (*Haftpflichtversicherung*) and are widely available from around €130 to €200 per year. Sometimes policies include legal cover (*Rechtsschutz*), which can also be useful in other circumstances.

Contract Termination

Most forms of contract in Germany are automatically renewable, which makes it all the more important for you to be aware of how to terminate a rental contract. Notice periods (*Kündigungsfrist*) are strictly enforced. Formerly the same periods and conditions applied to both tenants and landlords, but recently the law has been changed to the advantage of the tenant. Three months' notice is now the minimum for terminating a lease as well as the maximum notice period a tenant needs to give in the case of an open-ended contract. However, the longer you live in a property, the longer the notice period: after five years it becomes six months, and after eight years, nine months. Make sure you check the contract termination conditions before signing.

Transgressions of the terms of a contract – such as the landlord allowing the property to fall into a dangerous condition – may permit immediate termination, but you must follow the correct procedure. If you find yourself in this situation, it's usually best to consult a lawyer.

If you need or want to leave rented accommodation before the official notice period has expired, you can find someone to take over your contract. Normally, this means advertising for a replacement tenant at your own expense. If you find someone willing to take over and start paying rent before your notice period expires, then you're off the hook for your last few rent payments – provided your landlord approves of the person you've found. Alternatively, you can authorise your landlord to start showing the apartment, in the hope that he will find someone who wants to rent it. Make sure that you let your landlord know if you want to sell your kitchen or other appliances (such as a washing machine) when you move. If you're obliged to terminate your contract because your employer has transferred you elsewhere at short notice, you can (and should) expect help from him in terminating your contract or finding a replacement tenant.

When you move out of an apartment, you're expected to restore it to the same condition it was in when you moved in, i.e. not only clean it thoroughly but also carry out any necessary repairs or renovation (*Schönheitsreparaturen*). This includes stripping off any wallpaper you've put up, patching any holes you've made in ceilings or walls, and repainting walls and ceilings (usually white or off-white), sanding down and re-painting any wooden window sills and door frames, sanding and re-lacquering wood floors and even re-grouting the tiles in the bathroom and kitchen and replacing carpets (irrespective of their condition). You're usually also required to remove the entire kitchen (including the sink!) unless it belongs to the landlord or the next tenant is willing to buy it from you (see **Kitchens** on page 93).

Most contracts stipulate that these repairs (especially painting) must be done by a professional (*Fachmann*), and you may be asked to prove it with a receipt! This work must be completed before the end of your notice period, so you should schedule your move for a week or two before your contract ends. This partly explains why Germans don't move house very often!

If you move out without completing the renovation work, your landlord will arrange to have it done and bill you. In practice, this generally results in your forfeiting your deposit. If the landlord keeps part or all of your deposit, you're entitled to receive an itemised bill for all work done and you can request copies of invoices paid by your landlord to verify his expenditure.

If you encounter any problems with your landlord, you should go to the Tenants' Protection Association (*Mieterschutzverein*), an organisation that provides legal advice for a nominal fee (☐ www.mieterbund.de). It's a good idea to go there (or visit their website) to inform yourself about tenant's rights **before** a problem occurs.

BUYING PROPERTY

Buying a house or apartment in Germany is considered a 'major life decision' and it's something a newcomer should consider very carefully before doing. If you're staying only for a short term (say, less than five years), you're probably better off renting. Due to the chronic shortage of housing, the German government has tended to offer financial incentives to builders rather than to home-buyers. You may find that home ownership in Germany carries few of the tax benefits that you're used to in your home country, e.g. the interest paid on a mortgage or other property-backed loan isn't tax deductible unless you're letting the property.

An important factor to consider with regard to buying property in Germany is that it doesn't free you from most of the communal aspects of German life. If you buy an apartment, you must still deal with the building maintenance company and the onsite caretaker and are still subject to house rules (see page 108). It's highly likely that some or most of your neighbours will be renting their apartments and, in any case, house rules apply to everyone living in a building; some home-buyers are unpleasantly surprised to find that they cannot keep pets or must put up a certain type or colour of curtains, even in their own homes! Moreover, in addition to your mortgage or other loan repayments, you must pay the various incidental charges – for example, heating, hot water, building maintenance and the caretaker's salary. Even some single-family (detached) houses are part of a 'builder's community', and you may have a surprising amount of charges to pay at the end of each year.

The mix of tenants and owners in most buildings can complicate the house-hunting process. For example, you may find a property you want to buy, but the owner is letting it to long-term tenants, so it could be as much as a year after buying before you could actually move in. Of course, you'd be receiving rent from the tenants during this period, but you'd need to find temporary accommodation in the meantime.

Germans don't generally consider buying a home to be a good investment. Most properties in larger cities increase in value by only 2 or 3 per cent per year in real terms (after taking inflation into account), while those in undesirable locations may stagnate or even go down in value. The government's efforts to encourage the building of new housing may cause the price of existing housing to dip for several months or even years, which could lose you money. Add to this the fact that you're liable for capital gains tax if you sell a property within ten years of purchase (see page 306). On the other hand, 'experts' predict that property values will begin to increase – except in the eastern states – and buying a home may be more profitable in the next few years.

Property Prices

Property prices are are often quoted exclusive of land, as the cost of land varies greatly from place to place. While most land costs between €300 and €700 per m², in prime locations (e.g. in affluent suburbs or near a lake or river) it can go for as much as €2,000 per m², whereas in undesirable towns in east Germany it can cost as little as €70 per m². Property prices are calculated on the same basis as rental costs, i.e. per m². In a few areas, you might be able to find dwellings costing much less than the average price prevalent in the state or country as a whole, but they're likely to be in locations which are undesirable for one reason or another – in rural backwaters which have high unemployment or declining urban areas – or have serious problems necessitating major repairs and renovation, which would cost the earth because of the obligation to employ craftsmen. While you can get a new family house for around €190,000 plus the cost of the land, at the upper end of the market – e.g. in Stuttgart or affluent suburbs of Berlin – you can pay €10,000 per m² or more (i.e. €800,000 for a standard apartment).

Fees

You should be able to pay a deposit (*Eigenkapital*) of 10 to 25 per cent of the price. If you use a *Makler* to help find you a home, you must add 3 per cent (plus VAT) for his fee (see **Estate Agents** on page 96). There's also a 1-1.5 per cent notary fee (see **Conveyancing** below), 3.5 per cent property transfer tax (*Grunderwerbsteuer*), which must be paid to the tax office (*Finanzamt*), a 0.8-1.2 per cent registration of property fee and usually a 1 per cent mortgage fee from your lender.

Conveyancing

Conveyancing (or, more correctly, conveyance) is the legal term for processing the paperwork involved in buying and selling a property and transferring the deeds of ownership. In Germany, all transactions involving property ownership (*Grundbesitz*) must be registered in the official land register (*Grundbuch*) of the local authority (*Gemeinde*) for the area where the property is located. Contracts for the buying and selling of all property recorded in the *Grundbuch* must be handled by a public notary (*Notar*), who ensures that all applicable laws are observed and that the appropriate fees and taxes are paid and recorded. The notary is an agent of the state and acts as a neutral third party, representing neither the buyer nor the seller in the transaction but ensuring that the terms and conditions of the contract of sale (*Kaufvertrag*) have been met. It isn't unheard of for a notary to refuse to validate a contract because specific terms of the agreement haven't been settled between the buyer and seller. The issues you must decide before your appointment with a notary include:

- the exact selling price of the property;

- the payment schedule;

- who will pay the notary's fee or how it's to be divided;

- the exact date of transfer of the property;

- whether there will be any payment of rent between the parties if the transfer date doesn't coincide with the buyer's or seller's moving dates;

- what repairs or other work must be carried out prior to the hand-over;

- any unusual features or conditions of the sale, e.g. if the seller is leaving the kitchen or other appliances in place.

At your meeting with the notary (*Notartermin*), you must provide personal identification (usually your passport and residence permit, if you're a foreigner) and confirmation of your financing. Normally there aren't any restrictions or prohibitions on foreigners buying or selling property in Germany, although financing a property purchase is a complicated business (see **Mortgages** on page 297).

With all these documents and confirmations to hand, the notary draws up the sale contract and ensures that it's registered with the appropriate offices and bureaux of the local government. Notaries' fees are regulated by law and you should receive an itemised list of precisely what you're charged. Normally this consists of a fee for the preparation of the contract, which varies according to the selling price, plus four or five fixed fees for registering the sale with each of the various government offices and tax authorities. In general, you should plan on the notary's fees being around 1 to 1.5 per cent of the price of the property (see **Fees** above).

INCIDENTAL CHARGES

Whether you're renting or have bought a home, you must usually pay monthly incidental charges (*Nebenkosten*). A monthly allocation for incidental charges will be calculated when you move in, based on how many people will be living in the property and your estimated use of common resources based on the usage of previous tenants. At the end of each year (or, more usually, in January or February of the following year), your actual use of heat, water and other utilities is calculated. You'll receive a letter informing you of the date and approximate time of the official meter reading to determine your actual usage of communal services (usually water and heating costs). It's important that you're available to let the meter reader in on the appointed date or leave a key with a neighbour or give the caretaker authorisation to enter your home with the meter reader. The official meter reading is usually done by an independent company (the cost is added to your incidental charges), and if they need to make a separate trip to read your meters on another day, you must pay an extra charge.

Shared costs which cannot be metered or measured are apportioned to your property according to the size of your living space in relation to the building or complex. For example, the occupants of an 80m^2 apartment pay 80 per cent of the allocation of someone who occupies a 100m^2 apartment. If you've been paying too much towards your share of common costs, you'll receive a refund at the end of the year, and your monthly contribution for the next year may be reduced. On the other hand, if you haven't paid enough over the year you'll receive a bill and your monthly communal charges will be increased the following year. In any event, you'll receive a statement of your actual communal charges for the year, along with the calculations used to determine your share of each item.

For tenants, incidental charges are paid to the landlord each month with your rent. If you own a home that's part of a managed sub-division or housing estate, you make monthly payments directly to the builder or management company handling the property.

HEATING & HOT WATER

In most apartment buildings heat is supplied by a central heating furnace, usually oil or gas, which is the responsibility of the caretaker. By law, heating is switched on on 1st October and off on 30th April. Most modern buildings allow for the regulation of heat within each apartment, usually on a room-by-room basis. In buildings with radiators, there should be a thermostat and control on each one. Some new buildings have under-floor heating, but there's usually a means of controlling the heat in each room and it isn't uncommon to find under-floor heating combined with radiators in some rooms, particularly bedrooms. Forced hot-air heating is rare in German homes, which are solidly built so that insulation isn't usually a problem, particularly in new buildings.

If you can control the level of heat, there will be a meter (often several) somewhere in your apartment – usually in a cupboard or some other out-of-the-way spot. In some apartments there's a meter on each radiator. It's advisable to locate the meters before the meter reader is due to call! Note also that rental contracts hold the tenant responsible for maintaining an adequate temperature in the home to ensure that no damage occurs. If there's a cold snap while you're away on holiday, for example, you could be liable for burst pipes – not only for the damage to your own apartment but also for any damage caused to neighbouring apartments

Each apartment connected to a shared tank is metered separately, although it isn't uncommon to find that hot water costs are apportioned in relation to your overall water usage. In newer buildings there are sometimes individual hot water tanks in each apartment, in which case you pay directly for the heating of your water through your electricity bills.

In older houses and apartments you may find a small water-heating unit for each sink or basin where hot water is needed, and a larger water heater for the bath, which you may have to remember to 'fire up' before use. With this arrangement, you'll need to buy a water heater for your kitchen sink if there isn't one installed when you move in. Kitchen water heaters often allow you to rapidly heat a small amount of water to boiling point, which can be handy for making a quick pot of tea or filter coffee, instant soups or other convenience foods.

It may come as a surprise to some foreigners that household appliances in Germany, such as washing machines and dishwashers, are connected only to the cold water outlet. Appliances that require hot water have a built-in water heater and heat up just the right amount of water for a single cycle. (Incidentally, this means that even the most expensive dishwashers and washing machines require nearly an hour to complete a full cycle, due to the need to heat the water.) If you plan to import a washing machine or dishwasher, you should therefore check whether it will operate properly with a cold-water intake.

BUILDING MAINTENANCE

Individual residences (*Wohnung*) may be owner-occupied or let, but the builder or a property maintenance company retains the responsibility for the upkeep of the building (*Haus*), i.e. the common areas and grounds. Most large buildings have a resident caretaker (*Hausmeister* or *Hausdienst*). The caretaker is the on-site representative of a property maintenance company and usually functions as a general odd-job person for building repairs and maintenance. He is paid a nominal salary and given free or subsidised accommodation by the property maintenance company or builder. The job of caretaker is similar to that of a building supervisor ('the super') in the US but with one important difference; a caretaker isn't required to carry out repairs in individual apartments, which is the responsibility of tenants or owners. If your toilet leaks, you must call a plumber yourself, although your caretaker may be able to recommend someone. On the other hand, if your heating breaks down or you notice a problem in one of the common areas such as a crack in the wall or a broken entry door, you should contact the caretaker. The cost of the caretaker is included in incidental charges (see page 104) and apportioned to you according to the size of your apartment. At Christmas, it's traditional in some buildings to offer a small gift or tip to the caretaker, particularly if you've had direct contact with him during the year.

In small buildings without a caretaker, residents may be responsible for their own garden maintenance and snow removal in winter. Your contract or house rules (see below) will indicate whether this is the case. If you live in a multi-floor building, your contract or house rules may make you responsible for regular cleaning of the common areas on your floor. Generally this means that once a week the landing area and sometimes the steps up to the next floor must be washed or vacuumed. Some contracts also require tenants to clean hall windows on a regular basis. This duty is the shared responsibility of all residents on the floor, so if there are two other apartments sharing your floor, you should expect to be on cleaning duty every three weeks or so. How formally this duty is assigned and what happens when one or more apartments on the floor is vacant varies considerably.

In some areas of Germany, particularly in the south (Baden-Württemberg, for example), you may be subject to a maintenance ritual known as *Kehrwoche*. In addition to being required to clean your own floor's hall every so often, you'll be assigned a week when you have responsibility for cleaning **all** common areas in the building, in rotation with your neighbours. You're usually required to clean the hall windows, clean and polish the entry door to the building (a crucial part of the *Kehrwoche* routine in many buildings), wash or vacuum the entrance hall floors, and possibly clean the floors in laundry or drying rooms. Usually a schedule of *Kehrwoche* assignments and responsibilities is posted in the main entrance of the building. *Kehrwoche* is considered a part of the house rules and failure to do your assigned share (or even failure to meet local standards of housekeeping when you do!) may result in a formal reprimand by the building management, with or without an accompanying fine. Even if you aren't officially reprimanded, you'll draw considerable disapproval from your neighbours if you don't fulfil your share of the communal cleaning chores and complete them to everyone's satisfaction on the designated days.

Germans generally keep their homes immaculately clean and have particular (not to say peculiar) ideas about the appropriate 'tools' for cleaning tasks. Washing windows with a spray bottle and paper towels doesn't always meet with local approval; the Germans prefer to use soapy water and a squeegee (one of those rubber blades that scrapes the water off, sending it running down the walls onto the floor). Sponge mops are often considered inferior tools for washing floors by German housewives (*Hausfrauen*), who prefer to use cloth rags. The good news is that if you don't want to be bothered with *Kehrwoche* chores, you can hire a cleaning lady to do them for you, or if you already have your apartment cleaned periodically, ask your cleaning lady to add this to her routine for a small extra fee. In a small building, you may receive an enthusiastic reception from busy neighbours if you suggest sharing the cost of a regular cleaning person to relieve everyone in the building of these chores, which, in the hands of a professional, should take no more than an hour or two each week. Bear in mind that house rules sometimes require *Kehrwoche* chores to be completed over the weekend or by a certain day of the week.

HOUSE RULES

All apartment blocks have house rules (*Hausordnung*), some of which may be set by the local council and are enforceable by law (particularly those regarding noise and siesta periods). You should receive a copy on moving into an apartment or when you sign your rental or sales contract. They apply to everyone living in a building, whether a tenant or owner, so **it pays to check the rules before making an offer on an apartment that you're interested in buying**. If you don't understand them, you should have them translated. Some of the more common house rules are:

- a noise curfew between 10pm and 6am;

- a siesta, e.g. from noon to 2pm, during which you mustn't make any loud noise, play music or sing, or (most important of all) use any power tools. This is to allow young children and pensioners an undisturbed afternoon nap.

- no bathing or showering between 10pm and 6am. Sometimes there's even a restriction on flushing the toilet during these hours, lest you disturb your neighbours' slumber. If you work nights, however, you're exempt from this rule.

- no loud noise on Sundays and public holidays. In some areas (mostly the south), hanging out washing to dry and mowing the lawn are also forbidden on Sundays, even in detached houses. In some areas, hanging laundry to dry on balconies is prohibited if it can be seen from the street.

- restrictions regarding where children may play or ride their bicycles;

- restrictions on the storage of bicycles, carts, children's toys or other personal objects in hallways or ground floor entrances or on balconies;

- restrictions on the use of laundry or drying room facilities, including cleaning after use. Laundry hanging is often done in rotation, so it may be necessary to find out what day is allotted to you.

- responsibilities for cleaning common areas (see **Building Maintenance** above), gardening, snow removal or other maintenance chores;

- the requirement to keep the front door to the building locked between 8pm and 6 or 7am. Usually the occupants of the ground floor apartments are responsible for locking the front door at the appropriate hour in the evening.

- the requirement to separate and prepare rubbish for collection according to the town's regulations, with 'recyclables' separated into a number of categories (see **Rubbish & Recycling** on page 115).

Your neighbours will be familiar with the house rules and be only too happy to point out any transgressions. If in doubt, you should contact the caretaker for clarification.

INVENTORY

One of the most important tasks on moving into a new home is to complete an inventory (*Inventur*) and condition report (*Bestandliste*). This includes the state of fixtures and fittings, the cleanliness and condition of the decoration, and anything missing or in need of repair. The form should be provided by your landlord (or by the builder if you're buying or renting a new property), and any problems must be listed on this form, which you sign and return by the deadline stated. If the problems or damage noted aren't put right or repaired within a reasonable time, you may be entitled to a reduction of your rent for the period they're left unresolved. If you're buying a home, the condition report should be used to document any work or repairs that the seller has agreed to undertake. If possible, this list, along with the deadlines for completing the work, should be submitted prior to your meeting with the notary, so that it can be officially registered with the contract and sale.

If you're renting, a property should be spotless when you move in, as this is what your landlord will expect when you move out. Any damage that isn't noted on the condition report when you move in will be charged to you when you move out, so you should check a property thoroughly and return the reportr promptly to your landlord.

SECURITY & KEYS

Germans are highly security conscious and an important part of your apartment contract is the list of keys. Make sure you actually receive all the keys that you're entitled to. **If you lose any keys to your home, you'll be held liable for having the barrels of the locks changed, and if you lose a key to a common area you'll probably be expected to pay for your neighbours' new keys as well!**

The key to your front door may also open the main entrance to the building or there may be a separate key. If you have a common laundry room, where residents are expected to install their washing machines, there may even be a key to the electrical socket to prevent you from running your machine on your neighbour's power! The most important keys will probably be of a high-security type that you won't be able to have duplicated at a hardware store. You may need to carry your house key whenever you leave your apartment, as entry doors often lock automatically on closure.

In Germany, doors can be locked only with a key, from both sides; there's no handle or knob on the inside. Many people are tempted to leave a key in the lock at all times so that if there's a fire or another emergency they can quickly unlock the door and get out. If you do this, however, you should be aware that the lock won't operate from the outside. In fact, if someone tries to insert a key in the other side of the lock, both keys and the lock are likely to jam, and you'll have to call a locksmith to drill out and replace the lock (an expensive operation).

ELECTRICITY

Germany is one of the world's biggest consumers of energy, and not surprisingly, Germans pay some of the highest electricity rates in Europe. The electricity companies were privatised in early 1998 and, in theory at least, you're now able to purchase power from any supplier you choose. In practice, what has developed is a network of electricity brokers (*Strombrokers*), who purchase power from the large generating companies and sell it to individual consumers under a variety of tariffs and plans. Within two years of privatisation there were over 900 electricity companies, mostly brokers, in Germany. To find a list of local electricity suppliers, look in the yellow pages under *Elektrizitätsgesellschaften* or *Energie-versorgung* (energy supply).

Electricity is generated using a variety of fuels – primarily lignite, hard coal and enriched uranium. The heavy use of lignite was a major source of pollution in the former East Germany, while hard coal produced from German mines is expensive and uneconomical for privatised power companies. Although nuclear power stations supply around 31 per cent of Germany's electricity, the government is publicly committed to closing all nuclear plants, while at the same time encouraging energy conservation, private sector development of alternative and renewable energy resources, and the reduction of air and water pollution levels. Some brokers market themselves as purveyors of 'green' power generated primarily by wind or solar energy. Despite privatisation, it seems likely that electricity prices in Germany will continue to remain fairly high in comparison with other European countries.

Power Supply

The electricity supply is delivered to homes at 220 to 250 volts with a frequency of 50 Hertz (cycles). If you're coming from a country that operates on the same voltage, most of your appliances will require only a change of plug to fit German sockets (*Steckdosen*), which are recessed into the wall (particularly in modern buildings) and have two small earth contacts. German plugs (*Stecker*) have two round pins, usually with two earth (or ground) contacts on the side if an appliance requires an earth. Televisions and video recorders are the most notable exceptions, but this relates to the transmission systems in use rather than the power supply (see **Chapter 8**). North American or other 110V appliances aren't usable in Germany unless they can be switched or converted to the higher voltage (see **Converters & Transformers** below).

German plugs aren't fitted with fuses. Instead, the electrical circuits are protected by either a fuse box or a circuit-breaker panel. Most modern buildings have a circuit-breaker panel containing several switches, usually labelled to indicate the circuits or apparatus they control. When there's a short circuit or the system has been overloaded, the relevant breaker is tripped and the power supply is cut. To reset the circuit breaker, you must flip the switch to the 'off' position (when the circuit 'blows' the switch moves only to the half-way position) and then back to the 'on' position to restore power. **Before reconnecting the power, switch off any high-wattage appliances such as a washing machine or dishwasher.** If the power goes out while you're on the computer, it's advisable to switch off both the computer and the monitor before reconnecting the power. Make sure you know where the fuse or circuit-breaker box is located and keep a torch handy so that you can find it in the dark. In most apartment buildings, there's a circuit-breaker panel in the entrance hall or one in each main hall connecting apartments.

When you move into a new home, there will probably be no lighting fixtures but merely wires hanging from the ceiling or walls. These wires are colour-coded to match those in the lamp or fixture you attach to them. Inexpensive lighting fixtures are available in home furnishing, hardware and DIY stores, and the staff will explain how to connect them if necessary. Many hardware stores sell inexpensive screwdrivers with a lamp in the handle, which glows if the screwdriver touches a live wire but insulates you from an electric shock.

Converters & Transformers

Electrical equipment rated at 110 volts AC (e.g. from the US) requires a transformer to operate in Germany. Small, hand-held appliances, such as hairdryers or curling irons, may operate satisfactorily on small travel converters, but for long-term use it's advisable to buy a proper transformer. Some electrical appliances (e.g. electric razors and hair dryers) are fitted with a 110/240 volt switch. **Check for the switch, which may be inside the casing, and make sure that it's switched to 240 volts** *before* **connecting it to the power supply.** Add the wattage of the devices you plan to connect to a transformer and make sure that its power rating **exceeds** this sum by a comfortable margin. Transformers may generate considerable heat when they're connected to the mains, even if the electrical appliances themselves aren't running or switched on. Make sure that you either disconnect a transformer when it isn't required or install it where the heat generated won't be a problem. Transformers are available from most electrical retailers and can often be purchased second-hand from Americans returning home.

Computers often have a voltage switch, either on the back panel or inside the main unit. If your computer doesn't have a switch and is designed to run on 110v, the chances are it can be operated successfully using an appropriate transformer. Most other computer equipment can also be run on a transformer, but you should be particularly careful if you have a laser printer, which may require a separate transformer to handle its high power requirements. It's also wise to use a power surge protector (preferably one made for electronic equipment) when connecting your computer to a transformer. If you're bringing a portable (laptop) computer with you, check the charger unit to see whether it will accept a 240volt supply. Many laptop chargers are made to operate on both systems, with just a change of cable or an adapter plug.

An additional problem with some electrical equipment is the frequency rating, which in some countries, e.g. the US, is 60 Hertz (Hz) rather than Germany's 50Hz. Electrical equipment without a motor is generally unaffected by the drop in frequency to 50Hz (except TVs – see **Chapter 8**). Equipment with a motor may run satisfactorily, although with a 20 per cent drop in speed; however, electric clocks, record players and some tape recorders are unusable in Germany if they aren't designed for 50Hz operation. To find out whether a piece of equipment will work, look at the label on the back. If it says 50/60Hz, it should work. If it says 60Hz you may try it, but first ensure that the voltage is correct as outlined above. Bear in mind that the transformers and motors of electrical devices designed to run at 60Hz will run hotter at 50Hz, so ensure that equipment has sufficient space around it for cooling.

In most cases it's simpler to buy new appliances in Germany and sell them when you leave if you cannot take them with you. In any case, you may find it impossible to fit American appliances into German kitchens or laundry rooms. German appliances are generally of excellent quality, although they may be expensive in comparison with their American or British equivalents. However, the recognised German brands retain their value well over time, and there's an active market in used household appliances. Contact local expatriate clubs and employer organisations, which often hold sales or post advertisements from members for used appliances.

Suppliers & Tariffs

Before privatisation, you only had to go down to your local council offices (*Stadtverwaltung*) to sign up for your electrical (and most other) utilities. However, following the privatisation of the electricity market, hundreds of electricity brokers (*Strombrokers*) have sprung up, each offering an array of rates. The effect of so much competition has been lower prices, or at least those displayed in advertising – electricity rates in Germany are still among the highest in Europe. The differences in pricing structures, however, make comparison

Wieskirch, Bavaria
© Steve Richardson (www.shutterstock.com)

© Uschi Hering (www.shutterstock.com)

© Scott Pehrson (www.shutterstock.com)

Mercedes Benz © hfn8 (www.shutterstock.com)

Cherry blossom © koi88 (www.123rf.com)

▲ Potsdam, Brandenburg © Philip Lange (www.shutterstock.com)

◄ Market, Esslingen, Baden-Württemberg
© Sharon G. J. Ong (www.shutterstock.com)

▲ Dresden, Saxony © Inge Johnsen (www.shutterstock.com)

◄ Soccer fan © salamanderman (www.shutterstock.com)

▼ © Peter Hansen (www.shutterstock.com)

▲ *European Central Bank, Frankfurt-am-Main,*
Hesse © *Petronilo G. Dangoy Jr.*
(www.shutterstock.com)

▲ © *Elena Kouptsova-vasic*
(www.123rf.com))

▲ *ICE high-speed train* © *Bob Ford (www.123rf.com)*

▼ *German shepherd dogs*
© *Bonzami Emmanuelle (www.123rf.com)*

▼ © *Edite Artmann (www.123rf.com)*

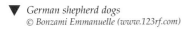

▲ Cochem, Rhineland-Palatinate
© Philip Lange (www.shutterstock.com)

▲ St. Bartholomae, Bavaria
© Kristen Speed
(www.shutterstock.com)

▲ © salamanderman (www.shutterstock.com)

◄ Cherry orchard © Olga Shelego (www.shutterstock.com)

▼ © Allan Groskrueger (www.shutterstock.com)

between brokers' rates and those of traditional utility companies almost impossible. Unlike brokers, most local utilities offer lower tariffs at night (*Nachttarif*) and many appliances are equipped with timers or start-delay systems so that thrifty Germans (and foreigners) can take full advantage of these.

There are other factors to take into consideration besides the price per unit at various times of the day, however: namely the minimum length of the contract you're obliged to sign up for and the notice period (*Kündigungsfrist*) you're required to give. German consumer magazines and other publications publish frequent comparisons of companies offering the lowest rates. A useful website is ⊟ www.stromtarif.de, where you can enter your estimated annual electricity usage, in order to bring up a list of the best offers currently available. For an average household (using around 1,500kwh per year) in April 2007 the best deal was around €277 per year with a 12-month contract and a six-week notice period, with a start-up fee of €48. The most expensive tariff was almost €440. For a household using twice as much energy the lowest tariff was around €475 and the highest almost €760. The most expensive tariffs are usually charged by companies using energy produced in environmentally friendly ways. **Note that some companies supply only within a certain area (e.g. western or eastern Germany).**

Sometimes the kwh rate depends on using a minimum amount each month or quarter and some brokers reduce the kwh rate if you agree to a higher monthly fixed fee. These plans may work out as being more economical for heavy electricity users, but it's difficult to evaluate competing claims if you don't know your usage. Brokers may require you to report your meter readings at regular intervals (with penalties for late reporting). Bear in mind the following when evaluating offers:

● It's unwise to sign a contract committing you to any power company for more than a year.

● The notice period for cancelling a contract or changing suppliers should be no longer than four weeks.

● Ensure that there are no conditions attached to the cancellation of your contract, such as a penalty payment or the need to produce a copy of a signed competitor's contract before you can cancel.

● Make sure that you read and understand all the small print regarding matters such as minimum consumption and your obligations to confirm or report meter readings.

Changing your electricity supplier consists only of the paperwork and there should be no need to turn off the power, change your meter or make any physical changes, although you must arrange a meter reading at the changeover date.

Bills

In your first year, a monthly or quarterly rate is estimated based on your family size and the size of the property you're occupying, and you're asked to transfer this amount each month or quarter via your bank to the local electricity utility. At the end of the year there's an official meter reading and you settle with the electricity company, which then sets a new monthly or quarterly rate for the coming year based on your actual usage.

GAS

Gas isn't widely available in homes in Germany, although local utility companies are starting to promote its use as a 'clean' fuel for heating. It's supplied by local companies (usually part of a town or regional utility); to find a list look in the yellow pages under *Gasversorgung*. Some make introductory offers to homeowners and builders who wish to install gas central heating in new properties or when renovating older buildings. In remote areas, homes may have a bottled gas cooker or heater. Most apartment buildings are designed to accommodate only electrical appliances in kitchens and it generally isn't possible to change to gas.

WATER

Water in Germany is generally hard, which means that you must have plenty of decalcification liquid on hand to keep your kettle, iron and other equipment and utensils clean. Tap and shower fixtures must be decalcified regularly. Distilled water or water melted from the frost build up in your refrigerator or freezer, should be used in some electric steam irons, although you should check the manufacturer's instructions; some brands of steam iron are made to be used with unfiltered tap water, and these have a decalcification system of their own which should be periodically cleaned or cleared. It also pays to decalcify dishwashers and washing machines from time to time. (Some detergents include decalcifying agents.)

There are a number of filter systems that can improve the quality of small quantities of water used in cooking and reduce or eliminate the calcium (*Kalk*) build-up on heating elements and in pots and pans. These normally require you to pour water through a filter into a pitcher or other storage container (such as Brita water filters) before using it. Other systems consist of a small filter fitted to a kitchen tap. Filters for both systems are available in supermarkets and other shops and generally need to be replaced every month or two. It's possible to install elaborate household decalcification equipment, although systems are generally expensive and aren't practical for installing in rented premises.

Water costs are included in the incidental charges (see page 104) for all apartments and most houses in Germany. Costs are based on your actual usage and there may be multiple meters, particularly if laundry or other washing facilities are located in a common cellar area.

RUBBISH & RECYCLING

The Germans have been sorting their rubbish for years and recycling is now a way of life. Most cities and towns require the sorting of household rubbish into several categories, including (at least) paper, cardboard, glass, plastic and metal. Many towns also collect organic waste (*Biomüll*) for composting and old clothes, bed linen and curtains for the poor (*Altkleidersammlung*). You should check with your local *Stadverwaltung* for the exact requirements for each category and how 'recyclables' should be prepared for collection, as this can vary from town to town. For example, some councils require that white paper be separated from coloured paper, while others insist only that brown cardboard be kept separate from paper. A few smaller councils require only that recyclable material be separated into 'round' (bottles, cans, jars, etc.) and 'flat' (paper, cardboard, plastic, etc.).

Most towns provide each building with standard-size coloured bins for each type of rubbish and recyclable waste. The collection of rubbish and recyclables is usually 'metered' for billing to building owners or maintenance companies, the cost being distributed to building occupants as part of their incidental charges (see page 104). Often bins have a bar-coded label which indicates the 'owner' of the bin, whether the homeowner or the management company of the apartment block. Each time a bin is emptied the bar code is 'swiped' and the owner is charged according to the size of the container. A large container costs more to empty each time, so many building owners try to make do with the smallest possible bins, even if they fill up long before the next collection day! **Leaving rubbish in plastic sacks alongside official rubbish bins is a violation of house rules (if not local laws) and you can be fined if you're identified as the culprit.**

Bottles

Knowing Germany's deposit (*Pfand*) rules is essential or you'll lose a great deal of money. Glass deposit bottles are standard throughout Germany for most juices and fizzy drinks, including beer (wine bottles are the main exception). The price of these drinks includes a *Pfand* to ensure the return of the bottle and the plastic crate (if you buy in bulk). When you return the empty bottles and cases to the shop where you made your purchase, you're refunded the deposit in cash or as a credit on your purchase (on the same visit). So-called one-way plastic bottles (*Einwegflaschen*) carry a €0.25 cent deposit and can be brought back to almost any supermarket and deposited in a machine, which dispenses a voucher to be claimed from the cashier. When a machine is unavailable you can return your bottles to a drink counter or to the cashier. Hard plastic bottles that you buy at kiosks (e.g. at railway stations) have a €0.15 *Pfand* but must be returned to the kiosk you bought them from (write it on the bottle!). Bottles made of polyethylene terephthalate (labelled *PET*) don't have a *Pfand*.

Non-deposit glass bottles (including wine bottles) should be disposed of in the appropriate glass recycling bin (e.g. for clear, brown or green glass). Many towns provide 'bottle banks' in car parks.

Packaging

German shops are required by law to take back packaging materials, e.g. cardboard boxes, plastic bags and Styrofoam, for every product they sell. Many supermarkets and other large shops provide a bin in the car park or near the main entrance to collect this material. If you have furniture or large appliances delivered to your home, the delivery service must take the packaging material away for you. In fact, if you have your household goods moved by a professional mover, they must offer either to take the packing boxes away with them after they've unpacked your belongings, or to pick up the empty boxes once you've unpacked them yourself. On the other hand, empty packing boxes (particularly heavy-duty ones used for international moves) can be sold for a couple of euros each to people who are moving or need storage boxes.

Other Recycling

Large objects, such as unwanted household furniture, broken appliances or building debris, may be collected once or twice a year on dates announced by your local council (*Stadtverwaltung*). In many areas, the evening before the pick-up you'll see people inspecting the items their neighbours have put out for disposal. By the time the trucks show up the next morning, many of the still-serviceable articles will have vanished, leaving only the real rubbish to be picked up. This form of 'direct' recycling is technically illegal but is tolerated by most local governments and residents.

You can usually request a collection of large items (for a fee) by calling your council offices. In some communities this is the only way of disposing of large or bulky items, so you may want to arrange a pick-up with one or more neighbours in order to share the cost.

Dead batteries mustn't be put in with regular household rubbish for collection but should be returned to shops, where they're collected for proper disposal (there's usually a box near the checkout). Shops are required to provide this facility if they sell batteries or battery-powered devices.

Other hazardous materials (paint, paint thinner, cleaning solvents, motor oil, etc.) should be taken to the local recycling and disposal centre. Information published by your local council will include the location of the nearest recycling centre, its hours of business and details of disposal requirements.

6.

POSTAL SERVICES

There's at least one post office (*Postamt*) in every German city or town, a total of some 12,000, although they're disappearing fast in small villages. As in many other countries, privatisation has put an end to the traditional role of the post office. The German Post Office (Deutsche Post AG) no longer operates the telephone system or offers banking services and it's now responsible solely for delivering post. When the post office was privatised, its banking and telephone operations became the Deutsche Postbank AG and the Deutsche Telekom AG respectively. However, it's still possible to open a savings or cheque account at a post office, deposit or withdraw cash, pay bills and perform a number of other banking transactions. Many post offices still have one or more telephone booths, although as they're no longer operated by the same company, there's a surcharge for using them.

Privatisation has had another negative consequence: the privatised postal service is trying to introduce the concept of customer care to its employees, although the process is far from complete. While many postal employees are courteous and helpful, some (known affectionately as 'stamp dragons') are notably less so! On the plus side, now that it has lost its responsibility for telecommunications and banking and can concentrate almost entirely on delivering post, Deutsche Post provides one of Europe's best postal services. Packages and express post are delivered by DHL, a subsidiary of Deutsche Post and the world's leading delivery network, though as a customer you aren't aware of using a different service.

Deutsche Post has an extremely useful and informative website (🖳 www. deutschepost.de – click on 'English' at the top right of the home page. It produces a number of free publications describing its products and services, the most comprehensive of which is entitled *Serviceinformationen*, available free from post offices.

BUSINESS HOURS

It's difficult to generalise about post office business hours, although offices usually open from around 8 or 8.30am until 6pm on weekdays and until noon on Saturdays. Generally, the larger the city, the longer the main post office (*Hauptpostamt*) remains open. Main post offices are usually located next to main railway stations (*Hauptbahnhof*) and are often open for a short time on Sundays. Smaller post offices may close for lunch, which is usually between 1 and 2.30pm. Post offices that are part of shops – a recent innovation – may open earlier or close later than ordinary post offices, depending on the business hours of the shops in which they're located.

Post office opening hours are given at the entrance to each building. However, should you need to establish the opening hours or locate the whereabouts of a particular post office in the country you can obtain the information by phoning ☎ 01802-3333 between 7am and 8pm on weekdays and from 8am to 2pm on Saturdays. The call costs €0.06 from an ordinary fixed line, irrespective of duration or where you're calling from in Germany. You can also use the search option (*Filialsuche*) on the 'Online Services' page of the Deutsche Post website (🖥 www.deutschepost.de).

LETTER POST

Ordinary letters posted at larger post offices before 9am are usually delivered the next working day anywhere in Germany. Delivery times to other countries are more difficult to estimate as a result of varying service standards in the country of destination but average 2.2 days for Belgium and the Netherlands, 2.3 days for the UK and 4.3 days for Italy – which says a lot more about the efficiency of Italy's postal service than Germany's!

Most post offices sell a variety of envelopes in various sizes, including 'bubble-pack' envelopes for sending fragile, but relatively flat items.

Rates

Postal rates for letters are based on a combination of size, weight, quantity (e.g. bulk deliveries), type of delivery, and even the content and purpose. A complete list of rates would be encyclopaedic and beyond the scope of this book, but the most common categories are listed below:

- **Postcard (*Postkarte*)** – €0.45 within Germany, €0.65 within Europe and €1 to the rest of the world;

- **Standard letter (*Standardbrief*)** – A 'standard letter' must be between 90 and 125mm wide and between 140 and 235mm long. It may be no more than 5mm thick and weigh no more than 20g. Postage is €0.55 to Germany, €0.70 to Europe and €1.70 to the rest of the world. American readers should note that the standard US 'business size' envelope (9.5 inches) is too long for this category of post. It's therefore advisable to use standard German envelopes.

- **Compact letter (*Kompaktbrief*)** – Despite its name, this has the same maximum width and length as a standard letter and can be slightly thicker and heavier: up to 10mm and 50g. It costs €0.90 within Germany, €1 within Europe and €2 to the rest of the world.

- **Large letter (*Grossbrief*)** – *Grossbriefe* may be between 70 and 250mm wide and between 100 and 353mm long, not more than 20mm thick with a maximum weight of 500g. The postage is €1.45 (within Germany only).

- **Maximum letter (*Maxibrief*)** – This is the largest size of letter than can be sent to domestic destinations. The length can be from 100mm to 353mm, the breadth from 70mm to 250mm, the thickness not more than 50mm, and the weight up to 1kg. It costs €2.20.

● **International maximum letter (*Maxibrief International*)** – the largest letter that can be sent abroad, which can be up to 600mm long or wide and weigh up to 2kg. Costs vary with weight, destination and the manner of shipment and range from €2 (to Europe) to €24 (to the ends of the earth).

A *Plusbrief* is an envelope with pre-printed postage. It's available at post offices and online and comes in packs of between three and ten envelopes costing between €2.40 and €6.50. They're stamped to the value needed for standard (within Germany), standard (rest of Europe), compact and large letter post and are available with or without windows.

Aerogrammes are available from stationery shops and cost €1 for worldwide delivery. They must not include enclosures of any kind.

Certain materials addressed to blind recipients, including Braille texts, audio tapes and similar materials, and weighing up to 7kg can be sent free. Particular rules apply – enquire at a post office for details.

Stamps can be purchased at any post office or from stamp machines outside post offices. **Note that when buying stamps from a machine, you receive your 'change' in stamps!** Alternatively, you can print postage vouchers via your PC (visit 🖳 www.deutschepost.de and go to 'Online franking (Stampit Web)' in the drop-down menu under 'Online Services').

Stamp collectors can order a variety of subscriptions and special issues via the extensive philately section on the 🖳 www.deutschepost.de website, as well as sign up for a free 'e-newsletter'.

Conditions

The correct format for addressing envelopes is as follows:

> Herrn Hans Handel
> Goethestr. 12
> D-65193 Wiesbaden
> Germany

Note that the street number follows the street name and the post code (*Postleitzahl*) precedes the name of the city. You may occasionally see envelopes with the post code and city name on the second line and the street address on the third. This is an old format and its use is discouraged due to the increasing mechanisation of post processing.

Mechanisation also requires that addresses begin no more than 14cm (around 5.5 inches) from the right edge of the envelope. This has the effect of moving the address considerably further to the right than is customary in many countries. Although senders of individual letters can safely disregard this rule, businesses sending mass mailings must be aware of it. The 'bible' for formats and rules such as this is the booklet *Gut in Form; ganz automatisch*, available free from post offices.

A list of post codes is available for inspection at any post office and on the Deutsche Post website (💻 www.deutschepost.de).

If you send a letter with insufficient postage it will be returned to you.

Registration & Insurance

There are various kinds of registered (*per Einschreibung*) letter. A letter which is recorded only by the postman (*Einwurfeinschreiben*) costs €1.60 plus postage. If you want a letter signed for by the recipient (*Übergabeeinschreiben*), who may not be the addressee, the cost is €2.05 plus postage. For greater security, materials sent as *Übergabeeinschreiben* may also be denominated *eigenhändig* for an additional €1.80. This ensures that delivery is to the addressee or his legal representative only, who must sign for the item. If you want a return receipt (*Rückschein*), which costs an additional €1.80, it must be signed by the recipient and is returned to the sender.

There are many categories of insurance for various kinds of post. Ask for details at a post office.

PARCELS

The most convenient way to send parcels is by using the standard boxes available in the *Packset*, an assortment of pre-cut and pre-folded boxes available from post offices. The designations, sizes and prices are as follows:

Designation	Dimensions	Cost
XS	22.5 x 14.5 x 3.5cm	€1.49
S	25 x 17.5 x 10cm	€1.69
M	37.5 x 30 x 13.5cm	€1.99
L	45 x 35 x 20cm	€2.29
F	37.5 x 13 x 13cm	€2.49

The F box is designed to take a standard bottle (e.g. of champagne). *Packset* boxes include address labels and (all but the XS size) sealing tape.

The variety of parcel-post categories and rates is even greater than that for letter post. Generally speaking, postage to domestic addresses on parcels weighing up to 2kg costs €3.90, 2-10kg €6.90 and up to 20kg €9.90. Sending packages between 5kg and 20kg to the EU (Zone 1) costs between €17 and €45. To the most distant parts of the world (Zones 3 and 4), it costs between €32 and €82. Packages sent within Germany normally arrive the next day.

EXPRESS POST

It's possible to send letters and parcels by express post. Express letters (*Express Briefe*) cost from €8 to €11 depending on the weight (the maximum is 2kg). Express packages (*Express Pakete*) can weigh up to 31.5kg and the price includes insurance up to €2,500 and an online tracking service, but there's no published tariff; you must take your package to a post office or ring ☎ 01805-345 2255 with the details to find out the price. Both letters and packages are delivered the next day, unless it's a Sunday or a public holiday. An extra fee of €31 (plus VAT) will ensure delivery on a Sunday or public holiday.

Postage for express post sent abroad is determined by weight and delivery zone. Zone 1 includes countries in western Europe, Zone 2 the rest of Europe, Zone 3 the US, Canada and the Middle East, and Zone 4 the rest of the world. Costs run from €38.35 for items up to 200g to a Zone 1 country to €437.15 for a 20kg shipment to a country in Zone 4.

COLLECTION & DELIVERY

Post boxes are yellow with a black stylised post-horn symbol and are usually mounted on building walls. Collections from boxes outside main post offices are usually made every hour or two, while in residential neighbourhoods boxes may be emptied only once a day (the days and times of collections are displayed on the front of boxes). A sticker on a post box in the form of a large red dot indicates that it will be emptied later than others in the area.

There's one postal delivery per day in most of Germany, from Mondays to Saturdays, usually in the morning.

If your postman requires a signature or payment of import duty, VAT or excess postage when you aren't at home, he will leave a form showing the address where you can pick up the item (not always the nearest post office). Pay particular attention to the entry on the card that begins '*heute jedoch nicht vor...*' followed by a time. You cannot retrieve the post before the time on the day (*heute* = today) you receive the notice.

Most post offices provide a *poste restante* (*Postlagernd*) service. Post is held for 14 days, and you may authorise others to collect it for you from the *Postlagernde Sendungen* counter (authorisation must be in writing). Post intended for such delivery should be addressed as follows:

```
[your name]
Postlagernd
[post code] [city]
Germany
```

Ensure that the address includes the correct post code for the post office where you want the post to be delivered. Try to ensure that your correspondents use the German term *Postlagernd* rather than the French *poste restante*, as the French term, while well known internationally, isn't generally used in Germany.

You can obtain a post office box (*Postfach*) at your local post office for a one-off registration fee of €15. There are no further charges. Post office box addresses should be in the following format:

```
[your name]
Postfach [box number]
[post code] [city]
Germany
```

The box number should be written with the digits grouped in pairs, e.g. Postfach 23 45 67. Note that the post code of your box is usually different from that of the post office in which the box is located!

CHANGE OF ADDRESS

If you're moving house, ask your local post office for a 'forwarding form' (*Nachsendeantrag*). Ordinary post can be forwarded to any country in the world for €15.20 (for six months) or €25.20 (for a year). You must make a request no later than five days before you want the forwarding of post to begin. For holidays and other temporary absences, it's often more practical to ask the post office to simply hold your post until your return. The form to use to request this is a *Lagerungsauftrag.*

POST OFFICE BANKING

Although the post office sold its banking operation when it was privatised, the banking company, Deutsche Postbank AG, transacts most of its business at post offices and has branches at many post offices in Germany, as well as 7,000 cash machines (ATMs) throughout the country, including those of Dresdner Bank, Commerzbank, Deutsche Bank and Hypovereinsbank.

Services available from Postbank include the following:

- bill payment (in person, by post or electronically), cash deposits and withdrawals;

- Postbank debit card free with account;

- Postbank MasterCard or Visa card – €15 for the first year and €20 for each subsequent year (€5 for those aged under 26) unless you open an account, in which case the first year is free;

- postage-paid envelopes for sending *Zahlungsverkehrsvordrucke* (see **Paying Bils** below) or other transactions;

- deposit insurance;

- option to open a savings account (*Postgirokonto* or *Postsparkonto*).

A *Postgirokonto* is among the cheapest bank accounts and, provided you deposit at least €1,250 per month you're eligible for a *Giro Plus* account, for which there's no maintenance fee. If you don't fulfil this condition, the monthly fee for a standard account is €5.90.

Electronic Banking

Manual transactions are well on the way to becoming obsolete, and extensive investment by Postbank in 'electronic banking' (the words are almost always written in English) has made it possible for you to do almost everything that can be done at a post office (except withdraw cash) from home via a computer and the internet. Both the major home-banking software packages, *Microsoft Money* and Intuit Corporation's *Quicken*, will enter account information directly from Postbank into your computerised chequebook. However the option most people choose (and one that doesn't require a software package) is *Online-Banking* through Postbank's own website (🖥 www.postbank.de), which allows you to carry out most transactions. One advantage of the online service is that transfers to and from EU countries are free.

Signatures are clearly impossible with online banking, but electronic payments are nonetheless quite safe. Postbank issues you with a personal identification number (PIN), which you must use to access your account, even if you wish only to check the balance. Transactions require additional numbers (TANs), which are each valid for a single transaction only; an attempt to re-use one generates an error message. The absence of a human element in this process increases the level of security but has the inevitable drawback that if you lose your PIN or TANs, no Postbank employee can help you and you must apply for new ones – a process that can take up to ten days.

For further information about banking, see **Chapter 14**.

Paying Bills

A red-and-white payment form (*Zahlungsverkehrsvordruck*) is usually included with bills you receive by post in Germany. With this form you can pay the bill, either in cash or as a direct debit from your bank account, at any post office or through any bank. There's no charge for the transaction provided you have a Postbank savings account or an account at the bank where you're making the payment. Most payment forms are partially completed with the payee's name, account number (*Kontonummer*), branch code (*Bankleitzahl*) and the amount owing, so you usually need only enter your own account number and branch code. **Make sure that you sign the form, however, or payment will be rejected.**

If there's no payment form enclosed with a bill, you should use your own, which Postbank provides free of charge. These are pre-printed with your name and account number, and the name and branch code of the Postbank branch that maintains your account. You must enter the payee's name and bank data, the amount and your signature. The payee's bank data (*Bankverbindung*) is shown at the bottom of the payee's letter or statement in the following format:

> **Dresdner Bank Stuttgart, BLZ 600 800 00, Ktonr. 987 654 321**

BLZ is the abbreviation for *Bankleitzahl* (branch code) while *Ktonr.* is the abbreviation for *Kontonummer* (account number). If more than one bank is listed, you may make the payment to any of them. It isn't strictly necessary to enter the name of the payee's bank on the form, but if you omit it you must be absolutely certain you've entered the branch code correctly.

If the creditor hasn't sent you a payment form and you have none left, you can obtain a blank one from a post office, although in this case you must complete everything yourself.

When writing figures in Germany (or anywhere in continental Europe), you should cross the down stroke of the number 7 in order to avoid confusion with the number 1, which is often written with a leading upstroke and resembles a seven to many non-Europeans. Germans (and other Europeans) write the date with the day first followed by the month and year, not as Americans do with the month first. For example, 1.7.08 is 1st July 2008 and not 7th January 2008. The conventional US form 1/7/01, with the month first and slashes between the digits, is unknown and must **never** be used.

POST OFFICE SHOPPING

German post offices also offer the following products and services:

- **Computer software** – for businesses;

- **Gifts** – A new venture between Deutsche Post and a number of German mail-order companies allows customers to order gifts ranging from flowers to books and CDs to wine, spirits and chocolates. Catalogues, entitled *Geschenkservice*, are updated every few months and available at any post office.

- **Lottery tickets** – for a single draw or an annual subscription;

- **Tickets** – for concerts, the circus, exhibitions and other major events;

- **Toys** – Collectors (and indulgent parents) can find an interesting and large selection of model trucks, buses, railway engines and historical postal vehicles for sale at larger post offices. These can also be ordered by post from Deutsche Post AG, Collection, Postfach 201208, 60642 Frankfurt, by telephone (☎ 0180-3246 042), or via the philately section of the Deutsche Post website (🖳 www.deutschepost.de).

7.

TELEPHONE

Until recently the German telephone network, operated by Deutsche Telekom (DT), was a state-run monopoly, and prices were among the highest in western Europe. In accordance with EU legislation, the German government privatised DT and offered 500m shares (representing around 26 per cent of the company) to the German public. Despite the reputation of Germans as cautious investors, the privatisation proved wildly successful and provided DT with much-needed capital to update and widen its range of services and prepare for competition, which was introduced to the German telecommunications market in 1998. Despite these changes, DT's customer service still has a 'public service' quality, perhaps because over 95 per cent of fixed lines are still owned and managed by DT.

Needless to say, DT doesn't appreciate the recent increase in competition and you may find that other providers can be somewhat slower at getting your telephone connected (as they must deal with DT). On the other hand they usually provide more personable service and attractive offers.

While DT investors have seen their shares take a roller-coaster ride after initially doubling in price, the outcome for telephone users has been a drop in prices. The downside is that there are now so many companies competing for your business (particularly in the long-distance and international markets) that keeping track of who offers the best deal has become a challenge.

INSTALLATION & REGISTRATION

The simplest way to get a standard telephone line installed in your home is to visit a DT office and complete an application form. The fee for installing a line in a property is around €60. DT often offers package deals (see **Charges** on page 136) that include this service in the price. If your property already has a line, you must usually wait just a day or two for connection rather than the couple of weeks it takes to install a new line. For the same price you can have either an analogue or a digital (ISDN) socket.

It's possible to rent or buy a telephone from DT or to have one included in a package deal, but this means you're committed to a 12-month contract. Alternatively, you can purchase one from a retailer. Basic phones cost as little as €20, although it's important to check that they conform to European specifications: a phone should have a CE and/or a BZT registration number, usually found on a sticker on its base. If a DT technician discovers 'illegal' phones, he will disconnect them and Telekom may refuse to continue providing a service to repeat 'offenders'. Almost any phone you purchase in Germany will be approved.

For analogue phones, it's the usual practice for DT to install only a TEA (European phone standard) connector and to leave it to the customer to decide what equipment to connect to it. However, Germans are rapidly switching to ISDN lines and the digital phone network is already extensive in Germany. DT markets a number of ISDN packages; the standard one costs around €25 per month compared with €16.50 per month for an analogue line, but an ISDN line allows subscribers to use two services simultaneously, e.g. phone and fax or internet.

To discontinue your phone service with DT, you must cancel the contract in writing and pay the final bill when it arrives. DT is infamous for pursuing ex-customers to the ends of the world to extract outstanding payments!

EMERGENCY & USEFUL NUMBERS

There are two nationwide emergency numbers in Germany: 110 for the police and 112 for fire and ambulance services. In some remote areas there are local numbers for ambulance services, although the fire department (on 112) will gladly put you through. You should be able to call either of these numbers free of charge from any public phone, including card phones, although with some old payphones you may need to insert coins first, which will be returned after the call. In many phone booths there's an emergency services 'lever' in a case near the phone. Pulling it to the green side automatically connects you to the police, the red side to the fire department – needless to say, misuse of this facility is punishable by a heavy fine.

Some other useful numbers to keep by your phone are listed below – those prefixed with an asterisk (*) are available only from a mobile phone.

Number	Service
030-40504050	Credit card cancellation (for all kinds of credit card)
*116116	Credit card cancellation
0761-19240	Poison control
0800-111 0333	To report child abuse
0900-1122499	ADAC (German motoring club) traffic report
*22499	ADAC traffic report

USING THE TELEPHONE

Using the telephone in Germany is much the same as in any other country, with a few German eccentricities thrown in for good measure. When dialling a number in your exchange area, dial the number only. When dialling anywhere else, you must add the area code before the subscriber's number. There's no standard method of writing German phone numbers. Some advertisements and company letterheads have spaces between each few digits, while others prefer to separate the area code (*Vorwahl*) from the rest of the number with a dash or full stop or put it in brackets. In this book, dashes are used to separate the code and spaces are inserted every three or four digits in the number itself.

Answering the Phone

Germans generally answer the phone by stating their last names; so don't expect a cheery 'Good morning' when you ring somebody. When making a call, Germans identify themselves first, before asking for the person they're calling, so if you don't want to be thought pushy or rude, it's best to do likewise. Similarly, it may be considered impolite to ring a private home between 1 and 3pm or after 9pm.

Listed below are some everyday phrases for use on the phone.

English	German
I'd like to speak to ___ .	*Ich möchte mit ___ sprechen.*
Could you connect me with ___ ?	*Könnten Sie mich mit ___ verbinden?*
___ is not in.	*___ ist nicht hier/im Hause.*
I will try again later.	*Ich versuche es später noch einmal.*
I would like to leave a message for ___ .	*Ich möchte ___ eine Nachricht hinterlassen.*
You've reached the wrong number.	*Sie sind falsch verbunden.*
Could you ask ___ to call me back?	*Könnten Sie ___ bitten zurückzurufen?*

Answering Machines

Answering machines cost from around €40, while the most expensive models cost around double this and have a range of special features, including automatic ring-back, call forwarding, remote playback of messages (only accessible using a code), and recording the date and time of incoming calls. Similar facilities (i.e. 'voicemail') are usually available from your telephone service provider and are normally included in your monthly fee. You simply dial a number to access your messages, and no extra device is needed.

Recorded Messages

Electronics, music and computer shops sell a variety of cassette tapes and CDs with pre-recorded messages in German for around €10. **Be wary of programming your telephone answering machine with a jokey message, which may not amuse Germans!** Listed below are some of the recorded messages you're most likely to hear.

German	English
Kein Anschluss unter dieser Nummer.	This number is unavailable.
Dieser Anschluss ist vorübergehend nicht erreichbar.	This number is temporarily unobtainable.
Diese Rufnummer hat sich geändert.	This number has been changed.
Bitte, erfragen Sie die neue Nummer bei der Auskunft.	Please ask Directory Enquiries for the new number.
Der Platz ist besetzt; bitte, warten Sie.	The extension is busy; please hold.

Nuisance Calls

Nuisance calls are rare. The best advice is to hang up as soon as you realise the nature of the call; most telephone pests soon lose interest if they fail to get a response. If the calls continue, you could blow a loud whistle down the line. If nuisance calls get out of hand, you can ask Telekom to use its call tracing service (called *Fangschaltung*), for which there's a fee. **You should also report the problem to the police.**

If you want to 'screen' calls before you pick up the receiver, you need a telephone that displays the caller's number or, preferably, an ID box which records this in its memory and gives you a permanent record of who has been phoning you. With the latter you can also associate numbers with names, so that the name of a caller appears on the display rather than just his number. The service doesn't apply to international calls, which are displayed as 'Number not recognised' (*Nummer unbekannt*). Caller ID boxes are available for around €30 from electronics shops such as Conrad (🖳 www.conrad.de) and from specialist phone shops. Nearly all telephones with digital displays have this feature.

SERVICE PROVIDERS

Since privatisation, a plethora of companies have started offering long-distance telephone services. This competition among carriers has resulted in the lowest phone costs in German history. Internet and cable providers compete with DT in offering telephone/internet combination packages, normally for a fixed monthly rate (*Flatrate* in 'German') for unlimited use. The major telephone and internet service providers are listed as follows:

- Alice – ☎ 0800-411 0411, 🖵 www.alice-dsl.de

- AOL – ☎ 01805-313 164, 🖵 www.aol.de

- Arcor – ☎ 0800-107 0220, 🖵 www.arcor.de

- Freenet – ☎ 01805-019 293, 🖵 www.freenet.de

- Kabeldeutschland – ☎ 01805-233 325, 🖵 www.kabeldeutschland.de

If you prefer not to be tied to a particular provider but free to switch according to which is offering the lowest prices at a particular time, you can use a 'call-by-call' service (the English term is used in German), although some providers require you to pay a minimum monthly fee and some require you to enter into an exclusive contract. To take advantage of a call-by-call service, you must dial a prefix (usually five digits) before the area code and phone number; you cannot do this from a phone connected by cable or, in some cases, ADSL. Some providers bill you independently of DT, while others (including most call-by-call providers) add their charges to your DT phone bill (see **Bills** on page 138).

In order to compare the prices and packages currently offered by each company (which change frequently!), go to 🖵 www.billiger-telefonieren.de or 🖵 www.teletarif.de. Alternatively, you can buy a 'call router' that selects the cheapest service provider for a given call, whether domestic or international. Some call routers are updated weekly by data transmission, although this is an optional service that costs extra. For those who must make regular long-distance or international calls and companies that rely on the phone for their business, these devices can save a considerable amount of money.

For more information on internet access see **Internet** on page 142.

CHARGES

How much you're being charged for a particular call is often almost impossible to calculate, as most telephone service providers offer only package deals, which may include the rent of a telephone, a certain number of 'free' calls or minutes, a discount on calls to mobile phones (*Festnetz zu Mobil*) or to selected countries (a benefit that may be called '*CountrySelect*' or '*CountryFlat*') and in some cases also internet access, cable TV services and/or a mobile phone contract. To further complicate the matter, there may be a variety of tariff periods, according to whether a call is local or national. Note also that all charges are based on one-minute intervals (*1-Minuten-Takt*), which means you pay for the full minute even if your call ends before the next 60 seconds are up.

In mid-2007, the cheapest national weekday peak time calls within Germany were via 01029 Telecom (access number 01029) and cost €0.0153 per minute. (Peak times are similar with most operators.) However, the cheapest for the weekday slot from 9pm to midnight were via Linkware (access number 01054), which charged €0.0166 per minute. The table below indicates typical rates charged for calls to selected overseas destinations in mid-2007.

Country	Price per Minute
Australia	€0.0183
Canada	€0.0137
UK	€0.012
US	€0.0139

The charges quoted below are DT's.

Local Calls

A local or 'city' call is a call within your code area (even if you don't live in a city!). You pay per minute according to the time of day, as follows (excluding VAT):

- **Daytime/Peak Rate** – Calls made on Mondays to Fridays from 7am to 7pm cost either €0.04 or €0.031 per minute depending on whether you sign up for DT's 'call plus' or 'call time' plan respectively.

- **Weekend/Off-peak Rate** – At all other times local calls cost €0.016 per minute with 'call plus' or €0.015 with 'call time'.

If you take out the 'XXL local' plan (costing €26 per month) or 'XXL fulltime' plan (€36 per month), all local calls are included in the monthly *Flatrate*.

National Calls

National calls (i.e. those outside your code area) are charged per minute or part of a minute. DT's rates (excluding VAT) are as follows:

- **Daytime Standard/Peak Rate** – Calls made between 7am and 7pm on weekdays cost €0.051, €0.046 or €0.04 depending on whether you sign up for the 'call plus', 'call time' or 'XXL local' plan respectively.

- **Weekend/Off-peak Rate** – National calls at all other times cost €0.03 with 'call plus' or €0.026 with 'call time' or XXL local'.

With 'XXL full-time' all national calls (from a fixed-line phone) are included in the monthly 'flatrate'.

International Calls

Rates vary according to the country you call. At present a call to the UK, US or Canada costs €0.126 per minute at any time of day with the 'call plus' plan and €0.046 with all other plans. You can request a 'country select' or 'country flat' service to get a cheaper price for the country of your choice – at extra cost, of course!

Other Calls

Calls to mobile phones are much more expensive than calls to fixed lines, costing between €0.159 and €0.234 per minute depending on which mobile network you call and which DT plan you have. Public telephone charges are €0.23 per minute for local and €0.34 per minute for national calls; calls to most western European countries cost €0.67 per minute, to the US and Canada €1 and to the rest of the world between €1.50 and €3.

BILLS

Your telephone bill (*Rechnung*) is issued monthly, whether by DT or another provider. It shows the charges for the previous month, based on units. For an additional fee you can request an itemised phone bill showing all calls made. A standard phone bill includes the following information (listed in alphabetical order):

German	English
Andere Dienstleistungen	Additional services provided by Telekom
Anschlüsse an . . .	Services to . . . (i.e. other providers' services)

bei Rückfragen Telefon	Telephone number to contact in case of billing discrepancies
Cityverbindungen	Local calls
Deutschlandsverbindungen	National calls (i.e. outside the local area)
Inlandsauskunft, Auslandsauskunft	Calls to information services
Kundennummer	Customer reference number
Mobilfunknetz	Connections made to mobile phone services
Monatliche Beträge	Monthly basic fee (including any rented equipment)
Rechnungsbetrag	Total amount due (including 16 per cent VAT)
Rechnungsdatum	Date of billing
Rechnungsnummer	Billing number
Regionalverbindungen	Regional calls
Rufnummer	Customer's telephone number
Weltverbindungen	International calls

Your telephone bill must be paid within 14 days of the date it was sent to you. If you're late, there's a penalty of €1; if you fail to pay after being sent two reminders, your service is disconnected, in which case, there's a fee to be reconnected and your telephone number is likely to change because your previous one may have been given to another customer. (It's no wonder DT customers are paranoid about paying their bills on time!) Payment can be made in advance of an absence by simply completing a form at your bank and paying the estimated amount for the period in question or using online banking to pay the bill. Any difference is adjusted the following month.

The most popular way to pay phone bills is by regular direct debit (*Dauerauftrag*). You receive a bill for information purposes. You can also settle your phone bill at a bank, but this means paying in cash, (often) waiting in a queue and, if you aren't an account holder at the bank, paying a fee.

PUBLIC TELEPHONES

Public phone boxes in Germany used to be easy to spot by their bright colour (yellow), but only a few of these remain. New booths are pink, and there are far fewer of them. Although DT claims to have 100,000 payphones in Germany, finding a public phone can sometimes be a challenge, although there's usually one (or more) at post offices, in hotel foyers, hospitals, restaurants and pedestrian areas of cities, outside the gates of military bases, at *Autobahn* service areas, airports and railway and bus stations, and near sports stadiums.

To use a phone in a post office, you must register at the counter, make your call from the assigned booth and then return to the counter to pay. If you're making an international call, go to the counter marked *Auslandgespräche*. **Note, however, that you must pay a hefty cash deposit for an international call – as much as €50 if you're phoning the US.** Germany's public phone system is fully automated; therefore operator-assisted calls aren't possible from phone booths, including those at post offices.

As elsewhere in Europe, most public phones in Germany no longer accept cash but require phone cards (*Telefonkarte*). These are available in denominations of €5 and €10 from DT offices, post offices and some newspaper kiosks. The cost of each call is subtracted automatically from the card. An increasing number of phone booths (currently 15,000 according to DT) accept international credit cards (*Kreditkarte*), particularly those at airports, railway stations and hotels. There is a €1 fee per call when you pay by credit card. The other payment option is a 'money card' (*Geldkarte* – see **Cash & Debit Cards** on page 294), which costs €0.10 per call. Only a few payphones, mainly at airports and railway stations, accept coins. See **Other Calls** on page 138 for the cost of calls.

Some phones have an illuminated counter indicating the credit remaining; when '*Bitte Zahlen*' flashes it's time to insert more money. Some phone booths, indicated by a bell logo, will receive calls – which is useful if you run out of money as you can ask the person you're calling to ring you back.

In addition to payphones, there are around 1,000 internet terminals (mostly in railway stations and airport terminals), where you can check email, surf the internet and send text messages. You can pay by credit card or telephone card.

TELEPHONE DIRECTORIES

Deutsche Telekom issues a handy free annual book of German and foreign area codes, entitled *Amtliches Verzeichnis der Ortsnetzkennzahlen* (inevitably abbreviated to *AVON*). To check international codes, you must know your country names in German, e.g. *Kanada* and *Ungarn* (Hungary). All DT subscribers are entitled to a free copy of *AVON*, along with their local telephone directory and yellow pages, but directories aren't delivered to your door. You must collect copies, normally from your local post office – subscribers receive a postcard explaining the procedure each year. Some post offices accept old directories for recycling, while others expect you to recycle them yourself.

Information about the phone system is provided in seven languages, including English, at the front of phone books. You can look up numbers in directories other than your own at a post office, although the quality of directories varies, as Germans have the inconsiderate habit of tearing out the pages they want. You can obtain a nationwide telephone directory on CD-ROM, which costs €15, or look up numbers (free) online at 💻 www.dastelefonbuch.de.

The yellow pages (*Gelbe Seiten*) are also available online, at 💻 www.gelbe seiten.de, where some 3,000 entries are updated every day.

Directory Enquiries

The phone number for domestic directory enquiries is ☎ 11833 and calls cost €0.20 for 'connection' plus €1 per minute. For international enquiries (☎ 11834) it's €1 per call and €1.19 per minute. For a service in English dial ☎ 11837.

MOBILE PHONES

Mobile phones (*Handys* – pronounced, more or less, as in English) range from around €200 to around €400 without a contract; if you take out a contract, the phone is usually 'free'. Needless to say, this apparent benevolence carries a sting in the tail. In the small print of the contract there's a clause committing you to a minimum period with a specific service provider. This will be at least a year and possibly three, which allows the retailer to recoup the cost of the phone in call charges and (he hopes) make a sizeable profit. A typical mobile phone contract requires you to pay at least €15 a month, even if you don't use your phone at all. Added to this are charges for each call you make, although some 'free' calls may be included in the monthly rental.

You can buy mobile phones from general shops, specialist dealers, and department and chain stores. Retailers have arrangements with service providers or networks to sell contracts along with phones, so you shouldn't rely on getting good or impartial advice from retail staff, some of whom know little or nothing about phones and networks. Ask friends and colleagues for their recommendations and shop around, comparing not only phone prices but also the features and additional services on offer (see below). Above all, compare the monthly fees and the charges for calls at different times.

There's an active market in second-hand mobile phones. Good places to look are in the shoppers' newspapers that are published once or twice a week, such as *SperrMüll* (💻 www.Sperrmuell.de), *Alles, Kurz & Fündig* and *Pinwand* (all three advertise on 💻 www.quoka.de) and *das Inserat* (💻 www.das-inserat.de). The German version of the eBay website (💻 www.ebay.de), which is as popular as its American and British counterparts, has a category '*Handy & Organizer*'.

There are three main mobile phone systems in Germany: *D-Net*, which operates on the GSM-900 band; *E-Net*, on the GSM-1800 band; and UMTS (also known as High-Speed Downlink Packet Access or HSDPA), a broadband service which allows you to access the internet and download and upload music, pictures, etc. but is more expensive (between around €40 and €50 per month).

D-Net has some 'black spots', where communication isn't possible, the location of which depends on the company providing the service. If you live outside a major city you must ensure that a company's cover includes the area(s) where you live and do business. The two main *D-Net* networks are D1 (operated by Deutsche Telekom) and D2 (run by Vodaphone). In eastern Germany, D1 is said to have better cover, whereas in western Germany the two networks are about equal. *E-Net* (run by O2 and E-plus) operates mainly in the main urban centres. All mobile phone companies also provide UMTS.

All three mobile phone systems conform to the GSM digital standard used by most foreign systems (the exceptions being Japan and most of the US). This means that people moving to Germany from another European country, Africa, Australia or most of Asia can use their existing GSM phone and must purchase only a new coding (or SIM) card or have their phone 'unlocked' (this can be done by your service provider, sometimes free, or you can do it yourself by finding the code on the internet – search for 'unlock mobile phone' – and giving the brand and model number of your phone and its International Mobile Equipment Identity (IMEI) number, which is normally found under the battery). Coding cards can be bought with pre-paid credits, which can be 'topped up' once the existing credit is used, or paid for via a monthly bill as with a fixed-line phone service. Dual-band and tri-band mobile phones work in Germany.

Mobile phone companies offer 'free' local calls as part of a *Flatrate* and partner contracts so that you and your partner can call each other at a low rate or free. One service called '*homezone*' offered by O2 allows you to designate a home (or work address) so that any calls you make from within around 1km of that location are as low as standard fixed line rates. There may also be a discount when you call another phone using the same network (e.g. *D-Net*).

Most mobile phone companies don't include a cancellation clause in their contracts, and all of them will pursue you to the ends of the earth (literally) if you fail to pay until the end of your contract. Short-term mobile phone contracts aren't common (or cheap) but are available.

INTERNET

There's a variety of internet service providers (ISPs), an abundance of access packages and four principal types of internet connection:

- **Analogue** – the slowest and least efficient but adequate for people who don't use the internet for more than around 20 hours per month;

- **ISDN** – a digital connection that allows you to use the telephone and the internet simultaneously;

- **ADSL** – a broadband digital connection over the telephone line with higher data transfer speeds than ISDN (as high as 24,000 kilobits per second);

- **Cable** – a broadband connection that can send up to 30 megabits per second.

Deutsche Telekom's internet service, T-Online (⌨ www.t-online.de), is currently the most widely used, and offers a variety of tariffs depending what kind of internet connection you choose. The most basic package, called 'eco classic', costs €5 per month and includes 20 'free' hours, each additional **minute** online costing €1.60. An ADSL connection costs between around €17 and €30 per month for unlimited access. The best deals usually involve a combination of telephone and internet connection (dubbed 'call and surf') and cost between around €35 and €65 per month (unlimited) depending on the speed you choose. For a list of other telephone/internet service package providers see **Service Providers** on page 136.

Both CompuServe and AOL provide services in Germany and both have large numbers of customers. To sign up, contact ☎ 01805-704070 for CompuServe (⌨ www.compuserve.de) or ☎ 01805-313164 for AOL (⌨ www.aol.de). You're likely to receive free promotional CDs from both of these ISPs in your post from time to time, and you'll certainly find them on the free CD-ROMs provided with most computer magazines. Hundreds of smaller ISPs advertise in local newspapers and magazines, on advertising posters and on TV and radio. Prices and services vary and **you should be wary of signing up with an 'unknown' new service, however attractive the offer, as many fail in their first few months, leaving users high and dry**.

You can also sign up with a free email service, such as Yahoo Mail (⌨ www.yahoo.com) or Hotmail (⌨ www.hotmail.com). One advantage of these services is that you can access your email from any computer with web access, e.g. at a library or a cyber café. **However, email sent to and from such services isn't necessarily secure.**

Any modem can be used on the German network.

TELEGRAMS & FAX

Despite mind-boggling recent advances in communications technology, it's reassuring to know that you can still send telegrams in Germany – but only to someone else in Germany! Telegrams can be ordered by phone (☎ 01805-121210), fax (▤ 01805-121211)or online (at ⌨ www.post.de), and delivery is the next working day. You have the choice of a plain cover or, for a small supplement, a festive design. Costs are high, starting at over €15 for a short message of up to ten words. There's an extra fee of €10.50 for delivery on Sundays or public holidays.

Fax is also still widely used in Germany. If your fax is connected to a dedicated line, you must register it; if it's connected to the same line as your telephone (or you have a fax-phone), you needn't. The registration process involves simply faxing a printed form to DT. Any fax machine using the G3 standard is adequate, but it must have either a CE or (older) BZT registration number to be legal. **If you bring a fax machine to Germany, there's no guarantee that it will work.**

You can send faxes from post offices, where fax machines may be located in the entrance hall (for which you'll need a credit card) or behind the counter (for which you must pay in cash). You'll also find public (credit-card operated) fax machines in busy places such as airports, railway stations and motorway service stations.

8.

TELEVISION & RADIO

Since the '80s, when broadcasting regulations were relaxed across Europe, many private broadcasters have set up in Germany, as a result of which there's as wide a choice of television (TV) and radio programmes as anywhere in Europe. TV and radio services are operated by both public and private broadcasting companies. The two 'national' public TV channels, ARD and ZDF, are run by a network of *Länder*-based broadcasters and funded by advertising and TV and radio licence fees, which are collected and distributed by an agency of the federal government. The regional authorities also produce and broadcast programmes targeted at their local audience using the so-called 'Third Channel' of public TV. There are nine Third Channels, whose regions don't correspond to Germany's 16 states; in some places it's possible to receive more than one Channel.

The public broadcasters are bound by European regulations requiring that at least 51 per cent of programming be European in origin, and there's an ever increasing amount of programming produced in Germany – everything from soap operas to drama series. One long-standing favourite throughout Europe has been *Derrick*, a German detective series (usually referred to as *Krimi*), which ended production only when the star of the series announced his retirement from the acting profession. *Derrick* can still be seen, however, dubbed into the local language or subtitled, throughout the continent. The ever-popular game shows can be useful for those learning the language, as many are based on word play or other language skills. The Germans also produce a wide range of talk shows, some of which are indistinguishable from their American counterparts, often right down to the sets used (but with different guests!).

German audiences are keen on news programmes and documentaries, particularly 'investigative reporting' or consumer-oriented *exposés* of overpriced tourist packages, food scares, shoddy builders and crooked estate agents. Late-night programming is often on the exotic (and erotic) side, with some documentary-type shows dedicated to exploring sexual themes. At weekends, don't be surprised to find soft porn films starting around midnight; you may be surprised that these are often poorly made or dubbed.

TELEVISION STANDARDS

The standard for TV reception in Germany isn't the same as in many other countries. Germany, together with much of the rest of continental Europe and Australia and New Zealand, uses a standard called PAL B/G. This differs from the PAL-I standard used in the UK, the SECAM-L standard used in France, the SECAM D/K used in Eastern Europe and many African countries, and the North American NSTC standard. This means that TVs imported from the UK, France or the US will be of little use unless they're multi-standard or equipped with a satellite receiver. Some TVs can be converted to PAL B/G, but in most cases it isn't worth the expense. The German mains supply is 220–240 volts at 50 Hertz (cycles), presenting an additional problem for those wishing to use equipment manufactured for the US market, which operates at 110 volts, 60 Hertz (see page 110).

The new European standard, PALplus, which includes a digital 16:9 (wide-screen) image and surround-sound transmission, is gradually replacing the older standards, so purchasing a PALplus set could be a worthwhile investment for anyone planning to remain in Europe. You should look for a model offering features such as teletext and a tele-synchronising clock – and particularly dual channel tone (not the same as stereo) – which will enable you to take advantage of the growing number of programmes transmitted in the original language as well as German.

For those planning to travel outside Europe after their stay in Germany, a multi-standard set-up is the best buy. Companies such as Bang & Olufsen and Loewe offer multi-standard compatibility across their entire range, while most other companies offer particular (generally more expensive) models only.

DVD Players & VCRs

PAL DVDs (including those from the UK) labelled 'region 2' work in German DVD players. North American DVDs are 'region 1' and won't work unless you have a region-free DVD player (see **DVDs & Videos** on page 155). You can play DVDs on your laptop or computer, but after three playbacks your player will be fixed to that region!

German video recorders (VCRs) are capable of playing back all PAL cassettes and some are equipped with an NTSC or SECAM playback capability. Many German TVs are capable of reproducing NTSC and SECAM video signals from NTSC or SECAM recorders/players. Older TVs, however, will only show such recordings in black and white (use the 'video out' and 'sound out' plugs on the recorder and the European SCART plug on the TV). British video recorders can also be used to play cassettes on German TVs provided you use the direct video/sound connection. American, French or British recorders cannot be used to record German TV off air, although British VCRs can be used to record from a TV's video output.

If you want to import a DVD player/video recorder made for the US market, check that it doesn't synchronise on the AC frequency, as the German mains frequency is 20 per cent slower than that used in the US.

TELEVISION LICENCE

It's mandatory for all TV owners in Germany to pay an annual licence fee (currently €204.36) to the Central Office for Licensing Fees for Radio and Television (Gebühreneinzugszentrale/GEZ). The licence fee goes toward maintaining the broadcast services of the ARD, ZDF and the regional channels. Registration forms (*Anmeldung*) are available from banks and post offices, or you can register (but not cancel) your TV licence over the internet (🖳 www. gez.de). The GEZ prefers bills to be paid by standing order from a bank account (quarterly, bi-annually or annually). As the TV licence fee also covers radios in your household, including your car radio (see **Radio Licence** on page 156), TV and radio registration are combined.

A separate licence isn't required for a second or additional TVs, provided they're in a room used by yourself, your spouse or your children under 18. If any other adult household member (including any of your children who are over 18) has a TV in their room, i.e. not in the main family room, they're expected to register it in their own name and pay a separate licence fee. **If you have a computer with internet connection it counts as a TV/radio, as you can receive broadcasts.** On leaving the country (or if you decide to live a radio- and TV-free life), don't forget to file the licence cancellation form (*Abmeldung*) to stop your standing order to the GEZ.

Registration should be made within two weeks of installing a TV. The registration form asks you for the month and year you first bought or installed your TV or radio and you may be asked to prove this date, either by producing a receipt for your TV or radio or verification of when you arrived in Germany. The GEZ is normally alerted to your presence as soon as you register your residence in Germany and sends you a letter requesting your registration as they assume that every human on the planet has a television or radio. You may also receive a surprise GEZ visit and, although GEZ staff have no right to enter your home without permission, they can sniff out a TV or radio at 100 paces. **You'll be fined if you're found to have a TV or radio without a licence.** If your TV is used only for video playback or as a computer monitor, no fee is payable, but you must be able to show that it's incapable of receiving any signals from broadcast, cable or satellite channels.

TELEVISION CHANNELS

Without cable or satellite TV (see below), you'll normally be able to receive only the three public broadcasters (ARD, ZDF and the local regional channel) plus perhaps the third channel of a nearby region. If you're in an area that receives more than one regional station, don't be surprised to find that both (or all) regional channels are showing the same programmes at the same time. Public stations are permitted to show advertisements (commercials) only during scheduled breaks between programmes and at certain times of day.

Most private broadcasters' programmes are available only by cable or satellite. There are channels dedicated to children's programmes (such as Ki.ka), to music (Viva Plus), shopping (Home Shopping Europe) and news (N-TV), as well as more general stations such as Pro7, RTL, Sonnenklar TV and Vox. Private stations are financed by advertising revenue and the limitations on the frequency and duration of advertising are much less restrictive than those for public broadcasters. Commercial breaks can extend to 10 or even 15 minutes. Private station broadcasts are dominated by American series and films, German talk shows and 'reality' and 'magazine' shows; science and nature programmes are also popular. Nearly all imported shows are dubbed into German. The German public is also fond of classic British comedy. Not only will you find frequent reruns of *Monty Python's Flying Circus* and *Fawlty Towers* episodes, but you can watch them in English, as they're subtitled rather than dubbed.

The American Forces Network (AFN TV) is available in areas where there are US military installations, but you need an NTSC standard TV or VCR to receive it.

Cable Television

In most cities and many rural areas, the majority of buildings are wired for cable TV, which enables households to receive over 30 TV stations and at least as many radio stations. In theory, you can request a cable connection to anywhere in Germany, but the cost in a remote rural area will be very high if cable TV isn't already installed locally – in any case it will cost far more than satellite TV. To have an existing cable connected is as easy as informing the building superintendent that you want it. In some apartment blocks, the entire building is wired for cable and all you need to do is connect your TV to the cable outlet. The cost of the connection is billed to you either as part of your incidental charges (*Nebenkosten* – see page 104) or directly by cable provider. Cable fees range from around €4 to €13 per month, depending on the options you choose. You can save a substantial sum by paying the charges annually or every six months in advance, rather than quarterly or monthly.

The downside of cable TV is that you have no choice of provider but must use whichever has the local contract. The selection of channels varies with the provider according to local needs and tastes, but the most popular stations, such as Kabel 1, Pro7, Sat 1, VOX, ARD, ZDF, RTL, MTV, VIVA, Eurosport, CNN International, are usually available. In border areas, you're likely to be offered public TV channels from neighbouring countries, as well as Arte (formerly a French-German co-operative channel but now becoming a pan-European enterprise).

Some stations are scrambled and require a decoder. An additional monthly fee is payable directly to the relevant broadcaster for this service (occasionally on a pay-per-view basis). For €4-6 extra you can get additional English channels: National Geographic, AXN, Extreme Sports, ESPN Classic, Playhouse Disney, Toon Disney, Boomerang, Sailing Channel, MTV Hits and Dance, VH-1 Classic, NASN, BBC Prime, and TCM (Turner Classic Movies). Details about how to subscribe to pay TV channels are available via TV adverts, in TV stores and on the website of your local cable provider.

Satellite Television

A large proportion of the satellite channels serving Germany are unencrypted, which means you need only a standard 85cm satellite dish to receive them, although a larger dish may be required for some areas for digital reception. Many satellite stations provide teletext information and most broadcast in stereo.

The two main satellite broadcasters are Astra (🖳 www.ses-astra.com) and Eutelsat (🖳 www.eutelsat.de). Among the many English-language stations available on Astra are Sky One, Movimax, Sky Premier, Sky Cinema, Film Four, Sky News, Sky Sports (three channels), UK Gold, Channel 5, Granada Plus, TNT, Eurosport, CNN, CNBC Europe, UK Style, UK Horizons, The Disney Channel and the Discovery Channel. Other stations broadcast in Dutch, German, Japanese, Swedish, Arabic, Spanish, Polish, Portuguese, Catalan, Italian and various Indian languages. The signal from many stations is scrambled (the decoder is usually built into the receiver) and viewers must pay a monthly subscription fee to receive programmes.

Eutelsat's stations are mostly non-English language and broadcast in Arabic, French, German, Hungarian, Italian, Polish, Portuguese, Spanish, Turkish, Rumanian, Russian, Serbo-Croat, Slovak, Czech, Swedish, Flemish, Greek, Kurdish and Macedonian. The English-language stations include Eurosport, NBC Europe, BBC Prime and BBC World (see below).

BBC Worldwide Television

The BBC's commercial subsidiary, BBC Worldwide Television, broadcasts on two 24-hour channels: BBC Prime (general entertainment) and BBC World (news and information). BBC World is free-to-air and is transmitted via the Eutelsat Hot Bird satellite, while BBC Prime, which is transmitted via Eutelsat Hotbird 6 (frequency 11,116 MHz, vertical polarisation, symbol rate 27,500), is encrypted and requires a Viaccess-compatible decoder.

Smartcards are available from BBC Prime, Customer Relations, PO Box 5054, London W12 0ZY, UK (☎ 020-8433 2221). The annual subscription costs £85 plus a one-off payment of £30 for the card and the inevitable VAT at 17.5 per cent. There are currently plans to make BBC Prime available in Germany via digital cable.

For more information and a programme guide contact BBC Worldwide Television, Woodlands, 80 Wood Lane, London W12 0TT, UK (☎ 020-8433 2000). A programme guide is also available via the internet (🖳 www.bbc.co.uk/schedules) and both BBC World and BBC Prime have websites providing further information (🖳 www.bbcworld.com and 🖳 www.bbcprime.com). When accessing schedules, you must enter the name of the country (e.g. Germany) so that they appear in local time.

German Digital Television

To watch digital TV you require a decoder, called a d-box, which you can buy either separately for around €100 or as part of a programme package deal. A list of digital satellite service providers can be found on 🖥 www.digitalfernsehen.de. By far the largest is Premiere World (☎ 0180-511 0000, 🖥 www.premiere-angebot.de), whose current best offer is '5er Combi', which includes all five available programme packages, such as entertainment, sports and blockbusters, for €35 per month. If you buy an interactive receiver for €1 you receive €30 credit on your account, which in effect cancels the 'activation' fee (also €30). The interactive receiver allows you to receive digital TV and radio programmes, and gives access to an onscreen programme guide and search function and automatic software updates. Individual programme packages cost €10 per month plus €7.50 for delivery of the decoder). Customers must usually sign up for two years. It's recommended that you have a phone line available if you want to use interactive services. **As with any contract in Germany, you should pay careful attention to the cancellation notice period, which is usually three months.**

Sky Television

You must buy a receiver with a Videocrypt decoder and pay a monthly subscription to receive Sky stations except Sky News (which isn't scrambled). Various packages are available, costing from £15 to over £43 a month (a package including Sky Sports 1, Sky Premier and Sky MovieMax costs around £42). You need an address in the UK. Subscribers are sent a coded smartcard, which must be inserted in the decoder to activate it (cards are periodically updated to thwart counterfeiters). Sky won't send smart cards to overseas viewers as they have the copyright to broadcast only in the UK and Ireland (overseas residents need to obtain a card through a friend or relative in the UK). However, a number of satellite companies in Germany (some of which advertise in the expatriate press) can provide (genuine) Sky cards. To watch Sky digital TV you require a Digibox and a dish.

Equipment

With a 1.2m or 1.5m motorised dish, you can receive hundreds of stations in a multitude of languages from around the world. If you wish to receive satellite TV on two or more TVs, you can buy a satellite system with two or more receivers. To receive stations from two or more satellites simultaneously, you need a motorised dish or a dish with a double feed antenna (dual LNBs).

You can import your own satellite dish and receiver and install it yourself. Otherwise, there are many satellite sales and installation companies in Germany, some of which advertise in the expatriate press. A basic Astra satellite system costs from around €200, excluding installation. Shop around as prices vary considerably. Before buying a system, ensure that it will be able to receive programmes from all existing and planned satellites.

Location

To receive programmes from any satellite, there must be no obstacles between the satellite and your dish, i.e. no trees, buildings or mountains must obstruct the signal, so check before renting an apartment or buying a home. In Germany, the Astra satellites are located at around 12° east of south at an elevation of 35° (depending on location, e.g. in Hamburg the elevation is lower than in Munich and the direction also varies). If you're in doubt, ask at your local TV shop, where they will be able to advise you on the local requirements. **Before buying or erecting a dish, check your lease or house rules regarding whether you need permission from your landlord or if there are restrictions on the size or visibility of a satellite dish.** You can now buy flat dishes in a variety of colours and patterns, which blend into the background.

Programme Guides

There's a bewildering choice of TV guides in Germany, some of which are published weekly and some fortnightly; they come and go with alarming frequency. Guides are available from supermarkets as well as newsagents' and are published early, so it's sometimes difficult to buy the current issue. Some magazines include satellite and cable programmes, others include radio programmes. Certain publications concentrate on films while others are dedicated solely to series, soaps or police series. The most popular guides include *HörZu*, *TV Movie* and *TV Today*.

The annual *World Radio and TV Handbook* (⌨ www.wrth.com) contains over 600 pages of information and the frequencies of all radio and TV stations worldwide.

There are a number of internet sites where you can design your own programme guides according to your tastes and the cable or satellite programmes you can receive. One particularly comprehensive website is ⌨ www.eurotv.com, which has the advantage of being in English, although it carries programme listings for nearly every European country. Nearly every TV station in Germany (and elsewhere) has a website, and some German websites offer some programme information in English.

Satellite Programme Guides

Satellite programme listings are provided in a number of British publications with names such as *What Satellite*, and *Satellite TV*, which are available on subscription. A number of satellite TV programme schedules can be displayed via German TV teletext.

DVDS & VIDEOS

DVDs are readily available to rent or buy in Germany. To rent a DVD, you generally must join a rental club and pay an annual fee, after which you can rent videos for as little as €1 (e.g. 'classic' films) or as much as €12 (for the latest Hollywood blockbuster). Another popular way to rent DVDs and videos is via the internet, e.g. Amazon (🖥 www.amazon.de), which offers rental DVDs for as little as €3 each, including delivery (prepaid envelope provided).

Almost every shop and petrol station sells DVDs at prices ranging from €10 to €25. You can buy English-language videos over the internet and through mail-order book and video catalogues. Check with local expatriate clubs for English-language videos available for sale or swap.

Double-check the language options before buying a DVD as some cheaper discs don't include an English audio track. Also check the 'region', as films intended for a North American audience (region 1) won't play back in a European (region 2) DVD player unless it has been modified, and region 1 versions often don't contain the alternate soundtracks and subtitling. There are multi-region or 'code-free' DVD players , and it's also possible to modify many single-region players to handle multiple-region DVDs.

RADIO

The good news for radio enthusiasts is that radios have the same standards the world over, meaning there are generally few problems with equipment compatibility. The only significant difficulties are likely to be experienced by Americans, who may find that their VHF radios with digital tuning don't work properly in Europe. The reason for this is that the American broadcasting standard calls for a broader tuning bandwidth than in Europe (10kHz rather than 9kHz). Many modern radios can be switched from 10 to 9kHz bandwidth, but not all.

FM (VHF) stereo stations flourish in Germany, to the extent that it's currently almost impossible to obtain a broadcasting licence due to the lack of available frequencies. Medium-wave (MW or AM) and long-wave (LW) bands are also in wide use throughout Europe. A short-wave (SW) radio is useful for receiving international stations such as the BBC World Service, Voice of America, Radio Canada and Radio Sweden. The BBC World Service and Voice of America are also available via cable and satellite (see below). Portable digital radio receivers are now widely available and provide good reception, particularly on short wave, and expensive 'professional' receivers are capable of receiving stations from almost anywhere. If you're interested in receiving radio stations from further afield, obtain a copy of the *World Radio TV Handbook* (Billboard).

Radio Licence

A radio licence costs €66.24 per year (€5.52 per month), but if you pay for a TV licence there's no additional fee for a radio licence. The registration procedure is the same as for TV licence registration (see page 149) and both registrations can be done at the same time. If applicable, the radio licence fee is payable monthly, quarterly or annually by bank standing order. It covers all radios used in your home by you, your spouse and your children under 18. It also covers a radio in your car(s), although if you have a company car or use your car for business, you're likely to have to pay extra. If any other adult member of your household (including children over 18) has a radio in his room, he must register it and pay an additional licence fee in his own name. If you register for a radio only, the GEZ is likely to send an inspector to your house to check whether you 'forgot' to register a TV as well. **Failure to register can result in a fine.**

German Radio

There's a wide choice of German radio stations, both public and private, although most are regionally orientated. All musical tastes are covered, from classical to youth and oldies' stations, although most stations broadcast a mixture of music. If you're near a US or British military base, you'll be able to pick up English-language stations – e.g. the British Forces Broadcasting Service (BFBS) of the Rhine Army (🖳 www.ssvc.com/bfbs) in the Lüneburg-Osnabrück area – while those living in central and southern Germany can receive AFN Radio, which caters to the American forces in Europe and is popular for its country-and-western music among German listeners, as well as homesick Americans. Deutsche Welle, the equivalent of the BBC World Service (see below), broadcasts on short wave and satellite in German and English (as well as in many other languages) across the globe.

BBC & Other Foreign Stations

The BBC World Service is simultaneously broadcast on short wave, medium wave, long wave and FM frequencies, and you should be able to receive a good signal on one of them. The signal strength may vary according to where you live, the time of day and year, the sensitivity and positioning of your receiver, and atmospheric conditions; the FM signal tends to be the best. Short-wave frequencies come into use at different times of the day, but 12095, 9410 and 6195kHz are usually worth trying. The medium-wave frequency, 648kHz, is only worth bothering about in north-west Germany, roughly north of Bonn and west of Osnabrück, although even here reception is variable. The long wave frequency, 198kHz, carries BBC Radio 4 during the day and the World Service between 1 and 5.30am and again this can get quite 'crackly'. A list of frequencies can be found on the BBC website (🖳 www.bbc.co.uk/worldservice). The BBC World Service (plus BBC Radio 1, 2, 3, 4 and 5) is available via the Astra and Eutelsat satellites (see **Satellite TV** on page 152). For a free BBC World Service programme guide and frequency information leaflet write to BBC World Service (BBC Worldwide, PO Box 76, Bush House, Strand, London WC2B 4PH, UK, ☎ 020-7240 3456).

Many other foreign stations offer worldwide broadcasts for expatriates desperate for news from home, including Radio Australia, Radio Canada, Denmark Radio, Radio Nederland, Radio Sweden International and the Voice of America. Don't forget to check broadcasters' websites, where you can often download and hear broadcast material as well as check schedules.

Satellite Radio

Both digital and regular TV satellite services offer a range of radio stations, often from around the world. For example, BBC Radio 1, 2, 3, 4 and 5, BBC World Service, Sky Radio, Virgin 1215, NPR (National Public Radio from the US) and many non-English language stations are broadcast via the Astra satellites. Satellite radio stations are listed in British satellite TV magazines such as *What Satellite* and *Satellite TV Europe* and schedules can also be found on the internet. If you're interested in receiving radio stations from further afield you should obtain a copy of the *World Radio TV Handbook* (🖳 www.wrth.com).

Cable Radio

If your apartment is wired for cable TV (see page 151), it will also be wired for cable radio, providing reception of more than 30 stereo stations. Many cable networks provide the BBC World Service, BBC Foreign Language Service, and Voice of America, in addition to a wide selection of FM stereo stations based in Germany and Austria. All you need do is connect your radio or hi-fi tuner aerial to a wall socket (cables and connectors are available from TV shops).

9.

Education

G ermany was one of the first countries to introduce compulsory schooling but has no national education system, as education is a responsibility of the individual states (*Länder*). Consequently, there are as many school systems as there are states (i.e. 16), all with differing structures and methodologies. This has led to some apparently bizarre conflicts, most prominent of which was Bavaria's refusal to recognise the grammar school diplomas of some other states, because their examinations were less demanding than its own. The introduction of a unified school system for the whole of Germany has been a perennial topic of discussion among the chattering classes but up to now little has come of it.

Until recently, Germany has been proud of its educational standards, but the 2000 OECD Program for International Student Assessment (PISA) study of the achievements of 15-year-olds in 32 mainly industrialised countries sent a tidal shock-wave across the country when German children came in around 20th in all areas. In the most recent results (PISA 2003) German children competed with 40 other countries and reached 21st in reading, 19th in maths and 18th in science. Each German state was assessed in a separate league table, at the top of which was Bavaria. But even Bavaria managed only to reach a mid-table position in international comparisons. The PISA studies also showed that German pupils were less positive about their school experience than their counterparts elsewhere and have given fresh impetus to proposals to change many long-standing educational traditions.

Education is compulsory in Germany for at least nine years (ten in some states), children beginning full-time education at between five-and-a-half and six-and-a-half, depending on the time of year they were born. Education in German state schools is free, from primary school through to – and including – university. Free education is also provided within the state system for the children of foreign residents in Germany, although non-resident, non-EU students require a student visa (see page 77).

Unlike some other Europeans, Germans have always viewed their education as almost entirely egalitarian. For example, kindergarten teachers aren't allowed to teach the alphabet or reading, so that all children start out on an even footing. The disadvantage of this system is that learning disabilities, such as dyslexia, often remain unnoticed or are ignored. Those with such difficultires are simply considered 'dumb' and put at the back of the class. There are special schools for those with perceived or genuine mental and physical disabilities, but every attempt to create special schools for exceptionally intelligent or gifted children has been met with fierce opposition, from both the general public and politicians. Nevertheless, the education system is highly competitive and selective and separates the brighter students from the less academically gifted on entry into secondary schools. Formal tests are conducted each year from primary school upwards, and the results carry considerable weight in determining the type of education (and hence the likely future career) a child can expect. And although there are no close equivalents of France's elite *Grandes Ecoles* or the US's Ivy League universities, there are nonetheless good and bad universities (the former recognised as such) – and the differences between them can be considerable.

Critics of the German education system complain that, unlike British and US schools, which emphasise developing the whole person, the German system (like the French) is focused entirely on academic achievement and consequent career advancement. Most German state schools offer little in the way of extra-curricular activities (see **State Schools** on page 164).

German teaching style is generally more formal than that in many countries, including the UK and the US, with pupils in eastern Germany still required to stand by their desks when a teacher enters and little contact between pupils and teachers outside classrooms. In some city schools, discipline has become a problem in recent years, owing partly to tensions arising from the high proportion of children from ethnic minorities, who constitute 50 per cent or more of the school rolls in some districts of large cities.

On the plus side, academic standards are generally high (the PISA results notwithstanding), with well qualified teachers and commendable results (at least by German standards), over 91 per cent of pupils achieve a school-leaving certificate and around 25 per cent the general university entrance qualification. German schools have also been quick to embrace the potential of new technology, most of the country's schools having ISDN connections, and each child, whatever his level of natural ability, is given the opportunity to study for a trade, diploma or degree.

A strong emphasis is placed on workplace training, and few school-leavers go into a job without it. Everyone up to the age of 18 must attend some form of educational institution (full or part time) and it's normal practice for those leaving school at 16 to attend a technical college or train as an apprentice. In today's highly competitive labour market, both parents and students are acutely aware that qualifications and training are of paramount importance in obtaining a good (or any) job, although these don't have to be academically orientated. In fact, a graduate of a *Fachhochschule*, where studies have a strongly technical bent, is more likely to get a job than a university graduate.

Further information about German schools, both state and private, can be obtained from German embassies and consulates abroad, and from foreign embassies, educational organisations and government departments in Germany. Local school information can be obtained from the municipal administration centre (*Stadtverwaltung*), or the education office (*Amt für Schule* or *Behörde für Schule, Jugend und Berufsbildung*), which is usually located at the *Stadtverwaltung* but may be in a separate building and usually supplies English leaflets.

ADAPTING TO THE SYSTEM

Generally, the younger your child is when he enters the German school system, the easier he will cope. Conversely, the older he is, the more problems he will have adjusting, particularly as the school curriculum is more demanding at a higher level. Teenagers often have considerable problems learning German and adjusting to German school life, particularly children from America or the UK who haven't learnt a second language. In some schools, foreign children who cannot understand the language may be neglected and just expected to get on with it. In your early days in Germany it's important to check exactly what your children are doing at school and whether they're making progress (not just with the language, but also with their lessons).

As a parent, you should be prepared to support your children through this difficult period. If you aren't fluent in German, you'll already be aware how frustrating it is being unable to express yourself adequately, which can easily lead to feelings of inferiority or inadequacy – in children as well as adults. It's also important for you to ensure that your children maintain their native language, as it can easily be neglected (studies show that the children of English residents in non-English-speaking countries tend to lose their ability to read and write English).

For many children, the challenge of living in a foreign country is stimulating and provides invaluable cultural as well as educational experiences. Your child will become a 'world' citizen, less likely to be prejudiced against foreigners and foreign ideas. This is particularly true if he attends an international school with pupils from many different countries, although many state schools, particularly in the larger cities, also have pupils from a number of countries and backgrounds. Before making major decisions about your child's education, it's important to consider his ability, character and long-term requirements.

Language

There are many considerations to take into account when choosing an appropriate school in Germany, not least the language of study. The only schools in Germany using English as the teaching language are a few foreign and international private schools (see below). For most children, however, studying in German isn't such a handicap as it may at first appear, particularly for those aged below ten. Many young children adapt quickly and some may become fluent within six months (if only it were so easy for adults!). However, all children don't adapt equally well to a change of language and culture, particularly children aged over ten (when children begin to learn languages more slowly), many of whom encounter great difficulties during their first year.

It should be borne in mind that the German state school system generally makes little or no concession to non-German speakers, e.g. by providing intensive German lessons. This can make the first few months quite an ordeal for non-German-speaking children. In areas with a large foreign population, schools may offer classes for those requiring German language lessons, but this is far from the rule. It may be worthwhile enquiring about the availability of extra German classes before deciding where to live. Note also that while attending language classes, children may fall behind in other subjects.

Foreign children are tested (like German children) and put into a class suited to their level of German, even if this means being taught with younger children or slow learners. In some states (e.g. Bavaria) they're tested before starting primary school (*Grundschule*) and held back a year if their German isn't considered good enough.

If your local state school doesn't provide extra German classes – and outside large cities this is likely to be the case – your only choice will be to pay for private lessons or send your child to another (possibly private) school, where extra tuition is available. Some parents send a child to an English-speaking school for a year, followed by a state school. Other parents find it easier to throw their children in at the deep end than to introduce them gradually. It all depends on the character, ability and wishes of the child.

Whatever you decide, it will help if your child has some intensive German lessons before arriving in Germany (see **Learning German** on page 182). It may be possible to organise an educational or cultural exchange with a German school or family before coming to live in Germany, which is a considerable help in integrating a child into the German language and culture.

STATE OR PRIVATE SCHOOL?

State education is generally perceived to be of a higher standard than private education, parents usually sending their children to a private school for religious or philosophical reasons, to get them off their hands if they're 'difficult', or if specific help is needed that's unavailable in a state school. If you're able to choose between state and private education, the following list of questions should help you decide:

- How long are you planning to stay in Germany? If you're uncertain, it's probably best to assume a long stay. Due to language and other integration problems, enrolling a child in a German state school is recommended only for a minimum of a year, particularly for teenage children who aren't fluent in German (see **Language** above).

- Do you know where you're going when you leave Germany? This may be an important consideration regarding your child's language of tuition and system of education in Germany. How old is your child and what age will he be when you leave Germany? What long-term plans do you have for his education, and in which country?

- How does your child view the thought of studying in German? What language is best from a long-term point of view? Is schooling available in Germany in his mother tongue?

- Will your child require your help with his studies and, more importantly, will you be able to help him, particularly with his German?

- Is special or extra tutoring available in German or other subjects, if necessary?

- What are the school hours and holiday periods, and how will these affect your family's work and leisure activities? Many state schools in Germany have compulsory Saturday morning classes.

- Is religion an important aspect in your choice of school? Most German state schools have compulsory religious education; most international schools, in contrast, don't.

- Do you want your child to go to a single-sex or mixed (co-educational) school? Nearly all German state schools are mixed.

- Are German examinations or the examinations set by prospective German schools recognised in your home country or the country where you plan to live after leaving Germany? If applicable, check that the German *Abitur* examination (see page 171) is recognised as a university entrance qualification in your home country.

- Does a prospective school have a good academic record? Most schools provide exam pass rate statistics.

- How large are the classes? What is the pupil-teacher ratio?

Bear in mind that the area where you choose to live will affect your choice of school(s). State school pupils usually go to nursery (*Kindergarten*) and primary schools near their home, but attending secondary school often entails travelling long distances. (One of the consequences of the depopulation of rural areas in the last few decades has been the closure of many schools.) If you choose a private day school, you must take into account the distance from your home to the school.

Obtain the opinions and advice of others who have been faced with the same questions and problems as you, and collect as much information from as many sources as possible before making a decision. Speak to teachers and the parents of children attending the schools on your shortlist. Finally, discuss the alternatives with your children before making a decision. See also **Choosing a Private School** on page 174.

STATE SCHOOLS

The German state education system has traditionally been very highly regarded, and is for the most part well organised and adequately funded (not that teachers would ever agree!). However, each state (*Land*) sets its own standards and objectives and develops its own education programme. The education ministers of German states meet periodically to debate current issues and establish minimum standards, although all attempts to institute a unified state education system have been vigorously opposed.

Co-education (mixed classes of girls and boys) is normal in German state schools and is even required by law in some states. There are very few all-male or all-female schools.

A general criticism of German state schools often made by foreigners is the lack of extra-curricular activities such as sport, music, drama, and arts and crafts. There's the occasional track-and-field contest, but state schools have few if any sports clubs or teams and, if your child wants to do team sports, he must join a local club. This means that you'll have to ferry children back and forth for games and social events (Americans will be used to this!). A list of organised activities for children and young people can usually be found at the town hall, and the local church may organise some activities.

Children at German schools are regularly tested in a range of subjects and each year receive two reports (one at the end of each term). Performance levels are traditionally indicated by a grade from 1 to 6, as follows:

Grade	Assessment	Meaning
1	*Sehr gut*	Very good
2	*Gut*	Good
3	*Befriedigend / Zufriedenstellend*	Reasonable / Satisfactory
4	*Ausreichend*	Sufficient
5	*Mangelhaft*	Deficient / Unsatisfactory
6	*Ungenügend*	Poor / Insufficient

Having made the decision to send your child to a state school, you should stick to it for at least a year to give it a fair trial. It will take a child at least this long to begin to adapt to a new language, the change of environment and the different curriculum.

Enrolment

Enrolling your child in a German school is usually straightforward. In fact, provided you're officially registered as German residents, your local school will write to you some time before the start of the school year inviting you to register your child for classes (this applies if you move to Germany from abroad or within Germany). You'll be told of any medical certificates that you must provide and any provisions you must buy (see page 168), and you're then required to visit the school during normal office hours to complete the necessary forms. Even if you've decided to send your child to another (e.g. private) school, you must notify your local state school and tell them what alternative arrangements you have made.

School Hours

Most state schools operate only in the morning and early afternoon from Mondays to Saturdays. Saturday may be a normal school day, reserved for extra-curricular activities or a completely free day, depending on the state. There's never school on Sundays. The standard school day is from 8am until 1pm, with a maximum of half an hour's variation either side of these times. The original rationale for this arrangement was that the afternoon and early evening would be devoted to a demanding homework regime, although, as the social climate has become more relaxed, children increasingly tend to look upon this as 'free time' for sport and leisure. Nevertheless, children are required to do at least two hours' homework per night, and parents are expected to help them – which places an additional burden on parents, who must also provide lunch for their offspring and supervise them during the afternoons.

All-day schools (*Ganztagsschulen*) were introduced by the Communist authorities in Saxony Anhalt and, partly as a consequence of the PISA results (see page 160), there has been huge pressure on federal and state governments to designate more *Ganztagsschulen*. The federal government has pledged €4bn to create around 10,000 *Ganztagsschulen* by 2009 and had already opened 6,400 by the end of 2007. All-day school include more extra-curricular activities and tutoring with homework. School continues until 4 or 5pm, sometimes with evening activities.

The situation is further complicated by the fact that school hours can vary from day to day. In most schools, children don't go to school in the early morning if they have no classes scheduled, and if their last class finishes before the end of the school day, they're free to go home. Similarly, if a teacher is off sick and the school cannot arrange a replacement (an increasingly common occurrence), children may be sent home without warning. Parents with two or more children face a scheduling nightmare, as each child may have quite a different school schedule.

Holidays

Summer holidays normally last six weeks but the start and finish dates vary from state to state. Before the introduction of this system, almost all Germans tried to have their holidays at the same time, causing monumental traffic jams on motorways and congestion on public transport. Each year a schedule for the whole of Germany is issued. In general, the northern and central states start their summer holidays in mid-June to early July, the eastern states in mid-July and the southern states as late as the end of July or early August. It's common for Germans to leave home the day after the school holidays commence and return the day before school starts again.

In addition to the summer holidays, there are the following school holidays:

- Two weeks in autumn, which used to be termed 'harvest holidays' and were originally intended to give children in rural areas time off school to help their parents with the farm work (nowadays the nearest most German children get to a harvest is the fruit and vegetable section of the local supermarket);

- Two to three weeks' at Christmas;

- Rose Monday (the day before Shrove Tuesday, i.e. two days before the beginning of Lent) and Hag Thursday (the Thursday of the week preceding Rose Monday). In regions where *Fasching* (Carnival) plays a major role, holidays can extend from Hag Thursday to Rose Monday or even Ash Wednesday.

- A one- to two-week break at Easter, which usually starts on the Monday before Easter and ends the following Friday;

- 10 to 14 days' holiday around Pentecost (in May or June).

There are additional short holidays of two to four days, the dates of which vary from state to state. Schools are also closed on church, state and national holidays that don't fall within a holiday period (see **Public Holidays** on page 54).

Some states allow you to withdraw your children from school for 'compassionate' reasons and/or to observe religious holidays that aren't provided for by the state. All absences from school (including those due to illness) must be justified in writing. It's wise to co-ordinate any planned absences with the teacher in charge of your child's class so that he doesn't miss any important activities or annual tests. **Removing your child from school for a period of more than a couple of days without prior agreement with school officials can lead to a substantial fine, and, for persistent offenders, imprisonment for parents and the placement of a child in foster care!**

Summer camps, so much a feature of a child's upbringing in North America, aren't part of the state educational system in Germany. There are, however, some summer camps organised by Boy and Girl Scout organisations, certain church groups and political parties.

Health & Accidents

As a rule, there's no school nurse in German state schools and health problems are generally referred to a family doctor (see page 257) or the hospital nearest to a school. Vaccination programmes exist in each state, but only a few are mandatory. In some states a school doctor makes regular examinations and provides vaccinations at a school, while in others healthcare is left to the discretion of parents. There are optional bi-annual dental checks at schools. All school health checks are free of charge.

Schools are insured for accidents that occur on their premises during school hours and on the way to and from school, provided children take the shortest route between their home and school, and don't interrupt the journey for any non-school-related reason. Other accidents should be covered by a family's health insurance, which is mandatory for all employees and some self-employed people (see **Health Insurance** on page 272).

Provisions

The items required to start school in Germany vary from state to state, although all pupils require the following:

- School bag (a rucksack is most commonly used);

- Pencil case, pencils, coloured pencils or crayons and a fountain pen (most German schools and teachers are opposed to the use of ballpoint pens during primary education and some schools insist on the use of fountain pens throughout a child's education);

- An assortment of lined writing pads or notebooks, graph paper for mathematics and plain (unlined) paper for drawing;

- Gym shoes (plimsolls), a T-shirt and a towel for sports and exercise periods. Some states also require a jogging suit. A sports bag is required if gym kit doesn't fit into the normal school bag.

There are mandatory schoolbooks for all ages, which are provided free by schools in some states while in others parents must pay for them. In some cases books are provided free of charge only if a child's parents earn less than a certain amount. If you have several children, it's therefore advisable to tell them to look after their books, so that they can be used by their younger siblings (the required book for a particular level seldom changes). Parents must also be prepared to cover the cost of materials for cookery and handicraft lessons.

Children may need a sleeping bag for the annual school excursion, which may be a day trip to a nearby site or a few days of camping or staying at youth hostels. Excursions, which aren't free, tend to get longer the older the children get, and a week's holiday abroad (e.g. in Majorca) just before graduating from secondary school isn't uncommon.

School uniforms are extremely unusual, although students usually devise their own 'uniform' and in some areas the theft of designer clothes by gangs is widespread and has resulted in children being told to dress down and not wear expensive clothes to school.

Parents are required to provide their children with food for mid-morning breaks, although snacks may be available from vendors who visit schools during breaks or from local shops. School cafeterias are rare, as most children are home by lunchtime. Some schools offer a 'milk-for-breakfast' programme, through which parents can arrange for their children to be given warm milk or a chocolate drink during break periods.

Nursery School

Attendance at nursery school (*Kindergarten*, meaning literally 'children's garden'), from the age of three, is voluntary in Germany and parents are required to pay a fee, although subsidies are available to those on average and low incomes from the Youth Authority (*Jugendamt*) – look in your yellow pages or on the internet for details of your local *Jugendamt*. While there are sufficient nursery school places to meet demand in the eastern states, in some western areas there aren't nearly enough. Indeed, some parents enrol their children at birth to ensure a place. Nursery school generally lasts from two to three hours in the morning, although children can be taken care of for up to nine hours or at other times (e.g. for shift-working parents) if required; the fee is naturally higher for longer hours.

Children normally attend nursery school from Mondays to Fridays, although some nursery schools are also equipped to look after the children of weekend workers. Nursery school is generally a good way to integrate your pre-school children into German life. Note, however, that in many nursery schools all children from the ages of three to six play together, with no attempt to segregate them into groups or activities. This means that children must be prepared to face a degree of rough-and-tumble; as one expatriate parent in Germany commented: "Kindergarten is wonderful for the children – they really learn how to defend themselves!"

In some towns there are *Kinderkrippen*, a kind of crèche for children under three, providing the same service.

Primary School

Children start primary school (*Grundschule*) between the ages of five-and-a-half and six-and-a-half depending on the month they were born. In some states they can start at five. A child may be held back one school year due to health, insufficient German knowledge or other factors (such as lack of maturity).

The first day of primary school is considered a very important event in a child's life in Germany and a degree of ceremony accompanies it, including pictures by professional photographers. It's customary to provide children starting school with a bag of sweets (*Schultüte*) resembling a colourful dunce's hat upside-down with an inscription such as 'my first day at school'. These bags can be purchased at stationery shops and supermarkets in a variety of colours and sizes but are sold empty and must be filled with treats purchased separately.

The total number of weekly lessons at primary school varies from 20 to 30 depending on the class (i.e. the age of the child). The main subjects are reading, writing and arithmetic. In addition, children receive a basic introduction to other subjects they will be studying at secondary school, including history (*Geschichte*), geography (*Erdkunde*), social studies (*Sozialkunde*), biology (*Biologie*), physics (*Physik*), chemistry (*Chemie*), music (*Musik*), art (*Kunsterziehung*) and sport (*Sport*). Religious education (*Religionslehre*) classes, which focus on Christianity, were mandatory everywhere with the exception of some eastern states, where a non-religious equivalent was substituted called 'ethics'. Nowadays, with a growing immigrant population, many of whom are Muslims, ethics is an option at nearly every school; however, this can cause an unhealthy segregation between Christian and non-Christian students. There's a strong Catholic tradition in southern Bavaria and, if your child attends a state school in this region (except in Munich, which is more cosmopolitan), you'll probably have to accept this as part and parcel of his education. Despite a recent ruling by Germany's supreme court that crucifixes on the walls of classrooms infringe on religious freedom and should be removed, there's hardly a classroom in the area without one.

Primary school normally lasts for four years (six in Berlin and Brandenburg). In Bavaria, however, *Grundschulen* and *Hauptschulen* (see **Secondary School** below) are amalgamated into *Volksschulen*. After this, in most states, parents receive a recommendation from the child's teachers concerning the type of school most appropriate for his continuing education. This is based on the teachers' assessment of the child's performance, abilities and interests, and teachers can veto the admittance of a child to a *Gymnasium* or *Realschule* if, in their view, he hasn't achieved the necessary standard. In some states, failing to pass a year (grade) precludes a child from attending a *Gymnasium*, and failing the same year twice or any grade three times means that a child is automatically enrolled in a special school for slow learners.

Secondary School

After primary education, children normally go to one of three types of school: a *Hauptschule*, a *Realschule* or a *Gymnasium*. In some states, however, there are *Gesamtschulen*. These four types of secondary school are described below.

Hauptschule

This type of school is designed for those who are less academically gifted, who are expected to enter a manual trade on leaving school. The main subjects studied are German, arithmetic, history, work studies (*Arbeitslehre*) and crafts. In some states, the *Hauptschule* curriculum includes a foreign language (normally English, French or Russian). The number of weekly lessons (each of which lasts 45 minutes) is between 30 and 33.

After five or six years, a *Hauptschule* graduate generally enters an apprenticeship (*Lehre*) in a manual trade, although those with very good grades may apply for an apprenticeship in a commercial or medical profession. Once a *Hauptschule* student has achieved his school certificate (*Hauptschulabschluss*), he can go on to study part-time for vocational qualifications at a *Berufschule*.

Realschule

Realschulen are designed for those who will be entering an apprenticeship in a commercial trade or medical profession such as nursing. Here the emphasis is more on mathematics and language skills than on crafts. In most states, at least two foreign languages (usually English and French) are taught, the number of weekly lessons being between 30 and 34. *Realschulen* include specialised schools such as trade schools (*Handelsschule*). The leaving certificate, awarded after a final examination, is called the *Mittlere Reife*.

Gymnasium

Equivalent to a British grammar school, this is the type of school for students with the most academic promise and is designed to prepare them for university or a 'high-end' apprenticeship. This is the most demanding type of schooling, with lots of homework and pressure to perform and between 32 and 40 lessons per week.

Classes at a *Gymnasium* consist of a group of mandatory subjects, including English, French, German, mathematics, chemistry, physics, history and religion/ethics, and a group of optional subjects (electives), such as advanced chemistry, advanced physics, advanced mathematics, Greek and Latin. The optional subjects selected depend on the career intentions of the student (a classical language, for example, may be compulsory for those hoping to pursue a career in medicine).

Gymnasium concludes with the *Abitur* examination, the number of subjects examined varying with the state. Upon passing the *Abitur*, a student is awarded the *Zeugnis der allgemeinen Hochschulreife*, which entitles him to study the subject of his choice at a university or equivalent institution (provided a place is available).

Because German university education is free, all but the best are 'filtered out' in *Gymnasien*, and it's possible that after one or two years your child's teachers may recommend that he transfers to a *Hauptschule* or *Realschule*. It may be wise to accept this suggestion, because in Germany it's much better to have a low-level qualification than no qualification at all. In most states, failing two years at any point in your school career automatically sets you back to a lower level education and in all states a child is allowed just two attempts to pass the final examination.

The *Abitur* is generally reckoned to be more demanding than UK A Levels but less so than the French *baccalauréat*. It's widely (but not universally) recognised as a university entrance qualification, although a student may also need to prove his capabilities in the relevant teaching language.

Gesamtschule

These are found in some parts of Germany (particularly the east) and are equivalent to a comprehensive school in the UK, where education for children of all abilities is carried out under one roof, with some common classes. The traditional three-track system (*Hauptschule*, *Realschule*, *Gymnasium*) still applies, leading to three levels of graduation, although there's more opportunity for a late-developing child to move to a higher level of schooling within a *Gesamtschule*.

PRIVATE SCHOOLS

There are various alternatives to the state school system in Germany, although most aren't strictly private and some claiming to be so are in reality dependent upon government funding and may operate under the same rules as state schools. Private schools normally have a higher standard of instruction but longer hours. Many new private schools are bi-lingual (English-German), which is a great advantage. At a semi-private school, the fees are determined on a sliding scale according to your income and the school cannot be elitist about entrance requirements, as they have to meet a foreigner/class quota. Most 'private' schools are in Bavaria and North Rhine-Westphalia, where, from time to time, a debate breaks out about reducing government funding to such schools.

The largest network of private schools in Germany is *Waldorfschulen*, which are 'alternative' schools based on the philosophy of Rudolf Steiner, known as anthroposophy. Similar in many respects to Montessori schools, which generally extend from kindergarten through to the early years of secondary education, Waldorf schools emphasise the importance of developing creativity in a child, and the curriculum places considerable emphasis on the arts. Waldorf schools have spread across the world since the first was founded in Stuttgart in 1919, but they're most heavily concentrated in Germany (although Steiner was Austrian), where there are around 206. A Waldorf school education is radically different from standard German (and most other European) schooling, and if your child must later change schools he or she may have trouble adapting. Students from

Waldorf schools may also face prejudice from traditional Germany university admission boards.

Religious schools can also be found throughout Germany, although most depend on state funding for their survival. They operate to a large extent like German state schools, although with a greater emphasis on religious and moral instruction. Catholic schools constitute the largest group in this category, although the Lutheran Church has a nationwide network, and there are Jewish and Moslem schools. Religious schools are heavily oversubscribed, as they're perceived as being more effective than state or other private schools. There's no need for a family to be practising members of a particular faith for their children to attend a religious school, but the children must show due respect for its beliefs and traditions and will, of course, be required to abide by its customs (e.g. concerning diet and dress).

A limited number of pupils can attend Department of Defense Educational Activity (DODEA) schools (called – for reasons known only to the DODEA – K-12 schools), run by the US Department of Defense, which are located on American military bases throughout Germany. Normally these schools are for the children of US (and some other NATO) military personnel and other government workers. All others must apply for permission and relatively few are approved (the admission criteria are – intentionally? – nebulous). Fees at K-12 schools are high, but they provide extensive sports facilities and instruction (basketball, American football, wrestling, track and field, and sometimes hockey and baseball) for both boys and girls. The comprehensive DODEA website (🖥 www. dedodea.edu) has sections of interest to parents and potential pupils (and to those seeking teaching positions), and is frequently updated with news.

Other private school options include international schools in Germany (see below), private day schools in neighbouring countries, e.g. France or Switzerland, and boarding schools abroad. There are only around 20 boarding schools (*Internate*) in Germany.

International Schools

Germany's 28 international schools can be found in cities or regions with a high concentration of diplomats or multinational firms. Most use English as their main teaching language and are based on the American educational system. Schools range from kindergarten level to secondary schools offering the American high school diploma or International Baccalaureate. Tuition fees are generally around €9,000 or €10,000 per year, other fees such as transport, registration and extra-curricular activities adding a further €2,500 or so. Among the most popular international schools are:

● Bonn International School (Martin-Luther-King Strasse 14, 53175 Bonn, ☎ 0228-308540);

- Frankfurt International School (An der Waldlust 15, D-61440 Oberursel, ☎ 06171-2020, 💻 www.fis.edu), which has a second campus in nearby Wiesbaden (see below). The brochure claims an average class size of 20 students.

- International School Berlin/Potsdam (Lentzeallee 12/14, D-14195 Berlin, ✉ info@private-kant-schule.de, 💻 www.berlin-international-school.de). This school has become very popular due to the relocation of the German government from Bonn to Berlin. Foreign embassies having moved their staff to Berlin accordingly, many pupils are from the families of diplomats.

- International School of Stuttgart (Sigmaringer Str. 257, D-70597 Stuttgart, ☎ 0711-7696 000). Many of the parents of pupils enrolled at this school, which opened in 1998, work at the Daimler Benz and IBM plants.

- International School Wiesbaden (Rudolf-Dietz-Str. 14, D-65207 Wiesbaden, ☎ 06127-99400);

- Munich International School (Schloß Buchhof, D-82319 Starnberg, ☎ 08151-3660).

Enquire at your country's embassy or consulate about international schools near where you'll be living.

Choosing a Private School

The following list of questions is designed to help you choose an appropriate private school:

- Does the school have a good reputation? When was it established?

- Does the school have a sound academic record? For example, what percentage of pupils receive good examination passes and go on to university?

- How large are the classes and what's the student-teacher ratio? Does the claimed class size tally with the number of desks in the classrooms? What are the classrooms like? For example, their size, space, cleanliness, lighting and furnishings – including computer equipment. Are there signs of creative teaching, e.g. wall charts, maps, posters and students' work on display?

- What are the qualification requirements for teachers and what nationality are they? Ask for a list of the teaching staff and their qualifications.

- What is the teacher turnover? A high turnover is generally a negative sign and suggests underpaid teachers and/or poor working conditions.

- What extras (e.g. art supplies, sports equipment, outings, clothing, health insurance, textbooks and stationery) must you pay for? Different schools have different policies.

- Which countries do most students come from?

- Is there religious education and, if so, in what faith?

- What language is used? Is tutoring in German offered to children who need it?

- What languages does the school teach as required or optional subjects?

- What is the student turnover?

- What are the school terms and holiday periods? These won't necessarily coincide with those of state schools.

- What are the school hours? Ask to see a pupil timetable to check the ratio of academic to non-academic subjects. Check the number of free study periods and whether they're supervised.

- What are the withdrawal conditions? A term's notice is usual.

- What does the curriculum include?

- What examinations are set?

- What sports instruction and facilities are provided and where?

- What are the facilities for art and science subjects, e.g. arts and crafts, music, computer studies, science, hobbies, drama, cookery and photography? Ask to see the classrooms, facilities, equipment and some students' projects.

- What sort of outings and holiday celebrations does the school organise?

- What medical facilities does the school provide, e.g. infirmary, resident doctor or nurse? Is medical and accident insurance included in the fees?

- How is discipline handled?

- What reports are provided for parents and how often?

Before making a final choice, it's important to visit the schools on your shortlist during term time and talk to teachers and students (and, if possible, former students and their parents). Try to find answers to the above questions in person and don't simply rely on a school's prospectus to provide the information. If you aren't happy with the answers, look elsewhere. Before enrolling your child in a private school, make sure you understand the withdrawal conditions in the school contract!

Having made your choice, keep a check on your child's progress and listen to his comments and complaints. Compare notes with other parents. If something doesn't seem right, try to establish whether the complaint is well founded or not and, if it is, take appropriate action to have the problem resolved. Don't forget that you (or your employer) are paying a lot of money for tuition.

Make applications to private schools as far in advance as possible. You're usually requested to send previous school reports (or transcripts), exam results and records.

APPRENTICESHIPS

The vast majority of German school-leavers go into an apprenticeship (*Lehre*) rather than straight into a job. There are around 375 state-recognised occupations in Germany, ranging from publisher to ladies' tailor, carpenter to dental surgery assistant and photographer to car mechanic. All require a two- to four-year apprenticeship, the exact length of which depends on the demands of the job. Participants who have passed the *Abitur* examination (see page 171) may have their apprenticeship shortened by six months or even a year if they perform exceptionally well.

An apprentice receives a low salary, which is increased annually. Roughly half the working week is spent on the job and the other half at a vocational school (*Berufsschule*), where the apprentice learns the theoretical and practical skills officially required for his occupation (although not necessarily used in the workplace!). The syllabus is set out in detailed national training regulations for each occupation drawn up by the relevant federal ministries in consultation with employers' organisations, business associations and trade unions with the aim of ensuring a uniform qualification for the practitioners of each occupation in Germany.

An apprenticeship concludes with an examination marked by a board of examiners comprising employer and employee representatives and vocational school teachers. Successful candidates are awarded a certificate of fellowship (*Gesellenbrief*) in manual trades, a business assistant's certificate (*Kaufmans Gehilfen Prüfung*) in commercial occupations, or a medical assistant's diploma (*Abschlussprüfung zur Arzthelfer/Apothekergehilfe*) in the case of medical assistants and chemists' assistants.

In recent years, there has been a marked shortage of available apprenticeship positions, which in certain cases has reached the point where a young man or woman wanting to be, say, a carpenter in Bremen might only be able to find a place as a men's hairdresser in Dresden. This has led to a kind of 'inflation' among educational qualifications, whereby only those with the highest grades and best qualifications are considered for even relatively lowly positions. Many banks, for example, are taking on trainee cashiers only if they have a top-level technical school qualification, or even an *Abitur*.

For those who have successfully completed an apprenticeship and want to obtain a higher qualification in their chosen field, there's the *Fachabitur*, which enables a student to attend a polytechnic (see page 179). A *Fachabitur* can be obtained by attending a vocational school, either full or part time.

The German labour office (*Arbeitsagentur*) offers cross-training programmes (*Umschulung*) for people trained in occupations that are gradually becoming obsolete, to enable them to move to another field with better prospects.

Master Programmes

After working for three years as a qualified tradesman (*Geselle*), you can attend classes to become a master tradesman (*Meister*). There are two types of *Meister* programme, one designed for someone wishing to run his own skilled trade business and the other for someone wanting to manage a company's apprentice programme. In most trades it's mandatory to have a *Meister* or engineer managing the business and an 'industry master' (*Industriemeister*) in charge of apprentices. There's no master tradesman qualification in medical or commercial professions. For the latter a licence (*Lehrberechtigung*) is required to train apprentices. Any doctor, dentist or chemist is authorised to train assistants. For those wishing to attend these classes full time but lacking the funds, there's a Federal Tuition Assistance Programme from BAFöG (see **Grants** on page 180).

HIGHER EDUCATION

Germany has over 400 higher education institutions, including state universities (traditional and technological), private universities and colleges of education, as well as a large number of specialised establishments, such as colleges of theology, colleges of art, polytechnics and colleges of public administration (the last admitting only graduates). Anyone who passes the *Abitur* (see page 171) is guaranteed entry to one of these institutions, which are attended by some 30 per cent of secondary students (around 1.8m).

The duration of higher education courses depends largely on students themselves. The period prescribed is usually four to six years, but most students take longer over their courses, which are completed at an average age of almost 28 in comparison with 25.5 in the US and 22.8 in the UK.

State Universities

German state universities include those at Augsburg, Bayreuth, Berlin, Bielefeld, Bonn, Bremen, Cologne, Dortmund, Dresden, Dusseldorf, Erlangen, Essen, Frankfurt, Frankfurt-an-der-Oder, Göttingen, Hamburg, Hanover, Heidelberg,

Kaiserslautern, Karlsruhe, Leipzig, Mainz, Mannheim, Marburg, Munich, Münster, Osnabrück, Passau, Potsdam, Rostock, Saarbrücken, Stuttgart, Tübingen, Ulm, Weimar and Würzburg. Germany's oldest higher education institutions are the universities of Heidelberg (founded in 1386), Leipzig (1409) and Rostock (1419).

Since 1960 over 20 new universities have been built in Germany and in the last few years the total number of students has fallen slightly; nevertheless, many universities suffer overcrowding, with lecture halls packed to the rafters and many courses heavily over-subscribed. The situation hasn't been helped by the budget cuts that many universities have been forced to make. Nevertheless, in international comparisons German universities still score well in terms of results.

Only students with the highest *Abitur* grades may choose the university they wish to attend; all others are allocated places by the Central Office for the Allocation of Study Places (Zentralstelle für die Vergabe von Studienplätzen/ZVS) in Dortmund. The allocation depends on two factors: your *Abitur* grades and the length of time you spend waiting for a place. The *Abitur* is graded from 1 to 6, where 1 is the highest pass and 6 is a fail; the better your grades, the better the university you'll be sent to. However, many fields of study have access restrictions. For example, if you wish to study medicine, you must usually have at least a grade of 1.5. If your grade is too low for direct admission, you can sometimes still obtain access to a university education by learning a related profession first. For example, doing a three-year apprenticeship as a medical technical assistant greatly improves your chances of getting into medical school if you have low *Abitur* grades. If you fail to gain admission at your first attempt, you can improve your chances by reapplying a term or a year or two later; presumably, the fact that you're prepared to wait for admission means that you're unusually keen to obtain a place – and the longer you wait the more likely you are to be accepted.

Foreign students number around 165,000 or just over 9 per cent of the intake to higher education establishments, over a third of whom obtained their university entrance qualification in Germany (so-called resident foreign students). Nevertheless, the government, anxious that the country will suffer academic isolation, is keen to attract more foreign students, and knowledge of German is no longer required. Many courses leading to internationally recognised bachelors and masters degrees are now available in English. Even for foreign students, tuition is free, and graduates are encouraged to remain in Germany to help bridge the country's skills gap.

If you wish to study at a German university but have non-German educational qualifications, your prospects will depend largely on whether your qualifications were awarded inside or outside Europe. All European qualifications (including British A Levels and the International Baccalaureate) are recognised as equivalent to the *Abitur* for the purposes of university admission. Non-European qualifications, however, including those from the US and Canada, require additional certification in order to be recognised. Each state's ministry of education has a different policy for evaluating such qualifications, with costs likely to include an administration fee plus the cost of official translations of school reports and other documents and the qualifications themselves. Without a BA, BBA or equivalent, an American will usually have difficulty obtaining a place at a German university.

Private Universities

Germany also has a number of private universities, which fall into three categories.

- **Private universities** – These are similar to state universities but usually affiliated to a religious organisation and focusing on subjects such as theology. You must pay the tuition costs yourself.

- **Elite, industry-sponsored institutions** – These are designed to train the second-level management of large corporations. Gaining access to these is even more difficult than to state universities but, once you're in, a glittering career in senior management is all but guaranteed.

- **International universities** – Mostly of US origin, these include the well known Schiller International University in Heidelberg (Bergstrasse 106, 69121 Heidelberg, ☎ 06221-45810, 🖳 www.siu.heidelberg.de). International universities mostly offer US-style diplomas, which aren't automatically recognised in Germany or the rest of the EU but are designed largely to allow American students a period abroad. Tuition fees are high.

Polytechnics

Polytechnics (*Fachhochschulen*) were originally intended to improve the skills of blue-collar workers but are now fully-fledged university-level institutions. However, one tradition remains, which is that only technical subjects are taught there. Some states insist that the diploma contains the letters *FH* to show that it was obtained at a *Fachhochschule*. Some graduates from traditional universities refer rather disparagingly to polytechnic graduates as 'narrow gauge scholars'. However, an *FH* designation often isn't a disadvantage for a graduate, but quite the opposite. Many employers seek those with *FH* degrees because of the practical skills and experience they have, and such individuals are more likely to find employment shortly before or after graduation than those from regular universities.

There are specialised schools for many fields of the medical profession; these are often private, meaning that students must pay for their board and tuition. Many firms and institutions (e.g. Deutsche Telekom) run their own polytechnics to train their engineers.

Accommodation

After gaining a university place, your first challenge will be to find a place to live. Although university and polytechnic courses are free, accommodation can be expensive and difficult to find. Many universities have halls of residence (*Studentenwohnheim*), but few have anywhere near enough places to meet demand and getting a room in a hall is almost equivalent to winning the national lottery! (Not many years ago, one university had to give homeless students 'containers' originally designed for earthquake victims.) If the cost of accommodation is likely to be a problem for you, as it is for many German students, you should apply for a place at a university in a smaller town rather than a large city, as rents are usually lower.

Degrees & Titles

There are essentially three types of degree: an MA, which is a purely academic qualification, usually in an arts subject; a *Diplom*, which is similar but in a science subject; and a *Staatsexamen*, which is taken by future teachers and tests their knowledge of the relevant school curriculum. Teacher-trainees must also take a second (*zweites*) *Staatsexamen* after practical experience in the field. After six terms (semesters), you take an intermediate exam (*Zwischenprüfung*), which is often regarded as the equivalent of a British BA degree, although it confers no qualification.

The highest qualification is a doctorate, which is highly prized – almost all Germans who have achieved a doctorate wish to be addressed as '*Herr/Frau Doktor*'. Those with doctorates from other EU countries have the right to use the title also, but those with an American PhD can call themselves 'Doctor' in Germany only if their qualification has been recognised by a state's Ministry of Education. The procedure for this can be more or less complicated, depending on the state. In some states (Berlin, for example) it's as simple as sending a copy of your diploma to the registrar's office, while in others you may feel as if you're doing your thesis all over again (and you must have documents translated by officially recognised translators at considerable cost).

Grants

Most German students were given grants until the early '80s, when funds were first limited to those who couldn't afford to study, then geared to the level of their financial needs, and finally converted into a loan which must be repaid (after finding a job). The situation that applies today is some way from the original intention, which was to allow anyone capable of studying at a university the opportunity to do so. Student subsidies are administered by the Bundesausbildungsförderungsgesetz (BAFöG), which roughly translates as Federal Promotion of Education Authority but is the name for the assistance it provides as well as for the body that dispenses it.

To qualify for a subsidy, you must be an EU citizen or have a parent who has worked in Germany for at least three years. You must be no more than 30 years old when you start your degree and 'earn' less than €377 per month if you live with your parents (or a parent) or €466 per month if you don't. To apply for a subsidy, you must provide statements showing not only your own financial resources but also those of anybody who may reasonably be expected to support you. Those under the age of 27 must provide earnings statements from their parents, and a divorced person may even be required to supply an earnings statement for his ex-spouse. If your means are below the qualifying limit, the state pays 50 per cent of your subsidy in the form of a grant and 50 per cent as an interest-free loan, which you have up to 20 years to repay (up to a maximum total of €10,000; exemptions and reductions apply to certain categories of student). Applications are processed locally in the town or city where you wish to study and full information is available (in German) on the BAFöG website (🖥 www.bafoeg.bmbf.de).

The qualifying limits haven't been increased in line with inflation for well over a decade, which means that anybody trying to survive on a subsidy will barely exist above the poverty line – in some cities (e.g. Munich, Frankfurt and Berlin) the BAFöG subsidy hardly covers the average room rent. Consequently many German students have at least one part-time job, which is one reason why they take much longer than their European counterparts to complete their studies.

DISTANCE LEARNING

Although magazines in Germany are filled with advertisements for correspondence schools, there's only one German state institution whose certificates are recognised by all European countries. This is the Fernuniversität Hagen (🖥 www.fernuni-hagen.de), which is roughly equivalent to the UK's Open University and broadcasts some lectures via the third TV channel (see **Television Channels** on page 150). The Fernuniversität is designed for people who cannot afford to take time off work to study, and conditions are a little more relaxed than at normal universities. The disadvantages are that it usually takes longer to earn a diploma than through a 'normal' university and the subjects available are somewhat limited.

Graduates of other distance learning universities, particularly those located overseas, may have trouble getting their qualifications recognised in Germany. However, because of the many distance-learning programmes throughout the EU, some of the stricter German rules regarding recognition are likely to be relaxed in the future.

LEARNING GERMAN

If you want to make the most of the German way of life and your time in Germany, it's essential to learn German as soon as possible. For people living in Germany permanently, learning German isn't an option but a necessity. Although it isn't a particularly easy language to learn, even the least linguistically talented person can acquire a working knowledge of German. All that's required is some hard work, help and, particularly if you have only English-speaking colleagues and friends, perseverance. **Your business and social enjoyment and success in Germany will be directly related to the degree to which you master German.**

Most people can help themselves a great deal through the use of books, tapes, DVDs (e.g. watching once in English and then in German), CDs and CD-ROMs and web-based courses. Many 'virtual classroom' courses allow you to speak to and interact with an online teacher, but for most people, attending a 'real' course (combined with one or more of the other methods listed above) is likely to be the best solution.

There's certainly no shortage of possibilities. German classes are offered by language schools (including branches of big corporations such as Berlitz), German and foreign colleges and universities, private and international schools, foreign and international organisations, local associations and clubs, and private teachers. Tuition ranges from language courses for beginners through specialised business-related or cultural courses to university-level courses leading to recognised diplomas. If you already speak German but need conversation practice, you may prefer to enrol on an art or craft course at the local *Volkshochschule* (see **Evening Classes** on page 331). You can also learn German via a telephone language course, which is particularly practical for busy executives and those who don't live near a language school.

There are language schools (*Sprachschulen*) in all German cities and large towns. Most run various classes, from which you can choose according to your language ability, how many hours you wish to study a week, how much money you have to spend and how quickly you want or need to learn. There are 'extensive' courses, comprising four to ten hours' teaching per week, 'intensive' courses (10-20 hours) and, for those for whom money is no object (hopefully your employer!), 'total immersion' courses where you study for up to nine hours a day for five days at a cost of between €1,500 and €2,000, depending on the school. Note, however, that not everyone benefits from such intensive study and it's generally better to spread your lessons over a longer period.

One of the most famous German-language teaching organisations is the Goethe Institut, now officially the Goethe Institut Inter Nationes (Dachauer Strasse 122, 80637 Munich or Postfach 19 04 19, 80604 Munich, ☎ 089-159210, 💻 www.goethe.de), a government-funded, non-profit making organisation with 142 branches in 81 countries across the world and 13 centres in Germany. The Goethe Institut runs general, specialist and intensive courses.

The recommended method (not always possible in practice) is to start with a course in your home country at level one (*Grundstufe 1*), followed by courses at levels 2 and 3 in Germany. Courses cover speech, pronunciation, reading, writing and grammar. All Goethe Institut instructors are university graduates with additional training in teaching German as a foreign language. Many have studied abroad or worked at an overseas branch, and the high quality of the teaching is widely acknowledged. Unfortunately the costs are high (e.g. a two-week immersion course costs €1,780) and so is the number of participants (up to 16!). The Goethe Institut publishes a free annual leaflet, *Learn German in Germany*, which contains up-to-date information about the courses available at its centres in Germany, with an overview of course content, dates and prices. The leaflet is available in American-English, British-English, French, German, Greek, Italian, Japanese, Polish, Portuguese, Russian, Spanish and Turkish.

You may prefer to have private lessons, which are a quicker, although generally more expensive, method of learning a language. The main advantage of private lessons is that you learn at your own pace and aren't held back by slow learners or left floundering in the wake of the class genius. You can advertise for a teacher in your local newspapers, on shopping centre/supermarket and university notice boards, and through your or your spouse's employer. Don't forget to ask friends, neighbours and colleagues if they can recommend a private teacher. Private lessons by the hour cost from around €50 at a school or €20 to €30 with a self-employed tutor.

Another possibility is to find someone who wants to learn (or improve) his English and work out some kind of reciprocal arrangement with them. This can be a very economical (or even free) way of learning German, although it depends on your having the time (and inclination) to give 'lessons' as well as take them.

UK citizens wishing to visit Germany to study the language and culture might be interested in programmes offered by the Central Bureau for Educational Visits and Exchanges, a division of the British Council. The Central Bureau also organises a range of international education and training exchange programmes, including the English Language Assistants' Programme, which enables Modern Language graduates and undergraduates to spend a year working as a language assistant in a foreign school. The Central Bureau publishes a range of guides, including *Home From Home – The Complete Guide to Homestays and Exchanges* and the annual *Working Holidays*. These guides contain practical information on a wide range of opportunities to work and study abroad. For information contact the Education Section of The British Council, 10 Spring Gardens, London, SW1A 2BN, UK (☎ 020-7930 8466, 🖳 www.british council.org) or its office in Germany at Hackescher Markt 1, 10178 Berlin (☎ 030-311 0990).

10.

PUBLIC TRANSPORT

Public transport (*öffentlicher Verkehr* or *öV*) in Germany is efficient, clean, safe, comfortable and comprehensive. Integration between different modes of transport is good, although perhaps not quite up to the standard of Switzerland. The main modes of public transport within Germany are air, train, tram, bus, and underground (subway). There are also river and lake ferries and cable-cars, although these tend to be localised and usually cater more for tourists than residents. Inter-city services are provided largely by air and rail, and inter-city bus services are virtually non-existent, although Germany is served by a network of international bus services provided by companies such as Eurolines. Frankfurt is the hub of both rail and air services within Germany.

In major cities – and to an increasing extent in rural areas also – public transport is organised and paid for by a public transport authority (*Verkehrsverbund*), which contracts services out to different companies and is responsible for integrating fares within the region, so that one ticket is accepted on all modes of transport within a city or region. Rural transport, by contrast, can be patchy, with infrequent services outside school starting and finishing times. Weekend services, particularly outside tourist areas, can be sparse.

Fares may be considered high by some foreigners (though not Britons). Rail fares aren't based simply on distances but may also take into account the quality and speed of trains, which means that money can be saved by choosing slower trains when time isn't of the essence. If you're commuting regularly, it's worth buying a weekly, monthly or even an annual ticket. Many transport systems grant extra privileges to season ticket (*Abo*) holders, such as allowing other family members to accompany them free of charge during the evenings and at weekends. In addition, these tickets aren't usually issued in an individual's name, which allows other family members or friends to borrow them and travel independently. The only drawback is that there's no automatic replacement if a ticket is lost or stolen. You can use these tickets for travel at any time on all modes of transport within the designated zone(s), with the exception of long-distance DB trains.

TRAINS & TRAMS

Newcomers are sometimes confused by the terminology used in Germany for rail systems, which include main-line railways (*Eisenbahn*), trams (*Strassenbahn*), underground (*U-Bahn*) and light rail (*Stadtschnellbahn* or more commonly *S-Bahn*) – all described below.

The railway (*Eisenbahn*) network in Germany is extensive and has seen huge investment in recent years, high-speed lines being built and others upgraded to cater for high-speed trains. Most main lines are electrified, as are suburban lines around the main conurbations. After unification, the railway systems of the former East and West Germany were merged to form Deutsche Bahn AG (DB AG). However, following directives from the European Union (EU) that were intended to increase competition, the operating arm of DB AG was split into several companies, the most important of which are DB Reise & Turistik AG (long-distance passenger services) and DB Regio AG (local passenger traffic). In 2006 DB broke all records by transporting 1.85bn passengers and 96.4bn tonnes of freight. This brought in €30bn revenue and DB announced that it will offer shares to the public in 2008 and become semi-privatised.

A huge investment (some €5bn) has recently been made in high-speed lines connecting Frankfurt and Cologne, reducing travel time between the two cities by an hour. High-speed lines aso run from Würzburg to Hanover, Mannheim to Stuttgart and Hanover to Berlin, while sections of the Nuremberg-Munich and Stuttgart-Munich lines have been upgraded. At Frankfurt, whose airport now has two stations (one for high-speed trains, the other for local trains), there's full co-ordination between trains and flights, so that passengers holding both rail and air tickets can check in their luggage at certain DB stations for direct loading onto planes in Frankfurt.

Internationally, rail links between Germany and other European countries continue to improve. The most exciting development in recent years has been the high-speed connection (300kph/186mph) from Frankfurt to Paris with a travel time of under four hours and a fare of under €100. Other German cities with high-speed connections to Paris are Kaiserslautern, Mannheim, Saarbrücken and Stuttgart. There's also a high-speed route between Brussels, Aachen and Cologne, linking with the new Cologne-Frankfurt line, which means that *Thalys* trains (operated jointly by France, Germany, Belgium and Holland) can run at 320kph (200mph) all the way from Amsterdam to Frankfurt. In Brussels, you can connect with the Eurostar service to London, providing high-speed rail connections between Germany and the UK for the first time. Other upgraded international links include Berlin-Prague-Vienna, Berlin-Poznan-Warsaw (with the potential for onward connections to Minsk and Moscow) and Paris-Strasbourg-Karlsruhe.

Investment isn't restricted to high-speed services. In many conurbations, a new generation of rolling stock for *S-Bahn* (see page 191) and regional trains has been introduced, providing new standards of comfort and security. Several rural lines are benefiting from tilting trains, enabling higher speeds in locations where new infrastructure cannot be justified.

Perhaps one of the most innovative local train services in Germany is in the Karlsruhe area, where specially-designed trams operate not only on the streets of the city but also on main DB lines to many surrounding towns and cities, providing a true centre-to-centre service. A few years ago, tramlines were re-introduced in central Heilbronn, allowing trams from Karlsruhe to travel all the way into Heilbronn city centre. The same idea has been used in Saarbrücken, trams running on tramlines in the city centre and on DB tracks outside the city. (A novelty here is that one of the lines crosses the border into France at Sarreguemines.)

The post-war history of Berlin meant that the railway network serving the city was split between its western and eastern halves. Since reunification, there has been major investment in a new north-south rail link, together with a completely new main station (*Hauptbahnhof*), sited near the historic *Reichstag* in the centre of the city. Additionally, the major interchanges at Berlin Ostbahnhof and Lichtenberg – both in the east of the city – have been completely rebuilt and now offer full facilities, including hotel accommodation at Ostbahnhof. Not to be outshone by the investment in mainline railways in Berlin, the *S-Bahn* network is rapidly being restored to its original extent, with the addition of new lines that have been opened in the east since the war.

In addition to DB, there are a number of private railway companies in Germany, operating branch lines or small self-contained networks. Many are fully or partly owned by the states and in several recent cases have been successful in obtaining operating contracts for regional passenger services from the *Verkehrsverbünde*, whereby they're now fully integrated into the local transport network. More competition was expected as new German and foreign companies took advantage of the EU open-access policy, but this has come to little so far.

First-class rail travel is popular in Germany, and not only among expense-account businessmen. One reason is that discount fares (see **Fares** on page 193) also apply to first-class tickets and many people consider the extra comfort and space well worth the extra cost.

General railway information is available on the DB website (🖥 www.bahn. de), which has links to many other information pages, plus timetables.

Types of Train

Passenger trains are classified according to their speed, the distance they cover, and the type of service they offer, as shown below:

● **InterCity Express (ICE)** – Deutsche Bahn's flagship trains travel at up to 320kph (200mph) on selected routes, usually with regular-interval timetables. Seating, entirely of the reclining variety, is arranged in either compartment or open-plan carriages (coaches), with panoramic windows and air-conditioning. You can plug a headset into the audio system in your armrest to access six music channels, while individual video screens and a copy of the *Financial Times Deutschland Kompakt* are available free in first class. First-class seats also have sockets for laptops and an amplified mobile phone signal for business travellers. In the latest carriages, the plush *ICE 3*, first-class passengers can sit in a lounge directly behind the driver with a view through the cockpit onto the track ahead. The *ICE T* is a tilting train that takes bends at up to 220kph (138mph). Needless to say, *ICE* trains are the most expensive to use.

ICE Sprinter services, introduced a few years ago, connect Frankfurt with Berlin, Hanover/Hamburg and Munich four times a day on weekdays, once on Saturdays and twice on Sundays, with a journey time of less than 3.5 hours. A complimentary snack, soft drinks and daily papers are available to passengers travelling in first class, which has three 'comfort categories'; other features include a 220V electricity socket and a service call button at each seat, not to mention card telephones. There are also a cocktail and espresso bar, and hire car bookings with Avis, Eurocar, Hertz and Sixt can be made from trains an hour before arrival. Your car will be waiting at the station on arrival. A second-class category has been added to what was formerly a first-class only service.

- **InterCity (IC)** – express trains operating on major internal routes at a speed of up to 200kph (125mph) at regular intervals and with first- and second-class carriages. They usually include a restaurant or bistro car.

- **EuroCity (EC)** – *IC* trains serving destinations outside Germany;

- **InterRegioExpress (IRE)** – limited-stop trains connecting regional centres, with a minimum two-hour frequency and an average speed of at least 90kph (55mph);

- **Schnellzug (D)** – other limited-stop fast trains, including international services, e.g. to Rome, Warsaw and Budapest;

- **StädteExpress (SE)** – limited-stop local trains linking with the main conurbations;

- **RegionalExpress (RE)** – local trains operating a limited-stop service;

- **RegionalBahn (RB)** – local trains stopping at all stations along their route;

- **S-Bahn** (originally **Stadtschnellbahn**) – suburban services inside the *Verkehrsverbünde* (see page 191).

Each train has a unique number (like the flight number for aircraft) which is prefixed by one of the above abbreviations, so there should be no confusion about the type of train or the fares applicable. Most trains have a sign on each coach giving its destination and route details. *ICE* trains usually have an on-board electronic display with the same information, as well as an information screen in the entrance area to carriages, which can be used to obtain details of connections and other information. When it isn't otherwise in use, the screen shows the train's speed.

Restaurant or bistro and trolley facilities are available on *IC*, *ICE* and *EC* trains. *IRE* trains also normally have a bistro car, as well as a trolley service. A small number of *RE* and *SE* trains offer a limited refreshment service from a trolley. As in France, double-decker trains are becoming increasingly common on *RE* and *SE* services. These trains have been in use much longer in eastern Germany and are often to be found there on rural services.

Sleeping Cars

You can take a sleeping car on many long-distance routes. Accommodation in sleeping car trains includes the following:

- *Ruhesessel* – a reclining seat, normally in an 'open' coach.

- *Liegewagen* – a couchette, first or second class, the former with four berths and the latter with six berths per compartment;

- Compartment – which may include from one to four berths, with or without washing facilities. 'Deluxe' compartments have air-conditioning and an electric socket.

Sleeping car carriages are attached to some international *D*-class trains. Dedicated sleeping car services include the following:

- **DB NachtZug** – offers the highest level of comfort and the biggest choice of routes (currently nine) within Germany;

- **EN (EuroNight)** – trains on international routes such as Berlin-Vienna-Budapest, Hamburg-Vienna, Cologne-Warsaw and Vienna-Ostend;

- **CityNightLine (CNL)** – trains to Austria, Holland and Switzerland in purpose-built couchette and sleeping cars, connecting Zurich with Berlin, Dresden, the Ruhr area (in summer also Nordeich-Mole) and Hamburg; Vienna with Dortmund; and Amsterdam with Zurich and Munich and (on winter weekends) Garmisch-Partenkirchen;

- **Urlaubs Express (UEX)** – seasonal trains to holiday destinations in Italy, etc..

Fares for these services can be found on 💻 www.dbnachtzug.de along with other information. Fares, which include breakfast, vary according to the type of accommodation and the time of year as well as the distance.

Car Trains

DB AutoZug operates a network of car-carrying trains from selected German stations to popular holiday destinations. The timetable differs considerably between summer and winter, the destinations offered in winter being mostly ski resorts. As most operate overnight, the trains consist of couchette and sleeper carriages (see **Sleeping Cars** on page 190) and double-decker, car-carrying wagons. Daytime accommodation is all first class.

Prices vary according to the date of the journey (peak holiday seasons are more expensive), the size of the car, the number of passengers travelling together and the type of accommodation (sleeper or couchette). Bookings can be made via the internet on ⌨ www.dbautozug.de, where you can view all possible permutations and pay by credit card.

Light Rail, Trams & Underground

Many large cities operate tram services, an increasing number being banished underground in city centres. Sometimes, as in Stuttgart, Frankfurt and Cologne, these have developed into an independent underground railway (*U-Bahn*) and the stations are distinguished by large signs showing a white 'U' on a blue background. In the Ruhr, high-speed tramlines are also referred to as the *U-Bahn* but confusingly often have the word *Stadtbahn* superimposed on the U. Only Hamburg, Berlin, Munich and Nuremberg have constructed genuine undergrounds from scratch, all other cities having upgraded from tramways.

Running alongside the underground network (or superimposed on it) may be the *S-Bahn* (an abbreviation of the original *Schnellbahn*). These often go underground in the city centre and can be distinguished by a sign showing a green circle with a white 'S' in the centre. Most *S-Bahnen* are operated by DB under contract to the local *Verkehrsverbund*. Stopping points are normally further apart than on the *U-Bahn* and trains are generally less frequent – every 15 to 20 minutes is typical – with routes extending into the surrounding towns and countryside. Nevertheless, both the *U-* and *S-Bahnen* are fully integrated into city transport systems and can be used with normal city transport tickets.

U- and *S-Bahn* services are both numbered, in contrast with similar services in other countries, where a line may have a name and/or a colour allocated to it. (In Germany, things are often numbered rather than named.) *U-Bahn* routes, not surprisingly, are numbered with a U prefix, *S-Bahn* lines with an S prefix. Peak hour or less-frequent services on branch lines have a different number, usually an extra digit; for example, the S11 may be a peak hour variation of the S1. At a main station the *S-Bahn* often runs from underground platforms (*Gleis*) separated from the main part of the station and accessible via an escalator or lift.

For more information on trams, see **Buses** on page 198.

Accommodation

Accommodation on trains varies with the train type. *ICE* trains have carriages that are mostly 'open', with two or three compartments at the end of each coach. *EC* and *D* trains have carriages with either compartments or open accommodation, whereas *IRE* trains have a mixture of compartments and semi-open 'bays'. On *ICE* trains, you can book a particular seat, whereas on other trains you can choose only between a compartment or an open carriage, a window or a corridor seat and (if you want two seats) facing or adjacent seats. In all cases, smoking or non-smoking is an option, although the number of smoking seats on *ICE* trains is relatively low. Note that you cannot choose a forward-facing or backward-facing seat, as many trains change direction during the course of their journey, although in older *IC* trains, seats in first-class 'open' carriages are reversible. Virtually all trains, including some *S-Bahn* trains (although not in Berlin), have both first- and second-class carriages.

On *Sprinter* trains (see page 188), accommodation is divided into four zones, which you choose when booking your ticket and seat:

● **Office Zone** – clear mobile telephone reception, fax service and business magazines for sale;

● **Silence Zone** – quiet atmosphere (mobile telephone- and computer-free), seats in rows, a choice of music programmes with headphones, and blankets and pillows available;

● **Club Zone** – individual choice of films (DVD players), clear mobile telephone reception, area for families with children and one coach equipped for disabled passengers;

● **Traveller Zone** – the second-class area, with none of the above comforts!

A few *S-Bahn* trains offer first-class carriages. If you want to take advantage of the exclusivity (it's rarely any more comfortable than standard class), you must buy a *Zuschlag* ticket from a machine.

The majority of coaches in *EC* and *IC* trains are air-conditioned, as are all *ICE* trains and the latest generation of *S-Bahn* trains. Many trains have toilets with wheelchair access. *ICE* trains have two toilets per carriage (male and female) in second class.

Tickets

You must buy a ticket before travelling by train. If you don't, you'll end up paying a higher fare or even a penalty. Bear in mind that ticket checks are routine, as each train usually has a team of staff rather than a single conductor. Tickets for rail travel can be purchased from a variety of sources, including the following (the last two being the cheapest):

● travel centres or booking offices at stations;

● authorised travel agencies (note that you may be charged an additional handling fee by the agency);

● ticket machines at stations. These are usually 'touch screen' and tickets may be purchased with cash (notes and coins) or by credit card.

● via the internet (⌨ www.bahn.de) using credit or debit card; tickets can be posted to you, collected at a nominated station, or printed at a machine by entering a personal identification number. You can also print them out on your computer at home if you're a *Bahncard* holder (see page 195) or have a credit card.

Tickets can be bought on board some long-distance trains, but a surcharge of between €2 and €10 is payable. Tickets cannot be bought on local trains operated by a *Verkehrsverbund*, and anyone discovered travelling without a ticket is regarded as a 'black traveller' (*Schwarzfahrer*) and liable to an on-the-spot fine. Fines vary according to the *Verkehrsverbund* but average around €40.

RE, *SE* and *S-Bahn* trains operating within major conurbations can be used with the same tickets.

Fares

DB's fare structure was intended to be simple but not everyone has found this to be the case, and a pocket calculator is a useful accessory for travellers. A wide range of fares is offered, and there are many discounts, some of which can be combined. Prices are based on the speed and comfort offered as well as the distance covered. Premium trains attract premium fares and there's no set per kilometre tariff; the further you travel, the lower the kilometre price. The most common fares are summarised below:

● **Standard (basic) fare** – These vary with the length of the journey, longer journeys costing less per kilometre. There are no discounts on these fares, except for those with *Gruppe & Spar* tickets (see below). You may either exchange your ticket for another or obtain a full refund if you decide not to travel, as long as you do this before the day of validity. No charge is made.

● **Kostenloser Kindermitnahme** – Children up to 14 can travel free when accompanied by their parents or grandparents. If they're on their own, they receive a 50 per cent discount. They can receive a further 25 per cent discount if they have a *Bahncard* (see page 195).

● **Mitfahrer-Rabatt** – One person pays the full fare and up to four others travel for half price. The minimum fares to which this offer applies are €30 in second class and €45 in first class. For groups of six or more the *Gruppe und Spar* tariffs apply (see below).

● **Dauer-Spezial** – Every Saturday at 10am the 'routes of the week' are posted on the DB website and tickets to theses destinations are available for as little as €40 (booked online only and subject to availability). You may start your journey any time from the next day (Sunday) to the following Saturday and must return within 14 days. Children up to 14 travel free.

- **Surf & Rail International** – For €19 one-way you can travel to many popular European destinations. Tickets must be booked online and travel must be completed within one month. Subject to availability.

- **Sparpreis 25 & 50** – These discounted tickets are subject to availability and, although you may cancel, a fee of between €15 and €30 is thereby incurred, depending on how late this is done. Two under-14s count as one adult. You receive a discount of between 25 and 50 per cent when you book three days or more in advance. You receive a 50 per cent discount only on weekends. This deal is also applicable with the *Mitfahrer-Rabatt* (see above).

- **Gruppe & Spar** – Fares apply to six or more people travelling together (two under-14s counting as one adult) and are subject to availability. There are three types of ticket:

  - **Gruppe & Spar 50** – Buy tickets at any time and get a 50 per cent reduction.

  - **Gruppe & Spar 60** – Buy tickets seven days in advance and get a 60 per cent reduction.

  - **Gruppe & Spar 70** – Buy tickets 14 days in advance to get a 70 per cent reduction.

- **Schönes-Wochenende-Ticket** – a 'good weekend ticket' valid on Saturdays and Sundays from midnight to 3am the following day, e.g. from midnight Friday/Saturday to 3am on Sunday, for unlimited travel on local trains (*RE, RB, SE, S-Bahn*) in second class. The cost is €28 for up to five people travelling together, or for parents or grandparents with an unlimited number of their own children or grandchildren up to 14 years of age. If you buy it aboard the train, you must pay 10 per cent extra. The *Schönes-Wochenende-Ticket* is also valid on the *U-Bahns*, trams and buses of many local transport systems. You can take a bike with you for an additional one-off payment of €3.

- **Länder-Ticket** – This is a 'rover' ticket for an entire federal state and costs from around €25 to €30. It's valid from 9am any weekday to 3am the following morning, on local trains (*IRE, RE, RB* and *S-Bahn*) in second class, along with the other forms of transport of many local transport authorities. Up to five people, or parents/grandparents with an unlimited number of their own children or grandchildren up to the age of 14, can use it. Some states offer single tickets for those travelling alone for €18 or €19. Conditions vary slightly from state to state.

- **Local transport system all-inclusive tickets** – Usually up to 72 hours' unlimited travel in a particular city and surrounding area, using the entire local transport network. Prices vary but are usually an excellent bargain; they're listed on the Deutsche Bahn website: pick the state and then the local area to view the details.

- **Other tickets** – Rail & Fly tickets are airline tickets that include free or reduced-price travel on German railways. Other tickets offer reduced prices for journeys to specific destinations at specific times, such as the annual carnival in Berlin. They're explained in detail on 🖥 www.bahn.de.

Bahncard

This card gives a 25, 50 or 100 per cent discount on all fares, including *Mitfahrer-Rabatt*, *Kostenloser Kindermitnahme* and the *Sparpreis* fares (see above). Get your calculator out!

- *Bahncard 25* – offers a 25 per cent discount cost €53 for second class and €106 for first class. When a parent buys one, the other parent and children are entitled to buy their own for €5 each. It also entitles you to a 25 per cent discount from DB-owned regional bus companies. An additional payment of €15 annually gets you *Railplus*, which means that *Bahncards* can also be used in 28 other European countries to get the same discount.

- *Bahncard 50* – entitles you to a 50 per cent reduction on fares and costs €212 for second class and €424 for first class (half price for partners, children and students, senior citizens and the disabled);

- *Bahncard 100* – allows you (and four of your children under 15) to travel anywhere at any time 'free' (it costs €3,400 for second class and €5,700 for first class!). *Bahncard* 100 holders receive a *Bahncard* 25 free for their spouses and children.

If you've invested in a *Bahncard* (see page 195), you may also be entitled to a cheaper fare if your journey within a conurbation involves train travel only (*S-Bahn*, *RE* or *SE* services).

Booking

Bookings can be made for all *ICE*, *IC*, *EC*, *IRE* and *D* trains from three months in advance to a few minutes before departure. The latest *ICE* trains have automatic booking systems allowing seats to be reserved even after a train has left its starting station. Bookings are highly recommended on inter-city routes, particularly on Fridays and Sundays, when trains can become very crowded, even in first class. In second class you're liable to find yourself surrounded by soldiers either going home for the weekend or returning to barracks at these times (you can tell which by whether they're cheerful or gloomy).

The current booking fee is €1.50. If you want to reserve a seat for a disabled person (and companions) contact the Mobilitäts Service Zentrale, whose telephone number is ☎ 01805-512512 (calls cost €0.12 per minute).

Bicycles

Bicycles can normally be taken on local trains (*RE, SE, S-bahn, RB*) and on the underground and stored in luggage and entrance areas, provided space is available, although in some cases their carriage is restricted to certain carriages (indicated by a bicycle logo). Bikes may be taken on some long-distance trains, indicated by a similar logo. Booking is recommended at peak holiday times between the beginning of March and the end of November. Reserving a place for your bike is obligatory on some long-distance trains but doesn't cost anything. DB provides advice and assistance on its cyclist's hotline (☎ 01805-151415 – €0.12 per minute). The current charges for cycles are:

● **International trains** – €10 (but €15 on some night trains, such as the 242/243 from Berlin to Paris);

● **Long-distance trains** (*ICE, IC, D* and sleepers) – €9 or with a *Bahncard* €6;

● **Local & regional trains** (*IRE, RB, RE* and *S-Bahn*) – €4.50 with some variations according to the *Verkehrsverbund*.

If you don't want the hassle of taking your own bike with you, you can hire one on arrival through DB's new 'Call-A-Bike' service. It's currently available in Berlin, Cologne, Munich, Stuttgart and Frankfurt. According to DB, more than 4,000 modern bikes with eight gears are available for hire. When you call the local Call-A-Bike office to register, you'll be given a code, which you enter into a gadget attached to a bike to release the lock. €5 will automatically be debited from your credit card and then deducted from your total at the end of the ride. Bikes can be found at major road junctions as well as the railway stations in the towns mentioned. When you've finished with your bike, you leave it at the station or any main junction. You lock it and de-register with another telephone call to the Call-A-Bike office. Bikes are thus available 24 hours a day. You're charged according to the exact amount of time you've spent with the bike (at €0.08 per minute – €0.06 per minute for *Bahncard* holders) and regular users can pay monthly. A seven-day hire costs €60. Further details can be found on 🖥 www.callabike-interaktiv.de/kundenbuchung. More traditional bike hire companies usually operate close to stations, but these aren't connected with DB and rates vary.

Luggage

Accompanied luggage up to 30kg (66lb) is carried without charge. (In fact, it's unusual for the weight to be checked unless an item is extra-large.) Luggage can be sent in advance using the *KurierGepäck* service, for which there's a standard fee of around €16 per 'normal' item (up to 30kg/66lb in weight and 165cm/65in in length) or €25 for 'special' items (cycles, skis, wheelchairs, etc.). With three or four items the cost for each item is around €20. The service is available door-to-door, with payment made in advance at a DB ticket office.

Station Facilities

The main station in each town is called the *Hauptbahnhof* (abbreviated to *Hbf*). In the major cities these offer a range of facilities, including a *Reisezentrum*, which is a large combined booking and information office, a left-luggage office, luggage lockers, a travel agency (often from the associated DER chain), a currency exchange counter (run by the in-house Deutsche Verkehrs-Bank) and usually a post office, plus a variety of book shops, magazine stalls, cafes, bars and restaurants. Another feature of large stations is the *Markt im Bahnhof* ('market in the station'), where you can buy fresh food and vegetables seven days a week, free of Germany's restrictive trading hours.

Luggage can be transported on trolleys located at strategic points in stations. You need a 50 cent or €1 coin, which is returned when you replace the trolley at a collection point. Alternatively, you can sometimes hire the services of a porter.

Recently, DB has been putting a lot of effort into improving station waiting areas with the introduction of 'DB Lounges'. These are quiet waiting areas for first-class passengers, similar to business-class lounges at airports (complete with comfortable seats, drinks, newspapers, magazines, television and a screen displaying train times) with adjacent office areas equipped with desks, telephones and sockets for laptops. Conference rooms for meetings or presentations are also available. The DB Lounges at Frankfurt, Frankfurt Airport and Cologne stations now offer a 'Rail&Mail' service, providing internet access. Laptops can be hired. DB Lounges now offer a 'Rail&Mail' service, providing internet access; laptops can be hired. DB Lounges can be found at the following stations: Berlin, Bremen, Cologne, Dresden, Dusseldorf, Frankfurt, Frankfurt Airport, Hamburg, Hanover, Leipzig, Mannheim, Munich, Nuremberg and Stuttgart. They're open every day from 7am to 9pm. Customers with Metropolitan or *Thalys* (Comfort 1) tickets can use the DB Lounge at Cologne, while Lufthansa customers (first class) have access to the lounge in Stuttgart.

Another innovation is the 'ServicePoint/ServiceTeam' facility. Located in over 90 DB stations, these are places where passengers can send faxes, post letters and arrange courier deliveries, etc. A DB Service Team is on hand to provide transport and local accommodation information.

Information

Information about train services can be obtained at all stations with a manned ticket office. In an attempt to help passengers orientate themselves at stations, large colour-coded metal figures (*Stahlmenschen*) display different types of information, as follows:

- **Blue** – welcome signs and temporary information;

- **Red** – timetables; sheets showing departures (Abfahrt) are yellow, while those showing arrivals (Ankunft) are white;

- **Yellow** – station plans showing facilities and city maps;

- **Green** – exhibitions and shows in the city and/or station.

Large electronic displays show train departure and arrival details and platform information. Note, however, that only a limited number of stops for any given route are shown on these. At the entrance to each platform is a display board indicating the next arriving or departing train, again with main (but not all) stopping points. On the platform itself there's usually a *Wagenstandanzeiger*, a diagram showing every carriage in each train stopping at the platform with its number (and destination, if different from the rest of the train), alongside a series of letters from A to E. These letters relate to sections (*Abschnitte*) on the platform surface, so that it's easy to see precisely where your carriage will stop. This is important on long platforms where trains may stop only for a few minutes and you won't have time to rush from one end to the other looking for your carriage. This information also appears in simplified form on the platform display screen.

An increasingly popular way to find train and bus information is via the internet. DB has an easy-to-use website in German and English (🖥 http://bahn. hafas.de), which provides extensive details of train times and categories of trains. If you don't want the expense of an *ICE*, for example, you can exclude this type of train, or any other, from your timetable search. It's also possible to make bookings and buy tickets online. DB's online information isn't restricted to Germany, and information about all European railways can be accessed via the website, together with a range of bus and other local transport information. DB's latest development is 'Surf and Rail' (🖥 www.surfandrail.de), where tickets purchased online can be printed via your computer.

BUSES

Regional bus companies are owned mainly by Deutsche Bahn (DB) and tend to offer inter-urban (although not inter-city) services, as well as services linking major towns to outlying villages. In most cases these operate in conjunction with regional train services and generally the bus terminus is adjacent to the railway station. However, services are severely limited on some rural routes, the frequency of buses being calculated per week rather than per day. Many services cater particularly for schoolchildren (although anyone can use them) and therefore operate only from Mondays to Fridays (sometimes also Saturdays) at the start and end of the school day, and not at all during school holidays.

In some towns, local bus services are also provided by a DB subsidiary company. Some can be identified by a variation on the old DB bus livery of strawberry pink and grey, although many companies are now introducing their own liveries. If you have a *Bahncard* (see page 195), you should ask whether the service is run by DB or a subsidiary, as you're entitled to a 25 per cent fare discount on all DB services.

In all major cities, and in many smaller towns, bus services are provided by a division of the local authority (*Verkehrsbetriebe* or *Stadtwerke*). The scale of these operations varies enormously, from the extensive route networks of Berlin, Hamburg and Munich to just two or three routes in small satellite towns. Services are mainly operated with buses, although trams (*Strassenbahn* – see page 186) are used in the larger cities and trolleybuses in Eberswalde (north-east of Berlin), Esslingen (south of Stuttgart) and Solingen (in the Ruhr). In Wuppertal there's the *Schwebebahn*, a suspended monorail operating along the River Wupper, which isn't merely for tourists but is an integral part of the local transport system.

In the major conurbations bus services are co-ordinated by the regional *Verkehrsverbund*, common fare systems and timetables covering all public transport within the area. The largest example is the Verkehrsverbund Rhein-Ruhr, covering an area of over 5,000km^2 (1,930mi^2) in the industrial Ruhr area, and incorporating more than 800 routes providing services to over 20 major towns and cities in the region. Such services are integrated with local trains (*S-Bahn*) provided by DB.

Bus (and tram/trolleybus) services don't generally operate between around 1 and 5am, but most larger cities have an hourly night bus service covering popular destinations (and charging a premium).

Fares & Tickets

Fare systems vary between cities and regions but generally operate on a zone basis, where a ticket remains valid irrespective of the number of changes you make, provided you remain within the designated zone(s). Normally, a central city area will be within one zone and therefore subject to a single fare. Ticket machines usually have a simplified route map showing the fare zones or a list of possible destinations with fares for each.

In most large towns and cities, it's compulsory to buy a ticket from a machine before boarding a vehicle – buying tickets from the driver is the exception, although it's more common on rural routes where traffic doesn't justify the cost of installing a machine at each stop. The rule is: if there's a machine, use it! Because of the differences in systems between cities, it isn't possible to give precise instructions for using machines. For example, in the Rhein-Main area (the area surrounding Frankfurt) you enter a four-digit destination code on a numerical keypad and then press one of around ten buttons for the type of ticket required. In other cities there's a route map, on which you simply press a button corresponding to your destination. In each case the fare is displayed on a screen and you must insert the required payment; an increasing number of machines accept banknotes and credit cards as well as coins. Change is usually given. When change runs out, a sign is displayed, usually in red.

In some cities, such as Munich and Berlin, you may find a ticket machine on board trams (more rarely on buses). These function in the same way as machines at stops and, as there are no conductors, you must use them. Having purchased your ticket, it's usually necessary – depending on the city – to validate (*entwerten*) it in a machine at the stop or aboard the vehicle. If a ticket has a space on it for a machine stamp (generally marked with an arrow), it probably needs to be validated. If in doubt, ask the driver or another passenger. **If you don't validate your ticket, you're riding illegally and can be fined.** There are random but regular inspections by teams of plain-clothes ticket inspectors.

Children up to five travel free, those aged 6 to 14 at a reduced fare (but usually more than half the normal fare); those 15 and over pay full fare. In many cities *Auszubildende* or *Azubis* (youths aged 15 and over in full-time education or training) are able to purchase season tickets at reduced prices, typically 20 to 25 per cent below the full fare. Many cities allow the transport of bicycles without an extra charge, although this may be restricted to off-peak times and may be at the discretion of the driver if the vehicle is full or small (such as a minibus).

Discount Tickets

Discounted tickets include 24-hour or day tickets (*Tageskarten*), which are excellent value for a day trip to explore a city. It's worth checking whether a ticket is in fact valid for a day (usually until the next morning at 6am) or for 24 hours, as the latter can be used on the following day up until the time printed on it. Take care when using these tickets, as in some cities they must be both validated and signed. The machine (or ticket) should tell you; if in doubt, ask. Group tickets (*Partnerkarten*) are economical when travelling with a group of up to five people. In some cities you can buy a short-distance (*Kurzstrecke*) ticket, usually for journeys of less that 2km.

Access

Germany is at the forefront of investment in easy-access buses and trams, normally referred to as *Niederflür* (low entrance) vehicles. These originally involved merely a shallow entrance step to the main seating area, but the most recent vehicles have a completely flat floor, with direct access to most seats from the low floor area. Most of the latest vehicles also have a retractable wheelchair ramp, usually at the centre door, and a wheelchair parking area with clamps. Many drivers obligingly lower ramps at stops, even for (apparently) able-bodied people. Modern buses and trams are usually also air-conditioned.

In general, access to buses and trams can be made through any door. The exceptions are buses on rural routes, where the driver may want to check your ticket or sell you one, and on city buses after 8pm, when you should enter by the front door.

When you want to get off a bus (and some trams), you normally just press the button marked '*Tür öffnen*' or '*Stop*', though some open automatically A sign, '*Bus hält*' (bus stopping), will be illuminated. On some city bus lines stops are 'on request' (*Halten auf Wunsch*) in the evenings, in which case you must inform the driver when you board where you'd like to get off.

It isn't usually necessary to signal the driver to stop if you're at a bus (or tram) stop, as there are few 'request stops'. Sometimes, however, a driver may not realise that you're intending to board, so it's wise to put an arm out if he doesn't seem to be slowing down.

FERRIES

There's a variety of ferry (*Fährboot*) services in Germany. Major rivers, such as the Rhine and Main, have a number of ferry crossings for cars and foot passengers, and some major cities include ferry services in their range of public transport services, which are usually covered by a standard ticket. Examples are the river services in Hamburg and the lake services in Berlin, each of which forms an integral part of the local public transport system. Ferry services on Lake Constance (*Bodensee*) are provided by the Stadtwerke Konstanz company. The *Bodensee Pass* gives 50 per cent reductions on transport in this area, including the ferries.

North Sea ferry services operate internationally from Hamburg/Cuxhaven to Harwich in England (see 🖳 www.dfdsseaways.co.uk for details and timetables), and there are services between eastern Germany and Sweden, Finland, Lithuania and Latvia across the Baltic. There are also good connections from the German mainland to the outlying Friesian islands, usually run in conjunction with trains or express buses.

A variety of companies provide tourist services on Germany's lakes and rivers. Trips range from a few hours to several weeks. The two biggest operators are the Weisse Flotte (White Fleet) in Dresden, specialising in vintage steamboats on the Elbe River, and KD in Dusseldorf, which mainly operates in the Rhine/Main/Mosel regions.

CABLE CARS & FUNICULARS

Cable cars (*Seilbahnen*) and rack railways (*Zahnradbahnen*) can be found in the more mountainous areas of Germany, particularly the northern Alps in Bavaria. Here you'll find the famous *Zugspitzbahn*, an electrified rack railway running some 18.6km (12mi) from Garmisch-Partenkirchen at an altitude of around 700m (2,300ft) to the top station at 2,650m (8,694ft).

Funiculars (*Drahtseilbahnen*) are found in several of the hillier towns in Germany and include the *Nerobergbahn* in Wiesbaden, operated by a water-balance system, the two-stage line in Heidelberg and an ancient line in Stuttgart. Stuttgart also has the only rack railway (actually a tramway) to be integrated into a city transport network (at Degerloch on Route 10). In summer, a trailer is attached for the transportation of bicycles. Dresden has a hill-climbing *Schwebebahn* (suspension railway) and a more conventional funicular.

TIMETABLES

Comprehensive timetables are published by the major public transport authorities and cover all services in a region, although they're usually in several volumes. Similarly, DB produces a national timetable known as the *Kursbuch,* in addition to more manageable regional timetables. DB and the major *Verkehrsverbünde* also publish their timetables on CD-ROM. However, the trend is towards publishing timetable information electronically, such as on the DB website (🖳 www.bahn.de), and most *Verkehrsverbünde* have websites. There's a move towards producing a co-ordinated national enquiry system, so that it will soon be possible to obtain 'door-to-door' timetable information between any two towns in Germany (and indeed Europe) from a single internet enquiry. It's possible to take out a subscription to receive updated information by email or by downloading files from a website.

Most transport authorities and DB have telephone enquiry services, sometimes providing recorded announcements for the most popular routes. DB has a single national enquiry number (☎ 11861). This enquiry service costs on average €1 per minute but can be accessed 24 hours a day throughout the year. There is also a freephone number (☎ 0800-1507 090) for spoken timetable information – spoken by a machine, not a person!

TAXIS

Taxis are easy to identify in Germany, where they're painted in a standard cream livery and have an illuminated '*Taxi*' sign on the roof. Many are Mercedes or other quality makes. Fares, which are fixed by local authorities, are shown on a meter inside the vehicle and usually consist of a minimum fare plus a variable kilometre or elapsed time rate. Rates for evenings and weekends are usually higher. Taxis can be hailed in the street or hired from an official taxi rank (stand), which are found at railway stations, airports and bus and tram termini, for example. Taxis can be summoned to your home by telephone for €1. Several public transport authorities offer the facility to book a taxi to meet a bus or tram at a nominated stopping point, particularly during the evening or at night. There's usually no extra charge for this service.

AIRLINE SERVICES

Germany is well served by airlines, both domestic and international, and boasts the second-busiest airport in Europe, as well as numerous smaller airports. As well as Lufthansa (see below), a number of large charter holiday airlines are based in Germany, as is Deutsche BA, a subsidiary of British Airways, which operates mainly from Berlin Tegel.

Lufthansa

Lufthansa, the national airline, is one of the world's largest passenger and freight carriers. It flies to around 340 cities in some 90 countries and operates over 430 aircraft. To strengthen its international ties, Lufthansa was the founding member of the 'Star Alliance' with 17 other major airlines, including Air Canada, Air New Zealand, British Midland, Singapore Airlines, SAS Scandinavian, Thai, United Airlines and Varig. One of its most successful innovations has been the 'Miles and More' frequent flyer reward programme, which also recognises air miles flown with other Star Alliance members. (More information is on 🖥 www.miles-and-more.com).

Lufthansa's hub is Frankfurt Airport and it has a secondary base at Munich International Airport. Flights within Europe offer business and economy classes, while intercontinental flights also include first class. Lufthansa aircraft are equipped throughout with leather seats, which can be widened in business class to give additional room. All flights are non-smoking. Passengers travelling in first or business class can make bookings via the Lufthansa website (🖥 www.lufthansa.com), which also provides flight information, timetables, news of offers and other details. Economy seats can be reserved only on intercontinental flights (on European flights seats are allocated at check-in). Flights are often full during school holiday periods, which are listed in most diaries and calendars, so you should book early.

In addition to check-in facilities at airports, Lufthansa provides a check-in service at the main railway stations in Cologne and Stuttgart, where you can hand in your luggage and receive boarding cards. On the return trip, you can check in your bags at the airport and pick them up at Cologne or Stuttgart station. Trains run hourly. You can check in over the telephone (☎ 0561-993399) and pick up your ticket at a quick check-in machine or counter or online, choosing your seat and printing out your own boarding pass. At Frankfurt, Munich and Dusseldorf, first- and business-class passengers (with or without luggage) may check in at drive-in desks outside the terminal building adjacent to the taxi set-down point. Valet parking and porter service is available here.

Over 50 airports around the world provide dedicated lounges for holders of Lufthansa first, business and frequent traveller cards, and at a further 80 airports you can use the executive lounges of its partner airlines. Most lounges have wireless access (known in Germany as W-LAN or wireless LAN – LAN standing for 'local area network', in case you were wondering; the term 'wi-fi' is rarely used).

CityLine, a Lufthansa subsidiary, offers some 500 flights per day to 60 destinations in continental Europe, mostly from Cologne and Bonn airports, with 93-seat Avro RJ85 and 50-85-seat Canadair Jets.

Condor is Lufthansa's holiday airline, most of whose flights are sold as part of a holiday package. It's the largest such airline in Germany and provides around 500 weekly flights during the peak season to over 70 international destinations. Its modern fleet consists of Boeing 757, 767, and Airbus A320 aircraft.

Airports

The main international airports in Germany are in Berlin (Tegel and Schönefeld), Cologne-Bonn, Dusseldorf, Frankfurt (see below), Hamburg and Munich. There are many smaller airports that provide limited international services, including Dresden, Hanover and Leipzig-Halle, some handling only charter flights. A small airport with a significant schedule is Hahn, served from Stansted in England by Ryanair and set to become its second continental hub (after Brussels). Lufthansa recently took the Irish airline to court over the latter's somewhat ingenuous description of Hahn as Frankfurt (Hahn); in fact it's over 80km (50mi) from Frankfurt. Ryanair also has bases at Bremen and Weeze.

Long- and short-term parking is available at all major airports, including reserved parking for the disabled, and all major airports have wheelchairs and ambulance staff on hand to help disabled travellers, although it's wise to make arrangements in advance. Lufthansa also provides flight attendant services for children over five who are travelling alone, for a fee. International airports have shopping centres that are usually open for 24 hours a day, seven days a week. The table below gives telephone numbers for flight information and details of bus or rail services to the city centre from the main airports.

Airport	Telephone	Transport to City Centre
Berlin Tegel	0180-500 0186	Express bus X9 or bus109 (20 to 25 minutes)

Cologne-Bonn	02203-400	Shuttle bus 170 (20 minutes)
Dusseldorf	0211-4210	*S-Bahn* S7 (13 minutes)
Frankfurt	069-6900	*S-Bahn* S8 or S9 (12 minutes) – see **Access** below
Hamburg	040-50750	Airport Express bus (25 minutes)
Hanover	0511-9770	*S-Bahn* S5 (12 minutes)
Munich	089-97500	*S-Bahn* S1 or S8 (40 minutes)
Stuttgart	0711-9480	*S-Bahn* S2 or S3 (25 minutes)

Frankfurt

Frankfurt International is Germany's most important airport and the second-busiest in Europe (after London Heathrow), handling well over 50m passengers a year. The airport is huge. There are two terminals (a third is being constructed), five 'halls' (A–C in Terminal 1, D and E in Terminal 2) and six floors (four in Terminal 1 and two in Terminal 2); finding your way around can be difficult and you may have to walk long distances. Every imaginable service is available – in theory. Finding unoccupied information desks isn't unusual, and airport staff are often less than helpful. Looking at the airport website (🖥 www.frankfurt-airport.de) is worthwhile, and printing the map of the airport recommended.

The two terminals are linked by the 'Sky Line Shuttle', a driver-less electric train, which runs every two minutes (also the length of the trip). The shuttle is free, but you cannot take luggage trolleys on it. The Sky Line 'station' in Terminal 1 is above Departure Hall B and in Terminal 2 it's on Level 4. You must take the shuttle to get from Hall C to Hall D.

For passengers requiring overnight accommodation, there's a Sheraton Hotel in the terminal complex and at least 15 other hotels nearby, many directly accessible by courtesy shuttle buses and taxis. There's a hotel information and booking desk in each terminal, but the one in Terminal 1 is open later than that in Terminal 2. Several hotels offer a 'Park & Fly' service, with a room rate combined with short- or medium-term secure parking.

Access

The airport is well served by public transport and has good road access.

● **Train** – There are two railway stations: Frankfurt Flughafen Regionalbahnhof and Frankfurt Flughafen Fernbahnhof, the latter also called the 'AIRail terminal'. The first is served by local and regional trains and the second by long-distance inter-city trains. The Regionalbahnhof is directly beneath Terminal 1 (Hall B) and offers *S-Bahn* trains serving Frankfurt city every 15 minutes and frequent trains to Frankfurt's mainline station (*Hauptbahnhof*), an 11-minute journey. As its name suggests (*fern* means far), the *Fernbahnhof* is almost half a mile from the airport, although with covered pedestrian access from Terminal 1, and is the terminus for the Frankfurt-Cologne ultra-high-speed railway line. Deutsche Bahn claims that all major cities in Germany – and many abroad – can be reached from here with no more than one change of train.

● **Bus** – There are bus stops at both terminals – opposite Hall C (on Level 0) at Terminal 1 and opposite Hall E at Terminal 2 – and serve many nearby destinations. Lufthansa operates regular buses to the neighbouring towns of Heidelberg, Heilbronn, Kaiserslautern, Mannheim, Saarbrücken and Sinsheim.

● **Road** – The airport is conveniently situated close to *Autobahn 3* (Cologne-Munich) and *Autobahn 5* (Hanover-Basle), with well signposted slip roads. However, local access is provided from the parallel but less-congested B43 dual-carriageway, which can be used for the entire journey when travelling to or from Frankfurt city.

There are multi-storey car parks in both terminals open 24 hours a day. Fees at both terminals are around €1.50 for 30 minutes, €3.50 for an hour and €25 per day. Facilities are available for the disabled, including designated parking places (currently in the P31 car park close to Terminal 1).

Taxis are plentiful and can be found on the forecourts of the terminals. Although you sometimes need to queue, you rarely have to wait long. At Terminal 1 taxis generally drop off at one of the Halls on Level 2 (departures) and pick up from Level 1 (arrivals). At Terminal 2, taxis usually stop on the terminal service road on Level 2. The fare from central Frankfurt to the airport is around €20 to €25 and the journey normally takes around 20 to 30 minutes.

Departures

Luggage trolleys are plentiful, a situation which has improved considerably in recent years, and some escalators accommodate them, saving constant loading and offloading. Large information boards show the location of check-in desks. Most Lufthansa flights use Terminal 1, where most Lufthansa check-in desks are in Hall A and other airlines' desks in Hall B, while Hall C (with the fewest facilities) tends to be the refuge of small charter and holiday airlines.

After checking in, you'll find the gate number for your flight (if known) on your boarding card. Gate numbers consist of a Hall letter (A to E) and a number. It's wise to locate your gate well in advance of the departure time, as it may be a long walk. You may be asked to switch a computer on, so it's wise to charge it up beforehand.

Arrivals

If you arrive on a flight with a high proportion of transit passengers, the airport staff may decide not to run the luggage carousel. If this is the case, you must go to the 'oversize luggage' (*Sperrgepäck*) claim area and ask whether your luggage is there. If your luggage doesn't arrive at all or is damaged, go to the 'baggage tracing' (*Gepäckermittlung*) kiosk and report your loss and show your baggage tags. If your luggage is damaged, this is likely to be the only opportunity you'll get to report it and claim compensation. Generally, lost luggage appears a day or two later and is delivered to you directly by the airline; you don't need to return to the airport to collect it.

11.

MOTORING

Germany has the highest level of car ownership in Europe after Italy, with over 46m registered cars – around 560 per 1,000 inhabitants. Not surprisingly, although the country has an excellent road system, which includes some 226,500km (140,312mi) of main roads, it's notorious for its traffic jams (*Staue*), which can be encountered at any time. In addition to the expected congestion during rush hours, roads are usually clogged on school and public holidays, when millions of Germans take to their cars. Add to this the German propensity for high-speed driving and, irrespective of your level of motoring experience, you're likely to find motoring in Germany a challenging, not to say nerve-racking, experience (unless you're Italian or Portuguese or Spanish...).

Germany's motorway (*Autobahn*) network covers 11,500km (7,132mi) and provides direct connections between most German cities. There's no official speed limit on motorways (although there are 'recommended' speed limits – see **Speed Limits** on page 230) except at junctions and other 'dangerous' areas. Speeds in excess of 160kph (100mph) are common and high-performance cars can be seen – if you don't blink – zooming by at well over 200kph (125mph). Not surprisingly, there are a lot of 'accidents' in Germany, where over 5,000 people are killed on the roads annually and over 400,000 injured. (Germany ranks 'behind' Italy in the western European league table of the number of road deaths relative to distance travelled by motorists but well 'ahead' of the UK.)

The German authorities are serious about traffic laws and police the roads assiduously and effectively, using not only patrol cars but also cameras, which are more common than in any other European country. Cameras are stationed at strategic points (such as traffic lights) throughout the country, and photographs show not only your number plate and the date, time and location but also your face (or the face of the person who has stolen your car)! You may not be aware that you've been caught on camera until a traffic ticket arrives in the post a few days later. (The pictures used to be sent to the offender's home along with the ticket, but this practice was dropped when many partners opened the envelopes and saw photos of their spouses with someone of the opposite sex whom they didn't recognise! Now, in order to see the incriminating picture, you must go to a police station.)

Traffic information is readily available thanks to regular radio and television (TV) announcements and German TV's teletext information service. Recorded traffic information is also provided by the German motoring organisation ADAC (☎ 224 99). Signs on motorways show the radio frequency on which road and traffic bulletins are broadcast. To find out whether alpine passes are open (you can even see live webcam footage) visit ⌨ www.alpineroads.com.

IMPORTING A VEHICLE

If you plan to bring a motor vehicle to Germany, either temporarily or permanently, you should be aware of any restrictions or requirements that may apply. All vehicles manufactured outside Germany must meet German specifications (see **General Operating Licence** on page 213) and may therefore need to be modified. The question of finding parts and service facilities for foreign-made vehicles should also be considered before deciding to import a car rather than buying one in Germany. Add to this the cost of import duty and VAT (see below) and you may think twice (or three times) about bringing a car with you!

You're permitted to drive an imported vehicle with foreign number plates for up to 12 months, provided the vehicle's registration remains valid (a registration document with a German translation is required), but duty and tax (where applicable – see below) must normally be paid after six months.

Duty & VAT

Vehicles registered in a non-EU country are normally subject to import duty (*Zoll*) and value added tax (*Mehrwertsteuer*), either when entering Germany or at a later date. There are two exceptions:

● Normally, vehicles imported for private use for a maximum of six months (which don't need to be consecutive) in any 12-month period are exempt from duty and tax. It's strictly forbidden to lend, hire, give or sell a temporarily imported vehicle to a citizen of an EU member country. If this exception applies, VAT must be paid at the time of import and it's refunded by the customs office upon departure.

● If you're moving from a non-EU country and establishing residence, your vehicle may be considered part of your household goods and therefore exempt from taxation provided the following criteria are met:

  – you can prove that you've been resident outside the EU for the last 12 months;

  – the vehicle has been in your possession and was registered abroad by you at least six months before your arrival in Germany;

  – you register your residence in Germany (see page 83);

  – the vehicle is for personal use only;

  – the vehicle is immediately registered with the local motor vehicle office (see **Registration** below);

  – the vehicle isn't given away, sold, lent or hired for a year after its importation.

If no duty or tax is payable, a customs exemption certificate (*Unbedenklichkeits bescheinigung*) is issued. This document is required when registering the vehicle in Germany (see below).

In the case of non-EU vehicles that don't qualify for exemption, the following charges are levied, irrespective of the type of vehicle being imported:

- import duty of 10 per cent, based on the purchase price (see note below) plus freight costs and insurance to the place of destination in Germany;

- value added tax at 19 per cent, based on the purchase price plus freight costs and import duty.

You're required to present a dealer's invoice as evidence of the purchase price of the vehicle. If, however, customs officials don't consider this a fair and accurate representation of the vehicle's market value, they may calculate their own figure by reference to a dealer's car buying guide (the standard one is the *Schwacke Liste*) or obtain a certified appraisal (*Wertgutachten*). Appraisals can be arranged in Germany with local branches of the Dekra organisation (listed in the telephone book), but the authorities recommend that private importers without a recent invoice for their vehicle or who ship an uncommon type of car should have their vehicle appraised before declaring its value.

Once payment has been made, a customs receipt or clearance certificate (*Zollquittung*) is issued, which is required when registering the vehicle in Germany (see below). Some shipping agencies complete the clearance and customs formalities on your behalf (for a fee).

TECHNICAL INSPECTION & EMISSIONS TEST

A regular technical inspection (*Fahrzeughauptuntersuchung* or *HU*) made by a certified expert is required by law for every vehicle registered in Germany. An inspection must be made when a car is imported or reaches three years of age and thereafter at least every two years. The Technischer Überwachungsverein (TÜV) and the private Dekra organisation (🖳 www.dekra.de) maintain test centres in most towns and cities, listed in telephone books. (If you have an older vehicle that may be due for some repair, folk wisdom suggests that you should take it to a Dekra centre, as they have a reputation for being slightly more lenient on older cars.) The inspection currently costs between €44 and 52, depending on which federal state you live in (Saxony is the most expensive), and re-inspection after a failure costs €10 to 30. The car's mechanical condition is checked for compliance with relevant safety standards, which cover brakes, lights, chassis, shock absorbers and tyres. The vehicle is also tested for general roadworthiness. You don't need an appointment and can just drive your car to an inspection centre and ask for the inspection to be carried out on the spot.

If your vehicle doesn't pass the inspection, you're told what repairs or alterations are necessary before it can be re-tested. When your vehicle is approved, a small circular sticker (*TÜVplakette*) is affixed to the rear number plate by the test centre and a certificate issued; these state the expiry date (the number in the inner circle indicates the year when the next inspection is due and that in the outer circle the month). If you're apprehended driving a vehicle with an expired inspection sticker, you can expect to be fined and given a short period in which to have the car tested; if it isn't tested within this period, you won't be permitted to drive it until it passes the inspection. You must also pay a premium of up to €40 for an overdue inspection. After any major alterations or accident repairs, a vehicle must be checked to determine whether the modifications or repairs influence its handling or operating characteristics, in which case its certificate can be revoked.

An exhaust emissions test (*Abgassonderuntersuchung* or *AU*) is required on import (imported vehicles usually have both inspections at the same time) or after the first three years and thereafter every two years for modern vehicles. Older vehicles (generally those manufactured before 1980) must be tested annually. The test costs around €37, which includes any necessary minor repairs, and is carried out by the same centres as the technical inspection (see above) as well as at authorised garages (displaying an *ASU* or *AU* sign). As with the technical inspection, you don't need to make an appointment and there's a penalty of up to €40 for an overdue test plus points taken off your licence (see **Penalty Points** on page 225).

Certificates for both the technical inspection and emissions test are required when registering a motor vehicle (see below) and must be carried with the vehicle or driver at all times.

REGISTRATION

You must register your vehicle if one or more of the following apply:

● the vehicle was purchased in Germany;

● you've imported a vehicle and plan to stay longer than 12 months;

● you've imported a vehicle whose foreign registration has expired.

Only residents and resident companies can register a vehicle, either directly or via an authorised representative with power of attorney.

General Operating Licence

Vehicles can usually be registered only if a general operating licence (*allgemeine Betriebserlaubnis*) for the model has been issued by the Federal Motor Vehicle Authority (Kraftfahrtbundesamt/KBA), which certifies that the model conforms to German technical, safety and pollution-control standards. The general inspection is usually instigated by the manufacturer or importer when a new model is launched, and the KBA issues a specification (*Kraftfahrzeugbrief* or *Kfz-Brief*) for each model, listing its principal technical features, a copy of which is automatically issued to car buyers by the manufacturer or a dealer. If you don't have one, a copy can be obtained from the local motor vehicle licensing office (*Kfz-Zulassungsstelle*). **You're strongly advised not to make any substantial modifications to a licensed vehicle without obtaining expert advice, or you could invalidate the general operating licence.** If you feel compelled to turn your hatchback into a roadster, you can engage a KBA-certified expert (*Kfz-Sachverständiger*) to issue the necessary title after performing a technical inspection, but be warned: such 'private' general vehicle inspections don't come cheap.

Even when an imported model has been granted a general operating licence, modifications are likely to be necessary to meet German safety and environmental standards.

Privately imported vehicles (particularly those manufactured in America and Japan, few of which are sold in Germany) don't usually have the required operating licence. If a licence hasn't been issued, it's your responsibility to supply the necessary technical data. To avoid the time-consuming and expensive procedure of establishing the technical specifications of a car via a general inspection, you should contact the manufacturer of your vehicle before shipping for information about the VIN (vehicle identification number), year of manufacture, vehicle type, and other technical data, including:

- engine capacity;

- power (in horsepower or kilowatts);

- maximum speed;

- emissions data;

- admissible wheel and tyre sizes;

- admissible gross front/rear axle weight.

You must also provide the date of the vehicle's first registration, which determines the standards that apply to it.

If the vehicle doesn't have valid number plates, you need to request temporary 'red plates' (*rote Kennzeichen*) from the local motor vehicle licensing office in order to drive it to the inspection station.

Procedure

To register a vehicle in Germany, you must apply at the local motor vehicle licensing office (*Kfz-Zulassungsstelle*) in the town were you live, with the following documents:

- proof of identity and residence, e.g. passport and registration card;

- a customs clearance certificate stating payment of, or exemption from, the relevant duty and tax (see **Duty & VAT** on page 211);

- proof of ownership, e.g. a bill of sale or commercial invoice;

- proof of liability insurance cover (*Privathaftpflichtversicherung* – see **Third-party & Legal Insurance** on page 281), which takes the form of a copy of your policy (*Versicherungsdoppelkarte*), obtainable from your insurer;

- an export permit (from your previous country of residence) if applicable;

- vehicle documents, including the specification (*Kfz-Brief* – see above);

- technical inspection and emissions test certificates (see above).

You must pay a fee of between €10 and €45 in cash (the authorities don't accept payment by credit or debit cards), and are given a receipt and your vehicle registration certificate (*Kfz-Schein*) as well as three stickers to be affixed to the number (licence) plates, which must be purchased (you're told where you can obtain them). Plates cost between €20 and €30, depending on their size (non-standard plates are available for certain makes of car). The stickers show the validity of the vehicle registration and that the vehicle has passed the technical inspection (on the rear plate, alongside the one issued by the technical inspection centre – see **Technical Inspection & Emissions Test** on page 212) and the emissions test (on the front plate). Nothing should be stuck on your windscreen. Be prepared to attach your plates before driving away!

When you buy a new car, a dealer can assist you with the registration process – all you need to do is provide the necessary documents.

Number Plates

The first one to three letters of a German number plate indicate the district (*Kreis*) where the vehicle is registered. Large cities generally have a single registration letter (e.g. F for Frankfurt and S for Stuttgart), while smaller districts have two or three letters. You can therefore tell whether a vehicle is 'foreign' to your district or region. Number plates must be changed if you move to a new district for longer than three months. Standard plates show the letter 'D' for *Deutschland* and the EU logo, so no country code sticker is required.

ROAD TAX

Vehicles registered in Germany are subject to an annual tax (*Kfz-Steuer*), which is payable soon after registration. An 'application' for the tax is filed automatically with your registration and you receive a bill (*Kfz-Steuerbescheid*), which should be paid to your local tax office (*Finanzamt*). The amount payable is determined by the size of your vehicle's engine as well as its environmental-friendliness (or unfriendliness).

Rates are high compared with similar taxes in other countries: the tax for cars is between around €7 and €27 for every 100cc (cm3) or part thereof, according to whether they're diesel or petrol-powered and, if the latter, equipped with a catalytic converter (the lowest tax for a diesel car is around €15 per 100cc). If you have a car with a petrol-engine (known in Germany as an *Otto* – the engine, not the car – after that internationally famous engineer, Nikolaus Otto, who presumably had something to do with its design and therefore has a lot to answer for) that meets European Standard 3, you pay the minimum rate, i.e. around €200 for a three-litre engine. A petrol-driven car with a similar size engine but only meeting Standard 1 would cost you €15.13 per 100cc or €453.90 per year, while a 'gas-guzzling' diesel could cost you a whopping €27 per 100cc – almost €1,000 per year for a three-litre car. A different calculation is used for lorries, depending on the size of the loading surface. Motorbike owners pay around €7.50 per 100cc irrespective of engine type. The transportation minister, Wolfgang Tiefensee, has announced that Germany will reform the levy system by the end of 2007, making it more closely linked to carbon dioxide emission levels.

BUYING A CAR

After you discover what's required to import a vehicle into Germany, you're likely to decide against bringing a car with you, unless you're pathologically attached to your existing car, and will therefore need to or buy one (or hire one – see page 219) in Germany.

New Cars

Germany is the world's third-largest producer of cars and possibly the largest producer of high-quality cars. German-made cars aren't cheap, however, nor necessarily cheaper to buy in Germany than elsewhere, although prices are generally lower than in the UK.

Haggling over the price of a new car is possible, although significant discounts aren't easy to negotiate; you may have more chance of success by saying that the price is acceptable only if some options are included. Note, however, that you should expect to pay not only the list price but also several fees, including 'dealer preparation' and VAT (*Mehrwertsteuer* or *MWSt*). Dealer preparation fees, which cover the cost of the final factory inspection of a car, are generally between €200 and €400.

In contrast with most other items sold in Germany, VAT isn't always included in the list price of new cars, so you should make sure you know the total price, including taxes and fees. There are, however, certain circumstances that allow exemption from VAT: diplomats and military personnel enjoy tax-free status irrespective of how long they remain in Germany; and non-EU nationals don't have to pay VAT on a vehicle if they leave the country within 12 months of the purchase date.

Registration fees (see page 213) and insurance premiums (see page 225) must also be paid before you can put a new vehicle on the road.

When considering a new car purchase in Germany, it's important to take into account your intended length of stay. If you expect to be in Germany for longer than six months or more, you're likely to be better off purchasing a car with German specifications in local currency. Those in Germany for a short period and expecting to qualify for a tax reduction or exemption may wish to consider a purchase scheme such as those offered by the dealerships of the Swedish car companies Saab and Volvo, which can save you up to 30 per cent on a new car. They also offer tax-free purchase programmes for EU nationals planning to leave Germany within the year for a non-EU country, as well as favourable terms for shipping a car abroad. Details are available on the respective websites (🖥 www.saab.com and 🖥 http://expat.volvocars.com).

Among the German manufacturers, Audi and BMW offer discounts for diplomats and other short-term residents, while BMW, Mercedes-Benz and Porsche offer a 'tourist delivery programme' for US residents through their dealers in the US. You pay for the car in the States, pick it up on arrival in Germany and, when you leave again, drop it off at a handling agent, who ships it to the US for no extra charge.

Used Cars

Buying a used or second-hand car (*Gebrauchtwagen*) in Germany usually represents good value, as vehicle inspection standards are relatively stringent, meaning that cars are generally maintained in good condition. Nevertheless, the precautions necessary when buying a used car are the same as in any country and, whether you're buying privately or from a dealer, you should check:

- that the car has valid technical inspection and emissions test certificates (see page 212) and preferably isn't due to be re-tested for a year or more;

- that it hasn't been involved in a major accident and suffered structural damage. You can ask for a written declaration that the vehicle is 'accident-free' (*unfallfrei*).

- that the vehicle identification number on the chassis is the same as the identification number on the vehicle registration certificate (*Kfz-Schein*);

- that the service coupons have been completed and stamped, and that servicing was carried out by an authorised dealer;

- that the price roughly corresponds to the *Schwacke Liste* value or some other reputable guide to used car prices (second-hand car prices are fairly standard throughout Germany, but you may be able to negotiate a better deal in the former eastern bloc states, as their economies are still not as strong as those in the west);

- that import tax and duty have been paid (if applicable);

- whether a written guarantee is provided.

You should obtain a written purchase agreement, even if the vehicle is purchased privately. The agreement should state the odometer (km) reading at the time of sale and confirm that it's accurate.

Whatever 'guarantees' or assurances you receive, you should have the condition of all major systems checked by a mechanic or someone with a good knowledge of cars. If you don't know someone who can help you check a car before buying it, the German motoring club ADAC (see **Motoring Organisations** on page 247) provides an inspection service (*Standart gebrauchtwagen-untersuchung*) for prospective buyers, costing around €55.

When buying a car from a garage, you have some protection if the dealer is a member of the German Motor Trade Association (Deutsche Kraftfahrzeug gewerbe). In addition to the items noted above, members should provide a detailed list of things that are checked before a used car is sold. A reputable garage should also provide a warranty or guarantee, typically three months or 4,000km (2,500mi). If you purchase a used car through a dealer, he can handle the paperwork and register the car in your name. If you buy privately, you must complete the registration procedure (see page 213).

A type of used car peculiar to the German market is the *Jahreswagen*, which is a vehicle bought at a discount by an employee of a large firm and sold after a year or so (*Jahreswagen* means literally 'year car'), usually at a low price and often in excellent condition. Some dealers publicise the fact that they sell *Jahreswagen* (*Jahreswagenvermittlung*).

SELLING A CAR

The main points to note when selling a car in Germany are the following:

- Either you or the new owner must change the registration of the vehicle. If you sell the car to someone you know and trust, it may be easier to let him register as the new owner of the car. However, if you have any doubts at all about the honesty of the buyer, you should cancel the registration before selling a car.

● Inform your insurance company once the registration has been changed. Your insurance for a vehicle is automatically cancelled when your registration is cancelled.

● Insist on payment in cash; this is standard practice in Germany.

● Include in the receipt the price paid, the car's odometer (km) reading and the fact that you're selling the car in its present condition (as seen) without a guarantee (*ohne Garantie*). The new owner may ask for a declaration in writing that the car is accident-free (*unfallfrei*). This refers to major accidents causing structural damage and not bumps resulting only in dents and scratches.

You can advertise a car for sale in local newspapers, on free local notice boards, in major newspapers (the Saturday editions are best) and in motoring newspapers and magazines. Many free newspapers consist almost entirely of lists of used cars (and possibly other items) for sale. There are also a growing number of internet-based advertising sites, such as 💻 www.autoscout24.de, 💻 www.auto-ankauf.com and 💻 www.autoanzeigen.de. If you belong to any clubs or organisations that publish a newsletter, they usually have a classified advertising section (even if you aren't a member, many will accept your advertisement for a small fee).

The best place to advertise a car depends on its make and value. Cheap cars are probably best sold in local newspapers, while expensive and collectors' cars are better advertised in the national motoring press. Buyers will usually travel a long way to view a car that appears good value (if nobody phones, you'll know why!).

CAR HIRE

The major international car hire (rental) companies, such as Avis (💻 www.avis.de), Budget (💻 www.e-sixt.de), Europcar (💻 www.europcar.de) and Hertz (💻 www.hertz.de), are all represented in most German cities, although Budget goes by the name of Sixt in Germany (and is popular for its 'budget' rates). Cars can also be hired from local garages and offices in most towns – look under *Autovermietung* in the yellow pages. Business hours vary with the location of the office, those at airports having the longest opening hours. There are no special number plates for hire cars in Germany, as in some other countries.

Although far from cheap, car hire isn't as expensive as in some other European countries. The daily rate with unlimited mileage for a VW Golf is between around €55 and €70. The same car can be hired for a week with unlimited mileage for around €210. Although some car hire companies offer lower daily rates, they generally charge for each kilometre driven, possibly with the first 100km (62mi) 'free', so the value will depend on the distance you intend to cover.

Hire costs not only vary between companies but also depend on where you hire a car. Hiring from an airport is generally more expensive (around 17 per cent); if you can get to a city by public transport, you'll almost certainly get a better deal, though it may not be worth the inconvenience for a short hire. Older cars can be hired from garages at lower rates than those charged by the national companies.

Most car hire companies in Germany require drivers to be over 21 and some even have a minimum age of 25. You must, of course, have a valid driving licence. It isn't necessary to hold a German driving licence unless you've been living in Germany for more than six months, in which case your home licence will no longer be valid in Germany (though it may be in your home country – see **Driving Licence** on page 221). By law, non-residents are required to possess an International Driving Permit (IDP), although few companies ask to see it.

It's usually necessary to pay for car hire with a credit card, which is preferable in any case, as it may cover your uninsured excess (deductible) in the event of an accident, in which case you don't need to pay for the (usually exorbitant) collision damage waiver (CDW) option. However, this may apply only to US-issued credit cards and you should check in advance. If you don't have a credit card and the company still allows you to hire from them, you should expect to pay a deposit of at least €150.

German hire cars usually have manual transmission (stick shift); if you want (or need) an automatic, you must state this when booking and be prepared to pay extra. You may also have to pay extra for an additional driver.

Most major companies allow you to collect a car in one city and drop it off in another for no additional fee, although if you want to do this you must check that it's permitted and whether there's a surcharge. If you plan to travel outside Germany, this must also be allowed and noted in the contract – and check that the vehicle is properly documented for international travel, even within the EU. Most companies permit travel to other western European countries but not anywhere east of Germany (except Austria).

Vehicles should be equipped with the necessary emergency equipment (i.e. warning triangle and first-aid kit) and you may want to check that you have a parking disk (see **Parking** on page 240). In winter, hire cars may be fitted with studded tyres and you can usually request snow chains and ski racks if you're heading for the mountains. Car phones and baby and child seats are available from many companies for a fee, e.g. €10 per day for a child seat, which is required in Germany (see **Rules of the Road** on page 232).

Remember to check what type of fuel a vehicle uses and the octane rating. Before venturing onto the road, you should ensure that you know where all the important controls are – they're likely to be different from those in your own car, especially if you're used to driving on the left. (It pays to be able to differentiate between the windscreen wiper control and the indicator switch before you get onto an *Autobahn*.) You should also check a car thoroughly for any damage, including any marks on the bodywork, and have them noted on the hire contract form.

As an alternative to a standard car, you can hire a four-wheel-drive vehicle, estate car (station wagon), minibus, luxury car or convertible. Vans and pick-ups are also available from major hire companies and some local companies by the hour, half-day or day.

If you want to hire a car but don't want to drive it yourself, the major companies offer various options. Sixt provides a chauffeur service for those who would rather concentrate on business (or sightseeing) than the road, and they offer a welcome service so that visitors can be picked up in style.

DRIVING LICENCE

Ensuring that you're licensed to drive in Germany can be very simple or infuriatingly complicated depending mainly on whether your licence originates from a country inside or outside the EU. Those in the former category should have few problems (see **EU Licences** below). On the other hand, for those coming to Germany from certain non-EU countries and planning to live there for longer than six months, obtaining a German driving licence (*Führerschein*) may be one of the most frustrating experiences of your stay.

EU Licences

Residents of the EU enjoy reciprocal recognition of driving licences for an unlimited period and you don't need to obtain a German licence even if you become a permanent resident in Germany – unless you have a driving licence of a category other than class B (e.g. allowing you to drive professionally or in an HGV) and want to exercise the same privilege in Germany, in which case you must obtain the appropriate German licence. However, you'd be unwise not to obtain a German licence in any case, as you can have a foreign licence revoked for anything other than a minor infringement of the road rules (see **Penalty Points** on page 225). You can obtain a German licence from a driving licence office (*Führerscheinstelle*) without needing to take a written or road test, a privilege known as *Prüfungsfreiheit*, although it will cost a small fee.

Non-EU Licences

If you have a valid non-EU driving licence, you can legally drive in Germany for up to six months. Once the six months have elapsed, you must have a German licence. Those with licences issued in the following countries or states (irrespective of their nationality) can obtain a German licence without having to take either a written or a road test, a privilege known as *Prüfungsfreiheit*: Andorra, the Channel Islands, Croatia, Isle of Man, Israel, Japan, Monaco, New Caledonia, French Polynesia, San Marino, Singapore, South Africa, South

Korea, Switzerland, Taiwan and some states of the US (see **American Licences** below). If you renew a licence issued in one of the above countries after becoming officially resident in Germany and cannot prove that you had a licence before the renewal, your transfer application will be denied.

Those with licences issued in another country must take a German road and written test (see **Driving Test** on page 224) in order to obtain a German licence.

In order to obtain a German licence, irrespective of whether your licence exempts you from German driving tests, you must have your licence transcribed within your first six months in Germany (see **Transcription** below). Therefore, **if you have a non-EU licence and plan to stay longer than six months, you should start the process of obtaining a transcription and applying for a German licence as soon as possible after your arrival**, as it can take some time. If the country or state where your licence was issued enjoys *Prüfungsfreiheit* (see above) but you fail to have your licence transcribed within your first six months in Germany, you must take German theory and practical tests.

American Licences

Some American states enjoy *Prüfungsfreiheit* (known to Americans as 'full reciprocity'), while others have partial reciprocity.

The following states currently have full reciprocity: Alabama, Arizona, Arkansas, Colorado, Delaware, Illinois, Iowa, Kansas, Kentucky, Louisiana, Massachusetts, Michigan, New Mexico, Ohio, Oklahoma, Pennsylvania, South Dakota, South Carolina, Utah, Virginia, Washington, West Virginia, Wisconsin and Wyoming, and also the commonwealth of Puerto Rico.

Holders of licences from the following states (which have partial reciprocity) are exempt from the practical test but must take the written examination: Connecticut, Florida, Idaho, Minnesota, Mississippi, Missouri, Nebraska, North Carolina, Oregon, Tennessee and Washington DC. This list has been growing, so check with a US consulate for the latest situation.

Holders of licences issued in all other states must take both the theory and practical test to obtain a German licence. The local driving licence office (*Führerscheinstelle*) will inform you of your situation when you apply, but it's wise to get an update from the consulate before you apply, as information on reciprocity agreements can take time to percolate down to local offices.

Transcription

To have your foreign licence transcribed you must take the following documents to the driving licence department (*Führerscheinstelle*) of your local district administration office (*Landratsamt*):

- a valid passport or identity card with a residence permit;

- confirmation from the *Ausländerbehörde* of how long you've been a German resident (*Bestätigung über Aufenthaltsdauer*), which costs €15;

- a passport-size photograph;

- a translation of your driving licence by a translator approved by the German courts or by a recognised German motoring club;

- the results of an eye test (*Sehtest*) not more than two years old stating that your eyesight is acceptable. You can have the eye test done at most opticians or optometrists for around €12 (you must take your passport with you).

- the original and one copy of your foreign driving licence.

If your foreign licence **wasn't** issued in a country enjoying *Prüfungsfreiheit*, you must take the following **in addition to** the items listed above:

- a certificate stating that you've participated in a training course on first-aid procedures at the scene of an accident. These courses are offered by many organisations and last for almost a full day. Many centres offer package deals, where for around €30 you receive a first-aid course and, during coffee breaks, can have your eye test performed and picture taken. Don't worry if your German isn't good; it only seems to matter that you sit in the room, bring the dummy back to 'life' when it's your turn and pay your fee in cash. Check in the yellow pages or with any driving school for a list of local course providers. If you want to take the course in English, contact the American Red Cross, which offers courses in conjunction with the US military (e.g. at its bases in Ramstein, Landstuhl and Kaiserslautern).

- the name of the driving school through which you plan to take your driving test (only a licensed driving instructor can register you to take the tests).

In a large city, the office is likely to be crowded and you'll need to take a number from a dispenser and wait for it to be called. The official will examine your paperwork and tell you if anything isn't in order. If your driving licence has been renewed since you arrived in Germany and the date your licence was first issued isn't printed, you'll need proof that your driving history pre-dates your arrival in Germany – either an expired licence or a letter from the licensing authority. If you cannot prove that you've held your existing licence for more than two years, you'll be given only a probationary licence. This will greatly increase your insurance premiums, so it's worthwhile obtaining proof of your driving history.

Once the paperwork has been deemed acceptable, there are some additional forms to complete and a fee of around €35 to be paid. You're notified when your paperwork has been processed and the licence can be collected (see **German**

Licence below) or, if required, the driving test taken (see below). This should take six weeks but can take 12 or more.

Driving Test

If you're required to take a German driving test, you can start studying for the written test and taking whatever driving lessons you require while waiting for the necessary paperwork to be processed. You aren't obliged to attend the classroom sessions that new drivers must attend but, depending on the degree of 'reciprocity' of your licence (see **Non-EU Licences** on page 221), you may have to take the written test as well as the road test, in which case a driving school can order a set of all the possible questions (in English) for you to study.

The written test consists of 30 questions taken randomly from the possible questions. Most are multiple choice but there are a few 'fill-in-the-blank' questions requiring you to know certain figures. The test is by no means easy. Each time you answer a question incorrectly you lose points, and to pass you may not lose more than eight points in total. The fee for the written test in English, which includes a test of German driving-related vocabulary, is €40. Don't forget to take your passport with you to prove your identity. If you fail the test at your first attempt, the fee for a re-test is much higher!

Only after you pass the written test are you permitted to take the road test. (You can register to take both tests on the same day but, if you fail the written test, you aren't permitted to take the road test and your registration fee of around €100 will be forfeited. Once again, remember to take your passport with you for identification.) The road test is administered by an examiner from the Technischer Überwachungsverein (TÜV), who sits in the rear right-hand seat and gives instructions. Your driving instructor sits in the front passenger seat, and, if necessary, can translate for you. The test takes place on public roads and lasts from 30 to 45 minutes. After you've finished, the examiner will tell you whether you've passed and, if not, why not.

Once you've passed, you're given a card stamped by the examiner as proof and must return to the *Führerscheinstelle* to obtain your German licence (see below). An instructor or other representative from your driving school may accompany you if you require help.

German Licence

Take your passport to the *Führerscheinstelle* to prove your identity and your foreign driving licence along with your test certificate (if applicable). You must pay a fee of €10 if you want a temporary licence valid immediately; otherwise you must wait around a week for your permanent licence to arrive.

The German licence-issuing authority considers that once you have a German licence, your original licence is no longer valid. Therefore they may ask you for your original licence and, if you have one, your IDP. They may then return your original licence to the issuing authority with a note stating that you now have a driving licence in Germany, or they may just stamp it to indicate that you also have a German licence and return it to you.

If all this bureaucracy sounds too much for you, Germany has an excellent public transport system (see **Chapter 10**)!

Penalty Points

As in many other countries, if you infringe the rules of the road, you're liable for penalty 'points' on your licence. Once you've amassed a certain number of these, you must attend a course designed to correct your bad habits and, if you continue to incur penalties, your licence can be withdrawn. **You should be particularly careful if you're driving with a foreign licence (see Driving Licence on page 221), as penalty points don't apply and you can have your licence withdrawn for even a fairly minor infringement**; there's no option to obtain a local licence and have the penalty points deducted from that, as in France, for example. See also **Drink & Drugs** on page 244.

CAR INSURANCE

Car insurance in Germany is strictly regulated by law and supervised by the state authorities. The following categories of car insurance are available:

- **Third party** (*Haftpflichtversicherung*) – the most basic insurance, which covers you for the cost of third-party damage or injury in accidents for which you're responsible. This cover is compulsory for all motor vehicles.

- **Part comprehensive** (*Teilkasko*) – known in the UK as third-party, fire and theft cover and similar to comprehensive cover in North America. It includes cover against fire, natural hazards (e.g. rocks falling on your car), theft, a broken windscreen and damage caused by a collision with animals. You can usually choose to pay an excess (*Selbstbeteiligung*), e.g. the first €200 to €1,000 of a claim, in order to reduce your premium.

- **Fully comprehensive** (*Vollkasko*) – as in the UK and equivalent to the combination of comprehensive and collision cover in North America. It covers everything included under *Teilkasko* and also damage to your own car for which you're responsible (e.g. by driving into a lamp post). Again you can pay an excess to lower your premium. Fully comprehensive cover is compulsory when you lease a car or purchase one on credit. Experts recommend this cover for new cars up to three years old, after which you need to consider whether it makes financial sense due to the high premiums and the lower value of the vehicle (unless it's a Bugatti).

To ensure that any passengers injured in your car are well provided for in the event of an accident, extra passenger insurance (*Insassenversicherung*) is recommended and costs only a little extra.

Although EU regulations allow you to insure your car with any EU insurer (and therefore possibly save money), a vehicle licensed in Germany must be insured with an insurer 'registered' in Germany.

If you take out third-party insurance with a German insurance company and wish to increase your cover to fully comprehensive later, you aren't required to do this through your third-party insurance company but may shop around for the best deal.

Motorists insured in any EU country are automatically covered by third-party insurance in all EU countries, as well as in the Andorra, Croatia, Iceland, Liechtenstein, Norway and Switzerland.

Green Card

Under recent EU regulations, possession of an international insurance certificate (commonly referred to as a 'green card', although in many countries it isn't green) is no longer compulsory within the EU. However, it's still wise to obtain one from your insurance company, as it can help prevent problems and delays in the event of an accident in another country, and if you're travelling outside the EU it may be obligatory. In most countries you need only inform your insurance company that you want a green card to prove your cover and they will provide one free of charge (some insurance companies provide them automatically). If you have fully comprehensive insurance, you should obtain a green card, as without one you'll be insured only for third-party damage. If you're insured in the UK, however, your insurance company may provide a free green card for a limited period only, e.g. 30 or 90 days. (This is to discourage the British from driving on the continent, where they're a danger to other road users – most of them don't know which side of the road to drive on!) Note that a green card must be signed to be valid.

Schutzbrief

Even if you're covered by your insurance policy when driving in other EU countries, the additional protection of a *Schutzbrief* (literally 'protection letter') can be well worth the extra cost. A *Schutzbrief* is offered by most insurance companies and motoring organisations (see page 247) and the benefits vary between companies. It usually covers breakdown assistance, repairs, the removal of a damaged vehicle, emergency car hire, the train fare home, the transport of you or your passengers to hospital if necessary, and repatriation by air of the sick and injured as well as the return of your car to Germany after an accident or mechanical fault outside the country rendering it unfit to drive. Costs vary quite widely but, you can get good coverage for around €33. Check before buying, however, as the price of most new cars includes protection similar to that afforded by a *Schutzbrief* for the first three years.

Premiums & No-claims Bonus

The cost of car insurance in Germany is high, although premiums vary with a number of factors – not least the insurance company. A male driver who has a child at home will pay less (apparently fathers are calmer drivers than childless men), especially if he's a civil servant, but, if he drives a car which thieves have a propensity to steal (e.g. a VW Golf), it will cost him more. Premiums are also higher for cars with expensive replacement parts but lower in areas with a low theft rate. A novice driver will normally pay 25 per cent more than the standard rate, while someone with the best possible record – usually 18 or 21 years without a claim – will pay just 30 per cent of the standard rate. (You must normally have a year of accident-free driving before you qualify for the standard rate.) German drivers must complete a two-year probationary period after passing their test, and during this period they must pay the highest rates. The rate for third-party cover can be as high as 240 per cent of the standard rate. If you're in this category, it pays to shop around, as there are huge differences in premiums between providers. The average standard rate across the 20 most popular new cars is currently around €300 per year for third-party insurance, €500 for part comprehensive and €650 for fully comprehensive.

When buying car insurance (or any other kind of insurance), it's wise to shop around a number of insurance companies and compare rates and cover. The same car, driver and circumstances can attract quotes which differ by over 30 per cent. Note that an insurer may offer excellent rates for certain classes of vehicle and/or drivers but may be uncompetitive for others. Some may offer discounts for such considerations as off-road parking, but others may have a lower rate even without a discount.

If you had a no-claims bonus with a previous insurer, this is usually taken into account by a German insurer, although German insurance companies aren't obliged to do so. To substantiate a no-claims record, you must obtain a letter from your previous insurer stating how many years you've driven without making a claim. In Germany, no-claims discounts apply only to third-party and fully comprehensive cover. You're placed in a 'no-claims class' (*Schadenfreiheitsklasse* or *SF*) according to your number of years without a claim. For each claim-free year you're automatically moved into a higher *SF* class, which usually leads to a premium reduction. If you're involved in an accident for which you're deemed wholly or partly responsible, you may lose some or all of your no-claims bonus and can expect your premiums to rise significantly the following year.

High discounts take longer to accrue in Germany than in some other countries, and you may need 21 years' claim-free driving to achieve the maximum discount of 65 or 70 per cent (compared with as little as five years in the UK, for example).

If you discover that you can obtain better rates in your particular classification from another insurance company, you're permitted to switch, but only at the end of your insurance year. If you're switching third-party cover, you must give written notice a month in advance, while terminating part or fully comprehensive cover requires three months' notice. Notice can be sent by fax but a fax should be followed by a registered letter (*Einschreiben*) requiring a signature to confirm receipt by your insurance company. Your new insurance must begin no later than one day after the last day of your old insurance. Be sure to arrange this well in advance of the date you need the policy to commence, in order to allow time for billing and payment processing. Bills are usually sent out 30 days in advance to ensure that payment is received by the due date.

BREAKDOWN INSURANCE

Breakdown insurance (*Schutzbriefversicherung*) in Germany and other European countries is provided by car insurance companies and German motoring organisations (see page 247), as well as by some car manufacturers. If you are or have been a member of a motoring organisation in another country, check with them before you move whether they have a reciprocal agreement with a German motoring club. If you've purchased a new car in Germany, you may already have breakdown cover, at least during the initial warranty period, which is provided through the manufacturer. Some credit card companies (e.g. American Express and Diners Club) offer this type of insurance for their members. If you have a company car, breakdown cover is usually provided by your employer. Some organisations also provide economical annual motoring policies for those who frequently travel abroad.

ROAD SIGNS

Germany generally adheres to the international road sign system. With a few exceptions, most signs conform to the following shapes and colours:

Design	Meaning
Red triangle	Warning
Red circle	Restriction
Blue circle	Requirement
Square/rectangle	Guidance

Diamond	Priority
Octagon	Stop

German road signs generally use words sparingly, but those you're most likely to come across are listed below:

German	English
Abblendlicht	Dipped headlights
Abstand halten	Keep your distance
Achtung	Warning
Alle Richtungen	All directions
Anfang	Start, beginning
An geraden Tagen	On even days (see **Parking** on page 240)
An ungeraden Tagen	On odd days (see **Parking** on page 240)
An Sonn und Feiertagen	On Sundays and holidays
Anlieger frei	Except residents
Anschluss	Junction
Ausfahrt	Exit
Bauarbeiten/Baustelle	Roadworks
Belegt/Besetzt	Full
Durchfahrt verboten	No through traffic
Einbahnstrasse	One-way street
Einfahrt	Entrance
Fahrbahnwechsel	Change lanes
Gefahr/Gefährlich	Danger/Dangerous
Glatteisgefahr	Risk of ice
Grenze	Border

Grenze Kontrolle	Border inspection
Haltestelle	Bus/Tram stop
Keine Einfahrt	No entry
Landschaftsschutzgebiet	Natural preserve
Licht einschalten	Switch on lights
Lieferverkehr frei	Delivery vehicles only
Links einbiegen	Turn left
Radweg kreuzt	Cycle path crossing
Raststätte	Service area
Rechts einbiegen	Turn right
Rechts fahren	Keep right
Sackgasse	Dead end, cul-de-sac
Seitenstreifen nicht befahrbar	Do not use hard shoulder
Sperrgebiet	Restricted area
Überholen verboten	No passing
Umleitung	Detour
Unfall	Accident
Verengte Fahrbahn	Lane narrows
Vorfahrt/Vorrang	Priority/Right of way
Vorfahrt beachten	Give way (Yield)
Vorsicht	Be careful
Zentrum	Town centre
Zufahrt frei	Access permitted

SPEED LIMITS

Maximum speed limits are posted on signs with red circular borders, while a blue circular sign with a number in it is a minimum speed limit. The latter most commonly show 60kph (37mph), the minimum speed on motorways. There are also blue square signs, which show 'recommended' maximum speeds (see below). Note that speed limits aren't always posted and it's up to motorists to know the prevailing speed limit in the absence of signs.

In cities and towns, the maximum speed limit for all vehicles is 50kph (31mph) unless otherwise posted. Many residential and school areas are designated as '30 Zone', where the maximum speed limit is 30kph (18mph); the 30kph limit remains in force until you pass a 30kph sign with a diagonal line through it, indicating a return to the usual 50kph limit. Even more restrictive are the traffic calming zones found on some residential streets, which are indicated by blue signs showing an adult playing ball with a child in front of a house. Traffic here is limited to walking speed, i.e. 7kph (4mph).

Outside cities and built-up areas (except on motorways), the speed limit for vehicles under 3.5 tonnes without trailers on a normal two-lane road is 100kph (62mph). For vehicles between 3.5 and 7.5 tonnes and those that are towing, the maximum permissible speed is 80kph (50mph); above 7.5 tonnes the limit is 60kph (37mph).

Despite their reputation as unregulated race tracks, German motorways are often subject to speed restrictions. Limits of between 90 and 120kph (56 to 75mph) are typical on stretches with constant heavy traffic, near urban areas, or with tight bends. Construction zones (*Baustelle*), which seem to be everywhere, can have limits as low as 60kph (37mph). There are also sections with night and wet-weather speed restrictions. Lorries (trucks) and vehicles towing trailers are limited to between 60 and 110kph (37 to 68mph) on all motorways; a truck or car with a trailer weighing less than 7.5 tonnes may travel at up to 80kph (50mph).

Where there are no signs stating otherwise, drivers are advised (although not obliged) not to exceed 130kph (82mph). The absence of a general motorway speed limit isn't without controversy. The Green Party, with its strong environmental platform, has pushed for a national speed limit as low as 100kph (62mph), claiming that the air pollution created by high-speed driving has caused widespread destruction of trees and forests. As a compromise, some limits have been set in heavily forested areas, but a general limit remains unlikely. It appears that the government fears the reaction of the millions of citizens who own luxury cars and have a predilection for high-speed driving. No matter how highly petrol is taxed, the cost doesn't seem to persuade many drivers to slow down.

In fog on any type of road, the maximum speed is reduced to 50kph (31mph).

Speed Checks & Fines

Speeds are checked by various methods. Some small towns use cameras controlled by a measuring system built into the road surface. More common are radar-linked cameras, which are found along various stretches of the motorway system (usually the busiest sections) and indicated by a large yellow or grey box showing an orange circle and a flash sign. They can take a picture at any time of the day or night showing you and your car, together with a record of your speed, the date, the time and the location. There are various rules about the distances between cameras and the location on the road where the picture is taken and, if you can prove that the camera that took your picture fell outside these guidelines, the evidence will be invalidated (good luck!). As in most of Europe, the use of radar detectors by motorists is illegal.

Police also set up temporary speed checks using radar or laser beams, which have a range of several kilometres, depending on the road. Green and white police cars are typically used for this type of control, and traffic often slows down 'mysteriously' when such a vehicle is spotted. Harder to spot are the unmarked cars used to check speeds in some cities.

Speeding fines range from €15 to €425 depending on the speed at which you were travelling, how far it was above the legal limit and whether you have any previous convictions. If you're stopped by the police (as opposed to having your picture taken by a camera), you may be asked to pay a fine of up to €35 on the spot; this applies particularly if you're a foreign visitor. If you don't have the money with you, you may be allowed to pay within a week, but you'll probably be required to pay at least a deposit immediately. If you cannot pay even this, your vehicle will be impounded (at an additional cost, of course). If you're caught significantly exceeding the speed limit, not only may the fine be the maximum of €425, but you could also lose your driving licence for a period – usually a month.

RULES OF THE ROAD

The following rules apply to driving in Germany generally:

● The Germans drive on the right-hand side of the road; it saves confusion if you do likewise!

● All motorists must carry a red breakdown triangle (*Warndreieck*), which must be stored inside the car within reach of the driver's seat and not in the boot (trunk), which could be damaged and jammed shut in an accident. If you have an accident or breakdown, the triangle must be placed behind the car at the edge of the road, at least 50m (160ft) away on secondary roads, 100m (325ft) on major roads and 200m (650ft) on motorways.

    Emergency telephones are located at 1.5 to 3km (1 to 2mi) intervals along motorways; black arrows on white posts along the hard shoulder indicate the direction of the nearest phone box. An operator will answer as soon as you pick up the receiver, so you should be ready to give the number of the motorway, the direction in which you're travelling and the identifying number of the telephone box you're using.

● You must also carry a spare bulb kit (*Ersatzglühbirnen*) and a first-aid kit (*Erstehilfekasten* or *Verbandkasten*). It's wise to buy the latter in Germany, as there are specific requirements for the kit's contents, e.g. they must include waterproof gloves to provide protection from HIV infection. Kits are available from the ADAC (see **Motoring Organisations** on page 247) and petrol stations.

- If you need to wear glasses or contact lenses when motoring, it will be noted on your German driving licence and you must always wear them and carry a spare pair.

- When you're motoring outside the country in which your car is registered, it must display either the new EU-style number plates, which incorporate a letter or letters showing the country of registration surrounded by the EU yellow stars, or a separate nationality sticker affixed to the rear. For vehicles registered in Germany the identification letter is D (for *Deutschland*). You can be fined on the spot for not displaying this, although judging by the number of cars which fail to do so, this law is seldom enforced. Cars must show only the correct nationality sticker and not an assortment.

- The wearing of seatbelts is mandatory and includes passengers in rear seats when seat belts are fitted. In the event of an accident, a German insurance company isn't obliged to pay the whole cost of damages when it appears that those injured weren't using their seat belts (benefits may be reduced by up to 50 per cent). The driver and each passenger who isn't wearing a seatbelt can be fined €30. Children up to the age of 12 or shorter than 1.5m (4ft 10in) are permitted to ride in a vehicle only in an approved safety seat that's appropriate for their size. They may not ride in the front seat if they can be accommodated in a back seat. The driver of a vehicle who is carrying children who aren't properly secured can be fined €40.

- All drivers must give way to police cars, ambulances and fire engines when these have their lights flashing or sirens wailing, and trams and buses when they're leaving stops. You may not pass a school bus when its red lights are flashing.

- On secondary roads without priority signs (a yellow diamond on a white background, used throughout most of continental Europe), you must give way to vehicles coming from your right. **Failure to observe this rule is the cause of many accidents.** The priority to the right rule usually also applies in car parks.

- Vehicles on a roundabout (traffic circle) have priority over those approaching it, who will be faced with a 'Give Way' ('*Vorfahrt beachten*') sign. Traffic flows anti-clockwise around roundabouts and not clockwise as in the UK and other countries where motorists drive on the left. Roundabouts aren't as popular in Germany as in some other countries, although they have become more common in recent years.

- Driving in bus, taxi or cycle lanes is prohibited unless it's essential to avoid a stationary vehicle or obstruction, and car drivers using these lanes must give priority to authorised users. For obvious reasons, you should stay clear of tramlines and outside the restricted area around them, marked by a white line.

- Dipped (low beam) headlights must be used in tunnels, fog, snowstorms, heavy rain and when visibility is less than 200m (640ft). It's illegal to drive only on side (parking) lights at any time. Front fog or spotlights must be fitted in pairs at a regulation height and should be used only when visibility is less than 50m (160ft). Only a single rear fog lamp is permitted (on the offside), to prevent following vehicles mistaking fog lamps for brake lights. **If your car has two rear fog lights, you must remove the bulb from the nearside (kerbside) lamp.** A vehicle's hazard warning lights (both indicators simultaneously) may be used to warn other drivers of an obstruction, e.g. an accident or traffic jam.

- Headlight flashing has different meanings in different countries. In Germany, it's likely to mean 'Get out of my $*@!# way!', which, of course, you aren't obliged to do.

- Within a city or town you must ensure that your vehicle can be seen when parked at night. This means leaving its side lights on if street lighting is inadequate or doesn't remain on all night – a red-and-white band around the post indicates a street lamp that doesn't stay on all night. (Many cars allow you to turn on parking lights on one side only, by using your direction indicator – in which case the offside lights should be switched on.)

- Traffic lights (*Verkehrsampel* or *Ampel*) are usually located on the same side of the road junction as the approaching traffic. They're often mounted above the road as well as to the left and right. The sequence of lights is: red, red and amber (yellow), green, amber, and back to red, as in the UK. Amber means stop at the stop line; you may proceed only if the amber light appears after you've crossed the line or when stopping may cause an accident. Red and amber together mean prepare to go, but you may not actually move off until the green light appears (although most drivers ignore this rule).

  Road junctions often have traffic lights that show arrows rather than full circles; these indicate the permitted direction(s) of travel. If the lights at a junction show arrows and you don't see one for the direction you want to go, travelling in that direction may not be permitted; look for other signs. Always give way to pedestrians and cyclists when turning left or right. There's often a flashing yellow signal with a pedestrian symbol to warn you that pedestrians have priority.

  At some junctions there are illuminated left-pointing arrows. A flashing yellow arrow indicates that you may turn left but should proceed with caution. A green arrow indicates that you have the right of way to turn left.

  Right turns on red aren't generally permitted in Germany. Such a turn is allowed only at junctions with a separate filter light to the right of the red stop light with a green arrow pointing right. If this is illuminated, you're allowed to make a right turn, but only after coming to a complete stop and giving way to other traffic and pedestrians.

Amber flashing lights are usually a warning to proceed with caution, for example, at roadworks and non-functioning traffic lights. They're also used to indicate speed restrictions, particularly on motorways. Many crossroads and road junctions have traffic lights that operate only during peak periods. At night and weekends in particular, lights may be switched off or the amber light may be set to flash constantly as a general warning to drivers to look out for other road users. When lights aren't functioning, control is provided by the traffic signs mounted to the right of the traffic lights. A flashing amber light will usually be accompanied by a give way or stop sign. There's no flashing red signal in Germany.

Rather confusingly, many locations (usually railway or tram crossings) have signals consisting of just red and amber lights – indicating that you should always take care! When neither red nor amber is lit, ignore the signal and obey any other signs or signals displayed; in the absence of these, proceed with caution.

- When two vehicles meet on a narrow mountain road, the ascending vehicle has priority and the other must give way or reverse as necessary. On roads where passing is difficult or isn't permitted, slow traffic is required to pull over when possible to allow faster traffic to pass.

- On-the-spot fines (*Strafgeld*) of up to €35 can be imposed for traffic offences such as minor speeding (see **Speed Checks & Fines** on page 231), not being in possession of your driving licence or vehicle documents (see **Vehicle Documents** on page 237), failing to remove the ignition key when leaving a vehicle unattended, not using dipped headlights at night, and parking infringements.

- If someone on the road annoys you, you'd be wise not to show it with finger or other hand signals. If it's proven that you showed a fellow driver a particular finger, or even tapped your forehead or passed a hand in front of your eyes, you can be fined over €1,000. If you call a police officer or other uniformed traffic official an idiot in German (or any other language that they can understand – Swahili is usually pretty safe), the fine is €1,500; in fact, if you so much as call him *du* (instead of *Sie*), you can be fined €500! (The German police have an official list of offensive phrases and corresponding fines – presumably derived from long experience of being insulted – though despite intensive research a copy was unable to be found for inclusion in this publication.)

- Using your mobile phone when driving isn't permitted in Germany (or Austria or Switzerland) and results in a fine of €40. If it's proved that you caused an accident while on the phone, your insurance may provide only partial cover and the courts will reduce damages due to drivers who have suffered as a consequence.

- If you witness an accident, you must stop and give assistance.

- Motorists must signal before overtaking and when moving back into an inside lane after overtaking, e.g. on a motorway.

- Take care when crossing railway lines, particularly at crossings with no barriers! Approach a level crossing slowly and STOP at the St. Andrew's Cross (*Andreas Kreuz*) as soon as the barrier or half-barrier starts to fall, as soon as the red warning lights are illuminated or flashing or the warning bell is ringing, or when a train approaches! Your new Audi or Mercedes may be built like a tank, but it won't look so smart after a collision with a 70-tonne locomotive.

- Be wary of cyclists and moped riders. It isn't always easy to see them, particularly when they're hidden by the blind spots of a car or are riding at night without lights (illegal, but it happens). When overtaking cyclists or motorbikes, give them a **WIDE** berth. By law there must be at least 150cm (59in) of space to the right of your vehicle when you overtake a cyclist or vehicle. If you knock a rider off his bike, you may have a difficult time convincing the police that it wasn't your fault.

- Drive at no faster than walking speed (*Schritt Tempo*) when passing a stationary tram or bus, particularly a school bus. Where passengers must cross a road to reach a footpath (sidewalk), e.g. from a tram stop in the middle of the road, you must stop and give way to them.

- In a city or town you may not use your horn except when attempting to avoid a collision.

The following regulations apply on German motorways:

- Vehicles with a maximum speed of less than 60kph (37mph) are prohibited from using motorways, as are bicycles, mopeds, and pedestrians.

- Overtaking on the right is prohibited, but you should move to the right to allow faster traffic to pass on the left.

- Stopping, parking, making a U-turn and reversing are prohibited, including on hard shoulders and entrance and exit roads.

- In traffic jams on motorways without a hard shoulder, motorists must leave a gap between the left-hand lane and the middle or (on a two-lane motorway) right-hand lane wide enough for emergency vehicles to pass between the lines of cars.

- It's illegal to run out of petrol on a motorway (you can be fined for doing so) or to use full beam (high beams).

- You must stop for a pedestrian waiting at a crossing if he shows any intention to cross the road. Pedestrian crossings that aren't at traffic lights are indicated by thick black stripes on the road known as zebra stripes (*Zebrastreifen*). It's prohibited to overtake on or near zebra stripes or to park your car on them.

For further information on traffic rules and regulations, you can purchase a driver's education manual at a driving school or obtain a copy of the *Strassenverkehrsordnung*, which is distributed by the Federal Transport Ministry and available from book shops.

VEHICLE DOCUMENTS

Under German law, you're required to carry yourvehicle registration certificate (*Kraftfahrzeugschein* or *Kfzschein* – see **Registration** on page 213) and driving licence at all times when driving a vehicle. It's wise to take copies of these documents (in case the car and/or your documents are stolen) and to keep the originals on your person or locked in the glove box. If you're stopped by the police without the required papers, you can be fined. When driving outside Germany, it's wise to have a green card from your insurance company with you (see page 226). It's also prudent to keep a blank accident report form (*Unfallbericht*) in your car; these can be obtained from your insurance company.

WINTER DRIVING

Most of Germany doesn't experience such severe winters as many of its neighbouring countries. Except in a few high altitude regions, such as the Bavarian Alps and the Black Forest, driving conditions aren't usually hazardous for prolonged periods during winter. However, most motorists who rely on their cars for regular transport fit studded tyres (*Winterreifen* or *Schneereifen*) at the start of the winter. In some rural areas, roads aren't cleared of snow by the authorities, making 'snow tyres' a necessity (when it snows). Snow tyres may be used on vehicles of up to 3.5 tonnes from 1st November until 31st March; vehicles are then restricted to 80kph (50mph). **If you have an accident on snow in a vehicle that isn't fitted with such tyres, you may be considered at fault if the other vehicles involved have snow tyres, irrespective of other circumstances.**

In towns and cities, many roads are salted or gritted during the winter. Due to the risk of corrosion, many motorists change to steel wheels with snow tyres already fitted in winter rather than change the tyres on their (expensive) alloy wheels. Shop around for the best buys in winter tyres and steel wheels, as prices vary considerably.

If there are signs showing a tyre covered by chains, it's compulsory to fit chains (*Schneeketten*) when there's snow. These signs are generally found only at the highest altitudes, but even if you don't see them it's wise to fit chains when there's thick snow. Buy good quality chains and practise putting them on and removing them before you get stuck in the snow; even getting the container undone can be a trial when you have numb fingers, let alone fitting the chains. Note that vehicles with chains may not exceed 50kph (31mph).

In mountainous areas, the edges of many rural roads are marked by two-metre high poles in case of snow.

Skis carried on roof racks should have their curved front ends facing towards the rear of a car.

GERMAN DRIVERS

Ever since Carl Benz invented the first practical motorcar in 1885, Germans have been in love with their cars and care for them like a member of the family (often better). Only Americans are more devoted to their cars, and it's said that depriving a German of his car is like amputating one of his limbs. On the other hand, the Germans, being more ecologically minded than many other Europeans, are prepared to forgo their cars for more environmentally friendly means of transport when practicable. The number of Germans who own bicycles and use them surprises most visitors, and it's common to see bikes on the top or back of cars on their way to a weekend or holiday destination.

Germans take it for granted that anyone driving in Germany will stick to the rules of the road, and the rigorous process of earning a driving licence contributes greatly to the general competence of motorists. Predictability is as important in this sphere as it is in every other in this country. Thus Germans drive precisely, if not always with any particular degree of courtesy or understanding beyond that specifically called for by the rules of the road.

Although Germans are proud of their driving skills, however, they come only fifth in the current ADAC league table of safe driving countries in the EU, top of the league being the British by a considerable margin (mainly because British traffic is at a standstill much of the time). Despite the high speeds permitted on German motorways, there are relatively few serious accidents on them. Most serious crashes occur on ordinary roads outside built-up areas, and speeding or impatience are frequently a prime cause. Sixty-four per cent of fatalities take place on such roads annually, although the number of minor traffic incidents is much greater within urban areas. Significantly, recent figures from the Federal Office of Statistics show that the city-states of Hamburg and Bremen have annual road-death rates of 24 and 35 per million inhabitants respectively, whereas the rate for the almost entirely rural state of Mecklenburg-Vorpommern and similar states is over 200.

Patience isn't common among German drivers and, although sounding your horn is prohibited within city limits (except in an emergency), this regulation is overlooked by many. Impatient and aggressive drivers are identifiable by their fondness for tailgating and reminding you with their horn that a red light may turn green at any second.

When driving on the motorway, you may feel that you've strayed onto a racetrack. Even if the traffic in the 'slow' lane is moving at the recommended maximum speed of 130kph (82mph), some drivers will constantly change lanes, often cutting in with no more than a few metres to spare, in order to gain a few 'places'. The one thing that preserves some kind of order in this potential chaos is the German respect for the 'car hierarchy'. In the outside lane, where tailgating is the norm, there's an unwritten code that a VW will yield to an Audi, which will yield to a Mercedes, which will yield to a BMW, while the kings and queens of the highway drive Porsches (Germans don't give way to foreign vehicles, whatever their make!).

MOTORCYCLES

To drive a motorcycle of up to 50cc (with a maximum speed of 45kph) on German roads, you require a class M licence and must be at least 16 years old. Obtaining a licence involves attending a driving school, as you must pass a written rules test and a practical test. If you already have a class A1, A, or B driving licence, however, you can ride any vehicle in class M without obtaining further permission. Most driving schools teach motorcycle as well as car driving, although specialist motorcycle driving schools exist. Once you're authorised to take your bike on the road, you can obtain a number plate from an insurance company at the same time as paying your road tax and obtaining the mandatory third-party insurance.

There are two classes of driving licence for motorcycles over 50cc: A1 and A. To apply for the A1 classification, you must be at least 16 and your motorcycle must have an engine capacity of no more than 125cc or an engine power not exceeding 11kW. If you're under 18, your bike must be capable of a speed no greater than 80kph (50mph). If you wish to drive a larger motorcycle, you must be at least 18 and have a class A licence. If you're aged 18 to 25, obtaining this is a two-stage process: first you must take instruction and pass written and road tests entitling you to ride motorcycles with an engine power not exceeding 25kW and a power-to-weight ratio of not more than 0.16kW/kg for two years after obtaining your licence; after two years' experience without any major accidents, you're permitted to ride any motorcycle. If you're over 25, you needn't undergo the two-year probationary period but may ride any bike after undertaking the required practical training and passing the corresponding test.

The registration procedure for a motorcycle is the same as for a car (see page 213). Your motorcycle must also pass a technical inspection and emissions test every two years (see page 212) and you must pay annual vehicle tax (see page 215).

All motorcyclists must use dipped (low beam) headlights and wear a crash helmet at all times when riding and must have at least third-party insurance.

PARKING

Once you've successfully navigated the roads, kept out of the way of other drivers and reached your destination, you may find yourself with a new challenge: finding somewhere to park. In most heavily populated residential areas and business districts, there's an acute lack of parking space. In many larger cities, areas are reserved for resident parking (as in other countries) during morning and afternoon rush hours. In order to park in places reserved for residents during these times, you must go to the town hall and prove your residence before you can buy a permit (*Anwohner Parkausweis*). (Recent legal challenges to this system led to the courts declaring it illegal, which caused much annoyance, but the authorities simply introduced new regulations that effectively restored the status quo ante!)

Parking is prohibited:

- on or within 5m (16ft) of a pedestrian crossing;

- within 10m (32ft) of 'Stop' and 'Give Way' signs and traffic signals, if parking would obstruct other motorists' view of the sign or signal;

- within 5m of a junction;

- within 15m (50ft) of a bus or tram stop;

- within 50m (160ft) of a railway level crossing outside a built-up area;

- within 5m of a pedestrian crossing in a built-up area;

- on a main road outside built-up areas;

- in front of entrances or exits;

- adjacent to a traffic island or roundabout;

- on railway level crossings (for obvious reasons!), taxi ranks and motorways;

- anywhere there's a 'No Parking' sign (a blue circle with a red border and a single red diagonal line).

Legal street parking is indicated by a blue sign with a white P, although wherever you park there must be at least 3m (10ft) between the middle of the street and your car. This may require that you park partly or completely on the pavement. When this is permitted (for vehicles up to 2.8 tonnes only), it's indicated by a sign with a P showing a car parked on two levels. There must be sufficient room left for pedestrians on the pavement. Cars may park on both sides of a one-way street, provided there's room for vehicles to pass between them. Parking is normally permitted only in the direction of the traffic.

Vouchers, Discs & Meters

If the time permitted for parking on a street or in a car park is limited, parking will be controlled by one of the following methods:

- **Parking voucher** (*Parkschein*) – When you see the sign '*Nur mit Parkschein*', you must buy a voucher from a nearby machine (*Parkscheinautomat*) before leaving your vehicle. The most modern machines accept debit cards and money cards (see page 295); otherwise, a notice will tell you what coins or notes are accepted. Vouchers must be placed behind your windscreen where they can clearly be seen, and you must return to your car before the expiry time printed on the voucher.

- **Parking disc** (*Parkscheibe*) – In shopping areas in particular, you'll often see a blue sign with a picture of a white parking disc and the white letter 'P', which denotes that the use of a parking disc is required. Discs can be obtained free or for a nominal cost from petrol stations, motor accessory shops, news-stands and kiosks, and from the ADAC and other motoring organisations (see page 247). You must turn the dial to indicate the time of your arrival (you may round it up to the next half-hour) and put it behind your windscreen. The time by which you must leave is automatically shown on the disc.

- **Parking meter** (*Parkuhr*) – These aren't as common as the other two methods and operate in the same way as in other countries. Coins must be put into the meter for the amount of time you wish to park. If a meter is defective, you're permitted to park with a disc. The maximum parking period is shown on the meter.

If you're caught exceeding your allotted time, you're fined between €5 and €40. It's illegal to return once your time has expired to insert more coins into a meter or to adjust a parking disc, penalties for which are similar to those for over-staying your time.

Car Parks

Blue-and-white 'P' signs not only indicate street parking but are also used to give directions to off-street car parks (*Parkplatz*). An inverted (and flattened) 'V' over the P (like a roof) indicates a covered car park (*Parkhaus*). In many larger urban areas there are electronic signs indicating which car parks and garages have spaces available (*frei*) and which are full (*besetzt*). These signs may also show the number of spaces available.

Most covered car parks are completely automated: you take a time-stamped ticket at the entry barrier, which then rises to allow you to enter. You take your ticket with you when you leave your car, and when you're ready to leave you find a payment machine (*Parkenkasseautomat*), which is usually near the pedestrian entrance. Insert the ticket in the direction shown by the arrow and the amount payable is displayed. Once you've inserted your payment, the ticket is validated and returned to you. You then have around 15 minutes in which to return to your car and leave the garage. At the exit gate, you insert your ticket into the machine and the gate will open (you hope). Payment at the exit isn't possible and you'll be extremely unpopular with the motorists behind you in the exit queue if you forget to pre-pay!

There are exceptions to this general principle, as some garages still have people who collect payments. Even so, they aren't at the exit gate but rather in a booth at a pedestrian entrance, so you still need to pay them and have your ticket validated before returning to your car.

Remember to check the opening hours if you're planning a late night, as some car parks close at 11pm or midnight and you'll have to wait until the next morning to retrieve your car if you fail to return in time!

Using a car park for up to an hour usually costs at least €3, although additional hours are cheaper.

ACCIDENTS

Knowing the correct procedure in case of an accident is very important in Germany, particularly as motorists who see an accident are required by law to stop and render assistance. **If you drive by the scene of an accident and are reported to the police, you can be severely penalised.** The basic procedure is as follows:

1. Stop and secure the scene of the accident.

2. Attend to the injured.

3. Call for help.

If you're involved in an accident, stop immediately and pull over to the side of the road if possible. Place your red warning triangle at the edge of the road at least 50m (160ft) behind your car on secondary roads, 100m (325ft) on major roads and 200m (650ft) on motorways. If necessary, e.g. when the road is partly or totally blocked, switch on your car's hazard warning lights and dipped headlights (low beam) and direct traffic around the hazard.

If anyone is injured, call immediately for emergency help. For an ambulance or the police, dial ☎ 110. If someone is trapped, or oil or chemicals have been spilt, dial ☎ 112 for the fire brigade. If someone has been injured more than superficially, the police must be notified. Don't move an injured person unless necessary, and don't leave him alone except to call for help. Cover him with a blanket or coat to keep him warm.

If there are no injuries and damage to vehicles or property is relatively minor, it isn't essential to summon the police. If the other driver has obviously been drinking or appears incapable of driving, call the police immediately! It's usually wise to call them in any case and obtain an official report; even if the other parties involved admit that they were at fault, they could 'forget' what happened when questioned by an insurance company. They may also give you false information. However, don't sign any police statements unless you're certain you understand and agree with every word.

Always use your insurance company form (*Unfallbericht*) to report any accident involving your vehicle. Don't forget to sign it and to obtain a new form in case it happens again.

Under no circumstances should you admit guilt, even if you know you did something wrong. Restrict yourself to telling what happened, and let the police and insurance companies decide who was at fault. **If you admit responsibility, either orally or in writing, it can absolve your insurance company from responsibility from paying a claim under your policy.**

If either you or the other driver(s) involved decides to call the police, avoid moving any of the vehicles unless they present a hazard. In such a case, try to record the positions of the vehicles before you move them. If there's a camera available take pictures; otherwise make drawings or mark their positions on the road. The accident form from your insurance company will require drawings of all the vehicles involved, so it's wise to make a record somewhere other than in your memory.

Check whether there are any witnesses to the accident and try to obtain their names and addresses, making a particular note of those who support your version of events. Note the registration numbers of all vehicles involved and their drivers' names, addresses and insurers. In return you'll be expected to give your details to any other drivers involved.

If you damage a parked car or other property, leaving a note with your name and address isn't sufficient. You can wait a reasonable amount of time for the other party to return, but if they don't you must note the registration number of the car involved (if applicable) and the nature of the damage and report it to the nearest police station.

If you're the victim of a hit-and-run accident, you should report it to the local police immediately and, if possible, summon them to the accident scene before moving your car. They will inspect your vehicle and take photographs and paint samples, which will help them to catch the culprit as well as assisting you with your insurance claim.

DRINK & DRUGS

The laws regarding drinking and driving are taken just as seriously as the beer in Germany. If you want to go out and enjoy a few drinks, it's wise to have someone with you who will remain sober to drive you home or to use public transport. Riding a bicycle isn't an acceptable alternative; **if you're caught riding a bike on public roads while over the legal limit for driving, your driving licence can be taken away**.

The legal limit in Germany is 0.5mg per 100ml of blood and the penalties for driving while over the limit are severe. Breath tests can be performed by the police at any time (even if you're driving correctly) and those found in violation of the law can lose their licence as well as being heavily fined.

If you have an accident while under the influence of alcohol, it will be expensive. Your insurance company isn't obliged to pay for damage to your car or any other vehicle that you damage. You can also be held personally liable for all medical expenses and property damage resulting from an accident. There will also be a fine, starting at several thousand euros, and if you're unable to pay it you may find yourself facing a jail sentence of up to five years! **The courts may decide that alcohol was a factor in an accident even when a driver's blood alcohol content was below the legal limit; anything above 30mg is likely to put you at fault.**

Driving under the influence of 'recreational' drugs isn't taken lightly either. If you're found to have been driving with traces of marijuana, hashish or cocaine in your system, your licence will be withdrawn for at least a year. You'll also incur penalty points, be fined and need to undergo a psychological examination before you receive your licence back.

It goes without saying that it doesn't make any sense to do anything but stay sober in Germany if you want to drive, or have alternative transport if you want to indulge!

CAR CRIME

Car theft is a significant risk in Germany, with well over 100,000 cars stolen annually. In addition, there are hundreds of thousands of incidences of items being stolen from parked cars. Of the stolen cars, some two-thirds are recovered, but usually not before they've been burnt out or badly vandalised. The police recommend that you observe the following rules, irrespective of where you park your car:

- Never leave handbags, cameras, mobile phones, wallets, cash or other items of obvious value visible in your car.

- Lock your car when parking, especially in quiet areas.

- Never leave your car windows or sun-roof open.

- When stopping overnight at a hotel, empty your boot (trunk) of all luggage and try to park in a brightly lit or secure area.

- If you have an alarm or other security system, get into the habit of turning it on each time you park.

FUEL

Unleaded petrol (*Bleifrei*) and diesel (*Diesel*) are available at all garages in Germany. (Leaded has been phased out.) Although diesel fuel is much cheaper than petrol, vehicle taxes for diesel cars are higher (see page 215). Typical current fuel prices are:

- Diesel – €1.15 per litre;

- Regular unleaded (*Normalbenzin*), 91 octane – €1.35 per litre;

- Super unleaded (*Super Bleifrei*), 95 octane – €1.40 per litre;

- Super Plus unleaded (*Super Plus Bleifrei*), 98 octane – €1.45 per litre.

Depending on where you fill up, the price of petrol varies by up to ten cents per litre. As you'd expect, petrol stations on motorways are the most expensive. The best places to fill up tend to be petrol stations associated with supermarkets, and, of course, those in areas where there's lots of competition.

Petrol stations in Germany are usually self-service; if you find one of the few exceptions, you'll pay extra for the pleasure of sitting in your car watching someone else fill the tank in the rain and splash petrol on his hands and shoes. Opening hours vary, but they aren't controlled like those of shops. Some are open from 7 or 8am until 10 or 11pm, others 24 hours a day. Many petrol stations are less interested in selling you petrol than goods (at high mark-ups), on which they make the bulk of their profits.

Payment is usually made after petrol has been purchased and to a person rather than a machine. Petrol pumps that accept credit cards are rarer in Germany than in neighbouring European countries. As long as a petrol station is open, it's usually manned by at least one person. When you've filled your tank, you go to the cashier and tell him the number of your pump. Unless otherwise stated, garages accept payment in cash or by debit card. Most petrol stations accept credit cards, although you shouldn't rely on paying by credit card in rural areas. If a garage is in an area with a high risk of robbery (especially after dark), you may be required to pay in advance; if you pay in cash, no change may be given, as all money is deposited directly into a safe (which the attendant is unable to open) to prevent robberies.

You're permitted to carry up to five litres of petrol, but only in an approved can. However, different rules apply in other countries, so check with a German motoring club before taking a can of petrol over the border. **It's illegal to run out of fuel on a motorway, for which you'll be fined if caught.**

The main operator of motorway petrol stations is the Tank & Rast company, which has over 700 outlets across the country offering (as the name suggests) facilities for relaxation as well as fuel. A free booklet, which includes a map showing the location of all services, is available at motorway service areas and from Autobahn Tank & Rast GmbH & Co KG, Andreas-Hermes-Str. 7-9, D-53175 Bonn (🖳 www.tank.rast.de – an English-language version is available).

GARAGES & SERVICING

As in most other European countries, servicing and repairs are offered by car dealers, private garages and petrol stations with workshops. If you require only an oil change, a new exhaust or tyres or some other minor service, there are numerous places you can take your car with little or no advance notice. Pit Stop is one of the most popular chains and has outlets in cities and towns throughout Germany. Don't expect to find a garage open on a Sunday, but otherwise opening hours are usually generous. Many service stations open as early as 7am (or you can drop your car off the evening before) and closing time is usually around 6.30pm, although special arrangements can usually be made. Many garages also open on Saturday mornings.

Prices vary, as does the quality of service, and it will pay to obtain recommendations if it isn't an emergency. Ensure that you obtain an estimate for any work to be done before you approve it, or you may be in for a nasty surprise when the bill is presented. Main dealers are typically the most expensive, but their work is guaranteed, although other reputable garages also offer a guarantee and can be much cheaper. Be wary of using 'back street' garages unless they're highly recommended by someone you can trust, as the money you save may well be exceeded by the amount you need to spend on repairing their work later.

If you need a car while yours is being serviced or repaired, most garages will hire you one for a nominal fee or make arrangements with a local car hire company.

Recent EU regulations forbid dealers to insist that cars they've sold are serviced by them in order for the warranty to remain valid and in theory this applies in Germany. However, the government has vehemently opposed this ruling and it may be slow to be implemented, so you're advised to check with your dealer whether you may have your car serviced elsewhere without invalidating its warranty.

ROAD MAPS

Good road maps are readily available in Germany and reasonably priced. Falk publishes an excellent hardcover atlas and CD which covers all of Germany and sells for around €25. The most popular street atlases are those published by Shell. The average hardcover Shell edition sells for around €15, with soft-cover versions available from €7 to €13. The ADAC motoring club (see **Motoring Organisations** below) publishes low-price maps which are widely available in Germany and abroad.

Street maps and atlases can be purchased at book shops, newsagents' and kiosks everywhere, while there are shops specialising in maps in the major cities. Other sources of maps include your telephone book, where you'll find local street maps with indexes, and tourist information offices.

MOTORING ORGANISATIONS

There are two main motoring organisations or clubs in Germany – the Allgemeiner Deutscher Automobil Club (ADAC) and the Automobilclub von Deutschland (AvD) – plus a few smaller organisations, such as Auto Club Europa (ACE). Their head offices are as follows (check your phone book for local branches):

● Allgemeiner Deutscher Automobil Club (ADAC), Am Westpark 8, D-81373 Munich (☎ 089-76760, 🖥 www.adac.de);

● Automobilclub von Deutschland (AvD), Lyoner Str. 16, D-60528 Frankfurt (☎ 069-66060, 🖥 www.avd.de);

● Auto Club Europa (ACE), Schmidener Str. 227, D-70374 Stuttgart (☎ 0711-53030, 🖥 www.ace-online.de).

The ADAC, which celebrated its 100th anniversary in 2003, is by far the biggest and best known, and provides products and services extending well beyond the usual motoring requirements. It has a large network of shops selling road maps and motoring accessories, and also maintains driving practice areas for learners and foreigners who need to take practical driving tests. The ADAC also provides translations of foreign licences and legal advice regarding accidents and other motoring-related problems, with the initial consultation free to members. You can purchase motoring legal protection (*Rechtschutz*) for around €46 per year, which covers your legal costs in the event of an accident. Many services aren't included in the standard membership fee, although members are usually entitled to a discount. Basic services offered by ADAC, AvD and the other smaller clubs include:

- emergency roadside assistance;

- assistance if you've locked yourself out of your car;

- estimation of repair costs and verification of repairs/servicing and bills;

- travel bureau and ticket office services;

- hotel finding and booking;

- road maps, tour guides and tourist information;

- advice on buying cars and valuations of used cars;

- car insurance;

- travel insurance.

There are two types of ADAC membership: standard (costing around €45 per year) and *Plusmitgliedschaft* (€80), the latter including a *Schutzbrief* (see page 226). If you want other family members to be covered, they need their own membership, although discounts are provided. Standard membership covers roadside assistance in Germany up to a value of €200 and towing without any monetary limit. The higher category of membership provides you with more extensive cover and assistance outside Germany through reciprocal agreements with other national breakdown services.

Basic annual membership of the AvD costs around €60. Entitlements vary with the organisation and, if you want anything more than basic emergency breakdown cover, it pays to shop around and compare the benefits offered.

If you break down on a motorway, go to the nearest emergency phone (indicated by arrows along motorways and other main roads), pick up the receiver and tell the operator you require assistance and which motoring organisation you belong to. Be ready to give your membership number. If there isn't an emergency phone nearby, the number to call is ☎ 222-222 on a mobile for the ADAC. The number to call from a fixed line is ☎ 0180-2222 222. The equivalent for the AvD is ☎ 0800-9909 909. If you aren't a member of a motoring organisation, the nearest available breakdown service will be sent to you and you must pay for it.

PEDESTRIAN ROAD RULES

Pedestrians (*Fussgänger*) must wait for a green light before crossing the road at a crossing with a pedestrian traffic light, irrespective of whether there's any traffic. You can be fined €5 for failing to do so or for crossing the road dangerously, although it's more likely that you'll simply be run over. Pedestrian crossings that aren't at traffic lights are indicated by thick black stripes on the road known as zebra stripes (*Zebrastreifen*). Although motorists must (and in Germany usually do) stop when you're waiting at a crossing if you show any intention of crossing the road, you should never assume that a car will stop.

If an accident results from your crossing the street without proper regard to traffic controls, you're liable for any resulting damage or injury, although, not surprisingly, you can take out liability insurance (*Haftpflicht*) against this eventuality.

MOTORING ABROAD

If you're travelling across the border into other European countries, you should make yourself aware of the rules and regulations that apply. The following general hints and tips are designed to help you survive a trip abroad:

- Don't forget your car registration and insurance papers, passports, identity cards, visas and inoculation certificates for pets. Make sure you have sufficient local currency for petrol, tolls, food, fines, bribes, etc. If you're planning to use Swiss motorways, you must buy a pass costing around €25.

- Check that you have valid insurance. A green card (see page 226) is compulsory for Andorra, Bulgaria, Poland and Rumania and strongly recommended for Greece, Italy, Portugal, Spain and Turkey. A green card is available at no extra cost when you're insured with a German insurance company.

- Holiday or travel insurance (see page 282) and breakdown insurance (see page 228) is recommended when travelling abroad. If you're a member of a German motoring organisation (see page 247) you'll usually be covered when travelling elsewhere in Europe through reciprocal agreements with national breakdown services. When motoring in some countries, it's wise to have legal protection insurance.

- Check that your car complies with local laws and that you have the necessary equipment, e.g. warning triangles, first-aid kit, fire extinguisher, petrol can (plastic cans are forbidden in some countries) and headlight beam deflectors (for the UK and Ireland). Check the latest regulations with a German motoring organisation.

- Make sure that you have sufficient spares such as bulbs, fan belt, fuses, and clutch and accelerator cables, particularly if you're driving a rare or 'exotic' model (e.g. most American and British cars).

- Note that the procedure following an accident isn't the same in all European countries, although most western European countries use the standard European accident report form (*Unfallbericht*) provided by German insurance companies. As a general rule, it's wise to call the police for anything other than a minor accident. **In eastern European countries you should always call the police.**

- Seat belts must be worn in all European countries. In Finland, Norway and Sweden, dipped headlights (low beam) must be used at all times.

- If you're planning a long journey, a mechanical check-up for your car is recommended, particularly if it's some time since its last service.

- The maximum legal blood/alcohol level is lower in some countries than in Germany, and the wine and beer may be stronger. The permitted level usually varies from 0.2 to 1mg of alcohol per 100ml of blood, although in some countries it's zero!

- An international driving permit (IDP) or a translation of your German or foreign driving licence is necessary in some countries (check with a German motoring organisation).

The most dangerous European countries to drive in include Portugal, Spain and Italy, but that doesn't mean you're safe in any other country. Driving in some European cities can be chaotic. If in doubt about your ability to cope with the stress or the risks involved, you'd be wiser to fly or take a train and use public transport on arrival.

12.

HEALTH

The German healthcare system is widely acknowledged as being among the best in the world, although it may not be as good as it once was. It provides near-universal cover and ensures that almost everyone, irrespective of income or social status, has the same access to healthcare. Statistics underline its excellence. The infant mortality rate in Germany is 4.2 deaths in the first year for every 1,000 live births, one of the lowest in the world. Around 30 mothers die in childbirth each year in contrast to over 1,000 as recently as 1960. Average life expectancy at birth is now 76.2 for a man and 81.7 for a woman, figures exceeded by few other nations.

The system is, however, an enormous financial drain on the government and private industry (which foots part of the bill) as well as individuals, and cost-cutting reforms have been implemented in recent years and more are in the pipeline or being urgently discussed in parliament. Such reforms (and proposed reforms) inevitably meet stiff resistance from a population unaccustomed to paying anything for their health and medical needs other than through their health insurance (see page 272). As in most developed countries, however, a declining birth rate has unbalanced the system so that a decreasing number of workers must pay for the extended life spans of an increasing number of retirees. Health insurance (*Krankenkasse*) contributions have now reached 14.5 per cent of gross income, with costs split between employees and employers, though the former must pay up to 0.9 per cent more than half. Nevertheless, for the time being at least, Germany has a surplus of hospitals and medical personnel, and waiting lists for treatment are rare.

When you register with the health authorities, you're sent a plastic identity card, which you must sign. There's a microchip in the card, where your medical data are stored. Children are covered for free until 18 under their parents' health plan. Medications and even some over-the-counter items are also free as long as they're prescribed by a paediatrician.

One area in which Germans are surprisingly less than health-conscious is smoking, over 27 per cent of the population as a whole and a massive 37 per cent of those aged 20 to 50 regularly breathing through burning tobacco – despite punitive taxes on cigarettes, etc.. Non-smoking areas are provided in only a few restaurants, many people ignore '*Rauchen verboten*' signs, and polls show that the great majority of Germans are opposed to legislation banning smoking in public places. Nevertheless, the government has now finally decided to implement a partial smoking ban in all 16 federal states by the end of 2007, assuming the bill is passed in both houses of parliament. The ban would cover all public buildings, including nightclubs, restaurants and pubs. Exceptions would be made for some small bars and premises with separate smoking rooms.

Paradoxically, despite their general salubrity, most Germans regularly worry about their health. They fear most medical problems known (and many unknown) to modern man and visit the doctor frequently – comforted by the knowledge that their health insurance will pay for everything. (Each German citizen visits the doctor almost once a month on average.) An employee need only inform his employer that he has a doctor's appointment to be allowed time off work, although current job market uncertainties are making employees less inclined to take advantage of the system. Employees are generally entitled to unlimited paid sick leave (after six weeks the payment is reduced) provided their doctor provides them with a sick note (*Krankmeldung*) stating that they're unable to work (see **Sick Leave** on page 56).

Perhaps the biggest health mystery in Germany is a 'disease' unknown to the rest of the world called *Kreislaufstörung*. This roughly translates as 'circulatory disorder' and covers everything from mild headaches and tiredness to heart problems. In some cases it can also mean 'I don't feel like going to work today but don't want to use any of my annual leave'. Since the disease is so vague and all-encompassing, some Germans claim a form of it regularly, and it's often difficult to determine how serious the underlying problem is – if indeed there is one.

EMERGENCIES

In a life-threatening emergency, you should call for an ambulance (dial ☎ 112 from anywhere in Germany), which will take you to the nearest hospital accident and emergency (A&E) department. Germany has a public ambulance service, which is efficient, and you're normally attended to without delay at A&E. If necessary, ambulance crew will begin treatment en route and, if you're able to, you should give them details of your health insurance (see page 272). When visiting a hospital or clinic, take proof of your health insurance, although you're unlikely to be refused treatment if it's urgently required.

If you need a doctor outside regular surgery hours, you should first try to contact your family doctor (keep the number by your phone). If the surgery is closed, there should be a recorded message telling you how to reach your doctor or a locum or service standing in for the practice. This, of course, will be in German, so it's wise to ask in advance how a practice handles emergencies. If you don't have a family doctor or yours cannot be reached, you can call the Emergency Doctors Service (*Ärztlicher Notdienst* or *Ärztlicher Bereitschafts dienst*), a free 24-hour public service. The number for your area will be at the front of your yellow pages. The GPs in a district usually take it in turns to act as emergency doctor (*Notarzt*) at night. They will offer advice and, if necessary, visit you or send an ambulance.

If you have a dental emergency or your pet is in dire need of medical attention, the numbers to call are listed in your yellow pages under *Zahn ärztlichen Notdienst* (dental emergencies) and *Tierärztlicher Notdienst* (veterinary emergencies).

ACCIDENTS

If you have an accident resulting in an injury, to yourself or to a third party, inform the following as required:

- a doctor if treatment is necessary;

- the police;

- your accident insurance company;

- your employer if it will affect your work (if you have an accident at work, report it to your manager or boss as soon as possible).

An accident report form must be completed for all accidents where medical treatment is necessary and which result in a claim on your insurance (e.g. car, health or third-party liability). Your health insurance policy will normally pay out for medical treatment only if you remain in Germany, and journeys abroad while undergoing a course of treatment as the result of an accident may require the consent of your insurance company.

HOSPITALS & CLINICS

Hospitals are denoted by the international sign of a white 'H' on a blue background. To find a list of hospitals in your area, look in your phone book under the heading *Krankenhäuser* (the singular is *Krankenhaus*). Hospital care is excellent in Germany, but you may notice a number of differences in admission and other procedures from those you're used to in your home country. Your family doctor requests a bed for you, but your care is taken over by a doctor at the hospital and you shouldn't expect to see your GP during your hospital stay. Either your medical records are transferred to the hospital or, if you're undergoing a regular procedure, you're given your records to take with you.

The kind of room you're allocated depends on whether you're covered by state or private insurance (see pages 272 and 278). A privately insured person is usually assigned to a single room, while those with state insurance usually share with up to three others; you can request a single room, but you're required to pay the extra cost yourself.

As a consequence of the growing concern over the cost of state-organised healthcare in Germany, patients are expected to pay a small proportion of hospital bills. Patients over 18 must pay a fee of €10 per day for a maximum of 28 days per year (i.e. to a maximum of €280), after which there's no further charge. They're also required to pay €5 to €10 of the cost of transport (by ambulance or taxi, for example) for necessary medical treatment. People on low incomes are exempt from these charges.

Some insurance companies are also ending the widespread practice of admitting patients the day before surgery, by refusing to pay the bill for the extra night unless it's shown to be necessary. Nevertheless, Germans stay in hospital longer than people in many other countries.

Because German doctors aren't usually inclined to discuss treatment with their patients, it may pay you to read up on your condition and possible treatment alternatives before entering hospital. If you don't speak fluent German and cannot find any useful books in English, you may wish to check the internet, where there's a wide range of English-language sites, including those of the American Academy of Family Physicians (💻 www.familydoctor.org) and Patient Information Publications (💻 www.patient.co.uk). German doctors will, of course, answer your questions or address any concerns you may have, but you must know what to ask. If language is a problem, you may also wish to take a German-English dictionary with you. Most doctors can speak at least some English, but nurses and other hospital personnel may not, although there will usually be someone around to interpret if there's a major problem.

Germans tend to be less concerned about privacy than most English-speakers. Gowns aren't issued during examinations, and there are usually no curtains surrounding beds. Therefore, if you don't wish to suffer 'exposure', be sure to bring a nightdress or pyjamas, dressing gown and slippers; you should also take towels and toiletries. Don't, however, bring too many things, as you'll have only a small locker in which to store them.

Visiting hours vary with the hospital, the level of care you require, and whether you're in a private room. In a hospital ward, visiting hours are usually from 2 to 8pm. Small children aren't welcome as visitors. If a child must go into hospital, a parent can usually spend the night. A telephone on which you can make outgoing calls is normally provided next to the bed, but to activate it you must buy a card from a machine in a public area on your floor. This can cost anything from €10 to €25 and there's a fee for just turning the phone on, after which charges for calls are deducted from the card. If you have unused time, the card machine will refund your money when you leave.

Meals and meal times in hospitals conform to the usual German practice, breakfast consisting of rolls or bread with jam, meat or cheese. (Expect to be woken up at crack of dawn.) Large hot meals are served at lunchtime and supper is a simple meal based on bread or rolls. There's usually a choice of menus and you may also keep your own food and drinks by your bed, unless you're on a prescribed diet.

DOCTORS

You should exercise the same care when selecting a doctor (*Arzt*) as you would in your home country. There are many excellent German doctors, although not all of them will be right for you. In general, German doctors aren't particularly open to discussion and questions about your treatment, so if this is important you may need to do some searching before you find someone who meets your needs – although it shouldn't be too difficult, given the current surplus of doctors. If possible, it's preferable to obtain recommendations from colleagues or friends. If you don't know anyone you can ask, start by checking at your consulate or in guides published by local English-speaking organisations. Doctors are listed by their specialities in the yellow pages under *Ärzte*. Many if not most doctors in

Germany have at least a basic level of English, but this isn't the case with nurses and nursing assistants. If appropriate, check before making an appointment. Doctors (and their specialisations) are listed on the internet (🖥 www.netklinik.de).

The healthcare system allows you to visit any doctor you choose, which means you may consult any doctor or specialist who will accept you as a patient. If you're unhappy with the diagnosis or treatment given by a doctor, you're free to consult another to obtain a second opinion. However, it can be difficult or impossible to obtain an appointment with certain specialists without a referral from a general practitioner (*Praktischer Arzt*).

Note that some doctors don't accept payment via the state system. Signs outside the surgery indicate this; if you're relying on the state system, look for '*Kassenarzt*' or '*Alle Kassen*', which indicates that patients from all the public health insurance providers or *Krankenkassen*, are accepted. Absence of such a sign indicates either that the doctor is a specialist or that he hasn't been able to obtain the official blessing of the *Krankenkassen* because the maximum number of doctors they'll recognise in that district has been reached. It doesn't necessarily indicate a higher quality of service.

Once you've found a doctor you like, it's preferable to consult only him (whenever possible) in order to establish a relationship with him and for the convenience of having your medical records in one place. Most people have a regular or 'house' doctor (*Hausarzt*).

Doctors' surgeries are usually open during normal office hours, with perhaps a late afternoon or early evening surgery one day a week. City doctors usually have longer surgery hours than those in small towns and villages, where hours may be more irregular. When you call a doctor's surgery for an appointment, you're usually given an appointment time (*Termin*) or occasionally told to come any time during surgery hours (*Sprechstunden*). The latter operate on a first-come-first-served basis but there's usually no difficulty in obtaining an early appointment.

When you register with a doctor, you must give your medical card to the receptionist, who will enter your details into a computer. If you're in the state health insurance programme, you're charged €10 per quarter for visits to the doctor, irrespective of the number of them or the reason for them. If you request a test that the doctor doesn't deem necessary, you may have to pay extra, depending on what your health insurance policy covers. Similarly, if you consult a specialist without a referral from your *Hausarzt*, you must usually pay the full cost.

If you're treated by anyone other than a *Kassenarzt*, you'll receive a bill that you must pay yourself, and the state health insurance scheme won't reimburse you. If you have private insurance, you must still pay and then submit the bill to your insurance company for reimbursement.

COMPLEMENTARY TREATMENT

Complementary medicine has a long tradition in Germany, although it isn't accepted as a viable alternative to regular medical care by more than a few.

Nevertheless, you may find the surgeries of both a doctor and an alternative practitioner (*Heilpraktiker*) in the same building, and it isn't unknown for someone who has first consulted the former to be referred to the latter (or vice versa). A small but growing number of GPs offer complementary therapies in addition to conventional medicine. Check in your local yellow pages, where these services are listed under the doctor's name.

The most widely available alternative therapy in Germany is homeopathy, which should come as no surprise given that it was founded by a German doctor, Samuel Hahnemann (1755-1843). Homeopathy operates on the controversial principle that a substance that's toxic in large quantities can act as a remedy in smaller measures – rather like a vaccination. Approval for homeopathic treatment in Germany dates back to a law passed in 1939, allowing a homeopath to practise in conjunction with an authorised medical doctor, provided he has passed a qualifying examination. Obtaining a diploma (after a two-year training course) is still necessary to establish a homeopathic practice in Germany.

Standard health insurance – whether state or private – normally doesn't cover the cost of treatment by a homeopath or other alternative practitioners. If, however, such a practitioner recommends or starts a treatment that's subsequently taken over by a GP, your insurance may cover the cost. (Some *Kassen* are more inclined to do this than others, so it's best to find out before choosing one – see page 272.) If you wish to turn to alternative medicine, there can therefore be a considerable financial advantage in registering with a doctor who offers such therapies, rather than going to an alternative practitioner who isn't medically qualified. Some doctors, however, might offer alternative therapies despite limited knowledge of them. If this is important to you, check before making an appointment.

Spas

The spa process is more of a ritual in Germany than in any other country in the world. The German word for spa (*Kur*) literally means cure. 'Take a cure' was originally made popular by noble families of central Europe, and the German bourgeoisie of the 19th century were behind the construction of the majority of spa resorts still found in Germany today. They were built around the dozens of mineral springs that had been discovered, the waters of which were thought to provide cures for arthritis, gout, hypertension and gynaecological problems. Today, there are over 300 health resorts with spas (*Kurort* – meaning literally 'cure place') in Germany, where the word Bad before the name of any town is an indication that it has a 'curative' spa (although 'bad', they're supposed to be good for you!). There are four types of spa in Germany:

● **Health resort with a mineral spring (*Kurbad*)** – These are springs with at least 1g of dissolved mineral substances per litre of water, where the water coming from the ground is at a temperature of at least 20C (68F). Various treatments are offered at these establishments, or you can simply bathe in the water.

- **Climatic health resorts (*Luftkurort*)** – These are health resorts situated in densely wooded areas that claim to have fresh air free of industrial waste gases. Landscaped trails are provided so that you can concentrate on enjoying the scenery, rather than the challenge of reaching your destination.

- **Kneipp spas (*Kneippkurort*)** – These spas are operated in accordance with a formula developed by Sebastian Kneipp in Bad Wörishofen. The treatment is based on strengthening the body's immune system and encouraging a natural and harmonious 'macrobiotic rhythm'. Cold water is used for stimulation and warm water for relaxation. There are five basic components to the system:

  - hydrotherapy for exercising the vascular and circulatory systems and for strengthening the immune system;

  - natural whole foods to ensure regular metabolism;

  - medicinal herbs to activate self-healing powers;

  - physical training and physiotherapy to improve cardiac activity and blood circulation;

  - 'adjustment' therapy to create a balance in life and harmony of the body and spirit.

- **Seaside spas** – Seawater, seaweed and mud are used in the therapeutic treatments here. Most of the patients at these resorts are being treated for circulatory problems, heart disease, post-operative weakness and skin diseases.

If you feel that you'll benefit from a spa treatment and can convince your GP, he can prescribe a visit for you. At one time, a visit to a spa was a pleasant little holiday at the expense of the *Kasse*, but recent health reforms mean that there must now be a clear medical reason for you to take a cure, or your insurance won't cover the cost. In any event, you'll have to pay a contribution. If you go for a cure, don't expect wild nightlife or a day filled with activities – you're meant to be recuperating and relaxing!

Even if you don't need a spa for medical reasons, it's well worth visiting one for a leisurely break. Many spa resorts have luxurious hotels where you can enjoy a fine meal, stay overnight and stroll around the beautiful grounds. Others have casinos, where you can gamble the night away. Casino and spa combinations are a long tradition in Germany, where resorts such as Bad Homburg, Baden-Baden and Wiesbaden have achieved worldwide fame and popularity (see also **Gambling** on page 325).

MEDICINES & CHEMISTS'

Prescription and most non-prescription medicines (drugs) are sold by chemists' or pharmacies (*Apotheke*), denoted by a sign showing a large red 'A' with a white symbol of a serpent and a dish on the left-hand side. Apart from throat lozenges, vitamin preparations and some therapeutic lotions, most medicines are (by law) available only from an *Apotheke*. This includes homeopathic products and items that you may be used to buying at your local corner shop or supermarket at home, such as aspirin and cold cures. As such treatments are expensive in Germany, it will pay you to bring an ample supply of non-prescription painkillers, cold remedies and other preparations with you. Even if it doesn't require a prescription, you must usually ask for a product you want by name. Alternatively, you can describe your symptoms, in which case the chemist (*Apotheker*) will offer a suggestion.

Chemists' opening hours correspond more or less with normal shop opening hours (see page 350), although if a number are located in one area they usually take turns in opening during the evening. In smaller towns and villages some chemists' are closed on Wednesday afternoons. Chemists' display a duty roster on their doors or windows and at least one will be available at night for emergencies. This information is also published in local newspapers under the heading *Apothekennotdienst*. Another alternative is to check the yellow pages for the number that provides a recorded list of chemists' open outside normal hours (again under *Apothekennotdienst*).

If you're privately insured, you must pay for all medicines and reclaim the cost from your insurer by sending the receipts. Some chemists offer a service whereby they keep your records on file and at appropriate intervals prepare a print-out of your purchases for submission to your insurance company (therefore encouraging you to visit them for all your medicines) in conjunction with a 3-5 per cent discount on over-the-counter items.

If you're insured under the state scheme, the process is simple. You can take a prescription to any chemist and, provided they have the medicine in stock, they will provide it. You must usually show your insurance card at the time of purchase and make a 'contribution' of between €4 and €5 depending largely on the package size. (This contribution is likely to increase in the near future.) Similar charges apply to non-prescription items. Not all medicines are covered, and if your doctor recommends you to use something that isn't covered by state insurance, you must pay the full price at the time of purchase.

Unlike an American drugstore, a *Drogerie* sells household goods, baby care items, cosmetics and personal hygiene products, but no medicines. You may be able to find some of these items at an *Apotheke*, but prices are generally higher. For health foods and other 'natural' food products, look for a *Reformhaus*; for perfumes and cosmetics, a *Parfümerie*.

DENTISTS

It's wise to be cautious when choosing a dentist (*Zahnarzt*) in Germany, as recent reforms to the state health system have greatly reduced the reimbursements for dental procedures. For example, preventative cleaning is no longer covered by state health insurance. Patients are therefore cutting back on treatment and even travelling to other European countries where costs are lower for 'dental work holidays'. This in turn has encouraged some dentists seeking to replace lost business to recommend procedures that may be unnecessary (a common practice in all countries). Many foreign residents schedule dental visits during trips home, (on the basis 'better the devil you know ...'). In any case, treatment is likely to be cheaper in your home country than in Germany (a check-up costs around €80, a cleaning €120-€170 and you can pay €4,000 for a set of dentures!). However, if this isn't possible or practicable and you need dental care while in Germany, try to obtain a recommendation from someone you can trust. If it's important to find a dentist who speaks English, check with your country's consulate or local English-speaking organisations to see whether they maintain lists. Dentists are listed in the yellow pages under *Zahnärzte*.

Before committing yourself to expensive treatment, it's wise to obtain a second opinion and in any case to ask for a written estimate of all costs, which you'll need in any case if you wish your insurance to cover some of the costs. Note, however, that two dentists rarely agree exactly on what treatment is necessary. It may be possible to negotiate the price with a dentist to some extent, but you shouldn't try too hard.

OPTICIANS

If you just want your vision checked, you can visit an optician or optometrist (*Optiker*), who can be found in most businesses selling prescription glasses and contact lenses. An optician will usually adjust your frames free of charge.

Ophthalmologists (medical doctors who specialise in examining and treating diseases of the eye) can also do a vision check but will charge more than an *Optiker*. Ophthalmologists are listed in yellow pages and other directories under *Augenärzte* (singular *Augenarzt*). You need a referral from a GP to visit an ophthalmologist and if you have state health insurance the cost is covered automatically (with private insurance you're reimbursed after paying the bill).

On the other hand, state heath insurance doesn't cover the cost of frames and lenses, both of which are expensive in Germany. You'll probably pay twice as much for glasses in Germany as you would for a comparable pair in the US, and Germans have been known to take their prescriptions with them on holidays to the States. The cost difference for contact lenses isn't as marked. Note, however, that there are several large optical chains in Germany selling glasses at lower prices than small shops, such as Fielman (probably the best-known name, thanks to its widespread advertising), and Apollo (a well established chain).

CHILDBIRTH

Although healthcare reforms have reduced benefits in many areas, pregnancy, childbirth and the aftermath attract increasingly generous benefits. Pregnant women and their babies receive excellent care in Germany and every effort is made to ensure the good health of mother and child. Once pregnancy is confirmed, which must be done by a gynaecologist (*Frauenarzt*), you're issued with a 'mother's passport' (*Mutterpass*), which is larger than a passport and contains all the important details of your pregnancy. It starts with your medical history and, each time you go for a check-up, information such as your blood pressure, weight and ultrasound results is recorded. Your *Mutterpass* must be taken to all pre-natal medical appointments and to the hospital for the birth itself. If you're pregnant, you're advised to carry your *Mutterpass* with you at all times in case of emergency.

In your home country, it may be customary to go to an obstetrician for pre-natal care and for him also to deliver the baby. However, this isn't always the case in Germany. A woman normally visits her regular gynaecologist or for pre- and post-natal care, and the baby is delivered at a maternity clinic by the medical personnel on duty there. It's possible to hire a midwife (*Hebamme*) to assist during the pregnancy, birth preparation and to accompany you to the hospital. All these services and prescribed medicine are covered by state health insurance, provided your doctor issues a prescription marked '*Gebührenfrei*'. If you're privately insured, you can arrange to be cared for throughout the pregnancy and birth by the chief obstetrician of the hospital's delivery team.

For the birth of your baby, you can choose between regular hospitals with maternity units, 'birthing centres' and your own home, under the supervision of a midwife. An invaluable magazine entitled *Wo bekomme ich mein Baby?* (Where do I have my baby?) is available from maternity clinics and gynaecologists' offices and provides a list and description of all the options in your area for having a baby, including information about the type of equipment available in the labour and delivery rooms, the anaesthesia and medication offered, ante-natal classes and post-natal services, and parking and public transport facilities. It's available only in German, so if you don't understand this and don't have anyone to help you translate, check with your local embassy or consulate to see if they have any information in English. Women's clubs, such as the American Women's Club (🖳 www.fawco.org) may also be able to help.

In addition to published information, most hospitals offer at least one 'open house' evening per month, when expectant mothers and partners can obtain details of the services available and inspect the facilities. After you've chosen the hospital or clinic for a birth, you must register with them.

When preparing your things to take to the hospital, you should include the passports of both parents and your marriage certificate. If the latter is in English, you'll need a certified German translation.

For a normal delivery, a woman usually spends five to seven days in hospital (7-12 for a caesarean). Recent changes in state health insurance law have increased the post-natal care to which a mother is entitled. All German health insurance plans now pay for a daily midwife visit for the first 11 days after a birth, plus a further 16 visits until a baby is two months old. Two house calls and two telephone conferences during weaning are also included. If recovering from a particularly difficult delivery or caesarean, you may be eligible for a free housekeeper (*Haushaltshilfe*) for the weeks following the birth.

The hospital will register the birth for you, but be sure to ask where it has been registered, as it may be necessary to go there in person to collect the birth certificate (*Geburtsurkunde*). If you're resident in Germany, it's essential also to register the child with your consulate or embassy, for which you'll require the birth certificate. Check the procedure with them, or a child may later be denied citizenship in your home country. US passport-holders must take their baby to a US consulate, as a Consul General must see it (though how he knows it's yours is anyone's guess!). It's wise to make an appointment as soon as the baby is born, as it can be a month or so before you receive an appointment. You must also register a baby with the German authorities at the *Einwohnermeldeamt* and apply for a residence permit on his or her behalf (see **Residence Permits** on page 71).

COUNSELLING & SOCIAL SERVICES

Counselling and general welfare assistance is widely available in Germany. In all major metropolitan areas, you can find help for problems such as alcoholism (Alcoholics Anonymous), drug addiction, compulsive gambling, marriage and relationship problems, and eating disorders. There are also dedicated centres for women or children who are suffering abuse.

For a list of professional counsellors, you can check first with your family doctor or, if you have health insurance in Germany, your insurance company. Also check the yellow pages under your local social services department. Key words to look for include *Jugendamt* (department for juvenile programs), *Sozialamt* (department of social services), *Sozialhilfe* (social help) and *Sozialdienst* (social work). If you need counselling in English, you may be able to obtain advice from your local embassy or consulate or an expatriate club, such as the American Women's Club.

HOME NURSING SERVICES

You can insure against the need for home nursing services by taking out a policy called (*Pflegeversicherung*). Policies are provided by the national health service and by private companies. The premiums for state insurance are deducted from your salary. If you have private health insurance, you must negotiate a separate home care policy with your insurer.

Since the introduction of long-term care insurance in 1995 (see page 273), there has been a rapid growth in the number of private home care agencies (*Pflegedienste*) in Germany. Your insurance company can assist you in choosing one and there are various seals of approval that indicate a high quality agency, such as the *Qualitätsgeprüfter Ambulanter Pflegedienst*.

The following services are usually provided by a home nursing service:

* body care – e.g. bathing, oral hygiene, hair care and shaving;

* nutrition – preparing food so that it can be easily eaten, and feeding;

* mobility – getting in and out of bed, getting dressed and undressed, help with standing, walking and stair climbing, accompanying on excursions outside the home;

* household needs – shopping, cooking, cleaning, dishwashing, and changing and washing bed linen.

A basic requirement for the cost of home nursing to be covered by insurance is that the patient requires help for a period of at least six months. The one exception to this rule is when the life expectancy of the patient is less than six months. The level of reimbursement depends on the amount of care required. There are three levels defined by law, and your insurance company will determine which applies according to the evaluations of qualified medical personnel.

DEATHS

If a foreign national dies in Germany, one of the first official steps is to contact the appropriate consulate or embassy. They will advise you of the options for burial (locally or in another country) and can also provide the names of morticians experienced in preparing the body for transport home, if desired. A consular report may be necessary for probate in your home country, but a consulate cannot issue this document until it receives an official death certificate (*Sterbeurkunde*) issued by the appropriate Registry of Births, Marriages and Deaths (*Standesamt*). You may also wish to request an International Death Certificate from the *Standesamt*, which are issued in several languages.

One important point to note is that a German death certificate (*Sterbeurkunde*) doesn't state the cause of death, without which you can encounter difficulty in settling insurance claims back home. To avoid this problem, you should ask a doctor for a 'cause of death' certificate (*Leichenschauschein*), which is normally issued only when a death occurred in suspicious circumstances. The *Leichenschauschein* and the *Sterbeurkunde* should be issued by the same doctor.

13.

INSURANCE

It's unnecessary to spend half your income insuring yourself against every eventuality from the common cold to being sued for your last cent, but it's important to insure against any event that could precipitate a major financial disaster, such as a serious accident or your house burning down. The German government and German law provide for various obligatory state and employer insurance schemes. These include health, pensions, unemployment, work accident and long-term care insurance – referred to as the five 'pillars' of the social security system, which was the world's first, established in 1883. Most working people and their families (over 80 per cent of the population) receive health treatment under the German social security system, although you may take out private health insurance if your salary exceeds a certain level (see **Health Insurance** on page 272). Social security also extends generous protection to students (if they aren't covered by their parents' insurance), the retired and trainees.

There are a few occasions in Germany where private insurance for individuals is compulsory. The most common is third-party car insurance (see page 225). Some landlords require tenants to have third-party liability insurance (i.e. to protect the landlord's interests) as a condition of the lease, and if you finance the purchase of a home, you're usually required to have life insurance to protect your lender. If you lease a car or buy one on credit, the lender will insist that you have comprehensive car insurance (*Vollkasko*) until the loan has been paid off. **You're responsible for ensuring that you and your family are legally insured in Germany.**

Forms of voluntary insurance include supplementary pensions, private health insurance, household insurance, certain third-party liability, and travel, car breakdown and life insurance. For information about car and breakdown insurance, see pages 225 and 228 respectively.

As with anything connected with finance, it's important to shop around when buying insurance. **Just collecting a few brochures from insurance agents or making a few phone calls could save you a lot of money.** Regrettably, however, you cannot insure yourself against being uninsured or sue your insurance agent for giving you bad advice!

If you wish to make a claim against an insurance policy, you may be required to report an incident to your insurer within prescribed time limits or in the exact manner and level of detail outlined in your contract or policy documents. Filing a claim may also require you to provide a list of receipts for articles damaged or destroyed, police reports or photographs of damage. Obtain legal advice for anything other than a minor claim. **German law is likely to differ from that in your home country or your previous country of residence, so you should never assume that it's the same.**

You should ensure that your family has full health insurance during the interval between leaving your last country of residence and obtaining health insurance in Germany. One way is to take out a holiday or travel insurance policy (see page 282). However, it's usually better to extend your present health insurance than to take out a new policy (most policies can be extended to provide international cover for a few months), particularly if you have a health problem, which may not be covered by a new policy. If you're coming to live in Germany without working, you're required to prove that you have adequate medical insurance with cover that's at least equal to the German state programme before you'll be granted a residence permit. Expatriate health insurance is provided by a number of international insurers, and group plans are available through some expatriate organisations and associations. See also **Private Health Insurance** on page 278.

INSURANCE COMPANIES & AGENTS

Insurance is one of Germany's major businesses and there are numerous companies to choose from, many providing a broad range of insurance services, while some specialise in certain fields only. The major insurance companies have offices or agencies throughout Germany. Some of the larger, better-known companies are Allianz, AXA and Zürich, but there are plenty of others. In most cities and towns there are a number of independent insurance agents and brokers (*Versicherungsmakler* or *Mehrfachagent*), who represent a number of insurance companies and allow you to compare policies from different companies. There are also a number of insurance consultants (*Versicherungs berater*), who will (for a fee) advise you on the insurance you require, in addition to finding you the best policies and rates. Some consultants, however, represent particular insurance companies and accept commission from them, so their advice may be biased and you should find an independent insurance consultant if you want impartial advice.

Many banks have insurance partners (for example, Versicherungskammer-bayern is the insurance partner of Stadtssparkasse bank) and include an analysis of your insurance cover as part of their financial advice and investment services. Quelle, the mail-order company (see page 365), provides its own insurance policies, including holiday, travel, car and life insurance, as do several department stores and hypermarkets. 'Telephone-only' insurance companies have appeared in recent years and usually offer competitive premiums, although there may be disadvantages to dealing with them; for example, it may be more difficult to obtain information or a decision regarding a claim over the telephone than face to face. In addition, you can find numerous insurance companies on the internet, many of which offer do-it-yourself price estimates and the facility to sign up online; lists of and comparisons between online insurance companies can be found on 💻 www.versicherungsvergleich.de and 💻 www.tarifchecks.de/versicherung.

Since mid-1994, the European insurance market has theoretically allowed insurers to offer cross-border policies. This means that, if you're coming from another EU country, you may be able to retain many of your insurance policies from that country (particularly life insurance and supplementary pension policies). However, in insurance, as in other matters, there's some discrepancy between theory and practice. Check with your insurance company before you leave to see if it will cover you in Germany and to determine whether cover is adequate or can be adapted to meet German requirements.

INSURANCE CONTRACTS

Read all insurance contracts before signing them. If you cannot get an English translation and you don't understand everything, ask a friend or colleague to translate it or take legal advice. Like insurance companies everywhere, some German companies will do almost anything to avoid honouring claims and will use any available legal loophole. It therefore pays to deal only with reputable companies (not that this provides a guarantee). Terms and cover can be difficult to compare, as insurers can now offer a whole range of excesses (deductibles), co-payments, conditions and exclusions even on 'standard' policies.

Always check the notice period required to cancel (*kündigen*) a policy. In Germany, insurance policies, like most forms of contract, are automatically extended for a further period (usually a year) unless cancelled in writing at least three months before their expiry date. Some types of policy must run for two or more years before they can be legally cancelled. You can cancel an insurance policy before the term has expired only if the premium is increased by more than 20 per cent, or if the terms or value of the policy are considerably changed. You won't receive a reminder of cancellation dates and, by the time you're notified that the premium is due, your cancellation date will be long past!

Most forms of insurance are paid via a single annual premium; if you want to make payments on a bi-annual, quarterly or monthly basis (assuming this is possible), you must pay considerably more. Most insurers require a bank transfer authorisation allowing them simply to deduct premiums from your bank account at the appointed times. If you don't pay, you can be sued for the whole premium, the credit collection agency's fees and interest.

The good news is that the insurance premiums you pay for the most common forms of insurance can be deducted from taxable income on your income tax declaration. This applies to life insurance, private health insurance, long-term care insurance, accident insurance and most forms of liability insurance. Social security contributions are automatically deducted from taxable income.

SOCIAL SECURITY

Germany has a comprehensive social security system for all employees, covering healthcare (including sickness and maternity benefits), injuries and illnesses at work, old age (pensions), unemployment,disability and death and, since 1995, long-term care insurance. The labour and social services budget comprises the largest item in the federal government's budget, and a large portion of spending has been directed toward bringing social services and pensions in the eastern part of the country up to a level comparable with that in western Germany.

Social security programmes in Germany also include a range of benefits and services available to those on low incomes, such as rent assistance, and food and clothing allowances. There's somewhat less stigma attached to accepting 'welfare' from the government than in some other countries; in fact Germans are justifiably proud of their social support network.

Social security cost-cutting measures have been (cautiously) introduced in recent years by politicians who, while anxious to increase contributions and cut costs, are well aware that they must maintain benefit levels if they wish to remain in power.

Employees' social security contributions are automatically deducted from their income by their employers, whereas the self-employed must pay their own contributions. Benefits aren't taxed.

The new Federal Ministry for Health and Social Security (Bundesministerium für Gesundheit und Soziale Sicherung) maintains a website (🖥 www.bmg.bund. de) containing information on social security and other programmes in German and a number of other languages, including English, although this and other government websites are being reorganised in line with changes to ministerial responsibilities. An excellent booklet in English called *Social Security at a Glance*, which provides a thorough overview of the German social security system, is available from the ministry's publications department online; simply click on 'Publications' and 'English'.

Eligibility

All employees and self-employed people in Germany are automatically enrolled in the state social security system, which also covers their immediate family members, i.e. spouse and children, as well as other dependent family members in the household. Students, trainees and apprentices are covered separately if they don't come under their parents' cover. Those drawing wage replacement benefits (unemployment, disability or old age pensions) are also covered, although they don't make any contributions. Your employer will provide you with a social security certificate, which serves to verify your enrolment and is required to claim certain benefits.

Social security agreements exist between Germany and over 30 other countries, including all EU nations and the US, whereby expatriates may remain under their home country's social security scheme for a limited period. For example, EU nationals transferred to Germany by an employer in their home country can continue to pay social security abroad for a year (form E101 is required), which can be extended for another year in unforeseen circumstances (when forms E102 and E106 are needed). Americans should be aware that the US social security agreement with Germany covers pensions only, and that medical and some survivor benefits under the US social security programme aren't payable to those living outside the US.

If you or your spouse work in Germany but remain insured under the social security legislation of another EU country, you can claim social security benefits from that country. If you must claim benefits in Germany and have paid contributions in another EU country, those contributions are usually taken into account when calculating your qualification for benefits. There's a mutual agreement between EU countries whereby contributions made in any EU country count as contributions in your home country when calculating benefits. Contact your country's social security administration for information. In the UK information is provided in a booklet, *Your Social Security, Healthcare and Pension Rights in the European Union* (reference number SA29). This can be obtained from the Department of Work & Pensions (formerly DSS), Centre for Non-Residents, Benton Park Road, Long Benton, Newcastle-upon-Tyne, NE98 1ZZ, or downloaded via the internet (🖳 www.dwp.gov.uk – from the section covering social security agreements with other countries); the downloadable version is entitled *Your Social Security Insurance, Healthcare and Benefits Rights in the EEA*.

Contributions

With the exception of work accident insurance, which is paid entirely by employers, social security contributions are split 50-50 between the employer and employee and are calculated as a percentage of your gross income – in some cases only up to a certain salary level. In general, you should expect around 21 per cent of your gross salary to 'disappear' in our social security contributions (treatment for shock is covered). Normally, the employer's share of the contribution is 'added' to your pay and then the full amount of the contribution (around 42.3 per cent) is deducted. The self-employed must pay the whole 42.3 per cent themselves – plus tax!

Health Insurance

Enrolment in the state health insurance scheme is mandatory for all employees earning less than a certain monthly salary, which in 2007 was €3,975 (i.e. €47,700 per year) in both western and eastern states. These limits are indexed for inflation each year. If your salary exceeds this level, you must choose between the state system and private health insurance (see **Private Health Insurance** on page 278). **If you choose private insurance, you may have difficulty getting back into the state scheme in the future.**

Health insurance is provided by some 600 non-profit-making funds (*gesetzliche Krankenversicherung/GKV*) working with the state to administer the national health programme, and you're free to choose among them; lists and comparisons can be found on 🖥 www.billig-krankenversicherungen.de, 🖥 www. krankenkasseninfo.de, 🖥 www.gesetzlichekrankenkassen.de. It pays to compare the offerings of a number of funds before making a decision because, although benefits are uniform across all insurers, costs vary significantly, the smaller companies (who are trying to boost their membership) usually being among the cheapest, although they may make low introductory offers and then raise their prices. Among the most popular funds are the AOK (Allgemeine Ortskrankenkasse), BEK, BKK, DAK and KKH, the AOK being among the cheapest and having the largest number of offices nationwide, which can be an advantage if you want to talk to a 'real' person about your cover.

Rates are determined according to your salary and cover all family members, irrespective of the number of children you have; in other words, a single person pays the same contribution as a married person with several children. The cost of state health insurance fluctuates between 11.9 and 15.8 per cent of gross pay (the average is around 14.5 per cent) up to the salary limit for mandatory state insurance (currently €3,975 per month – see above), of which the employee pays half plus around 0.9 per cent.

Statutory health insurance benefits are extensive and cover dentistry as well as medical care and even some spa treatments, if recommended by a doctor. However, orthodontics are usually covered only for children up to the age of 18 (when recommended by a dentist) and there's limited cover for spectacles and contact lenses. There's also a provision for the state to pay 70 per cent of your normal salary when you're absent from work due to illness, if your employer doesn't continue to pay you, although he's obliged to pay you for at least six weeks and will normally continue to pay you indefinitely if you have a doctor's certificate that you're unfit for work.

As the government tries to cut the cost of healthcare, co-payments (i.e. the portion of costs patients must pay) have been increasing for such basics as prescriptions, hospital stays, ambulance transport and dental care. However, for most doctors' appointments you simply show your health insurance card, which is sent to you automatically when you register with the national health service, and the doctor bills the insurance company directly. For more information see **Chapter 12**.

Long-term Care Insurance

Long-term care insurance (*Pflegeversicherung*) is the most recent addition to Germany's extensive social security benefits. Cover is mandatory and us linked to your health insurance plan. For those in the state healthcare system, the contribution is 1.7 per cent (plus 0.25 per cent if you don't have children) of your gross salary (up to €3,975 per month), with half paid by your employer. In Saxony, the contribution is 1.35 per cent (1.6 for the childless) but your employer pays only 0.35 per cent. If you're eligible for private health insurance, you can also shop around for long-term care cover, but you must prove to your health insurance provider that the cover you choose meets statutory requirements. The cost of private long-term care insurance obviously varies according to the benefits and options you choose. Whether public or private, the cover you select includes everyone in your family who doesn't have cover on their own behalf.

You're considered in need of long-term care if your health insurance company determines that you require frequent or substantial help with day-to-day activities for six months or longer (see **Home Nursing Services** on page 264). Long-term care benefits include holiday stand-ins for household helpers or caretakers, and extended social security cover for family members who reduce their paid employment in order to care for someone at home. Under the state programme, benefits can be tailored to individual needs, varying from cash reimbursement for private services engaged directly to contracting services from a social service agency. It's possible to receive nursing care training for family members or others to reduce or eliminate the need for outside services. You may also be eligible for grants for modifications to your home or car, when necessary.

Unemployment Insurance

Unemployment insurance (*Arbeitslosenversicherung*) is mandatory for all employees in Germany, the contribution amounting to 4.2 per cent of your gross monthly salary up to €5,250 in the west and €4,400 in the east, the employer paying half. In order to qualify for unemployment benefit, you must have worked (and paid contributions) for at least 12 months in the last three years.

Unemployment benefit is paid not only when you're unemployed but also when you're on short time or when an employer is unable to pay your wages, e.g. has gone bankrupt. Part-time employees are also entitled to unemployment benefit when wholly or partly unemployed.

To register for unemployment benefit, you must go to the local employment office (*Arbeitsagentur*) with personal identification, your tax card (see page 299), social security certificate and any documents previously issued by the *Arbeitsagentur*, such as your work permit or benefit claims. It's wise to register as soon as you become eligible (i.e. the day you become unemployed, provided you've made the required number of contributions), as benefit is paid only from the date you register; if you put off registering for a couple of weeks, you have no right to backdated benefit. If your employer has given you notice of your impending lay-off or termination, you can register for benefit up to two months in advance so that benefit take effect from the first day that you're unemployed. On the other hand, if it's your own fault that you're unemployed, e.g. you quit your job without good reason or were fired for good cause, the *Arbeitsagentur* can impose a holding period (*Sperrzeit*) of up to 12 weeks before starting your benefit. Again, this applies from the date you register as unemployed.

The benefit paid depends on your previous salary and whether or not you have children in your care, as noted on your tax card. Those without children receive around 60 per cent of their previous net pay up to a maximum benefit, which varies according to the tax class you were in during the previous year (see **Tax Card** on page 299). Benefit payments are made once a month directly into your bank account. Social security cover for pension, health, long-term care and accident insurance is maintained while you're drawing unemployment benefit.

How long you can continue to draw benefit depends on how long you've been working (and paying into the system) and your age. If you've been working only for a year, you're entitled to just six months' benefit. For those under 55, the maximum entitlement is 12 months' benefit and to qualify you must have been employed for at least 24 months in the last three years. For those aged 55 and over, with at least 36 months' previous employment, the maximum is 18 months' benefit.

After you've exhausted your unemployment benefit entitlement, you may be eligible for unemployment assistance (*Arbeitslosengeld II*) if you have no other means of support and no other working household member to assist you financially. Unemployment assistance is paid at 53 per cent of your previous net salary (57 per cent if you have children) up to the following limits: €676 per month for those with at least one child and €345 for the childless. Unemployment assistance is available indefinitely.

During the time you're drawing unemployment benefit, you must report to the *Arbeitsagentur* at least every three months or whenever they summon you to discuss a possible job opportunity or training to improve your employment prospects. Recent reforms by a government intent on reducing unemployment levels mean that officials have become much less relaxed about this. And it has become far more difficult to turn down work even though you might think it beneath you, unrelated to your area of expertise or inadequately paid. (No sacrifice is too great to improve a government's image – provided it's made by someone else!) You can also be required to attend classes or training programmes, all of which are provided free of charge.

Technically, you're required to check your letter box for information or requests from the *Arbeitsagentur* or your job counsellor at least once a day while drawing unemployment benefit, although you're entitled to take up to three weeks' holiday while unemployed, provided you notify the office in advance. If you miss an appointment, fail to turn up at classes or training programmes, or fail to follow up on job leads, you can be fined or have your benefit stopped for a number of days or weeks. You may be required to produce proof of your job-hunting efforts and you must notify the office immediately if you find a job or move house or your personal situation changes in any other way, e.g. you get married or divorced or find that you're expecting a baby. There are provisions for paying reduced benefit if you find part-time work while drawing unemployment benefit, but if you don't notify the *Arbeitsagentur* and continue to draw your benefit while being paid for full- or part-time work, you can be charged with fraud.

If you're a citizen of another EU country, you may be entitled to receive up to three months' unemployment benefit from Germany if you move to another EEA country to seek employment. To qualify, you must notify the *Arbeitsagentur* of your move and register with the unemployment office in your new country within seven days of your arrival.

Work Accident Insurance

Industrial accident insurance pays all medical and rehabilitation costs associated with injuries or illness occurring on the job, or while on your way to or from work. In the event of your death from a job-related injury or illness, your survivors receive a funeral allowance and pension benefits. This insurance also covers children in school, students attending university or vocational training, people who help at the scene of an accident, civil defence and emergency rescue workers, and blood and organ donors. The contribution is paid entirely by your employer, the amount being based on the employer's health and safety record. The employer is required to participate in various programmes to evaluate and improve health and safety conditions in the workplace as a condition of this insurance scheme. If you're self-employed and aren't required to have this type of insurance by law or under some other agreement, you can voluntarily obtain cover through the state system.

If you're unable to work (*arbeitsunfähig*) as a result of an injury or illness covered by insurance, 80 per cent of your wages (*Verletzengeld*) will be paid for up to 78 weeks after the statutory six-week period covered by your employer (see **Sick Leave** on page 56). In the event of long-term or permanent disability, you can receive occupational assistance, retraining and any necessary modifications to your car or home.

You must immediately notify your employer if you suffer an injury at work or on the way to or from work, or the educational establishment if the accident involves a child or student. The employer or school is responsible for filing a claim with their insurance provider. Statutory work accident insurance provides benefits irrespective of fault and exempts your employer from liability claims for work-related accidents or illnesses.

Pensions

'Pension insurance' (*Rentenversicherung*) is the German social security programme that covers old age, invalidity and death benefits for retirees, their families and survivors. All employees must make contributions to the state pension fund, as must trainees, disabled people employed by sheltered workshops, and those doing military or civilian service. Most self-employed people also pay into this plan, although there are some alternatives open to professions with their own social welfare plan (*Sozialkasse*). Artists and those involved in publishing may be exempt from contributions after five years provided their income doesn't exceed certain limits.

The state pension programme is easily the most expensive of the generous welfare plans in Germany and the one employers are most anxious to see reduced (at least their portion of the cost). The pensions system has come under considerable strain in the years since reunification, due both to high unemployment (particularly in the eastern region) and to the changing age structure of the German population as a whole. A voluntary private supplementary pension scheme has been introduced since, which it is obviously hoped will relieve the state of some of its burden (see **Supplementary Pensions** on page 279).

The pension insurance contribution is 19.9 per cent of gross salary up to a maximum of €5,266 per month (€63,000 annually) in the western states and €4,400 per month (€52,800 annually) in the east. As usual, employers pay half the sum and employees half (through payroll deductions); the self-employed must pay the full amount themselves.

In order to claim an old-age pension, you must have normally have contributed for at least five years. (Other conditions apply to those with occupational disabilities or work-related illnesses.) The normal retirement age (i.e. the age at which you can claim a full pension) for men and women is presently 65, but between 2012 and 2030 the retirement age will gradually be raised to 67: those born in 1946 will be the last to retire at 65, in year 2011 and those born in 1964 will have the dubious distinction of being the first to retire at 67, in 2031. However, those who have been working and paying into the system for 45 years may retire with full benefits at 65. Under certain circumstances, women, miners and those on unemployment or disability programmes are eligible for retirement at 60 or 63 with full benefits, although these exceptions are gradually being phased out. A reduced pension for early retirement is available from the age of 60 or 63 (according to your circumstances) and there are provisions for pensioners wishing to go on partial retirement so that they can continue to work part-time.

The pension scheme also provides pensions for surviving family members in the event of the death of an insured person, and partial pensions are available to compensate for reduced earning capacity in cases of long-term illness, injury or other forms of disability of an insured person.

The formula for determining the level of pension benefit is based on a fairly complicated points system, which takes into account your contributions (and therefore your salary level) and the length of time you've been covered. The total number of points earned is multiplied by a factor corresponding to the type of pension you're claiming (i.e. retirement, disability, survivor, partial, etc.) and your age. The resulting number of points is then multiplied by the current pension 'value', which is based on the monthly pension that an average wage earner would receive after paying contributions for a calendar year. The aim has traditionally been to maintain pensions at around 70 per cent of previous salary, although it's projected that the percentage will fall to around 67 by 2030. (Given the current financial situation, even this figure might be optimistic.) The pension in eastern Germany is currently around 87 percent of that in the west.

If you move to Germany after working in another EU country (or move to another EU country after working in Germany) your state pension contributions can be exported to Germany (or from Germany to another country). German state pensions are payable abroad, and most other countries will pay state pensions directly to their nationals resident in Germany. Non-EU nationals should check with their respective consulate, embassy or social security agency for details on claiming their national pension while living in Germany (or any other country). Under the terms of the pension-only social security agreements between Germany and certain countries, including the US and Canada, pension contributions made in Germany may count towards pension qualification or value in your home country.

Your pension cover is continued while you're on unemployment or other forms of income-replacement benefit, the relevant agency paying contributions on your behalf. Mothers and fathers on parental leave are automatically insured during their time off work, without having to make contributions.

PRIVATE HEALTH INSURANCE

If your salary exceeds the level where state insurance is mandatory (currently €3,975 per month or €47,700 per year), you may choose to purchase private health insurance instead of the statutory scheme (see **Health Insurance** above), although recent reforms have made this more difficult, as your salary must now have exceeded the specified limit for three calendar years in a row and you must give two months' notice to your insurance fund that you wish to go private. (The private insurers can also refuse you or make you pay through the nose for 'pre-existing' conditions.)

You also must notify your employer if you choose this option, in which case the monthly premiums will be deducted from your salary and remitted directly to your insurance company by your employer. Private health insurance provides much more extensive cover than the state scheme, including the option of private or semi-private hospital rooms, 'alternative therapies' such as acupuncture and herbal treatments, eye examinations, glasses and contact lenses, cosmetic surgery and other treatment that isn't usually available under the state plan.

You will also have a greater choice of medical practitioners with a private scheme, as some doctors restrict their practices to privately insured patients only (some because it's more profitable, others because the maximum number of GPs allowed to register in a particular administrative area with the *Kranken kassen* has already been reached and they have no option).

However, premiums for this cover can be considerably higher than for state cover, especially if you opt for cover that eliminates most co-payments. Note also that many employers limit their contribution to half the maximum statutory rate, so that all the extra costs are payable by you if you decide to go private.

Private insurers can refuse to cover 'pre-existing conditions', so this may not be a practical option if you or a family member has existing or recurring health problems.

Another important point to bear in mind when considering private health insurance is that, once you've opted out of the state health insurance system, you cannot go back unless your salary falls below the level where you're entitled to choose. In fact, if you're over 55 you aren't allowed to revert to the state system unless you're unemployed. Normally, you must make a decision on which health insurance *Kasse* you want to use within your first three months in a new job; if you aren't sure, it's best to sign up with one of the state insurers, as you can always go private later. At the end of each year there's an open enrolment period, when employees who are eligible for private health insurance can choose this option or change insurance companies.

If you wish to (or have to) stay in the state system but want to receive 'private insurance-level care' you can pay extra for supplementary insurance (*Zusatzversicherung*), either from your state provider or from a private insurance company. You choose the type of extra coverage you want, such as dental or homeopathic insurance.

SUPPLEMENTARY PENSIONS

Germans have traditionally placed considerable faith in the national pension scheme and supplementary private pensions were previously considered something of a luxury. However, with the cost of reunification and legislative moves to limit or even reduce state pension benefits, private pension insurance is slowly becoming more popular. Nowadays the government recommends a combination of state, company and private pensions – if you can afford it, of course. **If you already have private pension insurance in another country, it may not be necessary (or, in some circumstances, wise) to buy a supplementary pension policy in Germany, particularly if you will be moving on after a few years, and you should take expert advice.**

Technically, a private pension (*private Rentenversicherung*) in Germany is a form of life insurance investment, where you purchase an insurance contract for a set amount and a set term, usually 25 to 30 years. All policies for private pensions must run for at least 12 years to avoid being taxed as regular investments. At the end of the policy term, the accumulated benefits are paid to the insured person either as a monthly pension or in a lump sum. Where a private pension policy differs from a regular life insurance contract (see page 283) is in the manner in which proceeds are taxed after the death of the policyholder. When the pensioner dies, the remaining sum in the fund (or the face value of the policy if the policy hasn't yet matured) is paid to his heirs. While the pension payments made to the insured are tax-free, however, payments made to heirs after the death of the insured may be subject to tax (either inheritance tax or income tax, depending on the circumstances), whereas the proceeds of a life insurance policy are tax-free in all cases. On the other hand, you normally get a higher return on a private pension policy and there are other tax advantages.

Because of the dramatic impact the low birth rate is having and will increasingly have on the financing of the state pensions system, the government has recently introduced the state-assisted private supplementary pension. It's restricted almost entirely to those in the state insurance plan and is designed to soften the blow of future cuts in the state system on those who have been unable to take out a private supplementary pension and to prevent too wide a chasm emerging between the rich and the less-well-off. The system involves the government making 'bonus' payments into private pension schemes.

HOUSEHOLD INSURANCE

As few Germans and even fewer foreigners buy their homes, buildings insurance isn't usually a concern, but household contents insurance (*Hausratversicherung*) is essential for most people. Contents insurance normally covers your property in the event of damage by fire, burglary, vandalism, storms and water and usually replaces damaged items at their current value, including furniture, appliances, clothing and books, as well as jewellery up to certain limits. It also covers you for a limited amount of cash. Contents insurance may also include provision for refunding hotel or rent and transport costs if your home is rendered uninhabitable for a period by fire, vandalism or another form of insured damage. **It's important to make sure that your property is insured for its full value, or claims can be reduced by the proportion by which your property is under-insured.** For example, if it's determined that your insured property is worth €50,000 but you have it insured for only €40,000, a claim will be reduced by 20 per cent.

If you have possessions with a high value, it may be necessary to take out a separate policy or extension to cover them. These may include jewellery, antiques or financial documents (share certificates or bonds), where the value exceeds standard policy limits. As always, it's important to read and understand all the terms of a household insurance policy. 'Storm' damage, for example, is normally covered only when winds reach at least Force 8. You may also be required to show that you've done your best to minimise certain kinds of damage, e.g. by securing your possessions and home while you're absent, and some policies replace stolen articles only when there's evidence of forced entry. You may be able to obtain cover for 'mysterious disappearance' at an additional cost, but you should read the terms and conditions carefully.

Many household policies cover only items kept in your home and may not include garages, exterior storage areas or other off-site property unless specifically mentioned. It isn't uncommon to purchase a separate bicycle policy

(*Fahrradversicherung*) or to add such cover to your regular household insurance, particularly if you use your bicycle for day-to-day transport or have a particularly expensive model. This insurance covers the theft of your bicycle under most circumstances excluded by a regular household policy, although you must lock your bicycle whenever you aren't using it and store it in a locked area or bicycle shed when at home. Should it be stolen while in use, the theft must occur between the hours of 6am and 10pm for cover to be effective (apparently German insurance companies disapprove of late-night and early-morning bicycle riding).

If you have a non-family member (e.g. an au pair) living with you, you should check whether their possessions will be covered in a fire or other disaster. Non-related household members may need their own insurance cover for belongings, or your policy may require you to notify the insurer when you have a long-term house guest.

THIRD-PARTY & LEGAL INSURANCE

It's customary in Germany to have third-party liability insurance (*Privathaftpflicht versicherung*). To take an everyday example, if your soap slips out of your hand while you're taking a shower and jumps out of the window and your neighbour slips on it and breaks his neck, he (or his widow) will sue you for €1m (at least). With third-party liability insurance, you can shower in blissful security. If you're renting accommodation, your landlord may insist on seeing proof that you have this sort of cover so that he's adequately protected.

Third-party liability insurance covers all members of your family and includes damage done or caused by your children and pets (for example, if your dog or child bites someone). However, where damage is due to severe negligence on your part, benefits may be reduced or even denied. Many policies specifically exclude cover for claims resulting from certain dangerous sports or hobbies (sky-diving, power-boating or mountaineering, for example) or if you regularly keep explosive or inflammable material in or near your home.

Legal insurance (*Rechtsschutzversicherung*) pays for consultations with a lawyer and associated costs if you should require legal assistance or be taken to court. You can even obtain insurance for a particular type of legal assistance, e.g. for your employment, for traffic accidents or for your apartment or house lease. Legal insurance doesn't cover legal fees for most non-adversarial situations, however, such as inheritance planning, patenting inventions or starting your own business; as always, you need to read a policy carefully to ensure that you understand the extent of cover and how to file a claim.

Third-party liability insurance usually costs around €200 per year; legal insurance costs around €70 per year if purchased separately but only around €30 if added to a third-party liability policy.

HOLIDAY & TRAVEL INSURANCE

Holiday and travel insurance is available from a variety of sources, including insurance companies, banks and travel agencies, and can be purchased at airports and railway stations in Germany. Before taking out travel insurance, you should carefully consider the level of cover you require and compare policies. Most policies cover you for loss of deposit or holiday cancellation, missed flights, departure delay at both the start and end of a holiday, delayed and lost baggage and belongings, medical expenses (up to €3m) and accidents (including evacuation home if necessary), loss or theft of money, personal liability (e.g. €3m), legal expenses, holiday curtailment, and a tour operator going bust. Travel policies may also cover medical evacuation or repatriation of family members who fall ill or are injured while on holiday.

German state health insurance covers you for medical emergencies throughout Europe, but when travelling further afield you need additional insurance.

If you travel frequently, you may find it more economical to have a permanent annual travel policy with worldwide cover that includes health insurance than to purchase a travel insurance policy for each trip abroad. Annual policies are available from insurance companies that specialise in travel insurance, and some expatriate organisations offer attractively priced policies to members.

The Germans are renowned travellers and favour package holidays. As a result, a number of consumer protections are written into German law regarding full or partial refunds for holidays spoiled by overbooking, incomplete facilities, inflated advertising claims, etc., and you can often obtain a refund (in cash, possibly including compensation for the fact that you've wasted a holiday period) for such situations simply by asserting your rights (see **Consumer Associations** on page 368). For travel plans that go awry for other reasons, specific forms of travel insurance are available, including the following:

- **Travel cancellation insurance** (*Reiserücktrittsversicherung*) – refunds your holiday fees in full or in part if you need to cancel or cut short your trip due to serious illness or the death of a family member; offered by most travel agents;

- **Baggage insurance** (*Reisegepäckversicherung*) – covers damage to or loss of your bags while you're on holiday, which may be covered by a travel policy;

- **'Majorca policy'** (*Mallorca-Police*) – brings the cover on a foreign hire car up to German levels (see **Car Insurance** on page 225) and particularly recommended for travel in southern European countries, where minimum mandatory car insurance is considered wholly inadequate by Germans (hence the name). Before taking out such a policy, however, you should check your existing car insurance policy, as some German insurers include this cover in their standard policies.

LIFE INSURANCE

Although there may be worse things in life than death (such as spending an evening with a life insurance salesman), your dependants may rate your death without life insurance (*Lebensversicherung*) high on their list. You can take out a life insurance or endowment policy with numerous German or foreign insurance companies. If you already have a life insurance policy in your home country, it may be easier to maintain it, particularly if you're likely to be moving on after a few years in Germany.

German policies are usually for life assurance and not insurance. (An assurance policy covers an eventuality that's certain to occur, e.g. your death, so a life assurance policy remains valid until the day you die, whereas a life insurance policy covers an eventuality that may happen but isn't a certainty, e.g. that you should die in a car accident).

Most Germans consider life insurance a form of long-term investment or saving scheme for old age; when you consider the generous orphan, widow and survivor benefits most families are entitled to under social security insurance, this attitude makes sense. The most common sort of life insurance is called capital life insurance (*Kapitallebensversicherung*), which works much like an investment. You pay premiums for a certain number of years (a minimum of 12) and at the end of the agreed term receive the capital accrued, either as a lump sum or over a period as an annuity. Insurance companies promise differing rates of return over the term of the policy and it's important to evaluate not only the rate you're being promised, but also the company's performance over the last five or ten years. If the insured person dies before the end of the policy, the proceeds are paid to his beneficiaries. In most cases, the annual premiums on a life insurance policy are tax deductible and the proceeds are exempt from taxes whether paid to the insured or to his survivors. If a policy is cashed before 12 years have expired, these tax benefits don't apply and proceeds are treated like those from any other form of investment.

Another kind of life insurance is *Risikolebensversicherung* (also called *Versicherung auf den Todesfall*), which works like a term life assurance policy: if you die during the term of the policy, your designated beneficiary receives the value of the policy tax-free. There's no accumulation of capital, however, and if you cancel the policy or reach the end of the term alive, your cover ends with no return of the premiums paid over the years. If you borrow money, for example, to build or purchase a house or to establish a business, the lender may require you to purchase this type of life insurance to secure the unpaid balance of the loan in the event of your premature death.

It's wise to leave a copy of all insurance policies with your will and with your lawyer. If you don't have a lawyer, keep a copy in a safe deposit box – making sure your next of kin knows where it is! A life insurance policy must usually be sent to the insurance company upon the death of the insured, with a copy of the death certificate.

14.

FINANCE

One of the surprising things about the Germans to some foreigners is that they don't usually pay bills with cheques or credit cards, although this is changing – quite rapidly in some areas. Many prefer to pay in cash or with local debit cards called *EC Karten* and it isn't uncommon to find shops, restaurants and even some small hotels that don't accept credit cards. (However, most such establishments will happily point you to the nearest cash machine so that you can use your credit card to draw out the cash to pay your bill!) Compared with many other developed countries, particularly the UK and the US, Germany isn't a credit-oriented economy retail level. However, don't be fooled into thinking that this means the Germans are old-fashioned in their attitude towards money and avoid borrowing. The country has a highly efficient and dynamic banking system, which is one of the most advanced in the world.

When you arrive in Germany to take up residence or employment, ensure that you have sufficient cash, travellers' cheques, luncheon vouchers, coffee machine tokens, gold sovereigns and diamonds to last at least until your first pay day, which may be some time after your arrival. During this period you may also find an international credit card useful.

GERMAN CURRENCY

The euro (€) has the official currency of Germany since the mark's final bow on 1st July 2002. In April 2003, the euro reversed its decline against the dollar and pound (the Germans initially dubbed it the *Teuro* – a pun on *teuer*, meaning 'expensive') and is now worth more than at its launch. The euro exchange rates (*Wechselkurs*) against most major international currencies are listed in banks and daily newspapers, as well as on numerous financial websites (e.g. 🖳 http://cnnfn.com/markets/currencies).

As in most eurozone countries, locals still talk largely in old currency – i.e. marks (*Deutschmark* or *DM*) – and are likely to continue doing so for several years, so it's worth noting that two marks are roughly equivalent to one euro (officially €1 = DM1.95583).

The euro (*Euro* in both singular and plural) is divided into 100 cents (*Cent* in both singular and plural). Coins are minted in denominations of 1, 2, 5, 10, 20 and 50 cents and 1 and 2 euros. All euro coins have the same face, with a map of the European Union (EU) and the stars of the European flag. The obverse is different for each member country (designs on German coins include the Brandenburg Gate, an oak-leaf garland and an eagle – the state symbol), although all euro coins can be used in all eurozone countries – in theory, as minute differences in weight can cause problems with cash machines, e.g. at motorway tolls.

Euro banknotes are printed in denominations of 5, 10, 20, 50, 100, 200 and 500 euros. The design of the notes was subject to considerable debate and contention, and the winning designs depict 'symbolic' representations of Europe's architectural heritage. None of the images on any of the notes is supposed to be an actual building, bridge or arch, although there have been numerous claims in the press and elsewhere that the structures shown are actually landmarks in certain countries, including Germany.

When dealing with the euro, beware of counterfeit banknotes (especially €500 notes!), some of which are made with sophisticated colour laser copiers. Genuine banknotes contain a number of supposedly anti-counterfeit devices, including watermarks, a metallic reflection strip and special inks and printing techniques, which change the colours you see depending on the angle from which you view the notes.

The euro symbol (€) is generally available on most computer keyboards and calculators unless you're using pre-1997 (or so) equipment or software. Financial software in most of Europe can be easily upgraded to make use of the symbol if it isn't already incorporated into the current release, and the Microsoft website (▣ www.microsoft.com) has keyboard and operating system updates available for downloading.

IMPORTING & EXPORTING MONEY

You may bring into Germany or take out as much money as you wish in any currency, although you're obliged to report to the Bundesbank any movements of cash into or out of the country exceeding €12,500. When transferring or sending money to (or from) Germany, you should be aware of the alternatives, which include the following:

- **Bank draft** (*Bankscheck*) – Bank drafts aren't treated as cash in Germany and must be cleared, as with personal cheques. A bank draft should be sent by registered post. However, in the (albeit unlikely) event that it's lost or stolen, it's impossible to stop payment and you must wait six months before a new draft can be issued.

- **Bank transfer** (*zwischenbankliche Überweisung*) – A standard bank transfer should take three to seven days but in reality can take much longer, and an international bank transfer between non-affiliated banks can take weeks! Although German banks are among the most efficient in the world, it isn't unusual for transfers to and from Germany to get 'stuck' in the pipeline, which allows the German bank to use your money for a period interest free.

- **SWIFT transfer** – One of the safest and fastest methods of transferring money is via the Society of Worldwide Interbank Financial Telecommunications (SWIFT) system. A SWIFT transfer should be completed in a few hours, funds being available within 24 hours, although even SWIFT transfers can take five working days, especially from small branches that are unused to dealing with foreign transfers. The cost of transfers varies considerably – not only commission and exchange rates, but also transfer charges – but is usually between around €30 and €50. Britons should note that one of the cheapest ways to transfer money internationally is via the Co-Operative Bank's TIPANET service, although it takes up to a week (🖥 www.co-operativebank.co.uk)

● **Currency dealer** – It may be quicker to use a specialist currency dealer to carry out the transfer for you, and you may get a better exchange rate than from a bank, but there are usually value limits and other conditions.

If you routinely transfer large sums of money between currencies, you should investigate Fidelity Money Funds, which operate free of conversion charges and at wholesale rates of exchange.

Americans might like to investigate the Paypal system (see 🖥 www.paypal.com or the German version 🖥 www.paypal.de), which, although designed to facilitate international payments for goods bought via the internet, provides the cheapest means of making international dollar-euro transfers in general, although it's principally attractive for minor transactions, in which the exchange costs would otherwise be high in proportion to the sum transferred.

Some banks add a service charge to transactions originating outside Germany, irrespective of the currencies involved and despite the advent of the euro. The European Commission has registered this fact and similar developments elsewhere with distaste, and as a result introduced EU-regulation No 2560/2001, which states that the charge for an international payment in euros anywhere in the EU should be the same as if it were a domestic payment in the country in which it's made. This means that all such payments in euros within the EU should be free of charge – but don't bank on it.

Always check charges and exchange rates in advance and agree them with your bank (you may be able to negotiate a lower charge or a better rate). Shop around a number of banks and compare fees. Banks are often willing to negotiate on fees and exchange rates when you're transferring a large amount of money. **If you plan to send a large amount of money to Germany for a business transaction such as buying property, you should ensure that you receive the commercial rate of exchange rather than the tourist rate.** Some foreign banks levy a flat fee for electronic transfers, irrespective of the amount.

When you have money transferred to a bank in Germany, make sure that you give the account holder's name, the account number, the branch number and the bank code (the last two included in the IBAN number). If money is 'lost' while being transferred to or from a German bank account, it can take weeks to locate it.

Obtaining Cash

There are various methods of obtaining smaller amounts of money for everyday use. These include the following:

▲ Mask, Schömberg, Schwarzwald
© Carsten Reisinger (www.shutterstock.com)

◀ Chalk cliffs, Rügen, Mecklenburg-Western Pomerania
© Iryna Shpulak (www.123rf.com)

▼ Cologne cathedral,
North Rhine-Westphalia
© Bob Ford (www.123rf.com)

▲ Meersburg, Baden-Württemberg
© Rodion Rasputin (www.123rf.com)

▼ Frankfurters
© Torsten Schon (www.123rf.com)

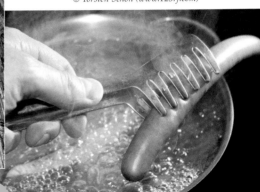

▲ Oktoberfest, Munich, Bavaria
© Mirenska Olga (www.shutterstock.com)

▶

Meissen, Saxony
© Olga Kolos (www.shutterstock.com)

▼ © Alexy Kryuchkov
(www.shutterstock.com)

▲ Office building, Berlin
© Nathan Wright (www.shutterstock.com)

▼ Berlin wall © Camilo Torres (www.shutterstock.com)

▲ Snowplough
© Manfred Steinbach (www.shutterstock.com)

◀ 'Traby' © David Harding (www.123rf.com)

▼ Eutin, Schleswig-Holstein
© Dagmar Schneider
(www.shutterstock.com)

▲ © Katharina Wittfeld (www.shutterstock.com)

▼ Warnemuende, Mecklenburg-Western Pomerania
© Stefanie Schoenebein (www.shutterstock.com)

▲ *Schloss Bellevue, Berlin*
© *Tobias Machhaus (www.shutterstock.com)*

◄ *Town hall, Munich, Bavaria*
© *Tan Wei Ming (www.shutterstock.com)*

▼ *Landsberg-am-Lech, Bavaria*
© *salamanderman*
(www.shutterstock.com)

▲ *Reichstag, Berlin*
© *Philip Lange (www.shutterstock.com)*

▼ *Vineyards*
© *Olga Shelego (www.shutterstock.com)*

- **Bureaux de change** – Most banks in major cities have foreign exchange windows, where you can buy and sell foreign currencies, buy and cash travellers' cheques, and obtain a cash advance on credit and charge cards. Banks tend to offer the best exchange rates and the post office the lowest charges.

  There are many private exchange bureaux at airports and main railway stations in major cities with longer business hours than banks, particularly at weekends. They're easier to deal with than banks and, if you're changing a lot of money, you can usually negotiate a better exchange rate. The most popular foreign currencies (e.g. US$, sterling and Swiss francs) can be changed into euros via currency machines at airports and major railway stations. **However, airport bureaux de change and change machines usually offer the worst exchange rates and charge the highest fees (e.g. handling charges).** Foreign currency (i.e. other than euros) can also be purchased from foreign currency dispensing machines at certain branches of major German banks, e.g. in shopping centres and at airports. Many German hotels and shops accept and exchange foreign currency, but almost always at a less favourable rate than banks. Never use unofficial moneychangers, who are likely to short change you.

- **Cards** – You can draw cash on debit, credit or charge cards but there's usually a daily limit. Many foreigners living in Germany (particularly retirees) keep the bulk of their money in a foreign account (perhaps in an offshore bank) and draw on it with a cash or credit card. This is an ideal solution for holidaymakers and holiday homeowners (although homeowners still need a German bank account to pay their bills). Exchange rates are usually competitive with those of exchange bureaux and banks, but there's a fee per transaction and a 1.5 per cent 'commission' charge. Some ATMs may reject foreign cards – if this happens try again or try another ATM.

- **Eurogiro** – Giro post cheques (Eurogiros) issued by European post offices can still be cashed (with a post cheque guarantee card) at main post offices in Germany. The maximum value per cheque depends on the country where issued. There's a charge for each cheque of between €3.70 and €11.80. You can also send money to Germany via the Girobank Eurogiro system from post offices in 15 countries in Europe and the US to some German banks.

- **Telegraphic transfer** – One of the quickest (it takes around ten minutes) and safest methods of transferring cash is via a telegraphic transfer, e.g. Moneygram (UK ☎ 0800-666 3947, 🖥 www.moneygram.com) or Western Union (UK ☎ 0800-833833, 🖥 www.westernunion.com), but it's also one of the most expensive, e.g. commission of 7 to 10 per cent of the amount sent! Western Union transfers can be picked up from a post office in Germany (and 100 other countries) just 15 minutes after being paid into an office abroad. Money can be sent via American Express offices by Amex cardholders.

- **Travellers' cheques** – If you're visiting Germany, it's safer to carry travellers' cheques (*Reisescheck*) than cash. (You can buy euro travellers' cheques, which can be used anywhere in Europe.) It's also advantageous, as all banks give a higher exchange rate for travellers' cheques than for banknotes. Fees and rates vary considerably when cashing travellers' cheques in Germany. Among the cheapest is the post office, which charges €6.50 per cheque. Buying large denomination cheques saves on per-cheque exchange charges. American Express and Thomas Cook offices don't charge for cashing their own cheques.

  Travellers' cheques aren't as easy to use for payment in Germany as in some other countries, e.g. the US, especially in rural areas. They aren't usually accepted by businesses, except perhaps hotels, restaurants and shops in major cities, which usually offer a poor exchange rate.

  Always keep a separate record of cheque numbers and note where and when they were cashed. American Express provides a free, three-hour replacement service for lost or stolen travellers' cheques at any of their offices worldwide, provided you know the serial numbers of the lost cheques. Without the serial numbers, replacement can take three days or longer. Most companies provide toll-free numbers for reporting lost or stolen travellers' cheques in Germany.

One thing to bear in mind when travelling anywhere is not to rely on one source of funds only.

Since the advent of the euro, there has been less demand for foreign exchange facilities in Germany, but you can still buy foreign currency, even in very small towns. However, it often pays to check in advance that they have the one you require. You can buy travellers' cheques from any German bank, usually for a fee of 1 per cent of the face value.

Happily you can donate any spare change weighing down your pockets to a variety of worthy causes when you pass through most airports in Germany and in much of the rest of Europe.

BANKS

There are three broad categories of bank in Germany: private commercial banks (*Kreditbanken*), public savings banks (*Sparkassen*) and credit co-operatives (*Genossenschaftsbanken*). The differences between the three types of bank relate principally to their legal forms and business structures rather than to the services they offer, and most banking institutions offer a full range of banking, investment and insurance services; many banks also provide advice regarding property rental and purchase and personal financial planning. It isn't unusual to find banks selling travel packages or tickets to local concerts and other events.

Private commercial banks include the so-called big three German banks: Deutsche Bank, Commerzbank and Dresdner Bank, often described as 'universal banks'. The private banking sector also includes almost 200 regional banks (e.g. Bayerische Vereinsbank, BfG Bank and Berliner Bank), the Postbank (see page 125) and numerous branches of over 300 foreign banks (including Barclays and Citibank).

Public savings banks include the 11 federal state banks (*Landesbanken*) and 11 federal building and loan associations (*Landesbausparkassen*) as well as the 500 or so local *Sparkassen* that are independently operated by town, district and municipal authorities. The *Landesbanken and Landesbausparkassen* don't do business directly with the public, but through the *Sparkassen*. When you buy a home, for instance, you can go to your *Sparkasse* and have them arrange it for you with the *LBS* or you can go directly to the *LBS* (whether you're a *Sparkasse* customer or not).

Co-operative credit associations, once limited to members of specific trades or professions, long ago evolved into full service banks, mostly operating under the names of *Volksbank* or *Raiffeisenbank*.

Choosing among the hundreds of banks available is no simple matter. One important factor to take into account is that some businesses have a preferential arrangement with a particular bank, which may result in lower bank charges for employees. Comparisons between banks can be found on 🖳 www.banken.de and 🖳 www.dooyoo.de/banken.

Opening Hours

Normal bank opening hours are from 8 or 9am until 4pm, though banks are sometimes open as late as 6pm, with no closure over the lunch period in some cities and large towns. The main offices of many banks tend to keep similar hours to the local shops and may even open on Saturdays, at least for some counter services. Most banks in Germany have automatic teller machines (ATMs) and statement machines available 24 hours a day in a secure area, so that customers can withdraw cash, make deposits and check statements at their convenience.

The banking industry in Germany is one of the most dynamic sectors of the economy. Twenty-four hour telephone banking has been available for many years and even the smallest banks now offer most services via the internet and even direct computer link as well as via fax.

Opening an Account

One of the first things you do on arrival in Germany should be to open a bank account. Simply go to the bank of your choice and tell them you're living or working in Germany and wish to open an account. You're normally asked to provide standard identification and it may be useful to be able to offer a letter of reference from your bank in your home country or from a German employer, although this isn't usually necessary.

If you prefer to open an internet-based account, you must generally complete a form on the bank's website, after which you receive an account information pack by post, although once you've opened an account you can perform most transactions online.

The 'default' method of paying bills in Germany is by bank transfer (see page 293) and cheques are rarely used. However, in order to be able to make a direct bank transfer, you must have a giro account (*Girokonto*), which can be opened at any bank, including Postbank (see page 125). Most banks allow giro account holders to overdraw their accounts (see **Overdrafts & Loans** on page 296).

After opening an account, don't forget to give the details (account number and bank identification number – *Bankleitzahl* or *BLZ*) to your employer if you wish to be paid, as your salary usually goes directly into your bank account. Some companies have a preferential arrangement with a particular bank, which may result in lower bank charges for employees. Your monthly salary statement is sent to your home address or given to you at work.

You can usually make arrangements with your bank to send statements to you as often as you like, e.g. monthly, weekly or even daily if you want to keep a really close track of your money. However, some banks have discontinued this service, as an increasing number of customers use the internet to check their accounts. There is, of course, a charge for the traditional statement service and the more frequently you wish to have a statement, the more expensive it is (most people receive monthly statements). However, most banks provide a machine in their lobby or alongside an ATM that permits you to print a bank statement whenever you want one, free of charge. You simply insert your bank card (at a branch of your bank), enter your personal identification number (PIN) and a statement is printed detailing all transactions on your account since the last time you requested a statement.

Your statement is often the only notification you receive from the bank about the charges they've deducted, so you should check it carefully. At the end of the year, your statement includes the annual totals required for tax and other reports. If you lose your copy of a bank statement, you must ask your bank for a duplicate, for which you're charged a fee. If you use a bank's online banking services, be sure to print the statements you need periodically, and don't forget to make a copy of files if you download your banking information.

German banks issue multi-purpose bank cards (see **Cash & Debit Cards** below), which also act as cheque guarantee cards – usually up to around €200. Don't keep your bankcard and chequebook in the same place; if you lose both your card and cheques at the same time, or they're stolen and cheques cashed, you may find that you're liable for any amounts debited from your account due to 'negligence'. Bank staff can be lax when checking signatures or identification. You're largely responsible for loss, improper use or forgery, and for mistakes due to missing or unclear designation of the amount or currency.

When writing figures in Germany (or anywhere in continental Europe), you should cross the down stroke of the number 7 in order to avoid confusion with the number 1, which is often written with a leading upstroke and resembles a seven to many non-Europeans (and Britons). Americans should note that Germans (like other Europeans) write the date with the day first followed by the month and year. For example, 1.9.08 is 1st September 2008 and not 9th January 2008. The conventional US form 9/1/04, with the month first and slashes between the digits, must never be used!

Bank Transfers

The usual and most common method of making payments within Germany is a bank transfer. There are essentially two kinds of bank transfer, depending on whether you're instructing the bank to transfer money from your account to another account (*Überweisungsauftrag*) or are authorising the bank to allow a third party (e.g. a utility company) take the money from your account (*Lastschriftverfahren*) – see below.

If you have an internet or other electronic bank account, you can usually establish, change and cancel single or regular payments over the internet or by fax or phone. Make sure that you keep copies of all transactions you authorise, plus the associated contracts or bills containing the bank account details and amounts. Your bank is responsible for correcting any errors made when transferring funds to or from your account, but corrections can be made much more quickly if you can produce documentation to back up your claim.

Überweisungsauftrag

An *Überweisungsauftrag* consists of a three-part form. You enter your name and account number and the identification number of your bank, and the name of the person or company you want to pay and their bank account and bank identification number. (This information must be printed on all bills and invoices sent to you for payment.) There's a space where you can enter the reason for the payment (whatever you put here will be printed on your bank statement) and another for the amount you want to transfer. You sign the form and keep one copy (the *Beleg für Auftraggeber*), giving the other two copies to your bank. You can either take or post the *Überweisungsauftrag* to your bank.

Often when you receive a bill in the post, it includes an *Überweisungsauftrag* form with the company's bank details and the amount already completed. You simply insert your bank details and sign the form before giving or sending it to your bank (don't send it back to the company!).

An *Überweisungsauftrag* form doesn't include the date – either the date you submit the form to the bank or the date you want payment to be made – and payment is normally made within two business days of the bank's receipt of the payment order. If you want the transfer to be made on a specific date, you must request this (in which case the transfer is called a *Terminüberweisung*). You may wish to mark the date on your copy for reference. It's also wise to keep your copies of *Überweisungsaufträge* you've submitted to the bank in the same place as your bank statements, so you can check that payments have been made.

Lastschriftverfahren

Instead of directing your bank to pay a creditor, a *Lastschrift* is an authorisation permitting a creditor to debit a specified sum from your account, usually on a specific date (*Lastschriftverfahren* is the term for this process). While either an *Überweisungsauftrag* or a *Lastschrift* can be used to make a single payment, *Lastschriften* are often used to settle recurring expenses, such as rent, utility charges, car insurance premiums, magazine subscriptions and other regular payments made monthly, quarterly or annually (see **Dauerauftrag** below).

Dauerauftrag

To arrange a regular debit from your account (*Dauerauftrag*) – which can be either an *Überweisungsauftrag* or a *Lastschriftverfahren* – contact your bank with the relevant payment information, including the bank account number of the person or company you want to pay.

Savings Accounts

You can open a savings account (*Sparkonto*) with commercial, co-operative and savings banks. Your employer may also offer a form of tax protected savings account at your own or another local bank. Most financial institutions offer a variety of savings and deposit accounts, with varying interest rates and minimum deposits, depending on the type of account and bank. In most cases the first €750 (€1,500 for a married couple) in savings account interest is exempt from tax (the amount is called the *Sparerfreibetrag*), and there are additional tax advantages for savings accounts established to buy a home. With deposit accounts (term deposits) you must be prepared to tie up your money for at least a month. The longer the term, the higher the return.

You receive a pass book (*Sparbuch*) for a savings account, where all deposits and withdrawals are recorded. If you take part in an employer-sponsored savings plan, you must take your pass book to the bank every few months to have the balance updated.

Cash & Debit Cards

German banks issue customers with a bank card which enables them to obtain cash from ATMs and obtain statements from a bank's statement machine. The bank card functions not only as a guarantee card but also as a debit card, and it can be used to make purchases (such as petrol) from outlets displaying the relevant service sign, where goods up to a certain weekly value can be paid for by card (€1,500 per week in the case of the Postbank card, for example, the sign to look for being 'Maestro'). You're also issued with a PIN. **Make a note of your PIN immediately and keep it in a secure place, as the ink on the form on which it's printed is designed to fade in a fairly short time.** Although you may make deposits without a PIN, you need it to make withdrawals. If you lose your bank card, notify your bank as soon as possible, as it can be used to withdraw cash and make purchases.

If you're banking with the Postbank (see page 125) or one of the associated Cash Group of banks (which includes the Commerzbank, Deutsche Bank, Dresdner Bank and the Hypo Vereinsbank), cash withdrawals are free at any of these banks. A withdrawal from the ATMs of other banks costs a minimum of €5. There's a maximum of €500 a day for Postbank Giro account withdrawals from any source.

A recent innovation is the 'money card' (*Geldkarte*), which can be used at outlets displaying a '*GELDKARTE*' sign. Cards are issued by your bank and can be 'charged' with up to €200 from your account. You can use them in cigarette and public transport ticket machines, in telephone booths and, sad to say, in McDonald's restaurants. If you use one to buy a trasnport ticket, you usually get a discount.

CREDIT & CHARGE CARDS

Credit and charge cards are referred to collectively as credit cards (*Kreditkarten*); in fact, most German 'credit' cards operate like charge cards in that payments for purchases are due when billed and cannot held over for months or years. It's sometimes possible to make deferred payments on travel costs (mostly air fares and hotel bills) charged to your card, but normally for up to three months only.

Although they've been slow to gain acceptance, there has been a marked increase in the popularity of credit and charge cards in the last decade, particularly due to their usefulness in shopping via the internet or abroad. The most common cards are Visa and MasterCard, which are available from most banks. American Express, Diners Club and Barclaycard are also popular.

While credit cards in Germany can cost you as little as €12 per year if you're a student, most other people must pay between €20 and €80 per year. Top-of-the-range cards (i.e. those with the greatest pose value), such as the American Express Centurion card, can set you back €400 annually. Some cards include travel or other forms of insurance as part of the annual fee; others provide free travel and accident life insurance when travel costs are paid for with the card.

Most credit cards allow you to withdraw cash from ATMs that are part of their network, although there's usually a hefty charge per transaction. In the case of the Postbank, which belongs to the Cash Group, for example, this is 2 per cent of the amount withdrawn and a minimum of €5. Before obtaining a credit or charge card, assess the costs and benefits.

As part of the sign-up process, you're required to indicate the bank account you wish to use to pay your monthly balance, and the contract includes an authorisation for the card company to debit payments automatically from your account. You receive a statement of your monthly charges around ten days before the date that the amount due is debited from your account, so you have an opportunity to review the statement and dispute any incorrect payments or charges. Like most other forms of contract in Germany, a credit card contract requires you to give formal written notification at least three months before its expiration date if you wish to cancel it and avoid paying the following year's fee.

If you maintain a bank account abroad, it's wise to retain your foreign credit cards. One of the advantages of using a credit card issued abroad is that your bill is usually rendered or your account debited up to six weeks later, therefore giving you interest-free credit – except when cards are used to obtain cash, when interest starts immediately. You may, however, find it more convenient and cheaper to be billed in euros than in a foreign currency, when you must wait for the bill from outside Germany and payments may vary due to exchange rate fluctuations.

If you lose a bank or credit card, report it immediately to the issuing office. You can insure against losing credit cards or you may be able to pay a fee to the card company, relieving you of any liability.

OVERDRAFTS & LOANS

Most banks allow giro account holders to overdraw their accounts by a specific sum as part of their general account terms. You may find that you're advanced round sums (e.g. €100 for an overdraft of up to that amount) and will be charged interest on the amount advanced at the current overdraft rate until the overdraft is repaid; it therefore doesn't pay to go overdrawn for a few euros only!

All German banks provide loans, although they aren't as free with their money as banks in many other European countries, particularly regarding business loans to foreigners. Loans are subject to your income and the amount of debt you already have. In Germany, the old maxim still applies: the best way to qualify for a loan is to convince a bank that you don't really need one!

It pays to shop around for a loan, as interest rates vary considerably according to the lender as well as the amount, the purpose and the period of the loan. Generally, loans of up to a year are considered short-term credit, loans for one to four years are medium-term, and anything longer than four years is long-term. Interest rates in mid-2007 ranged from around 6 to 9 per cent for a short-term loan, although cheaper loans could be arranged via the internet. German bankers are highly risk-averse and tend to prefer making loans where there's adequate collateral or where the borrower is also making a major investment from savings or other personal resources.

If you're making a major purchase, such as a car or an expensive household appliance, you may find that the vendor or manufacturer offers financing through a bank set up expressly for this purpose. These 'banks' are captive finance companies and don't offer any other banking services except for consumer credit for purchases of goods sold by their parent company. The deals they offer are usually quite competitive, but nevertheless it's worth shopping around and comparing interest rates and terms.

Borrowing from private loan companies, as advertised in newspapers, is expensive (i.e. interest rates are high). Use them only as a last resort, when all the other means have been exhausted. Even then, as a foreigner, you may find that the term of your loan is limited to the expiration date of your residence or work permit, or that you're required to repay the loan in full if you move abroad. In general, the more desperate your financial situation, the more suspicious you should be of anyone willing to lend you money.

MORTGAGES

Mortgages (home loans) are available from all major German banks, but the lending criteria may be rather different from what you're used to, particularly if you're from the UK or the US. Banks and other mortgage institutions base their loans on the value they assign to a property (the *Beleihungswert*), which may be derived from a published list of values or from an assessment, rather than to its actual purchase price and are permitted to lend only 60 per cent of this value as a principal mortgage, although you may be able to negotiate a higher *Beleihungswert*. In most cases the *Beleihungswert* is below the market value of a property (though if it's significantly lower than the asking price, you're probably paying too much!).

If necessary, a homebuyer must secure a second mortgage (at less favourable terms) for the remaining amount. It isn't uncommon for German employers (particularly family-owned companies in the *Mittelstand*) to lend money directly to employees making home purchases, or even to co-sign or otherwise support a second mortgage through the employer's bank. Note, however, that most British and American multinational companies specifically forbid the practice, although their German branch offices may ignore this.

Mortgage loans in Germany can be at either a fixed or a variable interest rate and most lenders require that all mortgages be repaid before normal retirement age. Add to this between 4 and 10 per cent of the purchase price in fees, taxes and transfer costs, and it's easy to see why most people in Germany prefer to rent their homes (see **Chapter 5**).

If you take out a mortgage, the lender may require you to purchase term life insurance (*Risikolebensversicherung*) to secure the unpaid balance of the loan in the event of your premature death (see page 283).

INCOME TAX

Income tax (*Einkommensteuer*) in Germany is the government's main source of revenue, providing around 35 per cent of its 'income', followed by value added tax (VAT), which brings in some 22 per cent. It's often contended that German income tax rates are high compared with the rest of Europe, but this was never entirely true and is now less true than it was, given recent tax reforms. The top rate is currently 45 per cent (for those who earn over €250,000 – poor them!) and the basic rate is 15 per cent. This is unlikely to still the clamour for more radical tax cuts from those who see these as the magic wand that will solve Germany's economic problems, so any subsequent rate changes will almost certainly be in the downward direction, although the German government faces the same dilemma as those of many other countries in wanting neither add to the tax burden of businesses nor to cut spending on welfare programmes or benefits, which become ever more costly.

As in many other countries, tax on employees' earnings (*Lohnsteuer* – literally 'salary tax') is deducted at source by their employers, i.e. pay as you earn (PAYE). The system used in Germany is extremely efficient and the amounts deducted usually cover your tax obligation almost to the cent, at least for those with no income other than from their regular employment. If you have no other source of income and no further credits or other adjustments to make for income tax purposes, you therefore don't even need to file an income tax return (see **Tax Return** on page 303).

The information below applies only to personal income tax and not to companies. Note that unmarried couples aren't treated (for tax purposes) in the same way as married couples, the latter enjoying certain tax advantages. **There are ruinous fines and possible imprisonment for those caught evading tax.**

Liability

Your liability for German taxes depends on where you're domiciled, which is usually the country you regard as your permanent home and where you live most of the year. A foreigner working in Germany who has taken up residence there is considered to have his tax domicile in Germany. A person can be resident in more than one country at a time but can be domiciled in only one country. Generally, people living in one country and working in another (known as 'border hoppers' – *Grenzenspringer*) pay taxes in the country in which they live.

German residents are taxed on their worldwide income, subject to certain treaty exceptions, while non-residents are taxed only on income arising in Germany. Most countries exempt their citizens from paying income tax if they're living outside their home country for a certain period. Germany has an extensive network of double-taxation treaties in order to ensure that income that has already been taxed in one treaty country isn't taxed again in another.

Americans should be aware that the US is the only country that taxes its non-resident citizens on income earned abroad and requires a tax return to be filed even if most or all of your income is exempt from taxation. US citizens can obtain information on tax filing requirements from an American embassy or consulate or via the internet (🖳 www.irs.ustreas.gov).

If you're in doubt about your tax liability in your home country, contact your nearest embassy or consulate in Germany.

Tax Card

Shortly after you register at your local *Stadtverwaltung* (see **Registration** on page 83), you receive a tax card (*Lohnsteuerkarte*) based on the information you provided on registration. You should check the information printed on the card, which includes your name, address, date of birth, church tax category (see page 83), and the number of children for whom you're claiming child credit or allowances. The tax card also shows your taxpayer identification number, which you should quote on all correspondence with the tax authorities, and your assigned tax class (*Steuerklasse* – abbreviated to *StKl*), which determines how much your employer must deduct from your pay for income tax.

If you're single, you'll probably be assigned to *StKl I*. (Single for tax purposes includes the divorced and widowed, and married people who are legally separated.) *StKl II* is for single people drawing certain types of assistance, which entitles them to income tax reductions. Married people are assigned to one of three tax classes according to whether their spouse is employed or not: *StKl III* is for a married person considered to be the primary breadwinner for the family. If a husband and wife are both employed full-time, both spouses will normally be assigned to *StKl IV*. *StKl V* is reserved for married people who need or wish to have extra taxes deducted from their pay each month to make up for the fact that their husband or wife is already assigned to *StKl III*.

You should give your tax card to your employer as soon as you receive it, as it serves as the basis upon which taxes are deducted from your pay. At the end of the year, your employer returns your card with a statement showing your income for the year and the social security payments and taxes deducted and paid on your behalf.

If your circumstances change (e.g. you divorce or have a child), you should contact your local authority immediately to have any corrections made, both on the card and in your file.

Tax Number

If you're freelance or own your own business you need a tax number (*Steuernummer*) instead of a tax card. In order to obtain a tax number, you must register your freelance status or company ownership at the tax office (*Finanzamt*). After around four weeks, you'll receive your number in the post. **It's against the law for any employer or contractor to pay you if you haven't received your *Steuernummer*.** If you're self-employed or freelance you must file a tax declaration every year and report all income if the total exceeds the base threshold (see **Tax Calculation** on page 301); you then receive a bill from the *Finanzamt*. Your future tax payments are based on your previous year's earnings and may be paid in instalments.

Taxable Income

You must report your income in relation to the following categories:

1. farming and forestry;

2. trade or business;

3. independent services (i.e. self-employment);

4. employment;

5. capital investment;

6. rents and leases;

7. other income, including annuities, maintenance payments (alimony) and similar legally mandated payments between spouses or partners.

The good news is that, if you receive payments that aren't defined in law as coming under one of the seven categories, they're tax-free! One of these is lottery winnings, which aren't subject to income tax in Germany. (Americans, however, are expected to pay income tax to their own government if they win the German lotto while resident in Germany!)

As mentioned above, your employer is responsible for reporting and paying the appropriate income tax on your employment income. Income from employment includes not only your salary, but also such things as overseas and cost of living allowances, profit sharing plans and bonuses, storage and relocation allowances, language lessons provided for a spouse, personal company car, payments in kind (such as free accommodation or meals), home leave or holiday (paid for by your employer), and children's education expenses. Your employer is required to value these benefits and services and include them on your pay slip each month when calculating the taxes to be deducted from your salary. They should also be included in the amounts reported for the year on your tax card.

Allowances

The tax payments your employer makes for you take into account certain standard allowances against income. The allowances listed below applied to 2007 income (most allowances are indexed annually). Social security contributions (see **Chapter 13**) are automatically deducted from taxable income.

- the cost of getting to and from your place of work, based on a flat rate per kilometre (currently €0.30) starting from 21km (16mi) – i.e. there's no allowance if you live less than 21km from work – unless you take a scenic route;

- a deduction for general employee expenses (*Arbeitnehmerpauschalbetrag*) of €920. You can deduct more (up to certain limits) if you have receipts to justify the larger amount.

- most insurance premiums, including life insurance, private health insurance, long-term care insurance, accident insurance and most forms of liability insurance;

- contributions (*Spenden*) to charitable, religious or scientific research organisations, generally up to 5 per cent but in a few instances up to 20 per cent of your income – if you're a philanthropist;

- costs incurred for 'extraordinary burdens' (*aussergewöhnliche Belastungen*) such as caring for a handicapped family member, hiring household help and private vocational training for a child;

- training or continuing education in order to change or enhance your career up to €4,000 (under certain circumstances);

- two-thirds of childcare costs, up to €4,000 per child;

- the first €750 of income from interest on investments or savings (€1,500 for a married couple filing jointly).

There are many other allowances, which usually change annually. Any that aren't allowed for by your employer can be claimed on your annual tax return.

Tax Calculation

The tax year in Germany is the same as the calendar year, from 1st January to 31st December. Families and married couples are usually taxed as a single entity; however, married couples can elect to file separate returns if they wish to claim individual tax credits and allowances.

Children under the age of 18 are included on their parents' (or a parent's) tax return. Children over the age of 18 can be included on their parents' tax return if they're enrolled in school or a vocational training programme. Earnings for the school year from part-time jobs or training schemes must be declared on the family's tax return, although they aren't generally subject to income tax.

The tax payable is calculated according to your taxable income minus allowances. Income up to the base threshold (*Grundfreibetrag*) isn't taxed (or, officially, is taxed at 0 per cent!). In 2007 this level was €7,664. Above the threshold, income is taxed progressively at between 15 and 45 per cent but on a sliding scale (up to €250,000) rather than in 'steps' as in most other countries, which means that you must wade through reams of income tax tables (*Einkommensteuer Tabellen*) to find out how much tax you owe.

In 2007, the tax burden for single taxpayers (or a couple filing separately) was as shown below.

Taxable Income	Tax Rate
Up to €7,664	0%
€7,665 to €12,739	15 to 23%
€12,740 to €52,151	24 to 41%
€52,151 to €250,000	42%
Over €250,000	45%

Married taxpayers (but not unmarried partners) filing jointly pay taxes based on so-called 'splitting tables' (*Splitting-Tabelle*), whereby their combined income is taxed at the rate that applies to half the total; for example, if a couple earns €100,000, they will pay tax on this amount but at the rate normally applied to an income of €50,000.

Credits

Once you've calculated your tax due, you can claim a tax credit (*Kinderfreibetrag*) for each dependent child of €1,824 (for a single parent) or €3,648 (for parents filing jointly). Divorced parents with joint-custody arrangements are generally entitled to half a credit each per child, provided the child lives in Germany. It's possible to claim a credit for a child living outside Germany if you're legally obliged to support the child, e.g. under a divorce or separation agreement, or some other form of child support decree.

Surcharges

Once you've deducted any credits due, you must add surcharges! Those who declare themselves affiliated to certain religions must pay a church tax, which is levied at 8 or 9 per cent of the amount of income tax due (see page 83). There's also a solidarity surcharge, imposed in 1995 to help finance the reunification of the former East and West German states, which is currently levied at 5.5 per cent of your income tax due; although the government claims to intend to reduce it further (it was originally 7.5 per cent of tax), there's currently no sign of this happening.

Tax Return

Some time in January, your employer returns your tax card to you, with the sections related to earnings, allowances, credits and payments completed for the year just ended. Normally you also receive a set of tax forms and instructions from the local tax authorities (*Finanzamt*), but if you don't you can pick up copies from your town hall or the *Finanzamt* itself. Some post offices and banks keep copies of the most common tax forms.

Employees who have had income tax deducted from their wages and who have no other source of income aren't required to file a return. Most employees can normally dredge up a few extra allowances, however, and generally wish to claim at least a small refund of taxes deducted – in which case they must file a return. Self-employed people, business owners and other non-employees must file a tax return if their income from all sources exceeds the base threshold (currently €7,664).

Unless your tax affairs are simple, it's prudent to employ a tax adviser (*Steuerberater*) to complete your tax return and ensure that you're correctly assessed, as the German tax system is somewhat complicated (especially if you don't have a good command of the language), and there are usually changes to allowances or allowable deductions each year. If you're self-employed or in business, finding a good adviser can mean the difference between success and failure, and his fee is tax-deductible! If you aren't self-employed, a cheap alternative to a tax adviser is the *Lohnsteuerhilfeverein*, a sort of club for tax advice (your local club can be found via an internet search). You pay a fee of around €100-150 per couple per year and get unlimited tax advice and a completed tax return.

If you decide to do it yourself, many books, websites, magazines and computer programs are available to help you understand and save taxes, prepare your tax return and calculate your final tax bill. You must, of course, understand German well (and possibly have a good business or legal dictionary handy!) to complete your tax return.

A general income tax form (*Hauptvordruck*) includes basic personal information such as your taxpayer identification number, name, address, occupation, spouse's name and his or her occupation. Most of this information will already be printed on the form if you received it by post from the *Finanzamt*. The tax authorities need your bank account number and the bank identification number (*BLZ*) for the account which you wish to use to pay your taxes or to receive any refund due; these can be found on your bank statement and on the back of your bank card.

German tax returns, not surprisingly, are complicated and contain specialist (i.e. obscure) terminology. You must not only declare your income on the appropriate form(s) – see below – but also document your rights to the various allowances and credits. The form (*Anlage*) you require depend on the types of income you have to declare and include:

- *AUS* – to report foreign source income and tax paid abroad;

- *AV* – to report retirement savings plans;

- *FW* – to claim certain benefits related to home ownership;

- *GSE* – to report income and expenses from businesses you own or from self-employment;

- *K* – to claim child credits (yes, these are separate forms!);

- *Kinder* – to identify the children for whom you're claiming credits;

- *KSO* – to report income from other investments (interest or dividends, annuities, mutual funds or any other income not otherwise reported);

- *N* – to report employment income and marketing costs (*Werbekosten*);

- *U* – to report maintenance payments (alimony) or other support payments between separated or divorced partners;

- *V* – to report income and expenses from the rental and lease of property;

- *VL* – to report capital investments (this form is usually provided by the investment institution).

The forms don't help you to calculate the amount of tax you must pay, but you can buy books and computer programmes that include the appropriate tax tables along with instructions on estimating your final bill. You must include your tax card with the return, so be sure to take a copy of your card, as well as a copy of your return and any additional documents included.

Tax returns should be filed on or before 31st May of the year following the tax year; for example, your return for the year 2007 should be filed by 31st May 2008. The tax office is authorised to grant extensions and normally does so on request, up to the end of the year following the tax year, which is the absolute deadline for filing (i.e. 31st December 2008 for the 2007 tax return). If you haven't filed a return by this time, you lose any claim you may have had to a tax refund. To request an extension, you normally need only include a letter with your return, stating the reason you couldn't file by 31st May. Acceptable reasons include work, travel or family commitments. However, the tax inspector can impose a penalty of up to 10 per cent of the taxes due, so it's wise to file your return on time if there's any possibility that you will owe additional tax. (Needless to say, the tax authorities won't pay you interest if you're late claiming a refund!) If you haven't filed your return by 31st May, it's usually wise to have a tax adviser file it for you (the tax adviser's fee is deductible on your next tax return).

Tax Bills

Within a few weeks of filing your tax return, the tax office sends you a tax assessment (*Steuerbescheid*). If a refund is due, they will advise you of the amount, which will be transferred automatically to the bank account you listed on your return. If you owe money, you'll be informed of the amount that will be debited from your account.

If you feel that your taxes haven't been correctly calculated, you have one month after receipt of the tax assessment to make a formal protest (*Einspruch*). To make a protest, you must have a specific complaint about the calculation and be able to show where and by how much the calculation is in error! The protest must be submitted in writing and you should either follow an established model or have a tax adviser prepare the letter for you in order to ensure that you follow the correct procedure.

VALUE ADDED TAX

Value added tax (VAT) is called either *Mehrwertsteuer* (*MwSt*) or *Umsatzsteuer* (*USt*) in Germany (and is usually the difference between a fair price and too expensive!). The two terms are used more or less interchangeably, although the legally correct term in Germany is *Umsatzsteuer*. Literally, it's a use tax rather than a sales tax, as it's levied on all goods and services used in Germany, irrespective of where they were purchased. If you buy goods by mail-order from outside the EU, you may be charged VAT by the post office when they're delivered, although on small purchases (under around €50 declared value) they often don't bother to collect the tax.

Most prices in Germany are quoted inclusive of tax (*einschliesslich Mehrwertsteuer/Umsatzsteuer*), although they're sometimes quoted exclusive of tax (*ohne Mehrwertsteuer/Umsatzsteuer*).

Germany has three rates of VAT: the standard rate of 19 per cent, which applies to most goods and services, and reduced rates of 7 and 4.4 per cent rate that apply to certain food products and 'necessary' social services. The only services exempted from VAT are those that are taxed in some other way, such as certain forms of life insurance that are actually investments.

There's no threshold for registering for VAT; if you're engaged in any 'economic activity' to earn a living rather than just as a sideline, you're normally required to register with the local tax office (*Finanzamt*) and charge VAT to your clients, even if you're barely making ends meet. This obviously adds to the bureaucracy of setting up as a self-employed person in Germany. However, 'small' businesses (*Kleinunternehmen*) can choose to opt out of paying VAT, in which case they may not charge their customers VAT (invoices should be marked as 'VAT exempt'). The disadvantage of doing so is that you don't have the benefit of deducting any VAT you've paid to your suppliers. A small business for VAT purposes is one which had a turnover of less than €17,500 in the previous year (VAT is included in this figure) and which expects its turnover to be no more than €50,000 (including VAT) in the current year. Once a small business has decided to become VAT exempt, it's required to remain so for five years.

Some professions are exempt from VAT, such as doctors, physiotherapists and insurance brokers. All other businesses must include VAT at the appropriate rate on all their invoices, bills and receipts. VAT payments are normally paid (or refunds claimed) every month but in some cases every three months.

It's the declared aim of the EU eventually to have just one rate of VAT for the whole community, although this will take some time to accomplish, particularly as only Denmark, Slovak Republic and Bulgaria have a single rate on everything at present, and other countries have at least two widely differing rates.

CAPITAL GAINS TAX

Capital gains from the sale of non-business assets (e.g. a second home) are generally exempt from tax unless they're considered to be speculative. In the case of property, a sale is considered to be speculative if it takes place within ten years of purchase. Gains from the sale of a substantial share (i.e. more than 10 per cent) in a company are also taxable. Capital gains tax rates are the same as those for personal income (see page 301).

INHERITANCE & GIFT TAX

As in most other developed countries, dying doesn't free you (or rather your inheritors) entirely from the clutches of the taxman. Germany imposes both inheritance tax (*Erbschaftssteuer*) and gift tax (*Schenkungssteuer*) on its inhabitants, although in Germany it's the inheritor or the recipient of the gift (the beneficiary) who's responsible for filing a return and paying taxes, rather than the deceased's estate or the donor.

Inheritance tax (called estate tax or death duty in some countries) is levied on the transfer of property from the deceased to his heirs. The amount of tax due depends on the value of the property inherited and the relationship between the deceased and the beneficiary. Gift tax is levied in much the same way on property that's granted or donated to another person before the owner's death.

A surviving spouse has a tax-free allowance of €307,000, while children and stepchildren are given an allowance of €205,000 and grandchildren or parents have a €51,200 allowance. Most other relatives (brothers and sisters, nieces and nephews) can claim only a €10,300 tax-free allowance, and all other beneficiaries receive an exemption of just €5,200. There are strict rules and regulations regarding how property (both land and buildings) is valued, based on rental values and the use of the property at the date of death or a gift. Buildings that produce rental income are considered particularly valuable assets at tax time.

Beneficiaries are grouped into three tax categories (*Steuerklasse*) according to their relationship to the donor. Category I includes the spouse and children; category II parents, siblings and other blood relatives; and category III more distant relatives or unrelated beneficiaries. The following tax rates apply to the amount of a gift or inheritance after the tax-free allowance has been deducted:

Taxable Value of Bequest	Tax Payable Category I	Category II	Category III
Up to €52,000	7%	12%	17%
€52,000 to €256,000	11%	17%	23%
€256,000 to €512000	15%	22%	29%
€512,000 to €5,113,000	19%	27%	35%
€5,113,000 to €12,183,000	23%	32%	41%
€12,183,000 to €25,565,000	27%	37%	47%
Over €25,565,000	30%	40%	50%

It's possible to purchase life insurance to cover the inheritance tax your heirs will have to pay.

If you inherit property in Germany from abroad, you should consult a notary (*Notar*) or lawyer who's familiar with international tax law and treaties, or contact the *Finanzamt* directly before claiming your inheritance. Under tax treaties, the German *Finanzamt* usually recognises taxes already paid on an estate overseas, but it's important to know what documents you require to verify this when repatriating an inheritance from abroad.

WILLS

It's an unfortunate fact of life that you're unable to take your hard-earned assets with you when you take your final bow (or come back and reclaim them in a later life). All adults should make a will (*Testament*) irrespective of how large or small their assets. The disposal of your estate depends on your country of domicile and, particularly if you own property (land or buildings), may also depend on where the property is located.

Under German law, you can indicate your final wishes regarding distribution of property and assets by drawing up a will. There are several kinds of will in Germany, but as with all official documents there are strict forms and rules to follow when writing a will. It's therefore wise to consult a lawyer or notary (*Notar*) to ensure that you leave your final instructions in a legally valid form.

If you choose a notarial will (*notarielles Testament*), you can tell the notary how you wish to distribute your property and he will draw up the legal documents for your signature. It's also possible to write your last wishes yourself and give them (sealed or not) to a notary, who will register the existence of your will and hold it until you pass on. The notary's fee is based on the value of your estate, irrespective of whether he actually writes up the document or just registers the existence of your sealed last testament.

You can also prepare a holographic will (*eigenhändiges Testament*) – simply one written in longhand – provided you follow the form and regulations carefully. A holographic will is a cheap way of making a will without using a notary or lawyer. The only catch is that someone has to know where it is after you've gone. If you decide to write a holographic will, it's important that you hand-write the entire text of the will and sign the document legibly at the end, indicating the exact date and place (i.e. town) of signature. No witnesses are required; in fact, this type of will shouldn't be witnessed or it will complicate matters.

It's possible for married couples to prepare a joint will, of which there are several variations, each with its own legal requirements and restrictions. A *Berliner Testament*, for example, must be hand-written by one of the spouses and signed by both in order to be valid.

It's possible to have two or more wills – one covering your property in Germany and others for property owned abroad – although it's important to ensure that they don't contradict each other, or none of them may be valid! It may be wise to have a German will that simply refers to another will in your home country or elsewhere. If you own property abroad, most legal experts advise you to have a separate will that's valid in the country where the property is located.

German law doesn't allow you to leave your property to anyone or anything you choose and you aren't permitted to disinherit entirely certain relatives, namely your direct descendants (children, grandchildren), your parents (if you have no children) and your surviving spouse. These privileged family members can claim their share of up to half the value of your final estate if they discover that you've left them out of your will. They have up to three years after your death to assert their rights and can even recover any gifts made in the ten years before your death. It's important to consider this requirement when drawing up your will, so as to avoid leaving your heirs squabbling over what's left when you're gone – unless that's your intention! Under German law, your heirs will inherit not only your property, but also any debts. However, if you die leaving more debts than assets, your heirs can choose to reject the bequest altogether, thereby avoiding all tax and debt issues.

If you don't have a will (i.e. die intestate), your estate will be divided among your heirs according to German inheritance law. Simply put, this means that your closest category of living family members will receive your property (and debts) to share among themselves. The exact division depend on your marital status, the degree of relationship to surviving family members and any property-sharing agreements or conventions that apply between you and your spouse (often based on the property laws at the date and place you were married).

Keep a copy of your will(s) in a safe place and another copy with your lawyer or the executor of your estate. Don't leave them in a bank safe deposit box, which in the event of your death is sealed for a period under German law. You should keep information regarding bank accounts and insurance policies with your will – but don't forget to tell someone where they are!

German inheritance law is a complicated subject and it's important to obtain professional legal advice when writing or altering your will.

COST OF LIVING

No doubt you would like to know how far your euros will stretch and how much money (if any) you will have left after paying your bills. First the good news: Germany has long been famous for having one of the highest standards of living in Europe. Wages are above average (particularly in technical and engineering disciplines), inflation was just 1.7 per cent in the 12 months to May 2007, which is historically around average, and the euro has become a strong and stable currency.

The bad news is that Germany has a high cost of living and high taxes, and the cost of many goods and services is higher than in most of the rest of Europe (housing is among the most expensive in the world). Fuel costs are also high, due primarily to heavy taxes, although in many urban areas it's possible (and often even desirable) to get by without owning a car at all. Your food bill will almost certainly be higher than in your home country or previous country of residence; German food prices can be almost double those in the US, for example, and up to 50 per cent higher than in southern Europe.

Shopping around for 'luxury' items such as hi-fi equipment, electronic goods, computers and photographic equipment at discount centres and bargain stores (see **Chapter 17**) can result in considerable savings. It's also possible to save money by shopping for wine and other products in France or neighbouring countries or shopping overseas (e.g. in the US) by mail-order and via the internet. Even in the most expensive cities, the cost of living needn't be astronomical and, if you shop wisely, compare prices and services before buying and don't live too extravagantly, you may be pleasantly surprised at how little you can live on.

Like all averages, an average cost of living encompasses a multitude of actual situations, determined by individual circumstances and lifestyles. There are also big differences in prices (and above all rents) between the major cities and more rural areas. For example, there's a considerable difference in property rental rates between western and eastern Germany, and rents in cities such as Berlin and Munich can easily cost double or triple the figures shown below.

A particularly detailed survey into precise living costs, the *Einkommens und Verbrauchsstichproben* (*EVS*) is carried out every five years, the last from which statistics are available being 2003. If these are updated for inflation, the monthly expenditure for an average household in mid-2007 was as follows:

Item	Cost
Food & drink	€315
Clothes & shoes	€120
Rent, heating & utilities and property maintenance	€770
Leisure	€275
Transport	€320
Health	€95
Household appliances & interior decor	€130
Education	€25
Newspapers & magazines	€70
Accommodation & restaurants	€110
Other goods & services	€100
Total	**€2,330**

In interpreting these figures you should bear in mind that only a quarter of households in Germany include children and that over 34 per cent are single-person households. Monthly costs for middle-class families with children would be considerably higher (up to €3,757 for a family of five).

15.

LEISURE

The Germans spend all their time sitting in beer gardens wearing *Gamsbart* hats and *Lederhosen*, drinking beer from huge Steins, eating radishes and sauerkraut, listening to an oompah band, and getting up only to dance polkas. This, at least, is the impression Hollywood and the Bavarian Tourist Office seem determined to peddle as far as German entertainment is concerned. The reality, however, is far more colourful and interesting, and leisure pursuits in Germany are as varied as in any country. It offers a huge variety of entertainment, sports (see **Chapter 16**) and pastimes and is blessed with a wealth of natural beauty – many tourists come to Germany to participate in outdoor sports, e.g. skiing and hiking, for which the country is famous – and historic cities and towns. Germany is particularly famous for its 'high' culture – theatre, concerts and opera – which rates among the best in Europe.

Wherever you are in Germany, you can reach most other regions on a day trip thanks to the country's excellent transport infrastructure – except at the end of school terms, when everybody seems to want to go on holiday and trains are over-crowded, airports over-run and the famously fast *Autobahns* converted into gigantic car parks. Of all the peoples in the world, the Germans seem to have the most highly developed herd instinct, and it sometimes appears that they will all decide to do exactly the same thing at the same moment. (Thankfully though, the different states stagger their annual school holidays.)

Leisure information is available from the German National Tourist Office (GNTO) and local tourist and information offices, many of which have a ticket agency, and a wealth of city and regional entertainment papers. Other information sources include local newspapers and radio programmes, and posters on those curious announcement pillars known as *Litfasssaülen*. Regional TV stations provide the latest entertainment news via their teletext services, including details of local concerts, plays and musicals, art shows, sports events, flea markets and much more. Tourist information can also be obtained from a plethora of excellent travel books (see **Appendix B** for a list) and from a multitude of websites, including 🖳 www.germany-info.org, 🖳 www. toytowngermany.com, 🖳 www.hotelstravel.com, 🖳 www.travel24.com and 🖳 www.donnerwetter.de (for weather forecasts), and most cities also have their own websites (e.g. 🖳 www.berlin.de and 🖳 www.munichfound.com).

TOURIST OFFICES

Most German cities have a tourist office or, at the very least, an information office (often located at the town hall), many of which also provide a hotel and event ticket booking service. They're usually open during normal business hours from Mondays to Saturdays and also on Sundays in cities and areas where tourism is a major industry. The German National Tourist Office/GNTO (Deutsche Zentrale für Tourismus, Beethovenstr. 69, D-60325 Frankfurt, ☎ 069-9746 4287, 🖳 www. germany-tourism.de) has offices in many countries including Australia, Austria, Belgium, Brazil, Canada, the Czech Republic, Denmark, Finland, France, Hong

Kong, Hungary, Israel, Italy, Japan, South Korea, Mexico, the Netherlands, Norway, Poland, Russia, South Africa, Spain, Sweden, Switzerland, the UK and the US (listed on the website). No matter what information you require, the GNTO will either be able to answer your question or give you an address or telephone number where you can find the answer. Local tourist and information offices are listed in guidebooks.

HOTELS

German hotels are generally spotless and efficient, and the standard of accommodation is invariably excellent, although the service may lack the eager friendliness one often finds in other countries. Don't expect the courtesies to go any further than a fleeting smile and an occasional '*Guten Tag*' in most hotels. You can expect to find every type of accommodation in Germany, including cosy rooms in private homes (look for '*Zimmer frei*' or '*Fremdenzimmer*' signs in windows), holiday rooms on farms and simple guesthouses (*Gästehaus* or *Pension*, the latter in Bavaria) up to five-star luxury hotels. A *Gasthof* is a unique German institution roughly equivalent to a traditional English inn (a bar/restaurant with rooms). Generally, the smaller the place, the friendlier the service – guesthouses are often particularly cosy (*gemütlich*) and homely places to stay.

Room rates usually include continental breakfast (basically coffee and rolls), while in some larger establishments a buffet-style cooked breakfast is offered for an extra charge. Hotels with restaurants offer half board (breakfast and dinner) or full board (breakfast, lunch, dinner) at favourable rates. A *Hotel Garni* provides breakfast and drinks.

The cheapest accommodation in Germany is provided by the Etap Hotels chain, which offers rooms from €25 a night in fairly central locations. Otherwise, rates vary from €30 to €50 per night for a single room (€50 to €70 for a double) in budget accommodation to over €350 per night at a top class hotel. The price charged for a room often has less to do with its quality or decor than with the amount of local competition (or lack of it). In some popular places, such as Frankfurt, even small guesthouses charge five-star rates during the popular trade fairs, and it's common for them to raise their prices steadily as the better establishments fill up. If you turn up in a city during a festival or international trade fair, you're likely to find yourself in poor quality, expensive accommodation on the outskirts of town, unless you've booked well in advance. Hotels outside the bigger cities are generally more affordable.

Those interested in history or architecture may wish to stay at one of the many castles that have been converted into hotels – though they should be prepared to pay dearly for the privilege. Information is available on the GNTO website.

Germany is a member of Motorbike Hotels International, Ignaz-Reder-Str. 3, D-97638 Mellrichstadt/Rhön, (☎ 097-7681 800, 🖳 www.motor-bike-hotels.com), the European network of hotels offering special services for those travelling by motorbike. Hotels are located in popular motorcycling areas and offer free maps plus safe parking areas, bike washing and maintenance facilities, boot polishing equipment, and heated drying rooms for wet gear. All hotel managers and many staff members are themselves keen motorcycle riders. First-time guests receive a 'biker's pass' which provides each tenth night free.

Most tourist guides contain a wealth of information about accommodation and there are a number of specialised hotel publications in English and German, including the *Michelin Red Hotel and Restaurant Guide Germany* and *Hotels Deutschland 2007* published by the Hotel Verband Deutschland.

Local tourist offices provide a wealth of information about accommodation at all price levels in their area and are happy to assist travellers in finding rooms and board in their towns. They also provide information for people with particular needs, such as those with children or pets, the disabled and those on particular diets. They may also have lists of bed and breakfast establishments (B&Bs) and rooms to let in private homes. Tourist offices that provide a room-finding service (*Zimmervermittlung*) may make bookings free of charge, while others charge a booking fee of €2 to €5.

HOSTELS

If you're travelling on a tight budget, the best way to stretch your financial resources is by staying at youth hostels (*Jugendherbergen*). Germany has one of the most extensive network of hostels in the world, with 550 throughout the country. The vast majority are operated by the German Youth Hostel Association (Deutsches Jugendherbergswerk/DJH, Haupverband, Leonardo-da-Vinci-Weg 1, 32760 Detmold ☎ 05231-99360, 🖳 www.jugendherberge.de) and indicated by a 'DJH' sign. The DJH publishes an annual *Handbuch der Jugendherbergen in Deutschland* listing all its hostels in Germany with descriptions, facilities, photographs, travel instructions and rates. **Although most hostels are open throughout the year, some are closed in winter and a number even close every other weekend.**

Hostel rates depend on the quality of the accommodation offered. Over 60 per cent of hostels fall into Category 4, which is the highest, and can charge up to €22 per night, but the average price is €15 and Category 1 accommodation costs only €9. Those aged over 26 pay €4 more and the prices for double rooms vary from hostel to hostel. Non-members of the International Youth Hostel Association (IYHA) must pay a surcharge in the form of 'welcome stamps' (an agreeable euphemism). Some hostels have only two large dormitories (one for men and one for women). All prices include sheets as well as breakfast. Other meals cost around €4. **Note that few German hostels have self-catering facilities**.

Priority is given to those aged under 27 and 'wrinklies' over 27 are supposed to be accepted only if a hostel isn't fully booked by 6pm, unless

they have a booking. In Bavaria, those aged over 26 aren't admitted to youth hostels unless accompanied by 'children' under 26. Bookings are held only until 6pm, unless the warden is informed that you'll be arriving late, 10pm being the latest check-in time. All hostels have a curfew, when the front door is locked, which may be as early as 10pm in rural areas, although it can be midnight or even 2am in large cities. The check-out time is usually 9am. The length of a stay at a youth hostel is limited to a maximum of three days, although this is usually enforced only when new arrivals would otherwise be prevented from getting a bed. However, some hostel wardens strictly enforce all rules – including some they make up as they go along!

Establishments run by the Friends of Nature Association (NaturFreunde Deutschlands e.V. Warschauer Straße 58a D-10243 Berlin (☎ 030-2977 3260, 🖳 www.naturfreunde.de) are similar to youth hostels, although targeted more at older people. There are some 500 of them in Germany, most in the countryside close to towns, and they provide accommodation in single and double rooms and/or small dormitories.

SELF-CATERING ACCOMMODATION

All tourist areas have self-catering accommodation (*Ferienwohnumgen*) and furnished apartments (*Ferienappartements*) available for short-term lease, which can be rented through agencies or in some cases directly from owners. While they all look good in the catalogues, the quality varies hugely, and a high rental charge is no guarantee of quality. Most are spotlessly clean but they're furnished and equipped to variable standards; some don't even supply toilet paper. If you don't bring your own bed linen and towels, you may be charged an additional fee for laundry services. If you plan to arrive on a Sunday, bear in mind that shops will be closed, so bring any necessities with you. Generally you're required to do your own daily cleaning, unless an apartment is part of a hotel complex where chambermaids are provided. In any case, you're usually charged a cleaning fee at the time of your departure! Apartments are normally leased on a weekly basis, from Saturday to Saturday, and you're required to vacate the premises before noon on the last day or face an army of cleaning ladies ready to remove you with the dustbins.

The best way to find self-catering accommodation is to write to the tourist office of the town where you wish to stay, which will send you a list of available properties and prices, sometimes with a map of the town showing the apartments' location. Prices vary considerably with the season, quality, size and location (e.g. closeness to amenities such as ski-lifts or tourist attractions). The rental agreement is likely to require a deposit (payable in advance) and should specify any additional costs. In some areas there's a 'spa tax' (*Kurtaxe*) of a few euros per day, which is designed to help maintain the local spas and isn't included in room rates. If you're planning to stay in a town whose name starts with 'Bad' you'll almost certainly have to pay this tax, which is also applied to each item you consume at restaurants or cafes in spa towns!

The Verband der Mitwohnzentralen, Schulterblatt 112, D-20357 Hamburg, Germany (☎ 040-19445) is an umbrella association for over 40 accommodation-finding services and can refer you to members in major cities throughout Germany.

CARAVANNING & CAMPING

Germany has over 2,000 official campsites, many in popular hiking and climbing areas, and camping anywhere else is frowned upon, although generally tolerated provided you have the permission of the landowner. Camping on public land is illegal, but you're permitted to spend one night in a caravan or mobile home in any public parking space.

Campsites are graded from 'good' to 'excellent' depending on their facilities, which range from basic washing and toilet facilities and perhaps a shop, to a wide range of amenities, including electricity connection, hot showers, sauna, washing machines, supermarket, lock-up storage for valuables and various sports facilities, which usually include a swimming pool (outdoor and/or indoor) and tennis courts. Sites may also have facilities for golf or crazy golf, volleyball, cycling, table tennis, canoeing, fishing and boating. Large campsites usually have a restaurant and a bar.

Prices are based on facilities and location, rates ranging from around €3 to €12 per person per night plus around €3 to €8 per tent, with extra fees for cars and caravans. Most campsites are full between June and September and you should arrive early in the afternoon if you haven't made a booking. Some camping areas are open only during the summer season, while others remain open all year round.

A free list of caravan and camping grounds can be obtained from German National Tourist Offices, and comprehensive guides are published by the German Camping Club (DDC, Mandlstr. 28, D-80802 Munich, ☎ 089-3801 420, 🖳 www.camping-club.de), the ADAC motoring organisation (*ADAC Reiseführer Camping*) and the Aral petrol company (*Aral Campingführer*).

Caravans and mobile homes can be hired from various companies throughout Germany.

FESTIVALS

Every German town, no matter how large or small, has an annual festival, which is normally organised by the volunteer fire brigade. Most people are familiar with Munich's *Oktoberfest* and some may even have heard of the *Cannstätter Wiesen* or the *Bad Dürkheim Weinfest*. There are many hundreds more, which although smaller, also possess that light-hearted, 'carousel-and-candy-floss' atmosphere. The larger festivals are invariably to celebrate the local beer and/or wine and you must usually pay a deposit on a beer mug at beer festivals or buy your own glass at wine festivals – the organisers have learnt from long experience that many glasses don't survive the evening or are taken home as souvenirs. **The number one rule on these occasions is never to drink and drive** but to use public transport; the local police may be ill-humoured at having to work while everybody else is having fun and apply the alcohol laws even more rigorously than usual.

There's also the carnival season (known as the 'fifth season'). *Karneval* or *Fasching* (pronounced 'fashing') is a Catholic festival normally beginning on Epiphany (this varies from region to region) and culminating on the day before Ash Wednesday, i.e. Shrove Tuesday (*Faschingsdienstag*). *Karneval* is most popular in the Rhineland and the party really gets going on *Weiberfastnacht* ('wives' carnival night') – the Thursday before Ash Wednesday – when women take control and run around cutting off men's ties. From Saturday to Tuesday parades take place in many towns, the most important of which are on Rose Monday (*Rosenmontag*), when most of the town shuts down and hundreds of thousands of people join in; things can get quite out of hand with revellers dressing up (political satire is an especially popular theme), drinking and trying to catch prizes that are thrown from floats. The biggest festivities are in Cologne, Dusseldorf and Mainz. Don't assume that all this is just fun and games, however – it's taken very seriously, particularly in the above towns and Wiesbaden. Once you get into the spirit of it, you may wish to join a *Fasching* club, where you'll discover that what looks like lots of fun to the visitor is actually considerable hard work and quite expensive. In fact, it's so costly that only millionaires can afford to accept the title of *Fasching* prince in the major locations. In Cologne it's estimated that the prince must spend around €60,000 just for the confectionery thrown from the parade's floats – a stiff bill for just 'three crazy days'.

There's a growing taste for medieval festivals, which are held in many parts of the country, particularly in the Angelbachtal and at Münzenberg Castle (near Butzbach) in spring or summer. An increasing number of people are drawn to this rather bizarre activity, which requires participants to make their own clothes, weapons and armour. Some of the groups involved, such the Society for Creative Anachronism (🖳 www.sca.org or 🖳 www.drachenwald.sca.org), take their hobby so seriously that they can hardly talk about anything else. Medieval festivals offer arts and crafts exhibits, jousting knights, jesters, wandering minstrels, an outdoor theatre, and plenty of hearty food and drink. **The castles are usually on hilltops, so be prepared for plenty of climbing.**

THEME PARKS

Germany boasts a number of theme parks, including the top-rated Phantasialand (☎ 02232-36200, 🖳 www.phantasialand.de) in Brühl, near Cologne, which has around 30 rides and seven shows, including some with animals. Free admission is provided for anyone visiting the park on his or her birthday (proof in the form of a passport or ID card is required). Movie Park (at Bottrop, north of Essen, 💻 www.movieparkgermany.de), where you can experience a car chase or dive into the Bermuda Triangle, is a must for all fans of Spongebob (a cartoon character, who teaches childred valuable lessons about friendship and loyalty). Holiday Park (Hassloch, between Mannheim and Karlsruhe, 💻 http://holidaypark.de) offers magic shows, a cypress garden and a waterski display, while Europa Park in the Black Forest (at Rust, near the city of Freiburg, 💻 www.europa-park.de) is set in an old castle park with a French quarter, an Italian section, a Russian corner and a Dutch village. German amusement parks (and zoos) are listed on 💻 www.themeparkcity.com/EURO_germ.htm.

You should plan to spend at least a day at any of these theme parks. All have plenty of parking, although coach trips are also offered by tour companies throughout Germany, usually on Saturdays or Sundays.

MUSEUMS

The diversity and range of museums in Germany is unequalled in any other European country, where it's said that every town with over 10,000 inhabitants has at least two museums (Berlin itself has over 100!). While most relate to the history of the local area (*Heimatmuseum*), others are national or even international, such as the Deutsches Museum in Berlin (💻 www.deutschesmuseum.de), the world's largest museum of technology and science, receiving around 1.3m visitors a year; the Pergamon Museum, also in Berlin, which houses remains and reconstructions of ancient monumental architecture, such as the Altar of Zeus from Pergamon and Ishtar Gate; and the Gutenberg Museum in Mainz (💻 www.gutenberg-museum.de), one of the oldest museums of printing in the world.

Details of all Berlin's museums can be found on 💻 www.smb.spk-berlin.de, and information about museums throughout Germany 💻 www.worldar tantiques.com/GermanyMuseums.htm.

State museums aren't always where you may expect to find them; for example, the Hessian state museum isn't in either Frankfurt (Hessen's largest city) or Wiesbaden (the capital of Hessen), but in Darmstadt, which was the capital until 1918.

One of the most remarkable museums is the Technik Museum in Sinsheim, where you can hire some of the vehicles on display and take them for a 'spin' – from a 1930s racing car to a Second World War tank – though the hire charges and insurance aren't exactly cheap. For those of a bloodthirsty disposition, exhibits at the Crime Museum (*Kriminal Museum*, 💻 www.kriminal museum.rothenburg.de) in Rothenburg o.d.T., open from April to October include chastity belts, neck violins, human cages, a witch's chair, and even the dreaded

Iron Maiden. Information is provided in English as well as German. There's also a humorous side to some German museums; anybody who thinks the Germans have no sense of humour need only visit the Karl Valentin Museum in Munich, where a bowl of water is labelled 'a splendid snow sculpture, until brought inside'. Other unusual museums around Germany include the Bee Museum (located in Weimar), the Chair Museum (Rabenau), the Chocolate Museum (Cologne), the Toy Soldiers and Tin Figures Museum (in Kulmbach) and the peerless Centre of Extraordinary Museums (ZAM in Munich), comprising museums of chamber pots, Easter bunnies and everything to do with torture.

Germany also has many interesting open-air museums and attractions, including the slate mines (*Schieferbergwerk Besuchergrube*) in Bundenbach/Hunsrück and the silver mines (*Reiche Zeche*) in Freiberg. If you're interested in architecture and 17th-century half-timbered buildings in particular, head for New Anspach (near Frankfurt) to see the open-air museum (*Freilicht Museum*) at Hessen Park.

Admission charges vary considerably, from around €2 to €6, some museums offering free admission, particularly those operated by a local authority or university. In most major cities, public transport tickets also provide admission to museums. Many museums close on Mondays (in eastern states many close on two days a week) and public holidays.

GARDENS, PARKS & ZOOS

Many of Germany's botanical and zoological gardens are world famous, such as the Ottobrunn Zoo in Munich and Frankfurt's Palmengarten. Almost every city has a zoo, sometimes called a *Vivarium* or *Tiergarten*. All charge an admission fee. In addition to general botanical gardens there are so-called 'teaching trails' (*Lehrpfade*) in some locations, designed to educate people about the local flora and agriculture. These are usually free unless the services of a guide are required. Garden lovers may also be interested in the German Federal Garden Show, held in a different city each year. A list of botanical gardens and zoos can be obtained from the GNTO and information can be found in most good guidebooks.

Many regions have areas designated as national parks or nature reserves, indicated by a triangular white sign with a green border reading '*Naturschutzgebiet*'. There are no admission fees, but the strictly enforced rules include no camping, no fires, no picking flowers, no disturbing the animals and no dogs running free, while in some reserves visitors are restricted to marked paths.

German zoos (and amusement parks) are listed on ▭ www.themepark city.com/EURO_germ.htm, and all the major zoos are listed on ▭ www.zoos-worldwide.de/land/europe/germany.html.

CINEMAS

Cinema flourishes in Germany, which has a long tradition of film-making, although the majority of films shown nowadays are American imports (dubbed into German). There are numerous cinemas (*Kinos*) in German cities, mostly with four to six screens (some have 16 or more) and most towns have at least one. Most cinemas show films only in German, although in most large cities there's at least one 'art-house' or 'alternative' cinema (*Kommunales Kino* or *Programmkino*) showing original-language versions, indicated by '*OF*' (*Originalfassung*) or '*OV*' (*Originalversion*). A foreign film with German subtitles is indicated by '*OmU*' (*Original mit Untertiteln*) after the title. In some cities, there may be a cinema showing only English-language films. There are strict age restrictions for many films, which are shown by the word *ab* (from) followed by a number and *J.* (short for *Jahren*, meaning 'years'), as follows:

Rating	Restriction
ab 6 J.	6 years and over
ab 12 J.	12 and over
ab 16 J.	16 and over
ab 18 J.	18 and over

Films suitable for all are classified *o. ALTB.* (*ohne Altersbegrenzung*). It isn't unusual for cashiers or ticket collectors to ask to see some form of identification if a person looks younger than the age limit, and anyone who cannot prove his age is refused admission. Tickets are usually quite expensive, e.g. €8 to €15 for a Saturday night showing of a first release, although discounts of up to 50 per cent are generally offered on one day a week (*Kinotag*). Most cinemas accept telephone and internet bookings and you can often buy tickets at box offices in advance. In most cities you can obtain information about programmes by calling a local hotline (numbers can be obtained from tourist offices) or checking entertainment websites. Some towns, e.g. Berlin and Munich, stage annual international film festivals, during which participating cinemas are open 24 hours a day.

THEATRE, OPERA & BALLET

High-quality theatre, opera and ballet performances are staged in all major cities, many by resident companies, which receive generous government subsidies (including over 400 theatre companies). This doesn't, however, mean that tickets are cheaper than in other European countries – indeed, the opposite may be true. In many cities it's possible to buy a subscription, which includes a seat at each production during a season. Tickets for popular theatre, opera and ballet performances at the most famous venues are in high demand and must be ordered well in advance. If you're planning to attend the annual Wagner festival in Bayreuth or the Passion Play held every ten years in Oberammergau, you must book literally years in advance.

Political and satirical *Kabarett* entertainment featuring monologues and short sketches is common in larger cities, particularly Berlin (where the musical *Cabaret* is set).

Top British musicals, such as those of Andrew Lloyd-Webber, are performed (usually in German) in some cities and have been extremely popular, so much so that an entire tourist industry has sprung up around them. Tour companies offer overnight or weekend package deals, which include transport, hotel accommodation and tickets to shows. These all-inclusive deals usually represent excellent value, often costing little more than the price of a pair of tickets alone if you buy them from the box office.

Theatre performances are generally in German except for occasional international workshops, tours by American or British companies, or community theatres such as the English Theatre in Frankfurt (Kaiserstrasse 34, ☎ 069-2423 1620, 💻 www.english-theatre.org). The Morale, Welfare and Recreation (MWR) division of the US armed forces sponsors English-language performances at its bases in Darmstadt, Hanau, Heidelberg, Giessen and Wiesbaden, which are open to the public. A website listing theatres in Germany is 💻 www.theaterparadies-deutschland.de.

CONCERTS

The birthplace of many of the world's greatest composers, Germany has a long tradition of classical music and opera performance. Every major city has a symphony orchestra and operatic company, many performing at the highest level. Classical concerts, music festivals and solo performances are regularly held throughout the country. Germany boasts not only some of the world's best concert houses, but three of its finest orchestras: the Berlin Philharmonic Orchestra (*Berliner Philharmoniker*), the Bavarian Radio Symphony Orchestra (*Symphonieorchester des Bayerischen Rundfunks*), based in Munich, and the Leipzig Gewandhaus Orchestra (*Gewandhausorcheter Leipzig*). Although all three perform almost nightly during the season, it doesn't mean that obtaining a ticket is an easy task and most concerts are sold out well in advance. If you wish to attend a concert, you should book as far in advance as possible.

Free concerts are often staged at the various Amerika Haus centres, such as those at Frankfurt and Leipzig, where Americans touring Europe 'stop off'. There are also many free classical and choral performances in parks and churches, some sponsored by local tourist boards. Look for notices in local newspapers and magazines and for posters in cities.

Many German cities (including Berlin, Essen, Frankfurt, Hamburg and Munich) are venues on the world tours of major popular artists and bands, some of which stage concerts in all five cities, while others take in only one or two. Tickets are available from record shops, local information offices and ticket agencies. In spring and summer, huge outdoor rock concerts are staged in major cities, attracting tens of thousands of fans. The price of tickets for pop music concerts is generally high and in the case of superstars and top bands exorbitant. Don't, however, neglect the wealth of home-grown talent; Germany has a thriving club scene where everything from blues and jazz to folk and rock can be enjoyed nightly.

SOCIAL CLUBS

Club life has a special place in German culture and most Germans belong to a number of clubs or associations, including sports clubs. There are many social clubs and expatriate organisations in Germany catering for both foreigners and Germans, including Ambassador clubs, American Women's and Men's Clubs, Anglo-French clubs, Business Clubs, International Men's and Women's clubs, Kiwani Clubs, Lion and Lioness Clubs and Rotary Clubs.

Expatriates from many countries run clubs in major cities, a list of which is often maintained by embassies and consulates (see **Appendix A**). Many local clubs organise activities and pastimes such as chess, bridge, art, music, sports activities and sports trips, theatre, cinema and visits to local attractions. Joining a local club is one of the easiest ways to meet people and make friends. If you want to integrate into your local community or German society in general, one of the best ways is to join a German club. Ask at the local town hall or library for information.

DISCOS & NIGHTLIFE

The availability, variety and quality of nightlife in Germany varies considerably with the town or region. In some small towns you may be fortunate to find a bar with live music or a discotheque, while in major cities such as Berlin, Hamburg and Munich, you'll be spoilt for choice and can party round the clock. The major cities offer a wide choice of entertainment, including jazz clubs, cabarets, discos, sex shows, music clubs, trendy bars, nightclubs and music halls. The liveliest places are the music clubs, which are infinitely variable and ever-changing with a wide choice of music from jazz to rock and funk to folk. The most popular clubs are listed in newspapers and entertainment magazines. For those with less tolerant eardrums, establishments such as *Tanz-Club*, *Tanz-Café*, or *Jazz-Club* may be more suitable.

Berlin and Hamburg are famous for providing opportunities for new groups and acts (it wasn't only The Beatles who made their name here). One place worthy of special mention is the Tiger Palast Club in Frankfurt (💻 www.tigerpalast.de), a successful combination of nightclub, circus and variety show. **Be warned that many such establishments have smoky atmospheres.**

Discos are very much part of youth culture in Germany, where the usual fare includes pounding techno music (Germany is its spiritual home) played at deafening volume. Many discos are selective about who they admit (unless business is slow), especially those with a fashionable reputation such as the P1 in Munich, where you must be either 'famous' or conform to a rigid (often outrageous) dress code to get past the doorman. Discos generally don't admit people under 18 after midnight and may ask them to leave (even if accompanied by adults) after that time. Places that cater only to teenagers aren't allowed to serve alcohol (although beer isn't reckoned to be an alcoholic drink in Bavaria!). Youth discos open as early as 7pm and generally close at midnight, while those targeted at adults often don't get going until midnight and close between 1 and 3am. The admission fee to discos (and other nightclubs) is usually from €4 to €10, although it can sometimes be as much as €20, which may include a 'free' drink or two, or there may be a minimum drink purchase. **Some clubs offer free entry, but drinks can be very expensive.** German discos are listed on 💻 www.discolist.de.

Germany is one of the world's more tolerant countries as far as homosexuality is concerned and most cities have thriving gay scenes. For listings of gay men's clubs consult *Gab Magazin*, a monthly magazine, while both gay and lesbian establishments are listed on 💻 www.die-andere-welt.de and can be found through the Lesben und Schwulenverband in Deutschland (LSDV) (Pipinstrasse 7, 50667 Cologne ☎ 0221-925 9610 💻 http://typo3.lsvd.de).

CASINOS & GAMBLING

Most states have at least one licensed casino, many of which are situated in spa towns. The casino (*Spielbank*) and spa combination is a centuries-old tradition in Germany, where resorts such as Baden-Baden (established 1810), Bad Homburg and Wiesbaden have achieved huge popularity, though casino clientele is much changed from the elite crowd that used to frequent Baden-Baden and Wiesbaden in the 19th century. Nowadays you can expect to find punters in casual dress and even wearing T-shirts and shorts during the afternoon. However, most casinos insist on formal attire in the evening or at the very least a collar and tie for men and a dress for women. All the usual temptations to part with your money are on offer, including roulette, blackjack, poker and craps, plus an endless array of slot machines. Most casinos have a high maximum stake and, if Lady Luck is with you, 'breaking the bank' is still a (remote) possibility – though, of course, you're far more likely to lose your shirt.

There's a nominal entrance fee of around €5 and you must show your passport or identity card.

Perhaps surprisingly, most gambling outside casinos is illegal. Among the few exceptions are the state and national lotteries, and slot machines limited to a small maximum pay-out per game. Sadly, the latter seem to be among the most addictive form of gambling in the world and no matter what initiatives are taken by the authorities (short of outlawing them), they're responsible for an increasingly large number of compulsive gamblers. State lotteries donate around half their profits to charities or community programmes (e.g. *Aktion Sorgenkind*, which funds programmes for mentally and physically disabled children) and pay out the other half in winnings.

The only other legal way to gamble in Germany is on horse races, where bets are accepted at courses and through the (government-controlled) national lottery outlets. Horseracing includes both trotting (the most popular form) and flat racing, most medium and large cities having at least one racetrack.

BARS & PUBS

There's at least one bar (*Bierlokal*) or inn (*Gasthof*) in every town and most villages in Germany, although they can be rather seedy establishments. If you're looking for a place with a bit of class, you should seek out a *Gaststätte* (called a *Kneipe* in some regions), which may open as early as 10am and close well after midnight – they must usually close by 2am, although *Kneipen* in Berlin must close for only one hour in every 24 hours for cleaning (and most are to be avoided)! While some are purely drinking establishments, others offer a variety of fairly basic, traditional dishes.

Irish-style pubs offering Guinness and other Irish beers are also common throughout Germany; to find one in your city go to 💻 www.irishpubs.hitsites.de. These establishments have almost a cult following and often offer live music. Darts can be played at many British and Irish pubs in Germany.

Southern Germany has a wealth of traditional beer halls known variously as a *Brauereikeller*, *Brauerei* or *Bierkeller*, where food is often served and consumption is often accompanied by a brass band (and possibly dancing if you can still stand). In many Bavarian beer gardens you're permitted to bring your own food and you're usually required to pay a deposit on your glass. As you will quickly learn, drinking toasts are extremely popular in Germany (too popular for some tastes), especially in beer halls and festivals, where the band invokes them by playing the *Prosit* song every three minutes (a sneaky trick to make you consume more beer). Toasting requires proper etiquette, which Germans are only too happy to teach you. The basic technique is as follows:

● When you get your drink, you must clink glasses with everyone within reach, while looking each individual in the eye, and say *Prost* or *zum Wohl*; do so whenever a new person comes to the table and gets a drink or simply whenever you feel like it. If you cannot reach someone, make eye contact and nod before drinking.

- Be sure not to 'cross glasses' with others, which is considered bad luck.

- In some regions you should bang the beer mat with your glass once before drinking.

- Never toast with water!

The main draught beer served in a bar or pub varies with the region but will generally be of one of the following varieties: *Pils* (Pilsen style), *Weizenbier* (wheat beer, mostly in Bavaria), *Berliner Weissbier* or *Kölsch* (Cologne style). Most bars have only one kind of beer on draught but a variety of bottled beers. In Bavaria, there are some beers that are served only at certain times of the year, such as around Christmas. One such beer is *Starkbier* (strong beer), which has an alcohol content of as much as 25 per cent, and needless to say, should be drunk very slowly. If you're a real beer fan, you may wish to visit the Brewery Museum in Cologne or, better still, a brewery (most of which offer private tours, including free tastings).

Bars also serve a variety of other drinks, including soft drinks, wine, spirits, champagne or German sparkling wine (*Sekt*) and the usual assortment of cocktails, although the prices of these can be astronomical. The wine list varies with the bar and the region, local wines usually predominating. In wine-growing areas (but rarely elsewhere) there are wine bars (*Weinstuben*) and cellars (*Weinkeller*).

When in Frankfurt you can hop aboard the Apple Wine Express, a vintage tram that winds through the city streets on weekends and public holidays. Apple wine (cider) is a Frankfurt tradition and the celebrated drink is produced only in a limited number of centuries-old, family-run establishments. Apple wine (called *Ebbelwei* in the local dialect), served in a blue-and-grey pottery jug called a *Bembel*, is made from a mixture of apples, water, sugar and yeast, and the cloudy, alcohol-rich result can make your head hurt for days if you drink too much. Apple wine pubs (*Apfelweinwirtschaft*) can be found throughout the old district of Sachsenhausen in Frankfurt, where customers sit outdoors at long wooden tables and toast each other with their apple wine glasses (known as a *Schobbeglas*). Those in the know order cheese in vinaigrette as an accompaniment.

German bartenders rarely demand payment after every drink, but note each drink on your beer mat, with the possible exception of popular tourist haunts and Irish and other 'foreign' pubs. Most bars close on one day of the week (*Ruhetag*), which is noted on a sign on the door. Most German bars will become smoke free by 2008.

You'll usually find at least one local newspaper and perhaps also a regional one in bars for customers to read. Card playing is permitted (although not if it involves gambling) as well as chess and draughts/checkers (boards are provided in many places). A popular card game is *Skat*, a three-player, 32-card game, which is an institution in Germany, where *Skat* clubs abound.

In most establishments there's a table reserved for regular customers called the *Stammtisch* – the locals may be upset if an outsider dares sit there, which particularly applies in Bavaria, where foreigners include everybody but locals.

CAFES

Cafes (*Café*) don't usually serve many alcoholic drinks, with the possible exception of sparkling wine and two or three beers. Instead, they offer a good selection of coffees, including iced versions, and teas. An establishment offering a wide range of fine cakes and pastries may be called a *Cafékonditorei*, while one specialising in ice cream, an *Eiscafé*. Usually you must go to the counter to choose your cake or pastry, which will then be served with the rest of your order. Snacks are available and usually include salads, homemade soups and simple toasted sandwiches, although you shouldn't expect much beyond this.

Cafes are an institution throughout Germany. They aren't simply a place to grab a cup of coffee or a bite to eat, but are meeting places, shelters, sun lounges, somewhere to make friends, talk, write, do business, study, read a newspaper or just watch the world go by. Germans spend a lot of time in cafes, perhaps nursing a single drink, and nobody will usually rush you to finish, unless it's the height of the tourist season and people are waiting for tables. Some are elegant places, visited as a Sunday outing. Some have a pianist or other entertainment and most (like bars) provide free newspapers for customers and possibly also a few magazines. Cafes generally close one day a week.

RESTAURANTS

The only field in which complete multicultural integration has been achieved in Germany is in its restaurants. No matter what cuisine you fancy, whether it's Chinese, Greek, Indian, Italian, Japanese, Spanish, Thai, Turkish, Yugoslavian or Vietnamese, you should be able to find it somewhere in the major cities. The quality varies widely, from Michelin-starred *haute cuisine* to fast food at its direst. Prices are comparable with those in other central European countries and service is generally good (and seldom provided by Germans).

Germany isn't noted for its food, though it isn't exactly a gastronomic wasteland, and, with the proliferation of ethnic restaurants, it has become increasingly difficult to find places offering traditional German cuisine. They do exist, however, and are well worth seeking out. Sausage (*Wurst*) is the most popular (virtually the national) dish in Germany, where it's possible to eat a different variety every day for more than four years. There are sausages made from beef, pork, veal or a combination of these, in a plethora of recipes. *Wurst* is usually accompanied by *Sauerkraut* (fermented cabbage cooked with apple, sometimes – in the cheaper varieties – with wine added to speed up the fermentation process), hot or cold potato salad, or dumplings.

Germany also boasts a number of regional specialities, and there are many books on German regional cuisine. In Bavaria a popular dish is leg of pork stuffed with red pepper, assorted minced meats and breadcrumbs; Berlin has its *Berliner Leber* (veal liver cooked with apples and onions); a Bremen speciality is chicken casserole simmered in cream, cognac and white wine; Frankfurt has its *Rippchen mit Kraut* (thick, salted pork chops, boiled in water, cooked with juniper berries and served with sauerkraut); Mecklenburg offers breast of duck with carrots and apples (flavoured with butter, pepper, sugar and marjoram); a Hamburg speciality is *Aalsuppe* (eel soup, with plums and vegetables); Saarland is noted for its rabbit cooked in red wine and garlic; Swabia for its sliced veal with cream sauce, served with noodles flavoured with juniper berries; and Thuringia is famous for its sauerkraut rice and sausage slices with onions, apple wine and paprika.

Germany isn't exactly a Shangri-la for vegetarians, but meat-free alternatives can be found. Among the best bets are Chinese restaurants (a *Buddhaplatter* is simply vegetables and rice) or Indian restaurants (where many rice dishes are served without meat, and vegetable curry is a favourite). Salad bars can be found at cafeterias in department stores and also at fancy hotels offering over-priced Sunday brunches. In fact, there's usually at least one meat-free dish on the menu at any German restaurant, although the quality is variable and most options are heavy on potatoes. True vegetarian restaurants are few and far between, although they do exist. If you don't have a restaurant guide, you can ask at a health food shop (*Reformhaus*) whether there are any vegetarian restaurants in the area. If you eat fish, you can get fish salads and sandwiches at the Nordsee fast food chain, but fresh fish isn't a regular item on the average German menu.

Restaurants are required to display their menu and price list outside the main entrance, so that you can see what's on offer and the price (which includes tax and service) before entering. You can buy a filling meal for around €10 at ethnic restaurants or by choosing the set menu of the day (see below), but for a good meal with wine you should be prepared to pay at least €20 per head.

Don't expect to be shown to a seat; you must find your own. In a busy restaurant in Bavaria, it's common for strangers to share tables and you shouldn't be surprised if someone asks to join you at your table. **Many restaurants allow dogs and it's common for customers to bring their dogs with them.**

A menu is called a *Karte* or *Speisekarte*, while a *Menü* (or *Tagesmenü*) is a set meal. Wine lists (*Weinkarten*) range from a few local house wines to the best French vintages at astronomical prices, but most good restaurants offer a selection of wines from around the world. Water isn't provided unless you ask for it and generally only sparkling mineral water is available (and charged to your bill). Bread is included only if stated on the menu; if you request it as an extra, it will also be added to your bill.

Note also the following regarding restaurants in Germany:

- Don't be surprised if you're presented with the bill (*Rechnung*) halfway through the meal, as this is common practice when staff are changing shifts, when the waiter (addressed as *Herr Ober* or *Fräulein* – Germans are **extremely** sexist) must balance his account.

- Tipping (*Trinkgeld*) isn't a big thing in Germany and you don't need to feel uncomfortable if you haven't got any change or just a few small coins; tips aren't a waiter's wages, but are considered a 'thank you' for a job well done.

- Many restaurants have a separate room that's provided free of charge for social functions, provided the participants book (you cannot just turn up with a party) and order plenty of drinks.

- Most restaurants close one day a week (*Ruhetag*), which is shown by a sign on the door.

- The best restaurant guides for Germany include the *Michelin Red Hotel and Restaurant Guide: Germany*, the *Schlemmer Atlas* and *Marcellino's Restaurant Report*.

FOREST HUTS & RECREATION AREAS

Most towns own a recreation area and/or a forest hut, which can be hired for a nominal fee for private parties and social functions. The actual fee depends on the amenities and services provided with the hut, which may include running water, toilets, electricity, basic appliances, and possibly beer mugs, glasses, cookery utensils and cutlery. Forest huts are excellent for those planning to throw a big party. You can build a log fire to keep warm and add to the atmosphere, you don't have to worry about spilled food and drinks on your carpet, and you can pump up the music as loud as your speakers (or eardrums) will stand. Anything short of burning down the hut is acceptable, but the bad news is that you must clean up the mess the next day or pay someone to do it. There are companies that specialise in catering for such outdoor parties, although this obviously adds considerably to the cost. Bear in mind that you must book months in advance, as almost everybody in town will want to organise an event there at some time, be it a birthday party or an office function.

LIBRARIES

Most towns have a public library and those that don't are usually served by a mobile library (*Bibliothek auf Rädern*), which also accepts orders from catalogues. Library opening times vary considerably and can be anywhere between 8am and 10pm Mondays to Fridays, and between 8am and noon on Saturdays. Many smaller libraries open only one or two days a week and are closed throughout the school holidays, while major libraries open six (or even seven) days a week. Most libraries offer CDs, DVDs and videos in addition to books. Generally there's a membership fee of €3 to €10 (costs are climbing fast) for those wishing to borrow books and you must show proof of residence to obtain a library card. In addition to public libraries, most school and university libraries are open to the public.

German libraries usually have a selection of books in foreign languages, including English, French, Italian and Spanish. In Munich, the Amerika Haus service (🖥 www.amerikahaus.de), a branch of the United States Information Service or USIS, and in Heidelberg the Deutsch-Amerikanische Institut (🖥 www .dai-heidelberg.de) provide an extensive English-language library complete with a reference section.

EVENING CLASSES

An inexpensive way to learn German or another language in Germany is at the people's high school (*Volkshochschule*), which originated in the early 20th century as popular education institution for the 'masses'. Schools were sponsored by left-wing political parties, including the Social Democrats, in a similar way to Workers' Educational Association (WEA) courses in the UK, though today they're government-run.

Volkshochschulen (*VHS*) offer courses in almost every imaginable subject, from basic basket weaving to offshore sailing. They run one-day seminars on topics such as tenants' rights and weekend courses on how to repair your bicycle. The most popular courses are foreign languages, but psychology, computers, health and 'new age' subjects are also widely available, some of which may have waiting lists. Course fees seldom exceed €200 per term, plus the cost of books and other course materials.

Each *VHS* publishes a course catalogue, many running to hundreds of pages, which are usually distributed free (but sometimes for a nominal fee) via bookshops and municipal buildings. There are three ways to enrol: in person at a *VHS*, by post or online (at 🖥 www.vhs.de). Enrolment periods and availability vary greatly. Places are limited, so you should book early. Some *VHS* courses offer an official certificate (e.g. in German proficiency) or a high school diploma; others are just for fun.

Private schools are less popular, probably because most Germans don't think that the quality of instruction justifies the generally high fees. Those that exist mostly survive thanks to government contracts and company clients such as international banks.

16.

SPORTS

Germany was largely responsible for sport's role in modern society, with the introduction of gymnastics into schools during the Napoleonic wars as a means of pre-military training and the development of a physical culture (*Körperkultur*) in the 19th century. In modern times, few regimes have attempted to exploit sport as a means of gaining international prestige as much as those of the Nazis and communist East Germany (although Hitler's 'Aryan' 1936 Berlin Olympic Games famously came unstuck when black American sprinter James 'Jesse' Owens won four gold medals).

Although not as successful as the East Germany of pre-unification days, which was a (drug-fuelled) superpower in world sports, the united Germany remains a force to be reckoned with. The most widely practised sports include football, tennis, gymnastics and shooting, while athletics, handball, table-tennis, horse riding, skiing and swimming are also popular. Hiking, cycling, hockey (including ice), basketball, squash, motor sports, watersports and aerial sports have many dedicated practitioners and followers.

Responsibility for sport is shared between the federal authorities, the states and the municipalities, the last being responsible for providing sports facilities. Most towns have a public municipal sports and leisure centre with a host of sports facilities, including a fitness centre. Facilities are excellent in the western states, although not so good in the eastern states, where sport was formerly an elitist pursuit. Participation in and spectating of some sports is expensive, but costs can be reduced through the purchase of season tickets or by joining a club.

The Germans are sports-crazy, as participants and spectators, and their enthusiasm is second to none (a number of TV stations are devoted solely to sports). Almost every sport is organised and performed somewhere in Germany, where there are almost 90,000 sports clubs (*Sportsvereine*) affiliated to the German Sports Federation (Deutschen Olympischen Sportbund/DOSB), which has 16 regional federations and numerous associated sports groups. Around one-third of all Germans (over 27m) are members of a sporting club, while a further 10m people enjoy sports activities outside formal clubs. Unlike those in many other countries, such as the UK and the US, German schools and universities don't compete against each other in inter-school/college sports competitions, and the main nurseries for professional sports in Germany are amateur club competitions.

The DOSB sponsors physical fitness programmes such as the long-running *Trim dich* (literally 'trim yourself') campaign and 'sport for everybody' (*Sport für Jedermann*), which has encouraged millions of Germans to abandon their TVs and take up active sports. Jogging paths and work-out areas abound throughout the country to assist in these aims, and the DOSB awards bronze, silver and gold 'badges', known as *Deutsche Sportabzeichen* (around 750,000 annually), to qualifying amateur sportsmen and women.

Various publications are available from tourist offices promoting sports events and listing local sports venues. Most states and cities publish comprehensive booklets listing local sports organisations, facilities and classes. The addresses of national and state sports associations in Germany can be obtained from the

DOSB, Otto Fleck-Schneise, 12, D-60528 Frankfurt (☎ 060-67000, 🖵 www. dosb.de), which also publishes a yearbook of sports (*Jahrbuch des Sports*). The yearbook, which contains almost 700 pages, is obtainable for around €20 (plus postage) from the Schors-Verlags-Gesellschaft, Schöne Aussicht 16, 65527 Niedernhausen, ☎ 06127-8029.

AERIAL SPORTS

Germany has many areas that are ideal for aerial sports, particularly gliding, hang-gliding, paragliding and hot-air ballooning. The Alps are a favourite spot due to the updraughts and the low density of air traffic (apart from all the gliders, hang-gliders and balloons!). Hang-gliding (*Drachenfliegen*) is especially popular in Germany, which has many schools, as is paragliding (*Gleitschirmfliegen*), which entails jumping off steep mountain slopes dangling from a parachute. Participants must have the proper equipment and complete an approved course of instruction, after which (if they survive) they receive a proficiency certificate and are permitted to go solo.

Ballooning has a small but dedicated band of followers. Balloon ownership is generally limited to the wealthy, but a ballon trip can be had for around €180 per trip. There is, however, no guarantee of distance or duration, and trips are dependent on wind conditions and the skill of your pilot. More information can be found on 🖵 www.ballonfahrten.de.

Light aircraft (including microlights) and gliders (sailplanes) can be hired with an instructor or (if you have a pilot's licence) without from most small airfields in Germany, where there are also many gliding clubs.

Free-fall parachuting (sky-diving) flights can be made from most private airfields, costing around €180-200 per jump (€450 for three jumps – if you think you'll survive the first two), including equipment. For further information, visit 🖵 www.tandemfun.de.

Further information about aerial sports is available from the German Aero Club (Deutsche Aero Club, Bundesgeschaeftsstelle, Hermann-Blenk-Str. 28, 38108 Braunschweig (☎ 0531-235400, 🖵 www.daec.de).

Before taking up the above sports, you're advised to make sure that you have adequate health, accident and life insurance and that your affairs are in order. Why not try fishing instead?

CYCLING

Cycling (*Radfahren*) is popular in Germany, not only as a means of transport and as a serious sport, but also as a relaxing pastime for the whole family. The country has over 170 long-distance cycling tracks totalling over 40,000km (25,000mi), forestry tracks (*Forstwege*), city cycling trails and tourist routes. Maps of scenic bike routes and suggested itineraries for bike trips can be obtained from the Allgemeiner Deutscher Fahrrad-Club (see below). Cycling maps (*Radwanderführer*) are published by Kompass.

Cycle racing has a huge following and races are organised at every level, including mountain-bike races. Germany has a good record in international racing, particularly track racing, though the world's premier cycle race, the Tour de France, has only once been won by a German, Jan Ullrich, in 1997.

Cyclists must use cycle lanes where provided and mustn't cycle in bus lanes or on footpaths. As required by law, German motorists generally give cyclists a wide berth when overtaking, but cycling in some major cities is still dangerous. If you cycle in cities, you should wear reflective clothing, protective headgear, a smog mask and a crucifix. **You must also take care not to get your wheels stuck in tram or railway lines.**

Bikes must be roadworthy and be fitted with a horn or bell and front and rear lights. They should also be fitted with an anti-theft device such as a steel cable lock (the only police-approved bike lock), although they're still not thief-proof. If your bicycle is stolen you should report it to the local police – but don't expect them to find it! Some insurance companies cover bicycle theft.

You can hire a bike from railway stations participating in the 'Call-A-Bike' scheme operated by Deutsche Bahn (see **Bicycles** on page 196). For other bike hire companies, look in the yellow pages under *Fahrradverleih*.

There are a number of cycling organisations in Germany, including the Allgemeiner Deutscher Fahrrad-Club (ADFC), Bundesgeschäftsstelle, Postfach 10 77 47, D-28077 Bremen (☎ 0421-346290, 💻 www.adfc.de), which publishes a free brochure, *Discovering Germany by Bicycle*, and the Bund Deutscher Radfahrer, Otto-Fleck-Schneise 4, D-60528 Frankfurt (☎ 069-9678 000, 💻 www.rad-net.de).

FISHING

Fishing (*Angeln*) is very popular in Germany, which has an abundance of well stocked waters. However, there are no free fishing waters in Germany (apart from the sea), as all inland water belongs to the state, private individuals or fishing clubs, and you must buy a licence and, if applicable, pay the owner of a stream, river, pond or lake a fee. A daily permit (*Tageskarte*) can be purchased for between around €5 and €20 for most waters, although some of the most famous and productive locations can cost as much as €60 per day.

German residents must complete months of instruction on fish habitat, biology, regulations and general knowledge and pass a test costing around €200 before they can become licensed anglers. They receive a certification card (*Fischereischein*), costing €10 to €15 per year. Non-residents aren't required to take a test but must have an appopriate fishing 'qualification' to obtain (from local tourist offices) a temporary licence to fish in Germany. Each state has different prices and different rules, e.g. a three-month licence for Bavaria costs around €15.

Germany's main sport fish are trout (rainbow, brown, brook), grayling and carp. Fishing for brown trout and grayling is popular in the mountain streams in the south, where Bavaria offers the best opportunities for fly fishing. The trout season usually runs from 1st May to the end of October, although in some waters the dates vary from year to year. There are strict regulations regarding the season, minimum size of catch and the number of fish that can be caught. For more information contact the Federation of German Sport Anglers (Verband der Deutscher Sportfischer, Siemensstr. 11-13, D-63071 Offenbach, ☎ 069-855006, 🖥 www.vdsf.de). The Landesfischereiverband Bayern (Pechdellerstr. 16, D-81545 Munich, ☎ 089-6427260, 🖥 www.lfvbayern.de) publishes a fishing guide for Bavaria entitled *Angelführer Bayern*. Angling competitions are organised in many areas.

Deep-sea fishing is possible in the North Sea and Baltic off Germany's northern coast, where boats can be hired from many ports.

FOOTBALL

Football or soccer (*Fussball*) is Germany's unofficial national sport, with literally thousands of amateur football clubs, and it's one of the most successful nations in the world at both club and international level. Germany has won the World Cup three times, in 1954, 1974 and 1990 (only Brazil and Italy have won it more often) and was the runner-up in 1966, 1982, 1986 and 2002; it has also won the European Championship three times, in 1972, 1980 and 1996. Germany hosted the World Cup in 2006 and finished third.

Like that of certain other nations, the national team is suffering from the large number of foreign players in its domestic league, which hinders the progress of home-grown talent. Conversely, many top German players play abroad – mostly in Italy but increasingly in the UK – which has affected the performance of top club teams in European competition, although German football clubs have a long and distinguished record here. Though not quite as rabid as Italian or Spanish fans, German fans can become rowdy, although it's generally safe to take your family to a football match.

The federal football league (*Bundesliga*) is Germany's premier competition, comprising 18 teams, among which the top dogs in recent years have included Bayern Munich, Borussia Dortmund, Bayer Leverkusen, Hamburg SV, Werder Bremen, FC Köln, FC Kaiserslauten and VfB Stuttgart. Bayern Munich (who play at the Allianz Arena in Munich) are Germany's most successful club side, but the current champions are Stuttgart. If you want to discover more or find details of forthcoming games, go to the *Bundesliga* website (🖥 http://bundesliga.de).

The football season runs from September to Christmas and mid-February to June (there's a mid-winter break), with most matches played on Saturday afternoons (although they're also played on Fridays and Sundays) and attended by an average of around 25,000 spectators. German cup (DFB) matches are usually played during the week, as are European competition matches. Tickets can usually be purchased at grounds on the day of matches or from ticket offices, and cost from around €15 for standing places (*Stehplätze*) and from €20 for seats. Tickets for big matches and internationals cost at least €50.

Almost every village or town has a football club, and there are local leagues throughout Germany. For local details and more information about the game as a whole, contact the Deutscher Fussball-Bund, Otto-Fleck-Schneise 6, D-60528 Frankfurt (☎ 069-67880, 💻 www.dfb.de).

GOLF

Although traditionally an elitist sport in Germany, golf (*Golf*) has enjoyed increasing popularity in the last decade, boosted by the success of Bernhard Langer, who has been in the top ranks of world golf for some 20 years. The country now boasts over 500 clubs with over 300,000 members, numbers that have increased by well over 70 per cent during the last ten years. However, most are private clubs with long waiting lists for membership and there are very few public golf courses in Germany. Club information is available on the internet (💻 www.golfeurope.com/euro_clubs/germany.htm). Most clubs admit non-members with a handicap card for a fee of around €25 per round during the week and €50 at weekends and on public holidays.

Three major golf tournaments are held in Germany annually: the BMW International Open (in Munich), the Deutschebank Players Championship of Europe and the Mercedes-Benz Championship (previously known as Linde German Masters). The Golf World Championship was held in Germany (Berlin) in 2000 for the first time.

For more information contact the German Golf Federation (Deutscher Golf-Verband, Viktoriastr. 16, D-65189 Wiesbaden, ☎ 0611-990200, 💻 www.golf.de).

HEALTH CLUBS

There are gymnasiums and health and fitness clubs (*Fitnessstudio*) in most towns in Germany. 'Working out' is becoming increasingly popular and many companies provide health and leisure centres or pay for corporate membership of private clubs for staff. In addition, most public sports centres have tonnes of expensive bone-jarring, muscle-wrenching apparatus. (Find out where the nearest hospital is before hiring any.)

To join a club, you must usually pay an initial fee, which ranges from €100 to €400 depending on the cachet of the club and the type of membership chosen, and then a monthly fee of €50 to €100. Normally, the higher the initial sum paid, the lower your monthly fee. You can reduce the fee by opting to use the facilities only during off-peak times, for example during the mornings or before 5pm.

In addition to gymnasiums, most clubs offer aerobics and keep-fit classes, a sauna and/or Jacuzzi and a swimming pool, and some also have tennis, squash and badminton courts (for which an additional fee is payable, depending on your membership). Other facilities may include a beauty salon (offering massage and aromatherapy) or spa area, and child care (usually from one year of age). Clubs allow you to buy a daily card (from around €20 to €40) or take a 'sniff' (*Schnupper*) day to assess whether you want to join. Clubs usually provide free personal training programmes for members.

Many top-class hotels have health clubs and swimming pools that are open to the public, although access to facilities may be restricted to certain times.

HIKING

Germans are keen hikers. Although the main hiking season is from around May to September, hiking isn't just a summer sport and most winter sports resorts keep trails open for walkers throughout the winter. Germany is a great hiking (*Wandern*) country, with over 100,000km (62,000mi) of marked hiking and mountain-walking tracks administered by regional hiking clubs (*Wandervereine*) and mountaineering groups. It has a national network of paths with routes of various degrees of difficulty, although most are fairly easy. Hikes take in romantic forests, beautiful landscapes and tranquil lakes, and most pass through picturesque villages where there's usually somewhere you can make an overnight stop.

Germany has some of the most beautiful hiking country in Europe, but the terrain isn't usually as rugged as in some other countries such as France or Spain. The most popular hiking areas are Bavaria and the *Schwarzwald* (Black Forest – the world's most famous forest, although it's actually the usual shades of green!), stretching from the resort town of Baden-Baden to the Swiss border. Other popular hiking areas include the Erzgebirge, the Thuringian Forest, the Harz Mountains, the Sauerland, the Rhön, the Fichtelgebirge and the Swabian mountains. Those who feel up to it may wish to try the challenging 60km (37mi) 'Allgäu high-level' route between Oberstdorf and the Oberjoch in the Alps, staying overnight in forest huts. Less ambitious are the organised 'social' hikes (*Volksmarsch*), usually of not more than 42km (26mi), which attract huge numbers of participants, who usually receive a certificate, badge or medal for making it to the end.

Those who are keen on Alpine walking should contact the German Alpine Association (Deutsche Alpenverein, Vohn-Kahr-Str. 2-4, D-80997 Munich, ☎ 089-140 030, 🖳 www.alpenverein.de), which maintains around 15,000km (over 9,000mi) of Alpine paths and some 50 mountain huts. It can provide courses in mountaineering and touring suggestions for both summer and winter routes, while a number of mountaineering schools offer courses ranging from basic techniques for beginners to advanced mountaineering. Mountain walking shouldn't be confused with hiking as it's generally done at much higher altitudes and in more difficult terrain. It's dangerous for the untrained and should be approached with much the same degree of caution and preparation as mountaineering.

Free hiking maps are available from tourist offices, although the best hiking maps (*Wanderkarten*) are the *Wanderführer* series published by Kompass. For more information contact the Federation of German Mountain and Hiking Clubs (Verband Deutscher Gebirgs- und Wandervereine, Wilhelmshöher Allee 157-159, D-34121 Kassel, ☎ 0561-938 730, 💻 www.wanderverband.de), the German People's Sports Federation (Deutscher Volkssportverband e.V, Fabrikstr. 8, D-845503 Altötting, ☎ 08671-96310, 💻 www.dw-wandern.de) or the Federation of German Ski and Mountain Guides (Verband Deutscher Ski und Bergführer, Untersbergstrasse 34, 83451 Piding, ☎ 08651-71221, 💻 www.berg fuehrer-verband.de).

RACKET SPORTS

Tennis (*Tennis*) is the second most popular participation sport in Germany (after football) and the German Tennis Association (Deutsche Tennis Bund) has over 2m members and the largest club network of any country, with over 10,000 tennis clubs, some 50,000 outdoor courts and more than 4,000 indoor courts. Tennis has flourished in Germany in the last few decades thanks to the success of stars such as Boris Becker, Steffi Graf, Michael Stich (all Grand Slam event winners) and Anke Huber. Prior to the success of Becker and Graf, tennis was considered an upper-class sport, although it's now played by people from all backgrounds.

Many towns have public courts (although they aren't as common as in many other countries), where you can book a court by the hour. Most courts are clay or Astroturf (artificial grass); hard (asphalt) and grass courts are rare in Germany. When playing on an indoor court you must wear shoes with non-marking soles – if you don't have any, they can usually be purchased or hired. Court fees vary from €15 to €30 per hour, depending on the season, day of the week and the time of day (they're usually cheaper before 5pm on weekdays), indoor courts being more expensive than outdoor courts. Local courts and clubs are listed in the yellow pages under *Tenniscenter* and *Sportanlagen*.

Germany stages a number of professional tournaments annually, among them the German Open in Hamburg (May), the BMW Tennis Open in Munich (April/May) and the Mercedes Cup in Stuttgart (July). Top German and foreign tennis players compete in the Federal Tennis League. For more information, contact the German Tennis Federation (Deutscher Tennis Bund, Hallerstr. 89, D-20149 Hamburg, ☎ 040-411780, 💻 www.dtb-tennis.de).

Squash and badminton are popular in Germany, although the country has yet to make any big waves in either sport. This could have something to do with the cost of playing: squash courts cost between €15 and €30 for 45 minutes, while badminton courts cost between €20 and €30 per hour, courts generally being cheaper before 5pm.

SKIING

Millions of Germans ski (*skifahren*, *skilaufen* or *schifahren/laufen*) regularly, although the majority head to neighbouring countries. Germany doesn't have many large ski centres and most are small, long-established resorts with 'traditional' lift systems. Where there are a number of nearby ski centres, you may be able to buy a pass covering all of them (although they're rarely linked by ski-lifts), sometimes including centres in Austria. German resorts are noted for their traditional architecture and the country doesn't go in for the purpose-built (i.e. concrete) resorts such as are common in France. Most resorts offer good *après-ski* and many have excellent facilities for other sports, including indoor swimming pools.

The Alps of southern Bavaria are Germany's main winter sports region, where Garmisch-Partenkirchen (720-2,966m/2,362-9,730ft) and Oberstdorf (700-2,224m/ 2,296-7,296ft) are the top resorts, both regular venues on the World Cup downhill circuit. Other Alpine resorts, suitable mainly for beginners and moderate skiers, include Bayrischzell, Berchtesgaden, Mittenwald and Schliersee. As an alternative to the Alps, you can ski in the Allgäu, Black Forest (*Schwarzwald*), Erzgebirge, Fichtelgebirge, Harz, Rhön, Sauerland (a cross-country paradise), Swabian mountains and the Thuringian Forest, although many resorts have just a few downhill (*Alpin*) runs or offer only cross-country (*Langlauf*) skiing. Among the most popular resorts outside the Alps are the Black Forest resorts of Furtwangen, Schonach, Todtmoos and Todtnau. The upper Harz (Hochharz) is also noted for its excellent cross-country skiing and ski hikes.

The skiing season runs from the middle of December to the end of March, although at higher altitudes such as the Zugspitze glacier near Garmisch (up to 2,830m/8,490ft), you can often ski from November until the middle of May.

Lift passes are fairly pricey, costing between around €14 and €37 for an adult for a day (€11-€23 for a child) and almost twice as much for two days. At the tope of these ranges is the Garmisch-Partenkirchen ski pass, which is valid for 28 lifts and provides access to 55km (34mi) of ski terrain, including the world famous ski runs of Kandahar and Olympia (both of which have snow-making equipment). Here, a five-day 'happy ski card', for the area around the Zugspitze, costs €142 for adults (€85 for children). Family passes (two adults and two children) are available in most resorts, costing from around €65 for one day. Off-season or 'white week' (*weisse Woche*) rates are offered by most winter resorts for cross-country and downhill holidays, which include bed and breakfast or half board plus ski lessons. Equipment (skis, poles and boots) can be hired for around €15 per day.

The ADAC motoring organisation (see page 247) provides a recorded 'snow conditions' telephone service for most regions. For further information about skiing in Germany, contact the German Skiing Federation (Deutscher Skiverband, Hubertusstr. 1, D-82152 Munich-Planegg, ☎ 089-857900, 🖳 www.ski-online.de).

SWIMMING

Swimming (*Schwimmen*) is very popular in Germany, where an estimated two-thirds of the population swim regularly. There are outdoor pools (*Freibad*) and indoor pools (*Hallenbad*) in most German towns and resorts, many open year-round. However, admission fees have been increased and the opening hours of many pools reduced in recent years. Swimming hats may be required at some pools and are usually sold at reception. There are a number of large indoor swimming centres and aquatic and water parks in Germany where the facilities may include hot-water pools, sulphur baths, thermal whirlpools, connecting indoor and outdoor pools, wave machines, huge water slides, solariums and saunas (many mixed sex). The entrance fee is high, e.g. €15 to €30, usually for a limited period, although they make a pleasant change from an ordinary pool. Spas (see page 259) throughout Germany have thermal or mineral-water indoor pools where day visitors can swim or relax in the water.

Germans are keen on nude bathing and many pools have days or times restricted to nude bathers; nudity is also permitted on certain beaches, shown by a sign reading '*FKK*' (for *Freiekörperkultur*). There are indoor sea-water pools in coastal areas and many lakes have swimming areas which are off-limits to other water-sport enthusiasts. Swimming in rivers, particularly the larger ones, isn't recommended and in some cases is prohibited ('*Baden verboten*'), due to shipping, pollution or dangerous currents.

Most swimming pools and clubs organise swimming lessons for all levels and run life saving courses. Children can join a swimming team (*Schwimmverband*) at a local pool that competes against other teams (competitions are organised by *Schwimmvereine*). For more information, contact your local swimming club or visit 🖳 www.dsv.de.

You can find a list of public swimming pools in your local area under *Freizeit-, Hallen- und Freibäder* in the journal section of the yellow pages. For further information, contact the German Swimming Association (Deutscher Schwimmverband, Korbacherstr. 93, D-34132 Kassel, (☎ 0561-940830, 🖳 www.dsv.de).

WATERSPORTS

All watersports, including sailing, motor boating, windsurfing, waterskiing, rowing, canoeing and sub-aquatic sports are popular in Germany, which has a good record in world and Olympic competition, particularly rowing and sailing. Boats and equipment can be hired on most lakes and at coastal resorts, where instruction is available for most disciplines. Windsurfing is particularly popular on Bavarian lakes, and rowing and canoeing is possible on most lakes and rivers in the country. Riversurfing has also become a popular sport in Munich on the Eisbach and Floßlände, which have 'standing waves' (rather like the Severn bore); in fact, Munich is one of the few places in the world to hold an annual river surfing competition, the Munich Surf Open. **Wetsuits are recommended for windsurfing, waterskiing and sub-aquatic sports, even during the summer.** A licence is required for a boat with an output of more than 3.6kW (around 5 horsepower).

The North Sea and Baltic coasts are a Mecca for sailors, as are the Bodensee (Lake Constance), Chiemsee, Müritz, Schweriner See and Starberger See (lakes). The most popular rivers are the Danube, Elbe, Main, Neckar, Oder, Rhine, Saale and Weser. There are some 200 sailing schools on the North Sea and Baltic coasts alone, where Kiel and Rostock are the main sailing centres.

For further information about watersports in Germany, contact the appropriate organisation:

- **Canoeing** – Deutsche Kanu-Verband, Bertaallee 8, D-47055 Duisberg (☎ 0203-997590, 💻 www.kanu.de);

- **Motor boating** – Deutscher Motoryachtverband, Vinckeufer 14, D-47119 Duisberg (☎ 0203-809 580, 💻 www.dmyv.de);

- **Rowing** – Deutscher Ruderverband, Ferdinand-Wilhelm-Fricke-Weg 10, D-30169 Hanover (☎ 0511-980940, 💻 www.rudern.de);

- **Sailing** – Deutscher Seglerverband, Gründgensstr. 18, D-22309 Hamburg (☎ 040-6320 090, 💻 www.dsv.org);

- **Waterskiing** – Deutscher Wasserskiverband, Gründgenstr. 18, D-22309 Hamburg (☎ 040-6399 8732, 💻 www.dwsv.de);

- **Windsurfing** – DWSV, Christophstr. 31, 74321 Bietigheim (☎ 07142-918 920, 💻 www.dwsv.net).

OTHER SPORTS & ACTIVITIES

The following is a selection of other popular sports in Germany. In addition to these, many foreign sports and pastimes have a group of expatriate fanatics in Germany, including cricket, American football (NFL exhibition games draw huge crowds), baseball, *boccia*, *boules*, croquet, polo, rounders, rugby football and softball. For more information enquire at community and tourist offices, embassies and consulates (see **Appendix A**).

Athletics

The country has excellent facilities and an excellent record in international competition. Germany stages three Grand Prix athletics meetings in early September – in Berlin, Cologne and Koblenz. Most German towns and villages have athletics clubs and organise local competitions and sports days. For more information, visit the website of the Deutscher Leichtathletik Verband (🖥   www. leichtathletik.de).

Basketball

The top teams participate in the European Clubs Championship. Professional basketball has a strong following, including both domestic and American (NBA) games. For more information, visit the website of the Deutscher Basketball Bund (🖥 www.basketball-bund.de).

Billiards & Snooker

Many hotels, bars and sports clubs have billiard or snooker tables and there are a few billiards clubs in the larger towns. English-style snooker isn't played in clubs in Germany.

Fencing

Germany has traditionally been very strong in international fencing competitions. For more information, visit the website of the Deutscher Fechter Bund (🖥 www. fechten.org).

Gymnastics

There are gymnastics clubs in all areas, even in small towns and villages. For more information, visit the website of the Deutscher Turner-Bund (🖥 www.dtb-online.de).

Handball

Germany is one of the world's top countries in handball terms. handball For more information, visit the website of the Deutscher Handball-Bund (🖥 www.dhb.de).

Hockey

Germany has enjoyed considerable success in world and Olympic competition in hockey (played on grass, not ice). It's equally popular among both sexes. For more information, visit the website of the Deutscher Hockey-Bund (🖥 www. deutscher-hockey-bund.de).

Horse Racing

A popular spectator sport in Germany, where the premier race is the German Derby held in Hamburg in late June, while the spring and autumn meetings at Iffezheim (near Baden-Baden) are fashionable occasions. Trotting is also popular.

Horse Riding

Germany is one of the world's leading equestrian nations, and there's a long tradition of horsemanship. This is usually expressed in competitive sporting terms in the show jumping arena, where Germans are always at or near the top of the rankings. Horse riding for fun is popular but expensive. There are numerous riding schools and equestrian centres (*Reiterhöfe*), although some insist on minimum riding proficiency. Some companies organise cross-country riding holidays, and information about riding excursions (costing around €20 per hour) can be obtained from tourist offices. The leading equestrian events are held in Aachen and Hamburg in June, while famous dressage displays take place in September and October in Celle. For more information, visit the website of the Deutsche Reiterliche Vereinigung (⌨ www.pferd-aktuell.de).

Motor Sports

Motor racing, particularly Formula 1, is extremely popular in Germany, where every kid's idol is the recently retired Michael Schumacher (whose brother Ralf is also a top driver) – even though he drove for the (Italian) Ferrari team. The German Grand Prix is held in August at Hockenheim (near Heidelberg), and the Belgian Grand Prix, a hop across the border at Spa-Francorchamps, is usually dominated by German spectators.

Rollerskating, Skateboarding & BMX

Rinks and circuits are provided in many towns for skateboarding and BMX cycles. Children can start at around seven, but it's difficult to hire equipment other than BMX bikes, as it's too easily stolen. Rollerskating rinks are available in many areas, sometimes using local sports and leisure centres. Skates can be hired and coaching is usually available. Many centres organise roller-discos for teenagers. Many cities organise rollerblade nights, when a few streets are closed to traffic from 8pm so that skaters don't have to dodge BMWs and trams. Keen rollerskaters and rollerbladers often play roller hockey.

Shooting

Rifle and pistol shooting ranges abound in Germany, where most towns and villages have a shooting 'federation' that organises local competitions. Many rifle clubs (*Schützenvereine*) have long traditions, including ceremonies and uniforms, and most have an enthusiastic social side. Crossbow shooting is also popular in Germany.

Many Germans enjoy shooting wild animals, although hunting with dogs isn't practised. There are few restrictions as to what may be shot (apart from other people) but shooters must take both a theory and a practical examination, preceded by a course lasting at least six months.

Ten-pin Bowling

There are ten-pin bowling centres in all major German cities and towns, and nine-pin skittles (*Kegeln*) is often played in rooms adjoining restaurants. *Kegeln* uses smaller balls with no finger-holes, just a large opening for your hand, and is performed on a long, narrow bowling lane (*Kegelbahn*). Booking is essential. To find a local establishment with facilities, look in the yellow pages under *Kegelbahnen* and *Kegelbahnenrestaurant*.

Trampolining

There are a large number of clubs (both junior and senior) throughout Germany, where courses are organised for all ages. For more information, visit 🖥 www. trampolincity.de.

Weightlifting

There are weightlifting clubs in most large towns in Germany, many using the facilities of local sports or leisure centres or a health and fitness club. For more information, visit the website of the Bundesverband Deutscher Gewichtheber (🖥 www.bvdg-online.de).

17.

Shopping

Germany offers a wide choice of shopping, ranging from ultra-sophisticated specialist shops and world-renowned department stores to traditional local farmers' markets and festivals featuring regional specialities. As with so many aspects of German life, commerce is subject to a plethora of rules, regulations and legal constraints, which influence when, where and how you can shop. On the other hand, the abundance of regulations also affords considerable protection to consumers and in general goods are of high quality, if rather expensive compared with many other countries, particularly the US. However, Germans are expert bargain hunters, particularly in the south of the country, where the Swabians claim to be European penny-pinching champions.

Much of the regulation of retailing stems from German labour laws designed to protect shop employees from exploitation. Shop opening hours are strictly controlled (see below) and staff can only be required to perform the job they were hired to do – and even then often apparently against their will. Even Germans joke about the surly customer service you can encounter in much of Germany, although standards are improving.

All prices advertised or quoted to individuals include value added tax (see page 305) and are the total price you pay.

Most shops accept exchanges or offer refunds (not always with a smile) unless they have an advertised policy to the contrary (in which case you should shop elsewhere!), but they usually require you to produce your receipt and, in some cases, the original packaging. However, as part of Germany's environmental legislation, all shops are required by law to take back the packaging from the goods they sell, so you should check that that the goods are in order as far as possible before leaving the shop. Some shops have recycling bins in their car parks or near entrances for cartons and other packing material. If you have goods delivered to your home, you can ask the delivery people to take the packaging material away with them.

The Germans are only sluggishly warming to credit cards, despite the fact that most issued in Germany are linked directly to a bank account and function more like debit cards. The situation is changing quite rapidly, but some shops still won't accept credit cards.

OPENING HOURS

Until recently, shopping hours were strictly controlled under federal labour law, which meant that everything was closed by 8pm Mondays to Fridays and all day on Sundays and public holidays. The 'liberalisation' of shopping hours that started in 2006 means that opening hours are now decided on a state level – and therefore vary from state to state. Nearly every state allows shop-owners to open on four to six Sundays/public holidays per year (usually during the Christmas season) and on weeknights and Saturdays they may remain open later than 8pm (e.g. 10pm). There aren't 'late shopping days' as in other countries. Bakeries can also open for a few hours on Sunday mornings to sell fresh bread and rolls. The exception is Bavaria, where the state government, shop owners and even the customers seem to prefer the status quo, so opening hours are more restricted. Smaller shops, particularly those in towns and villages, often close for an hour or so at lunchtime to allow employees to go home for their main meal of the day.

The only retail outlets that are exempt from normal shopping hours are those at airports, railway stations and petrol stations. Frankfurt airport, in particular, has an extensive underground shopping area, which includes a grocery store open all day Sunday and until late in the evening the rest of the week. Prices in airport shops are high, as you would expect, but most shops accept credit cards for almost any purchase. Petrol stations, particularly those on or near motorways, often run a convenience shop, where you can find most 'essentials' (at inflated prices).

PRICES & BARGAIN SHOPPING

There's minimal bargaining over prices in most shops, although some may offer discounts to members of a local sports club or other social or civic association. Prices aren't controlled, but retailers cannot easily change prices once posted, and most smaller stores adhere to the manufacturer's recommended retail price. A shopkeeper may reduce prices on a single line of products in order to sell off remaining stock, but such price reductions are limited to a small proportion of the total goods available and generally apply only where the product was a one-time purchase that won't be re-ordered.

Major sales normally occur twice per year: once at the end of the winter season (*Winterschlussverkauf*) and the other at the end of the summer season (*Sommerschlussverkauf*). The dates used to be set by regional authorities, but now shops are allowed to decide their own. In general the *Winterschlussverkauf* starts at the end of January and the *Sommerschlussverkauf* at the end of July. Price cuts during these sale periods are generous and it's an excellent time to stock up on seasonal merchandise, e.g. skiing and winter clothes in the end-of-winter sales, and swimming and holiday wear at the end of the summer. Goods purchased during end-of-season sales generally aren't returnable, so you should shop carefully at sale times.

Due to the high overall level of prices, there's an active market in Germany for second-hand goods, especially furniture (including complete kitchens) and appliances. Second-hand clothing and appliance stores can be found in almost every town with over 5,000 inhabitants and are listed in the local phone book and newspapers. Local newspapers contain classified advertisements for household goods, and several weekly publications devoted solely to such advertisements are sold at news stands.

Many towns run an annual flea market (*Flohmarkt* or *Trödelmarkt*), where the locals can set up a stall (for a small fee, payable to the town) to sell off used household and other items (they're a good source of toys and children's clothing).

Expatriate clubs are a good source of second-hand goods, which are either advertised in newsletters or sold at annual or bi-annual flea markets. Most cities in Germany are home to at least one (or usually more) British or American clubs with a high enough turnover of members each year to ensure a healthy exchange of used goods at reasonable prices.

Another place to purchase used clothing and books is the shops of British charity Oxfam, which has been steadily expanding in Germany after opening its first shop in Frankfurt in 1995 and now also has shops in Berlin, Bonn, Cologne, Mainz and Wiesbaden. Oxfam shops stock clothing, books, records, CDs and other small items, but most don't have sufficient space for larger objects.

Stiftung Warentest is a respected, independent and non-profit-making foundation which compares and tests products and services (rather like Which? and the Consumers' Association in the UK). Some 1,700 products (from grapefruit juice to hi-fi equipment) are tested each year as well as services related to investment, health, tourism, and transport. Companies whose products receive good or very good ratings indicate this in their advertising. Stiftung Warentest publishes two monthly magazines: *Test* for all types of consumer products and *FINANZtest* for financial products, such as insurance and property and banking services. You can buy a subscription to either magazine for €22.20 every six months or you can download the latest test from the website (🖥 www.test.de) for around €1 per topic, e.g. cars.

SHOPPING CENTRES & MARKETS

Germany has a variety of indoor shopping centres, located mostly in the larger towns and cities, and there's a wide range of shops and services in the underground passageways of most major underground and railway stations (e.g. in Frankfurt or Munich). The Germans haven't gone in for building vast indoor shopping malls on the outskirts of cities and towns, as are common in France and the US, although there are small clusters of large stores (usually hypermarkets and discount stores) in industrial and commercial estates on the periphery of many towns. These developments have a down-to-earth practical air but offer free parking, which is rarely to be found in towns.

Most German towns have a shopping street closed to traffic (*Fussgängerzone*) except for early morning deliveries. In most cases, it's in the centre of town and well served by public transport. Parking in the centre of most cities and towns is expensive and difficult, particularly on Saturdays and during sale periods and the pre-Christmas shopping season.

Most towns and all cities have regular open-air markets throughout the year. Most popular is the farmers' or food market, which is usually a weekly event at least (in Freiburg, for example, there's an open-air market six days a week in the Münsterplatz). These open-air markets aren't to be missed, particularly for regional and seasonal specialities such as white asparagus (*Spargel*) – available only in the spring – and the various types of wild mushroom (*Pilz*) – an autumn speciality. Other treats you'll find in open-air markets include locally produced honey (*Honig*), sausages (*Wurst*) and hams (*Schinken*), along with a wide variety of fresh fruit and vegetables. Market vendors set up at around 6 or 7am and shut up shop in the early afternoon.

In the run-up to Christmas, many towns hold *Adventmärkte* or *Christkindlmärkte* featuring local craft items, traditional Christmas ornaments and plenty of *Lebkuchen* (a form of gingerbread), *Stollen* (iced fruit loaf), *Spekulatius* or *Spekulatus* (an almond-flavoured biscuit) and other Christmas goodies, including *Glühwein* (mulled wine) to keep your Christmas shopping spirits up!

Other outdoor markets include flea markets (*Flohmarkt* or *Trödelmarkt*) and wine, crafts and other festivals organised by local authorities. Keep an eye out for posters around town announcing these events or ask at your local town hall or tourist office.

DEPARTMENT & CHAIN STORES

Germany has no shortage of excellent department stores, both indigenous and foreign, but after a long period of stability this sector has become the scene of mergers and takeovers in recent years. Kaufhof has partnered Horten, Karstadt has joined up with Hertie, and Kaufhalle has been bought by the Italian La Staedo group. These are all good-quality stores, but Germany's flagship store is KaDeWe in Berlin, the largest department store on the European continent and perhaps best known for its remarkable food department, where shoppers can sample exotic delicacies at the many gourmet counters and wash them down with champagne. In most large cities, there are foreign department stores such as H&M and C&A, while east Berlin even boasts a Galeries Lafayette in its new KuDamm shopping district.

Department stores offer a dizzying variety of high-quality merchandise, with all well known brands represented as well as usually a range of good-value own-brand items. Practically all department stores accept major credit cards, which isn't always the case with other shops. At some stores you can apply for a preferred customer card, which provides a discount and/or bonus points on all purchases after a qualifying period.

The department store chains of Hertie/Karstadt and Kaufhof/Horten have excellent food markets, typically on the ground floor or at basement level. Here you can usually find fresh, good-quality, pre-packaged foods, which is helpful if your German is basic and you're looking for something recognisable to cook for dinner.

Chain stores are popular throughout Germany, including US-style speciality chains, most notably Toys 'R' Us. There's at least one large hardware and DIY chain store (e.g. OBI) on the edge of most towns, and there are also a number of discount electronics chains where you can buy TVs, appliances and stereo equipment at competitive prices.

SUPERMARKETS & HYPERMARKETS

Most towns in Germany have one or more supermarkets offering a full range of food and drinks and some small household items. Among the major chains are Tengelmann, Edeka, Rewe, Metro (which also owns Real) and WalMart. Minimal is a well known smaller chain. There are many smaller international supermarkets, particularly Italian, Greek and Turkish, which can be good for unusual vegetables and specialist foods.

The American merchandising giant WalMart, which purchased the German chains Wertkauf and Interspar in 1997 and introduced a wider range of brands than were found in most German chains, including many American imports (though not American customs such as 'bagging' customer purchases and valet parking), has recently been forced to sell out to Metro, a huge 'cash-and-carry' retailer (discount retailer club), similar to Sam's Club in the US.

The large discount chains include Aldi, Lidl, PennyMarkt and Plus, where some amazing bargains can be found, although the selection can be limited and shops can become very crowded, especially when weekly special offers come out, so you may have to wait a long time at the checkout.

Supermarkets sell primarily food. Germany also has a wide range of hypermarkets, which are shops with over 2,500m² (27,000ft²) of floor space, selling electronic goods, household appliances, books, clothing and hardware as well as food, and are usually found on the outskirts of major towns and cities. The main hypermarket chains are Allkauf, E-center, Globus, Real and WalMart.

Although some of the brand names may be unfamiliar, most products are similar to those found in supermarkets in other countries and can meet most of your daily requirements.

Most supermarkets in Germany don't provide free carrier bags or pack your purchases at the checkout. You can usually buy plastic carrier bags for €0.10 to €0.30, but it's more economical (and ecological) to bring your own bags. At most supermarkets, a €1 coin (or similar size token) is required to unlock a trolley from a rack and is returned when you replace the trolley.

Service in some supermarkets and hypermarkets can be particularly brusque. Don't expect cashiers to wish you *Guten Tag* or even to smile, and don't be surprised to find full pallets of merchandise left in the middle of an aisle blocking access to shelves in some discount stores, where staff are at a premium. If you buy anything from the produce section, you're usually expected to weigh and label it yourself; don't make the mistake of arriving at the checkout without weighing your fruit or vegetables (a cardinal sin).

FOOD

When shopping for food, don't overlook the smaller specialist food shops, which include butchers', bakers' and greengrocers'. Fishmongers' are few and far between, except in coastal areas and cities with large foreign populations, and cheesemongers' can be found mainly in upmarket areas. Don't be surprised if you have to shop at three different places to find everything you need.

Germany boasts a fine range of *Wurst* (which translates as 'sausage' but also includes cured and smoked meats, salamis and processed meats) and cheeses. You may also be surprised at the variety of bread, rolls and buns on offer in even the smallest grocery shop. The Germans make bread from almost every form of grain – maize, wheat, rye, barley, etc. – typical German bread being heavy textured and thinly sliced. Foreign products, such as those dear to British tastes, aren't generally available, although stilton and peanut butter can be found in some shops.

The quality of fruit and vegetables varies from shop to shop. They're categorised from I (the highest quality) to III (the lowest). Some supermarket chains pride themselves on the quality (category I) and freshness of their produce, while in others the indifferent quality is matched only by the unattractive displays. Some stores stock only category II and III produce, as shown on labels. **Many fruit and vegetables are treated with fungicides and must be thoroughly washed before eating.**

Shops in rural areas often buy fruit and vegetables from local farmers, which is generally fresher and of better quality than that available in towns and cities and may even be cheaper. It helps to find out when your local shops receive deliveries and time your shopping trips accordingly. In general, Mondays are the worst days if you're looking for fresh produce or baked goods, and Saturday mornings are also to be avoided if possible, as this is the busiest time in most shops.

Eggs aren't generally washed or polished, giving them a more 'rustic' appearance than you may be used to; however, the fact that an egg doesn't shine doesn't mean that it's any less wholesome. Free-range eggs are available (marked *Bodenhaltung*). Milk is sold in three varieties: full-cream milk (*Vollmilch*), low fat/skimmed (*Fettarme Milch*) and heat-treated (*H Milch*). *H Milch* doesn't need refrigeration until it's opened, as it has been sterilised. If you plan to do any baking, note that the quality of flour is indicated by the 'type number' on the packaging: the less refined, the higher the number, e.g. cake flour carries the number 405, while wholemeal flour is in the 1600 range. Freshly ground coffee can be bought at most supermarkets.

DRINK

Drinking is a popular pastime in Germany, despite strictly enforced drink-driving laws and growing concerns over alcoholism. Beer is the number one tipple, although its popularity seems to be past its peak – in 2006, the average German consumed 115 litres compared with 153 litres in 1986 – but a possible shortage of beer, as was threatened a few years ago, can still bring the country to the brink of collective nervous breakdown. Wine drinking has grown in popularity over the last few decades, over 26 litres now being consumed per person per annum (the statistic includes the whole population, so the average adult drinks considerably more than this). Spirits are drunk in moderation, the most popular being Schnapps, which is also deemed to be the major cause of alcoholism!

Beer

Almost a third of the world's breweries – some 1,270 at the last count – are in Germany (and half of those in Bavaria), producing countless varieties of beer. Beer is brewed everywhere and styles differ considerably from area to area. Some of Germany's best brews are associated with monasteries, most notably the Kloster Weltenburg on the Danube, famous for its strong, chocolate-dark ales. *Roggenbier*, also from Bavaria, is brewed by the princes of Thurn and Taxis in the medieval city of Regensburg, using rye instead of barley; malted and effervescent, it's almost a meal in itself. Another Bavarian beer enjoying growing success in world markets is *Weizenbier* (wheat beer), also known as *Weissbier* (white beer), which is brewed using wheat, yeast and barley malts. Tangy, fruity and full, it's best drunk slightly chilled. From eastern Germany there's *Schwarzbier* (black beer), brewed using burnt barley malt, with a stout-like consistency and a toasted flavour. The speciality of Cologne is *Kölsch*, a light, dry pale brew with virtually no effervescence, typically served in small fluted glasses. Some people find that it lacks flavour compared with the nutty beers of southern Germany, but it's easier to drink and seems to bloat less.

Alt (old) beers are popular around Dusseldorf. The term doesn't mean that the beer has been 'aged' but that it's brewed according to traditional, top-fermenting methods. *Alt* beers are dark and can taste hops-bitter or malt-sweet, depending on the recipe. *Bock* beers, in contrast, which are particularly associated with Munich, are bottom-fermented and quite strong. They can be dark or light. *Pilsner* (or *Pils*) beer is the most widely brewed (and drunk) in Germany and has become famous in other parts of the world. Strictly speaking, the term describes a brewing method, first practised in the Bohemian town of Pilsen in 1842. The main ingredients of a *Pilsner* beer are pale malt, soft water, bottom-fermenting yeast and extremely aromatic hops. Most *Pils* is a pale golden colour, although you will occasionally come across a darker version, which has been brewed with dark malt.

German beer has a well deserved reputation for quality and flavour, which is due, at least in part, to the *Reinheitsgebot* (purity law) promulgated by the Duke of Bavaria in 1516. Brewing throughout Germany is still regulated by this decree, according to which beer made and marketed anywhere in the country may contain only grain malt, hops, yeast, water and, in some cases, sugar. Only natural ingredients are allowed, with preservatives and other additives strictly forbidden. The Germans successfully used the purity law to bar the import of almost all foreign-made beers until they were taken to the European Court of Justice by other EU members for unfairly restricting trade. A 1987 decision by the court forced Germany to accept foreign beers that didn't meet the purity criteria, although they haven't made much of a dent in the market, as Germans aren't generally willing to buy them.

Further information about German beer can be found on the brewing industry's website (🖥 www.bier.de – available in English).

Wine

The reputation of German wine has suffered in recent decades, although any visitor soon discovers that Germany offers much more than the saccharine *Liebfraumilch* so popular in the UK during the '70s and '80s. The German wine trade is currently reverting to older traditions and aiming for better quality wine of all types. Aided by a string of good vintages since 2001, German wines are reestablishing themselves, though inevitably (for climatic reasons) they lack the variety and range of French or even Italian wines.

Germany has 13 official wine-producing regions, all of which are located along rivers or around lakes: Ahr, Baden, Franken, Hessische Bergstrasse, Mittelrhein, Mosel-Saar-Ruwer, Nahe, Pfalz, Rheingau, Rheinhessen, Saale-Unstrut, Saxony and Württemberg. These regions are loosely grouped into areas, of which the principal two are the Rhine (whose wine is sold in tall, brown bottles) and Moselle (tall green bottles). Around 87 per cent of the country's vineyards are planted with white grape varieties, with just 13 per cent red. (A tiny amount of rosé wine is produced in the Ahr valley, but all of it is drunk locally.)

German wine is, by law, divided into two main categories, the lower of which is *Tafelwein* (table wine). Better quality wine is labelled *Qualitätswein*, which is roughly equivalent to the French *Appellation Contrôlée* and should signify a wine which is at least drinkable. *Qualitätswein* is further divided into *Qualitätswein eines bestimmten Anbaugebietes* (usually abbreviated to *Qualitätswein b.A.* or just *QbA*) and the best quality, *Qualitätswein mit Prädikat* (*QmP*), which literally means 'quality wine with a description'. *QmP* wines have six grades or 'attributes' corresponding to the ripeness (sugar content) of the grapes they were made from. These are, in ascending order of ripeness (but not necessarily sweetness), as follows:

- ● **Kabinett** – fine, usually light wines, made from fully ripened grapes. The lightest of the *Prädikat* wines, they're excellent with food or on their own.

- ● **Spätlese** – wines of superior quality made from grapes harvested after the normal harvest. *Spätlese* wines are more intense in flavour and concentration, but not necessarily sweet. They're good with richer, more flavourful foods or on their own.

- ● **Auslese** – wines made from selected, very ripe grapes. They're intense in bouquet and taste, and usually, but not always, sweet.

- **Beerenauslese** – wines made from selected overripe berries. These are rich, sweet dessert wines, which can also be enjoyed by themselves.

- **Eiswein** – wines of *Beerenauslese* intensity, made from grapes harvested and pressed while frozen (hence the name 'ice wine'). The flavour is unique, with a remarkable concentration of fruity acidity and sweetness.

- **Trockenbeerenauslese** (*TBA*) – wines made from grapes which are overripe and dried almost to raisins. *TBA*s are rich, sweet, luscious, honey-like wines.

QmP wines, which are made entirely with natural ingredients, include the finest Germany has to offer. However, it should be noted that a wine made from riper grapes isn't necessarily of better quality, simply one which is likely to be sweeter and/or stronger.

When buying, look for '*Erzeugerabfüllung*' or the new, more strictly defined '*Gutsabfüllung*' on the label, which indicate a wine bottled by the producer or estate. Wines without these words are likely to be blended from several producers. The grape type should also be indicated on the label; if it isn't, the wine is likely to be a blend of inferior grape juices and of poor quality. The classic German grape variety is *Riesling*, but some others can also be good, such as *Ruländer* (*Pinot Gris*) and the new varieties of *Kerner* and *Scheurebe*. Legally, however, a wine needs to contain only 85 per cent of the declared grape variety.

Alcohol levels tend to be low in German wines. Dry *Auslesen* generally have the highest alcohol levels, up to 15 per cent in some cases, while *Kabinett*s and even *TBA*s can come in at under 8 per cent. If a wine's sweetness isn't indicated on the label, it's likely to be slightly to extremely sweet, in rough proportion with the ripeness level. If you want a dry wine, look for one labelled '*trocken*' (dry) or '*halbtrocken*' (semi-dry). Wines up to *Auslese* level may be produced in a dry style.

Most wines of the *QbA* and *Kabinett* grades are ready to drink when marketed and are at their best when young; they should be kept for no more than five years. *Spätlese* may also be consumed young, but the wine is likely to be enjoyable up to ten years after bottling. The 'higher grades' (*Auslese* and above) are usually longer-lived, generally reaching their peak when seven to ten years old, and with good storage can remain at their best for many years longer. Wines from the Rheingau often take longer to reach their potential, while other Rhine wines – from Rheinhessen, Pfalz and Nahe – tend to mature faster. The wines of the Mosel-Saar-Ruwer are the most delicate, and the lesser grades from this region should definitely be drunk sooner rather than later. It's also wise to sample stored wines from time to time, so that they don't go past their best without your noticing.

A good source of information about German wine is the German Wine Institute (Deutsches Weininstitut, Postfach 1660, D-55116 Mainz, ☎ 06131-28290, 🖳 www.deutscheweine.de), which has branches in the UK (German Wine Information Service UK, Phipps PR, 33 Long Acre, Covent Garden, London WC2E 9LA, ☎ 020-7759 7405, ✉ german.wine@phippspr.co.uk) and the US (German Wine Information Bureau, 245 Park Avenue, 39th Floor, New

York, NY 10167, ☎ 212-792 4134, ✉ info@germanwineusa.org). Both provide a range of useful publications, including *Balance of Flavours – German Wine and Food Pairing Guide*. Wine buffs may also wish to visit the comprehensive German winegrowers' website (💻 www.germanwine.de), which covers everything anyone but a PhD student in viticulture could ever want to know about German wine and wine-making.

Schnapps

Schnapps (*Schnaps*) is served mainly as an aperitif or a digestive, although it's also sometimes drunk with a glass of beer – what Americans and Britons would call a chaser. Either way, it's normally served neat, at room temperature, in a one-shot glass called a *Kleine-kleine* ('small small'). Many regional brands exist, although they all look and taste much the same. Most are fruit-based, popular varieties, including apple (*Apfelschnaps*), pear (*Birnenschnaps*), plum (*Pflaumenschnaps* or, in Bavaria, *Zwetschgengeist*) and wheat (*Kornschnaps*). Others contain a high proportion of roots and herbs (arnica, angelica, bloodwort, etc.) and all have a high alcohol content (from 25 to 60 per cent) and should be consumed with caution. The extravagant health claims sometimes made for schnapps – that it cures everything from indigestion to infertility – should be taken with a large pinch of *Salz*!

Other Drinks

Supermarkets sell beer, soft drinks and mineral water by the crate, which usually represents excellent value. Due to the (many) ecological and recycling laws, you must pay a deposit (*Pfand*) on both the bottles and the crate, which is refunded when you return the empties to the store (see **Bottles** on page 115). Most supermarkets have a bottle return station, where you return your bottles and receive a credit slip to redeem at the checkout. Some shops are equipped with machines that do this automatically; you simply place the bottles on a turntable, press a button and the machine issues a receipt.

Many people arrange to have drinks delivered to their homes rather than struggle with heavy crates (although you'll be amazed at how many crates some people manage to transport by bicycle!). Deliveries are often made by the local brewery representative or the neighbourhood drinks market (*Getränkemarkt*) or supermarket.

CLOTHES

In general, Germans aren't known as flashy dressers, and people of all ages, male and female, dress roughly as people in the UK and North America, though perhaps a little more conservatively. One major factor in this is, of course, the climate. The winter months in most parts of Germany are cold and damp, and winter clothing, including warm gloves, hats, boots and waterproofs, is essential. Lightweight clothes are suitable for the summer, which rarely becomes uncomfortably hot.

Germans, it must be said, can be intolerant when it comes to unusual clothing. In some parts of the country, if you wear an unconventional outfit, such as a kilt or sari, you're likely to become an object of curiosity or even derision. Therefore, if you don't wish to stand out from the crowd you should observe how your German friends and neighbours dress and copy their style (it isn't, however, mandatory to wear *Lederhosen*). In some rural areas, Germans are still expected to wear their 'Sunday best' on Sundays, while in the cities attitudes are far more relaxed. For everyday wear, jeans and T-shirts are as popular in Germany as anywhere else and are acceptable for most leisure activities. At more expensive restaurants, men are usually expected to wear a jacket and tie in the evening, and many German women are highly fashion-conscious and wear stylish outfits to restaurants and the theatre, particularly in the larger cities.

Although conservative, the dress code for business is less rigid than it once was and is similar to that of North America and most northern European countries. Top management dresses more conservatively than those lower down the chain, and western Germans are generally more style-conscious than those from the east of the country. For men, a well made jacket (preferably dark) with contrasting trousers is acceptable, but a muted business suit is the best choice in most situations, and a tasteful tie is essential. For women, conservatively tailored suits and dresses are appropriate, and tight or revealing clothing should be avoided.

Clothing sold in Germany is generally of very good quality but tends to be expensive. All styles can be found in the major cities, but continental sizes may differ from those in other countries such as the UK and the US (see **Appendix D**). Britons and Americans may have difficulty in finding shoes that fit, as German feet tend to be wider and shorter. Shops selling Italian and Swiss footwear provide a wider range of sizes, although at higher prices.

German cities and larger towns have department stores offering extensive ranges of clothing and sportswear (see **Department & Chain Stores** on page 353), and clothing can be bought at specialist stores such as C&A, Hennes & Mauritz, and Peek & Cloppenburg. Peek & Cloppenburg, or P&C as it's known, is the place to go for stylish but conservative apparel. It stocks good quality brands, and prices are usually reasonable. Hennes & Mauritz, a Swedish chain, can be found throughout Germany and targets the young and trendy on a budget. C&A is also widespread, appealing to budget customers with more conservative preferences.

Winter sportswear is a best buy in Germany, where locally made garments are of excellent quality. Leatherwear is also a speciality, although the styling may not appeal to foreigners. The most interesting German traditional dress is that of Bavaria, where it's known as *Tracht* and Munich is the place to buy it. It consists, of course, of lederhosen – leather knee-breeches with suspenders – for men (and sometimes women), worn with high woollen socks and a knitted or leather jacket with big buttons over a linen shirt, topped with a felt hat sporting feathers or goat whiskers. Women wear peasant dresses called dirndls, with a close-fitting bodice, full skirt and apron. *Tracht* is worn for festivals and special occasions, while *Landhausmode*, the 'modern' peasant costume, is quite popular in southern Germany for all occasions.

NEWSPAPERS, MAGAZINES & BOOKS

Newsagents' and book shops are plentiful throughout Germany, and most supermarkets, hypermarkets and department stores sell a selection of books and magazines. There are no truly national newspapers in Germany, other than the *Bild Zeitung* (generally known as *Das Bild*), a low-brow tabloid. The leading serious newspapers are the *Frankfurter Allgemeine Zeitung*, generally referred to as the *FAZ*, and *Die Welt* (along with its sister publication *Die Welt am Sonntag*), both conservative, and their counterparts on the centre-left the *Süddeutsche Zeitung* (*SZ*) and the *Frankfurter Rundschau* (*FR*). These are available in 'national' editions throughout the country, although the *FR* includes a local news section in its Frankfurt edition; the same applies to the Munich edition of the *SZ*.

There are also numerous excellent regional newspapers, including the *Berliner Zeitung, Stuttgarter Zeitung* and *Westfaelische Nachrichten*. The newspapers with national scope tend to have fewer advertisements and fewer photographs, while regional newspapers (not surprisingly) provide more local information, including advertisements, cinema and theatre listings, and news of civic events. Regional or local newspapers are generally much easier to read than the *FAZ*, particularly if you're learning German. Many city and town newspapers distribute a free weekly edition containing selected articles and local shop and classified advertising through letterboxes and to apartment block foyers.

For decades, the major weekly news magazines in Germany were *Der Spiegel* and *Stern*. *Der Spiegel* is known for hard news and thorough analysis of issues and events, while *Stern* is a larger format magazine with more pictures and a softer news content that includes celebrity interviews and features. In the last decade, *Focus* has emerged as a competitor to its more established rivals. Modelled on the American-style news weeklies (*Newsweek* and *Time*), *Focus* combines hard news with more photographs, graphs and graphics than *Der Spiegel*, and has gained readers for that reason, although *Der Spiegel* remains one of the world's leading news magazines.

Many newspaper kiosks, even in small cities, sell major European English-language newspapers and magazines, including the *International Herald Tribune*, the *Financial Times Deutschland* and the London *Times*, as well as *Time* and *Newsweek*. Many are printed in Germany, with the content sent electronically from the originating country to German printers. There are international news kiosks in city centres and at major railway stations and airports offering a much wider range of foreign newspapers and magazines. Expect to pay a premium for English-language publications, particularly those that are available on the date of publication. In smaller towns, the issues on sale may be anything from a day to a week late, depending on the publication.

If you prefer to subscribe to your favourite publications, you must usually pay an overseas or airmail delivery charge in addition to the usual subscription price. In the case of US publications, this charge can amount to more than the subscription cost. Where a delivery charge isn't added, you usually receive a slimmed 'international' edition. *American Time, Newsweek* and *Business Week*, for example, are available only in international editions in Germany.

German publication subscriptions work somewhat differently from those in other countries. The subscription price for most magazines is slightly higher than the news-stand price. Most subscriptions are for a year and are automatically renewed unless written notice is given at least three months before the expiry date. Miss the notification date by a day and your bank account will be automatically debited for an additional year!

Most book shops in Germany, even those in fairly small towns, offer at least a small selection of English-language books. In major cities, large book shops such as H. Hugendubel have well stocked English-language sections, and most book shops selling technical or computer books stock a range of English-language titles. Prices for imports, as always, tend to be high, but competition from foreign mail-order and internet booksellers is starting to reduce prices a little. The leading internet bookseller is Amazon, which has German (🖥 www.amazon.de), British (🖥 www.amazon.co.uk) and American (🖥 www.amazon.com) websites. The German branch provides books in both German and English, with prices considerably below those charged by most shops. Delivery costs from the German branch are free, and your books should arrive much sooner. Using the German or UK site has the added advantage of avoiding import charges.

Anyone who loves books should visit the Frankfurt Book Fair (*Buchmesse*, 🖥 www.buchmesse.de) at least once. This is the world's premier publishing industry fair, held annually in early October. On Saturday and Sunday the fair is open to the public for a fee of €10 per day; at all other times, you need some form of 'professional' credentials to gain access, such as a business card with a title suggesting that you work in publishing, printing or book selling. The *Buchmesse* provides an opportunity to preview titles that aren't yet available in the shops.

FURNITURE & FURNISHINGS

Germans take great pride in their homes and furniture. The lounge or living room usually contains a large cupboard or sideboard called a *Wohnschrank*, made of solid wood and very heavy, which is used to store dishes and dinner services for entertaining, wine glasses, table linen, and perhaps a bottle of sherry or dessert wine. It also frequently serves as a home for the TV, video recorder and music centre. Even if you arrive in Germany with your own furniture, you may eventually decide to indulge in a *Wohnschrank*. If you're planning to take one home with you, consider first whether it will fit through the doorways!

Wohnschränke and other items of furniture are available in a wide variety of styles, quality and price ranges. German tastes range from traditional, massive wood-and-upholstered pieces to high-tech glass and stainless steel, often in bold colours and avant-garde designs. Prices in specialist shops tend to be high, but the quality is usually high and designs unusual. In many large cities you can find a branch of the upmarket chain Roche Bobois as well as several local furniture stores. If you're looking for serviceable furniture at more reasonable prices, there's a range of do-it-yourself and discount furniture retailers.

IKEA, the Swedish furniture manufacturer, has outlets throughout Germany where you can buy stylish, modern Scandinavian furniture at reasonable prices for home assembly. IKEA stores have free crèches and a restaurant, in case your shopping expedition takes longer than planned. There are also a number of German furniture chains and individual retailers who offer discount prices on a wide range of furniture and household goods.

If you're in the market for custom-made furniture, the town to visit is Kelkheim in south-east Germany, known as the *Möbelstadt* (furniture town), where craftsmen have been employed for centuries creating fine furniture. Local manufacturers sponsor an annual furniture exhibition (*Möbelausstellung*) in the autumn, at which local manufacturers proudly display their wares.

Most large items of furniture must be ordered, as shops don't keep them in stock, and some, such as upholstered chairs, are made to order, even at discount stores. Delivery takes from 4 to 12 weeks in most cases, unless you're buying a display item, in which case the shop will usually deliver within a week. Shops normally require a deposit when you order and expect you to pay the balance to the delivery people by cheque or in cash; therefore, if you plan to pay by credit card, you must pay the full amount in advance.

Carpets and curtains can be purchased at specialist shops, general furniture shops and department stores. Note, however, that many apartments and houses have external metal blinds, and the fashion is to have net curtains only inside. There are many oriental carpet stores, some of which seem to offer a 'this-week-only' deal or a 'going-out-of-business' (*Ausverkauf*) sale continually, despite laws forbidding this.

If you're bringing a bed from the UK or North America, you must bring bed linen (*Bettwäsche*) with you, as standard German bed linen (e.g. pillow cases, duvet covers and fitted sheets) is unlikely to fit; if you come without a bed, don't bother to bring sheets and blankets as they won't fit German mattresses. The Germans use duvets and huge pillows typically measuring 80cm x 80cm (31in x 31in). Bed linen sets contain duvet covers and pillowcases but you must buy a fitted sheet (*Spantuch*) to cover the mattress separately. Most fitted sheets cover mattresses ranging from 90 x 180cm (36in x 72in) to 100 x 200cm (39in x 78in), but check before buying. Typically, double beds have two separate mattresses with separate duvets (with no top sheet), and double duvets are hard to find; if you prefer sleeping 'together', bring your own with you.

Kitchens

One of the first surprises to hit many newcomers to Germany is the discovery that many rented apartments and houses don't include kitchen appliances or even cupboards and a sink unit. If you ask beforehand, it's sometimes possible to purchase the kitchen from the outgoing tenant, saving considerable effort on your part (as well as on the part of the departing tenant).

Most furniture shops and nearly all DIY stores offer kitchens and kitchen appliances in a wide range of styles and colours and various degrees of do-it-yourselfness regarding construction and installation, although a licensed plumber and electrician are required by law to connect appliances. IKEA offers attractive, good quality products at keen prices. The good news is that cupboards, cabinets and appliances come in standard sizes and can be taken with you if you move to another apartment or house. If you don't fancy doing the installation yourself, most furniture and kitchen stores will do it for you (it may even be included in the price). Those that don't do installation will recommend a local tradesman who can do the work for you.

HOUSEHOLD GOODS

Germany boasts a number of world famous manufacturers of high-quality household electrical appliances, including AEG, Bosch, Braun, Miele and Siemens. German products tend to be a bit more expensive than some of their lesser-known competitors, but German consumers expect reliable and well designed products, and the appliances you buy in Germany will last you a long (long) time. Before buying, however, check the efficiency rating, which is shown on all new appliances, to see how expensive an appliance will be to run; it may be worth buying a slightly more expensive model if it will save you money in the long run.

For Americans, who cannot understand how Germans function with such 'tiny' refrigerators, there's some good news: large American-style refrigerators (some even with ice and cold water distribution in the door or automatic ice making facilities) are coming into vogue in Europe and models conforming to the German electrical system can be purchased locally. However, they aren't among the most economical when it comes to running costs, and running water pipes to the refrigerator isn't an easy or cheap task. You may also have trouble fitting them into a standard German kitchen.

For information about importing foreign kitchen appliances, see page 93.

LAUNDRY & DRY CLEANING

All towns and shopping centres have dry cleaners' (*chemische Reinigung*), most of which also do minor clothes repairs, alterations and dyeing. However, 'express cleaning' may mean a few days rather than hours, even where dry cleaning is done on the premises. You usually pay in advance and charges are quite high, particularly for leather clothes. Note that, unless you purchase special insurance for your garments, the dry cleaner's liability for damage is limited to 15 times the cost of the cleaning. If you have expensive or particularly fragile items, be sure to mention this and enquire about insurance.

There are few self-service launderettes in Germany, other than in cities and large towns. Most German families have their own washing machines. Most of those who live in an apartment block have access to communal drying rooms, but the preferred method of drying clothes in Germany is to hang them in the fresh air outdoors, either on a clothes line or using a folding drying rack on a balcony or terrace.

Ironing services (*Bügelei*) are available in many areas. Look for signs in windows or announcements on shop notice boards, as this is a popular way for housewives to earn extra money in many small towns.

HOME SHOPPING

Shopping by post has long been popular in Germany and, given the stringent regulations and efficient postal system, is a safe and convenient way to buy many items. Catalogue shopping is dominated by three vast companies: Neckermann, Otto-Versand and Quelle, all long established and well respected. You'll see advertisements for these companies in many popular magazines and are likely to receive promotional leaflets in your letterbox. All three have established a reputation for their own brands, particularly for household appliances and electronic equipment, and are known for providing quality products at considerably lower prices than those in shops, with ironclad guarantees and warranties.

Neckermann, Otto-Versand and Quelle also have stores in most German cities and maintain agencies in smaller cities and towns where customers can consult catalogues and place orders. Many smaller items are delivered within 24 hours and even larger appliances and furniture are usually delivered quicker than by local stores, e.g. in a matter of days rather than weeks. All three companies provide a 24-hour ordering service, seven days a week via the internet (🖥 www.nèckermann.de, www.otto.de and www.quelle.de).

Many upmarket shops abroad publish catalogues and will send goods anywhere in the world, e.g. Fortnum & Mason and Harrods in the UK. Many provide account facilities or payment can be made by credit card. Although some mail order companies won't send goods abroad, there's nothing to stop you obtaining catalogues from friends or relatives and ordering through them. Buying goods by mail order from the US can result in huge savings, even after postage, VAT and import duty, although you should check exactly what charges will apply (see **Duty & VAT** below).

The German eBay site (🖥 www.ebay.de) is as popular as those elsewhere – and a good way of practising your German!

SHOPPING ABROAD

Shopping abroad can be a pleasant day out (or a nightmare) and can also save you money. Germany's neighbours include Austria, Belgium, the Czech Republic, Denmark, France (popular for food and wine), Luxembourg, the Netherlands, Poland and Switzerland. Don't forget your passports or identity cards, car papers, dog's vaccination papers and foreign currency where relevant. When visiting countries that are signatories to the Schengen agreement (see page 80) there are no border controls, and you won't need to change currency if you're shopping in France, Belgium, Luxembourg, Austria or the Netherlands. Most shops in border towns in other countries gladly accept euros (because they offer a poor exchange rate!), but it may pay you to use a credit card when shopping in non-euro countries, when you usually receive a better exchange rate (and can delay payment). You're also offered a certain amount of security if goods are found to be faulty.

When buying goods abroad, ensure that you're dealing with a bona fide company and that the goods will work in Germany. When you buy expensive goods abroad, always have them insured for their full value.

Although there are no restrictions, there are 'indicative levels' for certain items, above which goods may be classified as commercial quantities and therefore liable for import duty (if not prohibited altogether). People aged 17 or over may import the following amounts of alcohol and tobacco into Germany without question:

● 10 litres of spirits (over 22° proof);

● 20 litres of fortified wine (under 22° proof);

● 90 litres of wine (or 120 x 0.75 litre bottles or ten cases), of which a maximum of 60 litres may be sparkling wine;

● 110 litres of beer;

● 800 cigarettes, 400 cigarillos, 200 cigars and 1 kg of smoking tobacco.

There's no limit on perfume or toilet water. If you exceed the above amounts, you may need to convince the customs authorities that you aren't planning to sell the goods. There are huge fines for anyone who sells duty-paid alcohol and tobacco, which is classed as smuggling.

Duty & VAT

When buying goods overseas, take into account whether you'll be liable for duty and VAT. There's no duty or tax on goods purchased within the EU or on goods worth below around €50 purchased in most other countries, depending on the shipping method. If you make purchases from a mail order catalogue company or internet vendor outside the EU, you may receive a separate bill for VAT and/or customs duty, depending on the declared value of your shipment and the method of shipping. Parcels shipped from outside Europe by express mail services are more likely to be charged VAT, irrespective of their declared value, due to the customs clearing methods used by shippers. Where charges are due, the postman will collect them when he delivers the parcel or leave a notice in your letterbox instructing you to collect the parcel and pay the charges due at the local post office.

Duty-free Allowances

Duty-free shopping is available when travelling to and from non-EU countries (such as Switzerland). For each journey outside the EU, travellers aged 17 or over are entitled to import duty free:

- two litres of still table wine;

- one litre of alcohol over 22° volume or 38.8 per cent proof (e.g. spirits) **OR** two litres not over 22° volume (e.g. fortified or sparkling wines);

- 200 cigarettes **OR** 100 cigarillos **OR** 50 cigars **OR** 250g of tobacco;

- 60cc/ml (50gr or 2fl oz) of perfume;

- 250cc/ml (8fl oz) of toilet water;

- other goods (including gifts, souvenirs, beer and cider) to the value of €175.

Duty-free allowances apply on both outward and return journeys, even if both are made on the same day, so that the combined total (i.e. double the above limits) can be imported into Germany. Since 1993, duty-free sales have been 'vendor-controlled', meaning that vendors are responsible for ensuring that the amount of duty-free goods sold to individuals doesn't exceed their entitlement.

Duty-free goods purchased on board ships and ferries are noted on boarding cards, which must be presented with each purchase.

RECEIPTS

When shopping in Germany, make sure that you receive a receipt (*Quittung*) and retain it until you've reached home. This isn't only in case you need to return or exchange goods, which may be impossible without the receipt, but also to verify that you've paid if an automatic alarm sounds as you're leaving a shop or any other questions arise. When you buy a large object that cannot easily be wrapped, a sticker should be attached to it as evidence of purchase.

It's wise to keep receipts and records of all major purchases made while resident in Germany, particularly if your stay is for only a short period. This may save you both time and money when you leave Germany and are required to declare your belongings in your new country of residence and may be useful for tax reasons.

CONSUMER ASSOCIATIONS

Germans are usually well versed in the laws and other regulations that most affect them and, in the case of a dispute with a merchant, often all that's necessary is to quote the relevant law or regulation in order to receive satisfaction. On the other hand, if the law establishes a limit on the merchant's liability or responsibility, you're unlikely to sway him with any form of logic.

If you have a complaint against a retailer or manufacturer that you're unable to resolve with them, your first stop should be the local consumer association advice bureau (*Verbraucherzentrale*) to determine your legal position and rights. *Verbraucherzentralen* are found throughout Germany and, while privately owned and operated, are funded by the federal government and the states. For a list of your local *Verbraucherzentralen* go to 💻 www.verbraucher.de or contact the umbrella organisation, Verbraucherzentrale Bundesverband e.V., Kochstrasse 22, 10969 Berlin.

18.

ODDS & ENDS

This chapter contains miscellaneous information that may be of interest to anyone living or working in Germany, arranged in alphabetical order of subject from citizenship to tipping and toilets.

CITIZENSHIP

There are three ways of becoming a citizen of Germany: you can be born in Germany to a German mother or father, you can be naturalised (*Einbürgerung*) or you can exercise the so-called 'right of return' available to 'Germans' living in eastern Europe. Germans take the issue of citizenship and nationality very seriously, and for years Germany's citizenship laws were strictly based on the principle of *jus sanguinis* ('rights of blood' or nationality by inheritance rather than place of birth). Until 1975, a child born in Germany had to have a German father in order to claim German nationality and a German woman married to a foreigner could not transmit her nationality to her children. This changed in 1975, when the law was revised to permit either parent to transmit German nationality to their offspring, although the father's nationality is always registered automatically. **If you want your child (born in Germany) to have its mother's nationality you must make a formal request to the local authority.**

In 2000, the citizenship law was amended again to allow children born to foreign couples in Germany to be German citizens, provided one of the parents had been (legally) temporarily resident in Germany (i.e. with a *befristete Aufenthaltserlaubnis* – see **Residence Permits** on page 71) for at least eight years or held a 'permanent' residence permit (*unbefristete Aufenthaltserlaubnis* or *Niederlassungserlaubnis*) for at least three years at the date of a child's birth. It's also possible under certain circumstances for a child to have dual nationality (i.e. German and that of his parents or a parent).

To obtain German citizenship by naturalisation, you must have resided legally in Germany for eight years. You must be able to show that you haven't been convicted of a serious crime and can support yourself and your family without resort to public assistance (though naturalisation won't limit your eligibility for future assistance). Applicants for German citizenship must also demonstrate their proficiency in the German language and declare their allegiance to the German Constitution (*Grundgesetz*). The language test is very much practical rather than literary.

On taking German citizenship, you're expected to give up your previous citizenship. Most Germans don't believe that a person can properly honour an allegiance to two nations (and Germans who move abroad and take on a new citizenship are expected to give up their German nationality – unless they can demonstrate close personal or property ties in Germany). There are a few exceptions to the ban on dual nationality, including recognised political refugees, elderly individuals who would suffer 'unreasonable hardship' (such as the loss of their foreign pension rights), and cases where the other country imposes high fees or other unreasonably harsh conditions on anyone renouncing their citizenship. (This last provision is intended to address the problem faced by many Turkish residents of Germany, who can lose their rights of inheritance in Turkey on taking German nationality.)

A few countries refuse to accept the renunciation of nationality from a native-born citizen and it's possible you could receive your old passport back in the post. US citizens will find that even a formal renunciation of citizenship may not exempt them from their US tax obligations and it could result in their being denied entry to the US, even for just a visit. In any case, **renouncing your prior nationality is a grave step, which could have serious and life-long consequences**. If you're considering taking German nationality, make sure that you check with your country's embassy first so that you understand exactly what rights you may or may not be giving up along with your passport.

CLIMATE

Overall, Germany's climate is moderate, with warm summers and cool winters. Now and then Germany experiences a particularly hot spell in summer or a vicious cold snap in winter, but these phenomena are usually short-lived. In winter it can seem as if the country is almost upside down, temperatures in the north averaging several degrees higher than those in the south (which is more mountainous). Summers are damp and warm, and while many Germans like to spend their summer holidays on the beaches in the north of the country, the weather there is hardly as balmy as on the Côte d'Azur or in Majorca – both favoured spots among Germans. It's unusual to find air-conditioning anywhere in Germany and for the most part it isn't really needed.

The Alps are a major influence on the climate in the southern region, where winters are long and cold and snowfall is frequent. In Bavaria, annual rainfall can be as high as 200cm (79in), while in the rest of the country annual rainfall of 60 to 80cm (24 to 31in) is normal, summer being the wettest season. Ice and freezing rain are more frequent hazards in winter in most areas than heavy snow.

Germany isn't normally subject to catastrophic weather conditions such as tornadoes or cyclones. However, in spring there's always a danger of flooding, even in some of the minor river valleys, if heavy rains combine with melting snow from the mountains. In the north, storms sweeping across the Arctic Circle, referred to somewhat euphemistically as 'Icelandic lows', bring strong winds and gales to the coastal regions. These are moderated by the warm Gulf Stream, however, and winter temperatures along the North Sea coast average a degree or two above freezing. Centres of high pressure to the east of Germany can bring periods of cold, bright weather in winter.

When a low pressure system crosses the central part of Germany, conditions are ripe for the *Föhn*, a warm, dry wind from the south. Due to the changes in atmospheric pressure that create the *Föhn*, don't be surprised if you come down with a headache when the wind is from the south!

Average day-time maximum/minimum temperatures in Celsius and Fahrenheit (in brackets) for selected cities are show below:

Location	Spring	Summer	Autumn	Winter
Berlin	13/4 (55/39)	23/14 (73/57)	13/6 (55/43)	3/-3 (37/27)
Frankfurt	16/6 (61/43)	24/14 (75/57)	14/7 (57/45)	4/-1 (39/30)
Hamburg	13/3 (55/37)	22/13 (72/55)	13/6 (55/43)	3/-2 (39/28)
Leipzig	14/4 (57/39)	24/13 (75/55)	14/6 (57/43)	3/-3 (37/27)
Munich	14/3 (57/37)	23/13 (73/55)	13/4 (55/39)	2/-5 (36/23)

The German weather forecast is available via the TV teletext service and in all daily newspapers and also includes the pollen count (*Pollenbericht*) from March to July.

A quick way to make a rough conversion from Centigrade to Fahrenheit is to multiply by two and add 30 (see also **Appendix D**).

CRIME

Compared with some other developed countries, Germany had a low crime rate until the end of the '80s and, although a sharp increase occurred in the years following reunification, later figures showed a levelling out, with a fall in youth crime. Total recorded crime decreased by 3.6 per cent in 2005 and a further 1.37 per cent in 2006. Although the number of cases has declined, theft remains by far the most common (over 41 per cent) of all reported crime, followed by fraud and vandalism. Violent and sexual crime have decreased, but fraud, bribery and corruption (so-called white collar crime) have increased significantly and become a preoccupation of the authorities.

Germany is at the crossroads of Europe, not only for trade but also for organised crime, Berlin often serving as its centre of operations. Drugs are a major concern for law enforcement officials and the country is both a market for illegal narcotics and a transit point for the distribution of marijuana, heroin and cocaine to Scandinavia and the UK. Other activities associated with organised crime include car theft (particularly luxury models), counterfeiting, arms smuggling, prostitution and gambling. German tabloid newspapers and TV documentaries feature periodic *exposés* of white slavery rings, which are said to lure women to Germany with promises of office work or au pair positions, while actually selling them into prostitution. While such stories are sometimes sensationalised for the viewing audience, it pays to be aware that offers of easy employment, free from the usual immigration formalities, are unlikely to be legitimate.

During the '70s and early '80s, Germany developed something of a reputation as a centre for terrorist activity, mostly connected with radical left-wing groups such as the Baader Meinhof Gang and Red Army Faction (*Rote Armee Faktion*), which carried out attacks on government and business targets. By 1992, the left-wing groups had sworn off violence in pursuit of their goals, but the right-wing fringe had taken their place in the headlines with equally violent attacks on refugees and asylum seekers.

While racist violence is still a problem in Germany, there's no reason for undue anxiety or paranoia about 'ordinary' crime. Basic common sense and being 'street wise' should help you avoid most sources of trouble. Muggings and armed robbery are, fortunately, still rare in most of Germany, and you can safely walk almost anywhere, day or night. Larger cities, especially Berlin, have their seedy areas, which you should avoid (particularly after dark) – ask any policeman, taxi driver or local person which districts to avoid.

In cities, most apartments are equipped with sturdy locks and spy-holes, as well as a telephone entry system so that you can identify visitors before admitting them to the building. In contrast, in rural areas there are still villages and small towns where people don't lock their homes and cars, although these are fast disappearing.

GEOGRAPHY

Germany is the third-largest country in western Europe (after France and Spain), covering an area of almost 357,000km² (140,000mi²) and stretching 840km (520mi) from north to south and 620km (385mi) east to west. Germany shares borders with nine countries: Poland and the Czech Republic to the east, Switzerland and Austria to the south, France, Luxembourg, Belgium and the Netherlands to the west, and Denmark to the north. Land boundaries total 3,621km (2,250mi), while the coastline (which is entirely in the north bordering the North and Baltic Seas) extends for 2,389km (1,484mi).

Germany's geography has played a major role in much of its history and contributed greatly to the standing of the country within Europe. Located in the centre of the continent and sharing borders with so many other countries, Germany has long been a link between eastern and western Europe. The nation state of Germany has existed only since 1871, when Bismarck created the German Empire following the defeat of France. Prior to that, 'Germany' consisted of numerous small kingdoms, duchies, principalities and city states, some of which are reflected in the names and borders of the modern states (*Länder*). Although Germany is one of the few modern European states without overseas territories, parts of many of its neighbouring states have been German at one time or another.

Geographically, Germany consists of three principal regions. The south is mountainous, including the Bavarian Alps and the foothills of the Swiss Alpine mountain range. The Central German Uplands, in the centre, consist of forested black mountains and intermediate plateaux, which are part of the same formation as the Massif Central in France and continue east into Poland. The north of the country is part of the North European Lowlands, made up of marshes and mud flats extending to the coast and into Denmark. The country generally 'slopes' from south to north, starting with the Zugspitze, the highest point in the Bavarian Alps (2,962m/9,718ft), and dropping to sea level along the two sea coasts in the north. Germany is criss-crossed by many rivers, including the massive and spectacular Rhine, which forms part of its border with France.

A map of Germany showing the 16 states and state capitals is included in **Appendix E**.

GOVERNMENT

As its official name indicates, Germany is a federal republic. The current form of government was established in 1949, after it became clear to the occupying forces of West Germany (the Americans, British and French) that the Soviet Union wasn't going to reach an agreement with them on the future of Germany. Administrative structures had already been re-established by the occupying forces at state level (the *Länder*), so these were charged with selecting delegates to a council which would become the German Parliament. The Parliamentary Council drafted a constitution, called the 'basic law' (*Grundgesetz*), which was then approved by the states. The first national elections to the Parliament were held in August 1949.

Ten states comprised the former West Germany: Bavaria, Baden-Württemberg, Hesse, Lower Saxony, North-Rhine Westphalia, Rhineland-Palatinate, Saarland, Schleswig-Holstein, and the cities of Hamburg and Bremen. West Berlin was accorded non-voting status as an 11th state, as it has always been considered the 'real' capital city of Germany, although Bonn was established as the 'temporary' capital and seat of government. At reunification in 1990, the five eastern states were added: Brandenburg, Mecklenburg-Western Pomerania, Saxony, Saxony-Anhalt and Thuringia, Berlin (east and west) becoming a state in its own right.

Most governmental authority is vested in the states, each of which has its own constitution, parliament, judiciary, cabinet of ministers and even a Minister-President (although not every citizen knows who he is). With reunification, the German government could finally realise the long-held dream of re-establishing Berlin as its capital city. The move from Bonn to Berlin got under way in 1999, but several government agencies still remain there to placate the locals, many of whom opposed the change.

Parliament

The German legislature is a parliamentary system, consisting of two houses called the *Bundesrat* and the *Bundestag* (there's no word in German for both legislative bodies together). The *Bundesrat* is the upper house of parliament, made up of delegates selected by the state governments to represent the interests of the states. Each state has between three and six representatives in the *Bundesrat*, depending on the population of the state, The *Bundesrat* has the right of veto over legislation passed by the lower house (*Bundestag*), and they must approve certain types of legislation affecting the states.

Members of the *Bundestag* are elected by voters using a two-vote system combining proportional representation for political parties with the direct election of candidates within districts. Each voter has two votes in a parliamentary election. One is cast for individual candidates running within the legislative district, the winner gaining a seat in the *Bundestag*. The second vote is cast for a political party and all its state representatives (*Landesliste*), and the total number of seats each party receives in the *Bundestag* is determined by the result of this second vote.

In theory, there are two seats for each voting district in Germany, making a total of 656. However, if the results of the party vote differ from those of the individual elections, additional seats may be added to reflect the actual balance.

The *Bundestag* makes and changes federal laws, makes constitutional amendments, debates government policy, approves the federal budget and ratifies treaties dealing with Germany's external interests. It's the *Bundestag* that elects the prime minister, called the chancellor (*Kanzler*).

Chancellor & President

The chancellor (currently Angela Merkel) is the head of government and is responsible for setting the policy guidelines within which the federal ministers run their departments. The government is accountable to the *Bundestag* for its actions but (yet another demonstration of the German devotion to order and stability) the *Bundestag* can only unseat the chancellor in a vote of no-confidence if they've elected a new chancellor at the same time by an absolute majority. The *Bundestag* cannot unseat individual ministers.

There's also a federal president (currently Horst Köhler), who's the official head of state of Germany, charged with responsibility for appointing and dismissing federal ministers, judges, civil servants and officers of the armed forces. The post, however, is largely ceremonial, although recent presidents have wielded considerable influence over public opinion.

The next elections are in 2009.

Political Parties

Six political parties are represented in the *Bundestag*: the Christian Democratic Party (CDU), founded in 1945 by Konrad Adenauer; the Social Democratic Party (SPD), which has its roots in the working class movements of the late 19th century; the Christian Social Union (CSU); the Free Democratic Party (FDP); the Alliance 90/Greens (usually referred to simply as the Green Party); and The Left Party.

The CSU is primarily a Bavarian party and reflects the strong Catholic influence on the Bavarian state government. At national level, the CSU is aligned with the larger CDU, which has broad support in the business and agriculture sectors. Five of the seven post-war chancellors have been Christian Democrats, although the campaign funding scandal which broke in 2000 has eroded public confidence in the party.

The CDU is the party of Helmut Kohl, post-war Germany's longest-serving chancellor and once seen as the father of reunification. The current chancellor, Angela Merkel, also belongs to CDU and is the first woman to hold that office.

Alliance 90 was predominantly an East German environmental party, which allied with the western Greens in 1993. The Greens were an important partner in the coalition that strongly supported SPD Chancellor Gerhard Schröder.

The Left (*die Linke*), previously known as PDS/WASG, has its roots in the former state party of the German Democratic Republic and currently represents mostly east German voters, although it's working to expand its appeal in the west.

The FPD is a right-wing 'liberal' party, which tends to represent the interests of independent professionals and the owners and managers of small and medium-size businesses. Although small, it's politically important, as it often holds the balance of power.

There are a number of smaller parties active in the states, although none has been able to amass the 5 per cent vote needed for representation in the *Bundestag*.

German law permits the free establishment of political parties but requires parties to conform to democratic principles in their structure and to publicly account for the sources of their funding. Before it can nominate candidates, a new party must have a written constitution and a platform. Any party that seeks to impair or abolish the free democratic order or to endanger the existence of the Federal Republic of Germany can be banned. So far, the federal courts have banned two national parties, both in the '50s, one a far right-wing group and the other the Communist Party of Germany.

Of course, there's no longer a Nazi party in Germany and all literature, symbols, salutes and uniforms of the old National Socialist German Workers Party are banned, and there are heavy fines and jail terms for their use or display. Small groups of neo-Nazis have surfaced from time to time, particularly since reunification, and there's a fear that their numbers are on the increase. However, such groups are closely monitored and, in a number of cases, have been banned by courts in the states before they could organise on a national level.

States

The federal government derives its authority from the states, rather than the other way around. The states are responsible for their own legislation, government and the administration of justice, whereas the federal government is responsible for matters of national importance, such as defence and foreign policy.

Elections

German citizens are eligible to vote at the age of 18, provided they've lived in Germany for at least the three months before the election date. Those living abroad can vote by absentee ballot for ten years after leaving Germany. Citizens of the EU resident in Germany may only participate in local elections and vote and stand for election as representatives to the European Parliament.

Legal System

The German legal system is based on the civil codes enacted by the *Bundestag* (see above). The national constitution is called the 'basic law' (*Grundgesetz*) and spells out in minute detail the division of power between the individual states (*Länder*) and the national federation.

At times it seems that there are laws and regulations for literally everything, and many Germans jokingly explain the legal system with the phrase 'anything not expressly permitted is prohibited' (as opposed to the French system, where 'anything not expressly prohibited is permitted'). However, the Germans seem to find security and stability (*Ordnung*) in having laws or regulations to cover almost every conceivable situation.

Most book shops stock inexpensive editions of the various civil codes, popular legal reference books (*Ratgeber*) and analyses of laws and regulations by subject. A surprising number of Germans are able to quote chapter and verse from miscellaneous regulations governing rent increases, work rules and consumer rights.

Judges and prosecutors are appointed by the state and enjoy a status similar to that of a career civil servant. At federal level, judges are chosen by panels composed of the relevant federal ministry, the appropriate state ministries and deputies from the *Bundestag*. The court system is decentralised, and within each state there's a variety of specialised administrative, criminal and civil courts.

In a German court, it's a judge (or a panel of judges) who asks the questions and tries to determine the facts of the case. The prosecutor or defence counsel is permitted to ask questions or cross-examine defendants or witnesses, but this is rarely done (courtroom practice is considerably less dramatic than in the US). The judge determines the facts of the matter and then rules according to the law that applies. There are strict laws limiting publicity, both before and during a trial, so it's rare to see or read details about an ongoing case on TV or in the newspapers.

An unfavourable decision can be appealed against in a superior court, but only on points of law, not on the facts of the case. There are five federal courts that handle appeals in their respective areas of jurisdiction: the Federal Court of Justice (civil and criminal cases) in Karlsruhe; the Federal Administrative Court in Berlin; the Federal Financial Court in Munich; the Federal Labour Court in Kassel; and the Federal Social Court, also in Kassel. The Federal Constitutional Court deals solely with matters involving basic law, federal/state disputes and legislation on appeal from lower courts or the states. This 'supreme' court also rules on the constitutionality of political parties and on charges against the federal president. A decision in a superior court overrules a lower court's decision, but only for the facts and circumstances of that particular case, as German law doesn't recognise the notion of precedence, where a decision in one case is used as a model for future cases (as in the UK).

In Germany, a person is presumed innocent until proven guilty under the law and has the right to legal counsel. The judge will appoint a defence lawyer in cases where the accused is unable to pay for one, particularly in complicated cases or where a defendant is believed to be unable to defend himself. An accused person can only be imprisoned pending trial (i.e. on remand) where there's strong evidence that he committed a crime and a judge issues a written arrest warrant.

MARRIAGE & DIVORCE

As in many other developed countries, marriage in Germany is becoming less popular. Many couples prefer to live 'in sin' and the average age at which people marry for the first time is increasing (it's currently almost 30 for women and over 32.5 for men). The majority of weddings in western Germany are celebrated in church but only a small percentage of those in the east. In Germany, the civil wedding ceremony at the registrar's office (*Standesamt*) is the important one. A church wedding, which is optional, can take place only after the civil ceremony. Most friends and family members will, however, expect a big party to celebrate the wedding, irrespective of where the formalities take place.

To get married in Germany, you must apply at the registrar's office in the town where one or other of the partners is resident. If neither partner is resident in Germany, you can contact one of the central registrar offices, which can grant permission to any office in its district to perform a wedding for non-residents. There are four regional registrars: in Munich (for Bavaria), Baden-Baden (south-west Germany), Hamburg (northern Germany) and Berlin (eastern Germany).

The local registrar will tell you what documents to provide, but in all cases you need identification (national identification card or passport), documentation establishing your residence and marital status, and the names of your parents and their marital status at the time of your birth. For most Germans, this means obtaining a form from the local *Einwohnermeldeamt* (to establish their own residence and marital status), and providing an official extract from their parents' *Familienbuch*, which provides the necessary family history details.

Many registrars also require a medical certificate, which primarily involves blood tests to screen for congenital and other diseases. Foreigners planning to marry in Germany must provide a certified copy of their birth certificate, showing their parents' names and their marital status at the date of birth. If the prospective bride or groom is widowed or divorced, he or she will be asked to provide the appropriate certificates or decrees to prove this. All documents that aren't in German must be translated by a certified translator. Foreigners must also provide a so-called 'Certificate of No Impediment' from their home country. This is issued by the national authorities of the foreigner's home country and states that under the law of that country there's no reason why the person cannot get married. A number of countries (including the US) don't issue such certificates, in which case you must to apply to the President of the Higher Regional Court (*Oberlandesgericht*) for an exemption. The local registrar can draw up a request for this, so that you don't need to go to court. If you want the titles of any qualifications (e.g. an MA or a PhD) to be included in the wedding documents or announcements, you may be asked to provide the relevant certificates.

All this paperwork must be submitted to the registrar around four to six weeks before a wedding is planned. Germany no longer requires 'publication of the banns' – the practice of posting notice of an impending marriage on the *Rathaus* notice board for a week or two in case anyone wants to oppose your marriage or convince you to back out. Foreign nationals may also be required to notify their embassy or consulate of their marriage.

Marriage in Germany is legally considered like any other contract or legal obligation, so both partners must be of legal age (i.e. 18). It's possible for someone to marry at 16 with the permission of his or her parents, but only if the other partner is of legal age.

Some industry labour contracts provide for an extra day of paid holiday for the new bride and groom, and sometimes even for their parents.

Most couples take the traditional route and use the husband's last name as both their married names, but a married woman can keep her own name if she wishes. Either the husband or wife or both can use a double-name (*Doppelname*), by adding the wife's maiden name to that of the husband. On the birth of their first child, however, a couple must choose a single family name (*Familienname*), which will be the surname for that child and other children born within their marriage.

Unless they opt for a marital contract (*Ehevertrag*), a couple is covered by a form of communal property arrangement (*Zugewinngemeinschaft*), under which they automatically have joint ownership of the increase of the value of their assets since marriage. In the event of divorce, the household property (and any debts) acquired during the marriage are split evenly between the partners. However, it's possible to maintain complete separation of each partner's assets and debts by entering into a marital contract, either before or during the marriage, which must be drawn up by a notary or lawyer.

Marriage of a non-German citizen to a German citizen doesn't confer any preferential rights on the foreigner when it comes to taking German citizenship (see **Citizenship** on page 372).

Divorce

Any married couple resident in Germany can be divorced under German lawm which has largely abandoned the traditional need for one spouse to accuse the other of wrongdoing. The first step in getting divorced is generally that of establishing a separation (*Trennung*) between the partners, which involves not only the segregation of financial affairs but also the physical separation of the household. (It isn't always necessary for one of the partners to move out and it's possible to establish a separation with both spouses still living under the same roof.) Unless there are extraordinary circumstances, the couple won't be eligible for divorce until after at least a year's formal separation. If both parties are agreed to the divorce at that time, a court reviews the division of property and rules on any child support claims, after which the divorce becomes final. Where one of the partners isn't willing to go through with the divorce, the court will intervene to determine the state of the marriage and rule whether or not to finalise a divorce.

After three years' separation, a divorce will be granted automatically unless there are grave extenuating circumstances (such as serious illness or mental problems of one of the partners).

MILITARY SERVICE

Since 1994, German troops been permitted to participate in various military operations under UN auspices with the approval of the *Bundestag*, and Germany currently has peace-keeping forces in Afghanistan.

Defence spending – currently almost €30bn per year or around 10 per cent of the federal budget – is a sensitive political issue given Germany's recent history. There's constant pressure to reduce it, but in the aftermath of the US-Iraq war, the government is considering revising Germany's defence strategy from that of national territorial defence, using heavy armoured formations, to one of readiness to intervene anywhere in the world to defend the country's interests, with much lighter, more mobile forces.

Germany's armed forces (*Bundeswehr*) consist of around 250,000 military personnel. Men are subject to conscription between the ages of 18 and 25, although this can be postponed in cases of family or job-related hardship, the obligation being ten months' service. An alternative is to do 13 months' civilian service, usually in a hospital or other health care facility.

Military service is generally considered excellent preparation for the working world, and many young men display their service records proudly on their CVs when looking for their first job. Women aren't subject to the draft, although there are around 13,000 serving in various roles in the military.

Soldiers in the German military can join a soldiers' union, although they aren't permitted to go on strike. They even have a parliamentary ombudsman (*Wehrbeauftragter des Deutschen Bundestages*) to whom they can take their complaints without having to go through other channels.

PETS

If you plan to take a pet (*Haustier*) to Germany, it's important to check the latest regulations. Make sure that you have the correct papers, not only for Germany, but for all the countries you'll pass through to reach Germany. Careful consideration must be given before exporting a pet from a country with strict quarantine regulations. If you must return, even after just a few days in Germany, your pet may have to go into quarantine, which, apart from being expensive, is distressing for both pets and owners.

The UK has particularly strict quarantine laws, which were originally introduced to prevent the importation of rabies from continental Europe. However, the Pet Travel Scheme (PETS) replaced quarantine for qualifying cats and dogs and now includes rabbits, mice, rates, guinea pigs and ferrets. Under the scheme, pets must be microchipped (they have a microchip inserted in their neck) and vaccinated against rabies, undergo a blood test and be issued with a health certificate ('passport'). **The PETS certificate isn't issued until six months after all the above have been carried out.**

The scheme is restricted to animals imported from rabies-free countries and countries where rabies is under control; this includes all EU countries plus Andorra, Gibraltar, Iceland, Liechtenstein, Monaco, Norway, San Marino, Switzerland and the Vatican as well as Canada and the US and several islands. The quarantine requirement still applies to pets coming from Africa, most of Asia and South America.

The new regulations cost pet owners around £200 (for a microchip, rabies vaccination and blood test), plus some £60 per year for booster vaccinations and approximately £20 for a border check. Shop around and compare fees from a number of veterinary surgeons. To qualify, pets must travel by sea via Dover or

Portsmouth, by train via the Channel Tunnel or via Heathrow or Gatwick airport (only certain carriers are licensed to carry animals, one of which is Lufthansa). Before doing anything, check the current regulations with the Department for Environment, Food and Rural Affairs (DEFRA) in London. Their UK helpline (☎ 0870-241 1710) is manned between 8.30am and 5pm (UK time). Further information can be obtained from the DEFRA website and via email (🖳 www. defra.gov.uk/animalh/quarantine/index.htm and ✉ pets.helpline@defra.gsi. gov.uk).

You can take up to three dogs, cats rabbits or hares into Germany. (A female cat or dog with a litter of kittens or puppies under the age of three months counts as a single animal.) You must have a certificate for each animal showing that it was vaccinated against rabies within the last 12 months and at least 30 days before your arrival in Germany. The certificate must be issued by a licensed veterinary surgeon or state veterinary agency and indicate the address of the issuer clearly as part of the seal or stamp. Reptiles, aquarium fish, hamsters and guinea pigs aren't subject to import restrictions.

Up to four parrots or parakeets can be imported into Germany, provided they have a health certificate issued no more than ten days before their departure. All other birds require an import permit from the highest veterinary authority of the state (*Land*) where you enter Germany. **Birds from countries with outbreaks of avian flu are strictly prohibited.**

You should contact the state veterinary authority if you're planning to import an animal that hasn't been mentioned above. The German consulate can provide you with a list of the veterinary authorities for each state (also listed on 🖳 www.tierarztadressen.eu/98-1-tieraerzte-deutschland.php), who can usually provide bi-lingual forms for your vet to use for vaccination or health certification.

Dogs & Cats

If you own a dog which belongs to what could possibly be deemed a dangerous breed, you must check with the authorities whether you're allowed to bring it into Germany. The government has passed legislation analogous to the British Dangerous Dogs Act, and for similar reasons, which prevents the import into Germany or the breeding there of certain types of dog. The states also have varying regulations on the subject. German diplomatic missions can provide detailed information if you think these restrictions might affect you.

Dogs must be licensed in Germany, which involves having a rabies certificate. The cost of a dog licence varies from town to town, e.g. between €70 and €100 per year, the fee for two dogs often being double.

Dogs are considered a potential nuisance in Germany, with their tendency to make noise and foul pavements. Dog owners are expected to train their dogs, keep them on a lead in public areas and (most importantly) pick up any mess they make. A well trained dog, however, is usually welcomed everywhere, and it shouldn't surprise you to find a dog quietly dozing under a table in a cafe or restaurant while its owner is enjoying a meal or a beer. Shops which don't permit dogs usually post a polite message asking your dog to wait for you outside (evidently most German dogs can read) and sometimes providing rings on the wall for you to attach your pooch to in case it's tempted to disobey.

Cats needn't be licensed in Germany, although if they roam free it's wise to keep them up to date with the recommended vaccinations, particularly rabies. An outdoor cat should also have a collar and identification tag so that the local animal shelter (*Tierheim*) can contact you if your pet is lost.

POLICE

Police (*Polizei*) forces in Germany are organised and maintained by each state and include several specialist services. The *Schutzpolizei* are responsible for general law and order, traffic control, patrolling of streets, and much of the on-site investigation of crimes and accidents. The *Kriminalpolizei* get involved in serious crimes and 'remote' investigations into murders, robberies, organised crime and terrorism. The *Bereitschaftspolizei* is a national unit formed from state ranks which is controlled jointly by the states and the federal government. It provides security in the event of natural disasters or catastrophic accidents. It also assists with crowd control at demonstrations, sporting events and other large gatherings, major traffic control procedures and other large-scale police operations.

The police in Germany wear green uniforms and police cars, which range from small Opels to Porsches, are green and white and marked prominently with the word *Polizei*. It isn't unusual for a police car to sport a powerful loudspeaker system, which is used to tell you exactly where and how to pull over and stop when you've been driving too fast or have committed some other offence. If you start to turn the wrong way into a one-way street you may hear what sounds like a voice from on high barking out a command in German to 'Halt!' It's rather unnerving the first time it happens, but it can save you from a nasty accident. All German police are armed (so be polite to them).

In general, Germans have a lot of respect for their police, as they represent the law and help maintain order, which is so important in German society. Most of the time, your dealings with any member of the police force will be formal, precise and strictly according to the rules and regulations, as prescribed by law. German police don't have a particularly 'warm and friendly' image, but they also aren't normally considered brutal, prone to abusing their powers or corrupt. You should **never** try to bribe a police officer or offer money or anything else to 'forget' a transgression if you've been stopped, which is a particularly serious offence.

POPULATION

The population of Germany is some 82.4m, with an average population density of 230 inhabitants (*Einwohner*) per km^2 (598 per mi^2), one of the highest in Europe. However, population density varies enormously from region to region. The highest average density is in the industrial belt of North Rhine-Westphalia (528 per km^2) and the lowest is in Mecklenburg-Western Pomerania (77 per km^2) in the east. The 12 largest cities in Germany account for almost 15 per cent of the population, Munich (third-largest with 1.3m) being the country's the most densely populated city with over 4,200 inhabitants per km^2. The largest city in Germany, not surprisingly, is Berlin, with nearly 3.4m inhabitants and a density of just under 3,800 per km^2. The next largest cities are Hamburg (1.75m), Cologne (986,000) and Frankfurt (648,000). In the east, the largest cities are Dresden and Leipzig, with populations of 504,000 and 506,000 respectively, although Leipzig's high population density makes it much more crowded than Dresden.

Since reunification, many easterners (known as *Ossies*) have relocated to the west in search of jobs and the rumoured good life, with only limited movement to the east by westerners (*Wessies*); the population in the east in 2000 was around half a million less than in 1991, while the west was home to around 3m more people. Most of the 2.2 per cent overall growth in population in the '90s is attributed to the influx of foreigners and the native population of Germany is declining.

Average life expectancy in Germany is 81.7 for women and 76.2 for men, and increasing. Meanwhile, the birth rate is declining. Over two-thirds of households in Germany comprise just one or two people and the number of households with three or more is falling fast.

There are currently around 7.5m foreigners officially living in Germany or some 9 per cent of the population, plus an estimated half a million who aren't registered as residents. In the '60s and '70s, the Federal Republic recruited large numbers of foreign workers, mostly from Mediterranean countries, who were euphemistically called 'guest workers' (*Gastarbeiter*), in response to labour shortages. Many guest workers stayed at the end of their contracts, so that by the end of 1994 there were over 2m foreigners employed in western Germany, the largest national groups being (in diminishing order) those from Turkey, the states of the former Yugoslavia, Greece and Italy. The now defunct German Democratic Republic recruited a number of Vietnamese workers, several thousand of whom now live and work in what was formerly East Germany. Today, immigrants from Thailand and China still make up the fastest-growing segment of the foreign population. According to official statements, half the foreigners in Germany have lived there for over 20 years, while a third of them have lived in the country longer than 30 years. Until recently it was extremely difficult even for long-time residents of Germany to obtain German nationality (see **Citizenship** on page 372).

Negative attitudes towards foreigners in Germany attract considerable attention abroad from time to time, but immigrants' experiences vary widely and many are highly positive. In general, foreigners from the EU are accepted throughout Germany, although a small segment of the population still harbours visceral attitudes that can only be described as racist, mostly directed towards Greek and Italian immigrant groups. Americans (who are known as *Amis* or *Amies*) have decreased in popularity in the wake of the Iraq war. Attitudes towards some other non-Europeans (and Turks) can be hostile, although it must be emphasised that this is on the popular rather than official level.

Germany has justly prided itself on having some of the most liberal and open policies on political asylum in Europe. When the former Yugoslavia disintegrated, for example, Germany took in far more refugees and asylum seekers than most of its neighbours, despite already having enormous financial commitments with the reunification of the two German states. However, in recent years popular pressure has led to the tightening of asylum legislation and the German government has attempted to meet the needs of those it considers legitimate refugees, without encouraging permanent settlement in the country.

RELIGION

Some 70 per cent of the population are Christian, split fairly evenly between the Roman Catholic and Protestant faiths. The remaining 30 per cent includes some 3.2m Moslems, around 106,000 Jews and those claiming to have no religion at all, at least as far as church tax registration is concerned (see page 83).

The northern part of Germany is primarily Protestant, while the southern states (particularly Baden-Württemberg and Bavaria) are predominantly Catholic. Bavaria, in particular, takes its Catholicism seriously, in both political and educational matters, and the southern states observe additional public holidays, thanks to the influence of the Catholic Church (see **Public Holidays** on page 54).

The Jewish community in Germany tends to be Orthodox, with little remaining of the Conservative or Reform branches of the religion more common before the war. Berlin, Frankfurt and Munich have the largest Jewish communities, and there are smaller communities in at least 80 other towns throughout Germany. The government of Germany considers itself under a moral obligation to accept and welcome Jewish immigrants from eastern Europe.

While there's no official state religion, recognised churches receive funding from the state in exchange for operating a variety of public services, such as hospitals, nursing homes, day care centres and workshops for the disabled. Because of the relatively recent arrival of Islam in Germany, the state hasn't got around to officially recognising the Moslem faith and mosques are only now beginning to receive public funds, although Moslems are exempt from church tax.

Freedom of religion and a ban on discrimination based on religious observance are incorporated into the German constitution and rigorously enforced. Religion is taught as a subject in state schools, where children normally attend Christianity-focussed religious education classes, although parents can choose to have their children take an ethics course instead.

Adherents of Scientology should note that the practice is strongly discouraged in Germany and they're likely to encounter official hostility.

SOCIAL CUSTOMS

All countries have their social customs and Germany is no exception. As a foreigner you'll probably be excused if you accidentally insult your host (though but you may not be invited again!), but it's better to know what constitutes acceptable and unacceptable behaviour in advance. Keep in mind that there's variation from region to region and, by and large, small towns and conservative states in the south adhere more closely to tradition than cosmopolitan cities elsewhere.

- When you're introduced to a German, you should address him or her as Mr (*Herr*) or Mrs (*Frau*) followed by his or her family name and shake hands without gloves (unless it's 20 degrees below freezing). When saying goodbye, it's customary to shake hands again. Note that *Frau* is used nowadays for most women over the age of 18, whether or not they're married.

- When you're introduced to someone, always use the formal form of address (*Sie*). Don't use the familiar form (*du/ihr*) or call people by their first names until invited to do so. If you've previously been on formal terms with someone, there's often quite a bit of ceremony attached to the decision to change to the familiar form of address (*duzen*, as opposed to *siezen*), often involving going out for a drink (and sometimes three or four!) to celebrate.

- Especially in small towns and conservative cities, it's customary to say good day (*guten Tag*) or good morning (*guten Morgen*) – in Bavaria, God greets you (*grüß Gott*) – on entering a small shop or arriving at your place of work, and to say goodbye (see below) on leaving. However, if you do this in a more progressive city, such as Hamburg, where it isn't usual to greet strangers at all, you may get some strange looks (or you'll simply be 'dismissed' as a southern peasant).

- The Germans are well known for their 'wish' greetings among friends or close associates. Rather than saying simply good-bye (*auf Wiedersehen* – literally 'until seeing again'), it's considered more sociable to wish someone a good evening, a good weekend, even a good meal! At lunchtime in many workplaces, people say *Mahlzeit* to each other; this literally means 'mealtime' but is code for 'have a good lunch'. On leaving work in the evening, the usual expression is *Feierabend* (literally, 'quitting time' or 'evening off'), and on Fridays people wish one another a *schönes Wochenende* (literally 'beautiful weekend'). If someone is leaving on holiday, you should wish them *schönen Urlaub* or (if you know they're off on a trip) *gute Reise*. Other options are *viel Spass* ('have fun') and *kommen Sie gut Heim/nach Hause* ('have a safe trip home'). The all-purpose response *gleichfalls* ('same to you') is usually appropriate.

● When you're dining with another person, whether he is a family member or a stranger, you shouldn't begin to eat until you've wished him *guten Appetit*.

● Don't arrive late for an invitation and don't overstay your welcome. The Germans are extremely punctual and will invite you for exactly the time they expect you to arrive. If the invitation states a finishing time, you're expected to make your move for the door at the appropriate hour.

● If you're invited to someone's home, it's usual to take along a small present of flowers, a plant or chocolates. If you take flowers, there must be an odd number (in some places), and you should unwrap them before handing them to the hostess. Flowers can be tricky, as there are specific meanings attached to certain kinds of flowers, and these may differ considerably from what you're used to. To Germans, who take these things seriously, carnations mean bad luck, chrysanthemums are for cemeteries and roses signify love. For newcomers, a potted plant or a box of chocolates could be a safer bet.

● It's a good idea to close inside doors behind you when visiting someone's home. The Germans keep all inside doors closed when rooms aren't in use, including toilets and bathrooms. You should also get into the habit of turning off lights as you leave a room.

● Always identify yourself before asking to speak to someone on the telephone and don't call people at meal times or after 9pm unless you're sure they're night people (or foreigners). Incidentally, goodbye on the telephone is *auf Wiederhören* ('until hearing again').

● If you're planning a party, you should notify your neighbours so that they don't call the police and complain about the noise. Some people will advise you always to invite your neighbours, and in some areas there's an unofficial policy of not calling the police the first time someone throws a noisy party, provided the neighbours have been invited. If you're the one who calls to complain, you could find yourself the neighbourhood pariah – at least for a few weeks afterwards.

● It's considered bad luck to wish someone a happy birthday (or happy anniversary of any kind) or give them a present before the actual date. Stay up late and wait until just after midnight or catch them the next day.

- If you live in an apartment with a communal clothes line (outdoors or indoors), check whether each apartment has a scheduled day and time for using it. There's certainly no quicker way to alienate yourself than to use communal facilities out of turn. If you hang your laundry out to dry on your balcony or anywhere that's visible to the public, check whether there are any local by-laws against drying clothes on Sundays or public holidays, which are most common in small towns in the south of Germany.

TIME DIFFERENCE

Like most of the continent of Europe, Germany is on Central European Time (CET), which is Greenwich Mean Time (GMT) plus one hour in winter and two hours in summer. The Germans change from winter to summer time and vice versa at the same time as the rest of central Europe (i.e. at 2am on the last Sundays in March and October). Time changes are announced in local newspapers and on radio and TV so that you don't forget.

The time in selected major cities when it's noon (in winter) in Germany is shown below:

LONDON	JO'BURG	SYDNEY	AUCKLAND	LOS ANGELES	NEW YORK
11am	1pm	10pm	Midnight	3am	6am

Times (e.g. in timetables) are usually written using the 24-hour clock, when 10am is written as 1000 *Uhr* and 10pm as 2200 *Uhr*. Midday is 12 *Uhr* and midnight is 24 *Uhr* or *Null Uhr*. The 24-hour clock is also often used in speech; for example, 7pm may be referred to as *neunzehn Uhr* (1900) rather than *sieben Uhr abends*. Be careful if people say they'll meet you at *halb acht*, because in German this is 7.30, not 8.30, and they won't be happy if you turn up an hour late! Similarly *Viertel acht* ('quarter eight') is 7.15 (a quarter of the way to 8 o'clock), unless clearly stated as 'quarter to' (*Viertel vor*) or 'quarter past' (*Viertel nach*) the hour.

TIPPING

Most restaurants and hotels include a 12 to 15 per cent service charge in their prices, so leaving a tip (*Trinkgeld*) is optional. Normally, if you want to show your appreciation for the service, you round up the price you're quoted to the next whole euro, permitting staff to keep the change. Rounding up to the nearest five or ten euros is a way of indicating that you found the service exceptionally good, and of course is always appreciated. If you're out with a group of people, each person (or couple) is normally expected to settle his own part of the bill. Obviously, if every member of a large party rounds up his portion of the bill, the waiter will have been suitably rewarded for his efforts.

Although tipping is optional in most other situations, it's traditional to leave a couple of euros for the maid when you check out of a hotel room. Taxi drivers normally receive around 10 per cent of the fare, a tour guide a few euros at the end of a tour, and at the hairdresser you should leave a couple of extra euros for the shampoo girls (often trainees or apprentices). Porters, toilet attendants and cloakroom personnel often advertise their charges, so it's open to question whether a tip is necessary.

TOILETS

Public toilets (*Toiletten*) in Germany can be in exasperatingly short supply. When you're in a town and need one, your best bets are large department stores, cafes and restaurants or the foyers of large hotels. On the motorway, rest areas (*Raststätten*) with public toilets are clearly marked (*Toiletten*), although cleanliness varies. A bathroom is a *Badezimmer*, although this term is never used for a toilet. Public toilets are usually labelled *Herren/Männer* (gentlemen/men) and *Damen/Frauen* (ladies/women) or simply *H* and *D*.

Pay toilets are normal in Germany, particularly in railway stations and many department stores, although urinals (*Pissoir*) are sometimes free. The fee ranges from 10 to 50 cents, usually collected by means of a coin-operated lock, so be sure you always have some change with you. Some toilets have a sign indicating the charges for various 'services' such as using a urinal or WC and washing your hands with hot water. Some toilets have an attendant, whom it's usual to give a 'tip' on your way out.

The traditional German-style toilet may come as a bit of a surprise to unsuspecting newcomers. For some reason, the main part of the toilet bowl is rather shallow, forming a sort of platform. When you flush, the water flow from the tank (often concealed in the wall) pushes anything on this platform to the front of the bowl, where it's carried away down the disposal pipe. Some claim that this unique design caters to the German obsession with monitoring their health.

19.

THE GERMANS

Who are the Germans? What are they really like? Let us take a candid (and unashamedly prejudiced) look at the German people, tongue firmly in cheek, and hope they forgive my flippancy or that they don't read this bit (which is why it's hidden away at the back of the book).

The typical German is a green, a businessman, proud, bureaucratic, subservient, militaristic, punctual, competitive, a unionist, chauvinistic, private, a sun worshipper, angst-ridden, unsympathetic, organised, perfect, superior, honest, industrious, hygienic, a workaholic, taciturn, healthy, tidy, frugal, selfish, well educated, insecure, rigid, arrogant, affluent, conservative, authoritarian, formal, malleable, responsible, self-critical, a pacifist, stoical, materialistic, ambitious, intolerant, reliable, a beer lover, conscientious, obstinate, efficient, enterprising, unloved, obedient, liberal, stolid, orderly, insensitive, xenophobic, meticulous, inventive, prejudiced, conventional, intelligent, virtuous, egotistical, dependable, law-abiding, a good footballer and infuriatingly Teutonic.

You may have noticed that the above list contains 'a few' contradictions, which is hardly surprising, as there's no such thing as a typical German. Modern Germany is a patchwork of former feudal states with enclaves and cities reflecting the tribalism and eccentricities of the former dukedoms and principalities. Germans are first and foremost inhabitants of a particular city (Berliners, Dresdeners, Frankfurters, Hamburgers, Müncheners, etc.) followed by Bavarians, Friesians, Hessians, Prussians, Saxons, Swabians or whatever. They're Europeans third and Germans a distant fourth – and only then among foreigners and because it says so on their passports. However, while it's true that not all Germans are stereotypes (some are almost indistinguishable from 'normal' people), I refuse to allow a few eccentrics to spoil my arguments ...

There has long been a north-south divide; the more conservative northerners dismiss the less inhibited southerners as lazy and soft, while the southerners reciprocate with taunts of 'dour' and 'dull'. There's a less tangible divide between the parochial Saxons in the east and the cosmopolitan Rhinelanders in the west, although this has been sharpened by the reunification of the inhabitants of the former West Germany (*Wessies*) and East Germany (*Ossies*). To the *Ossies*, west Germans are seen as arrogant and greedy colonisers, while east Germans are viewed by *Wessies* as lazy socialists, more than happy to live off state handouts.

Although not always the xenophobes they're painted, Germans don't exactly like foreigners (particular those living in their country) but respect most English-speakers as equals, including (some) Americans, Australians, Britons – all of whom are 'English' to Germans – Canadians, Irish and New Zealanders. They also have a grudging regard for Austrians, French, Dutch, Scandinavians and Swiss (most of whom are more 'Germanic' than the Germans). They tolerate the people of other countries in the European Union (because they have to and they like to holiday in the sun) but are generally somewhat prejudiced against southern or eastern Europeans, not to mention non-Europeans.

Unlike many other countries with a large foreign population, Germany isn't an ethnic melting pot but a jumble of splinter groups living entirely separate lives with their own neighbourhoods, shops, restaurants, clubs and newspapers. The Germans' attitude to foreigners is typified by their name for foreign workers, 'guest workers' (*Gastarbeiter*), who were supposed to leave once they'd done the jobs they were invited to do. However, millions of foreigners, particularly Greeks, Italians, Spaniards, Turks and former Yugoslavians (plus Vietnamese in eastern Germany), failed to do so, and many 'guest' families are now into their third generation. Germany has an ageing population and a low birth rate, which makes immigration (especially of low-paid workers) essential if the natives are to maintain their high standard of living.

However, very few people immigrate in the true sense of the word, making a permanent home in Germany, changing their names to Fritz or Frieda and acquiring citizenship (which is still not that easy). Germany is also a magnet for the homeless and dispossessed, and it has attracted huge numbers of refugees and asylum seekers in the last few decades, whom it initially welcomed with open arms but is now less enthusiastic towards.

Germans pride themselves on their lack of class-consciousness and, apart from some with aristocratic names (surnames beginning with *von*) and a few who still live in castles, Germans generally consider themselves to be middle or working class. However, Germany is far from being a classless society and status is as important there as it is anywhere else, although it's invariably based on money rather than birthright. Germany generally has no 'old school tie' barriers to success (unlike the UK and France) and almost anyone, however humble his origins, can fight his way to the top of the heap – although ethnic barriers aren't so easy to overcome.

There's no truth in the rumour that laughter is forbidden (*Lachen ist verboten*) in Germany, although you may sometimes wonder whether there's a tax on humour. To Germans, humour is something to be taken very seriously – they don't even laugh when you tell them they have no sense of humour! Germans have no sense of sarcasm, although the misfortune of others is a source of much pleasure – called *Schadenfreude* and similar to what everyone else in the world feels when the German national team loses at football. Of course, not all Germans lack a sense of humour, although foreigners are unlikely to understand their complex 'jokes' and locals who appreciate a good jest have usually been corrupted by working too long with frivolous foreigners.

It's difficult to become close friends with Germans – even for other Germans – and Germans from other parts of Germany living in small towns and villages can remain 'outsiders' for decades. You may even be unaware that you have German neighbours, except when they complain. But once you've broken through the barrier, you normally have a loyal and lifelong friend and can call on them (and be called on) unannounced (when Germans entertain a stranger, everything must be spotless and in perfect *Ordnung*).

In business, Germans can be even more formal. In older, conservative companies, colleagues who have worked together for years may still address each other as Herr Schmidt or Frau Müller, using the formal *Sie* form of address. In international companies, *du* is often used among colleagues (usually of the same level), although it's safer to start with *Sie* until told otherwise. Germans aren't usually so strict with foreigners and, if you speak to them in English, you may find yourself on first name terms after a relatively short period. Like most people, they're less formal and more relaxed when entertaining guests in their own homes, although you may not receive an invitation right away.

Germans are law-abiding (except when it comes to speed limits) and follow all rules and regulations (except speed limits) to the letter. Anyone loitering in town at 3am is more likely to be waiting for a green light to cross the road than preparing to rob a bank. The Germans not only slavishly follow all rules and regulations but also delight in pointing out others' transgressions. In Germany, there are rules for everything – which, no matter how trivial, certainly aren't made to be broken. If you use an IN door to exit or park a few centimetres over a line, it will invariably be brought to your attention by an upstanding German citizen. It's often said that in Germany everything that isn't illegal is forbidden (*verboten*), while everything else is compulsory.

On the surface, Germans appear to be reasonably healthy, but in reality they all suffer from something, even if it's 'only' stress brought on by worrying about their possible or latent health problems (and whether they will ever have enough money to be able to retire). Fortunately, Germany has a lot of spas, which are a cure for everything from *Kreislaufstörung* ('circulation disorder' or generally feeling under the weather) to the common cold. However, there's no cure for the national plague of anxiety (*Angst*), which permeates all facets of Germans' lives.

The Germans worry about every aspect of their lives, from their diet to their bank balance, their appearance to their sex lives, their careers to what their friends and neighbours really think of them. But their *Angst* extends far beyond their own lives and they worry incessantly about the environment, their country's image and place in the world, the national football team, mad cow disease and the melting of the glaciers that will bring about the end of the world ... This constant worrying leads to another unique German complaint, *Weltschmerz* (literally 'world pain'), which roughly translates as weariness of life or sheer pessimism.

Germany isn't exactly noted for its food and there's no such thing as German cuisine. German food consists mostly of sausages (*Wurst*), pork, dumplings, potatoes, cabbage, sauerkraut, black bread and cake, washed down with numerous steins of beer. Not for Germans some prissy *nouvelle cuisine*; they want simple, hearty peasant food – and plenty of it. One thing Germans never worry about is starving. They're among the world's most committed carnivores, and vegetarians are thin on the ground. On the other hand, Germans are often particular about what they eat and are careful to avoid anything remotely connected with a health scare.

The Germans also know a thing or two about drinking and are among the world's most prolific consumers of alcohol, particularly beer, although you'll rarely see a legless German – unless it's at a *Bierfest* (and even then he's likely to be a foreigner). They produce a vast variety of beers, all of which are made to standards and with ingredients laid down in the 16th century (foreign beer is labelled to warn consumers that it's 'unclean'). In stark contrast to their excellent beer, most of Germany's wine is 'plonk' and leaves much to be desired (do people still drink Liebfraumilch?), although there are a few notable exceptions.

Germany is renowned for its excellent motorway network and the Germans are second only to Americans (and possibly Australians) in their worship of all things automotive (provided they're made in Germany). They have a passionate and enduring love affair with their cars, which are more important than their homes, spouses and children (put together). In Germany, you are what you drive: Mercedes are for doctors, politicians and captains of industry (and football managers); Porsches are for flashy media types, pop stars and football players; while BMWs and Audis are for middle managers, engineers and hairdressers. The peasants drive Fords, Opels and Volkswagens, although those who are really beyond the pale drive foreign cars.

However, even worse than a foreign car is a dirty car – anyone who doesn't pamper his car (usually a foreigner) doesn't deserve to own one! In Germany your car says more about you than what you wear, where you live or even how much money you have. When they aren't stuck in traffic jams, it's mandatory for Germans to drive everywhere at over 200kph. A German car must above all be reliable and, if one should ever break down, it's likely to be blamed on the *Gastarbeiter* who built it.

Sport is a source of great national pride or shame, depending on whether the Germans are thrashing everybody in sight – usually the case – or unluckily losing narrowly to opponents who cheated, bribed the referee or caught the Germans on a bad day (Germans are **never** beaten by superior opponents). Sports stars are icons and national heroes, and feted wherever they go, and are to be found on chat shows at all times of day and night expounding on a variety of topics, including (sometimes) sport.

The German attitude towards sex is open and up-front, and they delight in flaunting their bodies (and body hair) at every opportunity. German newspapers, magazines and television are obsessed with sex and routinely carry out surveys of the nation's (and other nations') sexual habits, while late night TV is dominated by explicit sex scenes. Germans are unembarrassed about discussing sex with strangers and will relate the most intimate details of their love lives at the drop of a pair of *Lederhosen*. Sex clubs, bars and shops abound in most towns, mixed nude bathing and saunas are commonplace, and Germans are enthusiastic naturists.

Germany isn't exactly a land of milk and honey for the dedicated career woman, who is considered something of an eccentric in the western states (in eastern Germany most women lost their jobs after reunification) and very few receive equal pay with their male colleagues or make it to the top of the heap. Although women theoretically have equal rights with men, in reality this often isn't the case, and they usually must be at least twice as qualified and three times as smart as men to compete on an equal footing. Until fairly recently, women didn't even have rights over their own bodies: abortion was legalised only in 1974 (it was punishable by death in the '30s).

However, most women don't appear overly concerned about the status quo and many seem to enjoy their subservient role, provided they're treated as ladies. Many German men still believe that a woman's place is in the church or home, cooking or taking care of the children – a position summed up by the three words *Kinder, Küche, Kirche.*

The Germans' seemingly permanent prosperity and stability was first jolted in the early '90s by the recession and reunification, which has cost (and is still costing) the Germans far more than they ever bargained for. On top of that, they're the highest financial contributors to the poorer EU countries, whose entrance to the EU they whole-heartedly supported. They're encumbered by myriad petty rules and regulations, and beset by red tape at every turn. Among the biggest concerns facing the nation are unemployment and job security, asylum seekers and refugees, drug addiction and crime, intolerance and racism, the environment, pensions, burgeoning social security costs, housing shortages, high taxation, corruption, increasing competition and high labour costs (not necessarily in that order). Germans can no longer afford to live in the past and many are fearful of what the future may hold.

To be fair, Germans do have quite a few good things going for them. They're excellent footballers, master brewers, and superb architects, engineers and designers, and their products are famous worldwide for their quality and reliability. They're generally slow to make changes, both individually and as a nation, but they're quick to embrace new technology, particularly when it will make them rich(er). Their society is a model of functionality and orderliness compared with many other countries, and they have a strong sense of community and social justice. Germany enjoys a high standard of living, low inflation, relatively good industrial relations, and a very impressive economy (despite the pessimism and unemployment).

They have superb public services, excellent social security benefits (although the country can barely afford them), superb health services (which they constantly complain about) and hospitals (no waiting lists), efficient local government, exceptional working conditions and employee benefits, and a first-class transport system with magnificent motorways and among the world's fastest trains. They also have a rich cultural history and have produced many great artists, composers, poets, philosophers and writers, including such world-famous names as Bach, Beethoven, Brahms, Brecht, Duden, Dürer, Goethe, the Grimm brothers, Handel, Hegel, von Humbolt, Luther, Mann, Marx, Mendelssohn, Nietzsche, Schiller, Schubert, Schumann and Wagner, to name but a handful. Today, Germany remains at the forefront of the arts, particularly classical music, and has some of the world's leading conductors, composers, musicians, orchestras, theatres, galleries and museums.

While doing battle with German bureaucracy is enough to discourage anybody, Germans are generally welcoming, and, provided you're willing to meet them halfway and learn their language, you'll invariably be warmly received. Contrary to popular belief, Germans aren't baby-eating ogres and, although they can be difficult to get to know, when you do get to know a German you invariably make friends for life. The mark of a great nation is that it rarely breeds indifference in foreigners – admiration, envy, hostility or even blind hatred, but seldom indifference. By that standard, Germany is indisputably a great nation. Love it or hate it, it's a unique, vibrant, civilised, bold, sophisticated and challenging country. Germans enjoy one of the world's best lifestyles and an enviable quality of life, and although foreign residents may criticise some aspects of German life, most feel privileged to live in Germany and very few seriously consider leaving.

Auf Deutschland!

20.

MOVING HOUSE OR LEAVING GERMANY

When moving house or leaving Germany, there are numerous things to be considered and a 'million' people to inform. The checklists contained in this chapter are intended to make the task easier and may even help prevent an ulcer or nervous breakdown – provided of course you don't leave everything to the last minute.

MOVING HOUSE WITHIN GERMANY

When you're moving house within Germany, you should consider the following points:

- You must usually give your landlord at least three months' notice before vacating rented accommodation (refer to your contract). If you don't give your landlord sufficient notice or aren't leaving on one of the approved moving dates, you must find someone to take over the property (see page 101). Your resignation letter must be sent by registered post to reach your landlord by the third day of the month or the notice period will apply from the following month. Arrange a date with your landlord for the hand-over.

- You'll need to inform the following:

  - your employer;

  - your present council a week before moving house and your new council within a week of taking up residence (see **Registration** on page 83);

  - your electricity, gas, telephone service, internet access, cable connection and water providers;

  - your insurance companies (e.g. health, car, house contents and private liability); banks, post office, stockbroker and other financial institutions; credit card and hire purchase (credit) companies; lawyer; accountant and local businesses where you have accounts;

  - your family doctor, dentist and other health practitioners – health records should be transferred to your new doctor and dentist, if applicable;

  - your children's schools. If applicable, arrange for schooling in your new community. Try to give a term's notice and obtain a copy of any relevant school reports or records from your children's current schools.

  - all regular correspondents, publications to which you subscribe, social and sports clubs, friends and relatives. Give or send them your new address and telephone number. Address cards are available free from post offices. Arrange to have your post redirected by the post office (see **Change of Address** on page 125).

- your local consulate or embassy if you're registered with them.

• If you have a German driving licence or a German registered car, you must contact the driving licence office (*Führerscheinstelle*) of your local district administration office (*Landratsamt*) and the local motor vehicle branch (*Kfz-Zulassungsstelle*) in your new town;

• Return anything borrowed (e.g. library books).

• Re-register your dog with your new council.

• Arrange removals or transport for your furniture and belongings.

• Arrange for a cleaning company and/or decorating company for your apartment, if necessary (see page 101).

• If applicable, ensure the return of the deposit from your landlord.

• Cancel newspaper and other regular deliveries.

• Give notice to your employer, if applicable.

• Contact Deutsche Telekom to cancel your contract and pay the final bill when it arrives.

• Ask yourself (again): 'Is it really worth all this trouble?'

LEAVING GERMANY

Before leaving Germany for an indefinite period, the following items should be considered **in addition** to those listed above:

• Check that your own and your family's passports are valid.

• Check the entry requirements for your country of destination, e.g. regarding visas, permits and vaccinations, by contacting its embassy or consulate in Germany. An exit permit or visa isn't required to leave Germany, but forms may need to be completed before arrival. If you've been living in Germany for less than a year, you're required to re-export all imported personal effects, including furniture and vehicles (if you sell them, you must pay duty).

• You may qualify for a rebate on your income tax and pension insurance. Your employer and council will assist you with these. Tax rebates are normally paid automatically.

• Your private company pension contributions may be repaid in full. Before your pension fund will repay your funds, you must provide a statement from your council stating that you've de-registered and are leaving Germany.

- Arrange to sell anything you aren't taking with you (e.g. house, car and furniture). Find out the exact procedure for shipping your belongings to your country of destination.

- If you have a German registered car that you plan to take with you, you must import and re-register it in your new country of residence within a limited time.

- Pets may require vaccinations several months in advance of your move or need to go into quarantine for a period on arrival in the new country.

- Arrange health, travel and other insurance (see **Chapter 13**).

- Depending on your destination, you may wish to arrange health and dental check-ups before leaving Germany. Obtain a copy of your health and dental records and a statement from your health insurance company stating your present level of cover.

- Terminate any German loan, lease or hire purchase (credit) contracts and pay all outstanding bills (allow plenty of time as some companies are slow to respond).

- Check whether you're entitled to a rebate on your road tax, car and other insurance. Obtain a letter from your German motor insurance company stating your no-claims bonus.

- Check whether you need an international driver's permit or a translation of your German or foreign driving licence for your country of destination.

- Give friends and business associates in Germany an address and telephone number where you can be contacted.

- If you'll be travelling or living abroad for an extended period, you may wish to give someone 'power of attorney' over your financial affairs in Germany so that they can act on your behalf in your absence. This can be for a fixed period or open-ended and can be limited to a specific purpose only. **You should, however, take legal advice before doing this.**

- Buy a copy of *Living and Working in* ******** before leaving Germany. If we haven't written it yet, drop us a line and we'll get started on it straight away!

Gute Reise!
Have a good journey!
And farewell to the old style!

APPENDICES

Appendix A: FURTHER INFORMATION

Embassies & Consulates

Foreign Embassies In Berlin

The following list includes the major embassies and consulates in the capital Berlin (telephone code 030). Many countries also have consulates in other cities (listed in the yellow pages under *Konsulate*).

Afghanistan: Taunusstrasse 3, Ecke Kronbergerstr. 5 10117 Berlin (☎ 206 7350).

Albania: Friedrichstrasse 231, 10969 Berlin (☎ 259 3040).

Algeria: Görschstrasse 45-46, 13187 Berlin (☎ 437 370).

Angola: Wallstrasse 58, 10179 Berlin (☎ 240 8970).

Argentina: Kleitstrasse 23-26, 10117 Berlin (☎ 226 6890).

Armenia: Nußbaumallee 4, 14050 Berlin (☎ 405 0910).

Australia: Wallstrasse 76-79, 10179 Berlin (☎ 880 0880).

Austria: Stauffenbergstrasse 1, 10785 Berlin (☎ 202 870).

Azerbaijan: Axel-Springer-Strasse 54, 10117 Berlin (☎ 219 1613).

Bahamas: Flottenstrasse 14-20, 13407 Berlin (☎ 4090 04107).

Bahrain: Klingelhöfer Strasse 7, 10785 Berlin (☎ 868 77777).

Bangladesh: Dovestrasse 1, 10587 Berlin (☎ 398 9750).

Belarus: Am Treptower Park 32, 12435 Berlin (☎ 536 3590).

Belgium: Jägerstrasse 52-53, 10117 Berlin (☎ 206420).

Benin, Republic of: Englerallee 23, 14195 Berlin (☎ 2363 14710).

Bolivia: Wichmannstrasse 6, 10787 Berlin (☎ 263 9150).

Bosnia-Herzegovina: Ibsenstrasse 14, 10439 Berlin (☎ 8147 1210).

Brazil: Wallstrasse 57, 10179 Berlin (☎ 72628600).

Brunei Darussalam: Kronenstrasse 55–58, 10117 Berlin (☎ 206 0760).

Bulgaria: Mauerstrasse 11, 10117 Berlin (☎ 201 0922).

Burkina Faso: Karolingerplatz 10-11, 14052 Berlin (☎ 3010 5990).

Burundi: Berlinerstrasse 36, 10715 Berlin (☎ 234 5670).

Cambodia: Benjamin-Vogelsdorff-Strasse 2, 13187 Berlin (☎ 4863 7901).

Canada: Leipziger Platz 17, 10117 Berlin (☎ 203120).

Cape Verde: Stavangerstrasse 16, 10439 Berlin (☎ 2045 0955).

Chile: Mohrenstrasse 42, 10117 Berlin (☎ 726 2035).

China, People's Republic of: Märkisches Ufer 54, 10179 Berlin (☎ 275880).

Columbia: Kurfürstenstrasse 84, 10787 Berlin (☎ 263 9610).

Costa Rica: Dessauerstrasse 28-29, 10963 Berlin (☎ 2639 8990)

Croatia: Ahornstrasse 4, 10787 Berlin (☎ 2362 8955).

Cuba: Stavangerstrasse 20, 10439 Berlin (☎ 4473 7023).

Cyprus: Wallstrasse 27, 10179 Berlin (☎ 308 6830).

Czech Republic: Wilhelmstrasse 44, 10117 Berlin (☎ 226380).

Denmark: Rauchstrasse 1, 10787 Berlin (☎ 5050 2000).

Dominican Republic: Dessauer Strasse 28/29, 10963 Berlin (☎ 2575 7760).

Ecuador: Joachimstaler Strasse 10-12, 10719 Berlin (☎ 800 9665).

Egypt: Stauffenbergstrasse 6-7, Berlin 10785 (☎ 477 5470).

El Salvador: Joachim-Karnatz-Allee 47, 10557 Berlin (☎ 206 4660).

Equatorial Guinea: Rohlfsstrass. 17-19, 14195 Berlin (☎ 8866 3877).

Eritrea: Stavangerstrasse 18, 10439 Berlin (☎ 446 7460).

Estonia: Hildebrandstrasse 5, 10785 Berlin (☎ 2546 0600).

Ethiopia: Boothstrasse 209, Berlin 12207 (☎ 772060).

EU Commission: Unter den Linden 78, 10117 Berlin, (☎ 2280 2000).

Finland: Rauchstrasse 1, 10787 Berlin (☎ 505030).

France: Pariser Platz 5, 10117 Berlin (☎ 5900 39000).

Gabon: Hohensteinerstrasse 16, 104197 Berlin (☎ 8973 3440).

Georgia: Heinrich-Mann-Strasse 32, 13156 Berlin (☎ 484 9070).

Ghana: Stavangerstrasse 17-19, 10439 Berlin (☎ 547 1490).

Great Britain: Wilhelmstrasse 70/71, 10117 Berlin (☎ 204570).

Greece: Jägerstrasse 55, 10117 Berlin (☎ 206260).

Guatemala: Joachim-Karnatz-Allee 47, 10557 Berlin (☎ 206 4363).

Guinea: Jägerstrasse 67-69, 10117 Berlin, (☎ 2007 4330).

Haiti: Meinekestrasse 5, 10719 Berlin (☎ 8855 4134).

Honduras: Cuxhavenerstrasse 14, 10555 Berlin (☎ 39749710/09).

Hungary: Unter den Linden 76, 10117 Berlin (☎ 203100).

Iceland: Rauchstrasse 1, 10787 Berlin (☎ 5050 4000).

India: Tiergartenstrasse 17, 10785 Berlin (☎ 2579 5611).

Indonesia: Lehrterstrasse 16-17, 10557 Berlin (☎ 478070).

Iran: Podbielskiallee 67, 14195 Berlin (☎ 843530).

Iraq: Remeisterstrasse 20, 14169 Berlin (☎ 814880).

Ireland: Friedrichstrasse 200, 10117 Berlin (☎ 220720).

Israel: Auguste-Viktoria-Strasse 74–76, 14193 Berlin (☎ 8904 5500).

Italy: Dessauer Strasse 28-29, 10963 Berlin (☎ 254400).

Jamaica: Schmargendorferstrasse. 32, 12159 Berlin (☎ 859 9451).

Japan: Hiroshimastrasse 6, 10785 Berlin (☎ 210940).

Jordan: Heerstrasse 201, 13595 Berlin (☎ 369 9600).

Kazakhstan: Nordendstrasse 14-15, 13156 Berlin (☎ 470 0711).

Kenya: Markgrafenstrasse 63, 10969 Berlin (☎ 259 2660).

Kirghizstan: Otto-Suhr-Allee 146, 10585 Berlin (☎ 3478 1338).

Korea (North): Glinkastrasse 5–7, 10117 Berlin (☎ 229 3189).

Korea (South): Stülerstrasse 8-10, 10787 Berlin (☎ 2606 5433).

Kuwait: Griegstrasse 5–7, 14193 Berlin (☎ 897 3000).

Laos: Bismarckallee 2a, 14193 Berlin (☎8906 0647).

Latvia: Reinerzstrasse 40/41, 14193 Berlin (☎ 8260 0222).

Lebanon: Berlinerstrasse 127, 13187 Berlin (☎ 474 9860).

Lesotho: Dessauer Strasse 28-29, 10963 Berlin (☎ 257 5720).

Liberia: Pücklerstrasse 8, 14195 Berlin (☎ 8410 9007).

Libya: Podbielskiallee 42, 14195 Berlin (☎ 200 5960).

Liechtenstein: Mohrenstrasse 42, 10117 Berlin (☎ 5200 0630).

Lithuania: Charitestrasse 9, 10117 Berlin (☎ 890 6810).

Luxembourg: Klingelhöferstrasse 7, 10785 Berlin (☎ 263 9570).

Macedonia: Königsallee 2-4, 14193 Berlin (☎ 8906 9511).

Malawi: Westfälischestrasse 86, 10709 Berlin (☎ 8631 3450).

Malaysia: Klingelhöferstrasse 6, 10785 Berlin (☎ 885 7490).

Mali: Kurfürstendamm 72, 10709 Berlin (☎ 319 9883).

Malta: Klingelhöferstrasse 7, 10785 Berlin (☎ 263 9110).

Mauritania: Kommandantenstrasse 80, 10117 Berlin (☎ 206 5883).

Mauritius: Kurfürstenstrasse 84, 10787 Berlin (☎ 2639 3610).

Mexico: Klingelhöferstrasse 3, 10785 Berlin (☎ 269 3230).

Moldova: Gotlandstrasse 16, 10439 Berlin (☎ 283 5237).

Monaco: Klingelhöferstrasse 7, 10785 Berlin (☎ 263 9033).

Mongolia: Dietzgenstrasse 31, 13156 Berlin (☎ 474 8060).

Morocco: Niederwallstrasse 39, 10117 Berlin (☎ 206 1240).

Mozambique: Stromstrasse 47, 10551 Berlin (☎ 3987 6500).

Myanmar (Burma): Thielallee 19, 14195 Berlin (☎ 2061 5710).

Namibia: Wichmannstrasse 5, 10787 Berlin (☎ 254 0950).

Nepal: Guerickestrasse 27, 10587 Berlin (☎ 3435 9920).

Netherlands: Klosterstrasse 50, 10179 Berlin (☎ 209560).

New Zealand: Friedrichstrasse 60, 10117 Berlin (☎ 206210).

Nicaragua: Joachim-Karnatz-Allee 45, 10557 Berlin (☎ 206 4380).

Nigeria: Neue Jacobstrasse 4, 10179 Berlin (☎ 212300).

Norway: Rauchstrasse 1, 10787 Berlin (☎ 505050).

Pakistan: Schaperstrasse 29, 10719 Berlin (☎ 212440).

Palestine General Delegation: Michaelkirchstr. 17-18, 10179 Berlin (☎ 206 1770).

Panama: Joachim-Karnatz-Allee 45, 10557 Berlin (☎ 2260 5811).

Paraguay: Hardenbergstrasse 12, 10623 Berlin (☎ 3180 2725).

Peru: Mohrenstrasse 42, 10117 Berlin (☎ 229 1455).

Philippines: Uhlandstrasse 97, 10715 Berlin (☎ 864 9500).

Poland: Lassenstrasse 19-21, 14193 Berlin (☎ 223130).

Portugal: Zimmerstrasse 56, 10117 Berlin (☎ 5900 63500).

Romania: Dorotheenstrasse 62-66, 10117 Berlin (☎ 2123 9555).

Russian Federation: Unter den Linden 63-65, 10117 Berlin (☎ 229 1110).

Rwanda: Jägerstrasse 67-69, 10117 Berlin (☎ 2091 6590).

Saudi Arabia: Kurfürstendamm 63, 10707 Berlin (☎ 889250).

Senegal: Dessauer Strasse 28-29, 10963 Berlin (☎ 856 2190).

Serbia: Taubertstrasse 18, 14193 Berlin (☎ 895 7700).

Seychelles: Rauchstrasse 26, 10787 Berlin (☎ 3190 7660).

Singapore: Friedrichstrasse 200, 10117 Berlin (☎ 2263 4318).

Slovak Republic: Friedrichstrasse 60, 10117 Berlin (☎ 889 26200).

Slovenia: Hausvogteiplatz 3-4, 10117 Berlin (☎ 206 1450).

South Africa: Tiergartenstrasse 18, 10785 Berlin (☎ 220730).

Spain: Lichtensteinallee 1, 10787 Berlin (☎ 254 0070).

Sri Lanka: Niklasstrasse 19, 14163 Berlin (☎ 8090 9743 49).

Sudan: Kurfürstendamm 151, 10709 Berlin (☎ 890 6980).

Swaziland: Neue Promenade 8, 10178 Berlin (☎ 2809 6250).

Sweden: Rauchstrasse 1, 10787 Berlin (☎ 505060).

Switzerland: Otto-von-Bismarck-Allee 4a, 10557 Berlin (☎ 390 4000).

Syria: Rauchstrasse 25, 10787 Berlin (☎ 501 770).

Tajikistan: Otto-Suhr-Alllee 84, 10585 Berlin (☎ 347 9300).

Tanzania: Eschenallee 11, 14050 Berlin (☎ 303 0800).

Thailand: Lepsiusstrasse 64–66, 12163 Berlin (☎ 794810).

Tunisia: Lindenallee 16, 14050 Berlin (☎ 364 1070).

Turkey: Rungestrasse 9, 10179 Berlin (☎ 275850).

Turkmenistan: Langobardenallee 14, 14052 Berlin (☎ 3010 2452).

Uganda: Heinrich-Heine-Strasse 18, 10179 Berlin (☎ 2404 7556).

Ukraine: Albrechtstrasse 26, 10117 Berlin (☎ 288 8710).

United Arab Emirates: Hiroshimastrasse 18-20, 10785 Berlin (☎ 516516).

United States of America: Neustädtische Kirchstrasse 4–5, 10117 Berlin (☎ 238 5174).

Uruguay: Budapesterstrasse 39, 10787 Berlin (☎ 263 9016).

Uzbekistan: Perlebergerstrasse 62, 10559 Berlin (☎ 394 0980).

Vatican City: Apostolische Nuntiatur, Lilienthalstrasse 3a, 10965 Berlin (☎ 616240).

Venezuela: Schillstrasse 9–10, 10785 Berlin (☎ 832 2400).

Vietnam: Elsenstrasse 3, 12435 Berlin (☎ 5363 0108).

Yemen: Budapester Strasse 37, 10787 Berlin (☎ 897 3050).

Zambia: Axel-Springer-Strasse 54a, 10117 Berlin (☎ 206 2940).

Zimbabwe: Kommandantenstrasse 80, 10117 Berlin (☎ 206 2263).

German Diplomatic Representation Abroad

The following is a list of German embassies, consulates or diplomatic missions in selected countries.

Australia: 119 Empire Circuit, Yarralumla, Canberra, ACT 2600 (☎ 6270 1911).

Canada: 1 Waverly Street, Ottawa, ON K2P 0T8 (☎ 613-232 1101).

Ireland: 31 Trimleston Avenue, Bootersown, Blackrock, Co. Dublin (☎ 01-269 3011).

New Zealand: 90–92 Hobson Street, Thorndon, Wellington (☎ 04-473 6063).

South Africa: 180 Blackwood Street, Arcadia, Pretoria 0083 (☎ 012-427 8900).

United Kingdom: 23 Belgrave Square, London SW1X 8PZ (☎ 020-7824 1300).

United States of America: 4645 Reservoir Road, NW, Washington, DC-20007-1998 (☎ 202-298 4000, 🖥 www.germany-info.org).

Government Offices

The principal federal ministries (*Bundesministerien*) and other government services in Germany are as follows (BM is short for *Bundesministerium*):

Chancellery (Bundeskanzleramt), Willy-Brandt-Strasse 1, 10557 Berlin.

Foreign Office (Auswärtiges Amt), Werderscher Markt 1, 10117 Berlin (☎ 030-50000).

Ministry for Consumer Protection, Food & Agriculture (BM für Verbraucherschutz, Ernährung und Landwirtschaft), Wilhelmstrasse 54, 10117 Berlin (☎ 030- 20060).

Ministry of Defence (BM der Verteidigung), Stauffenbergstrasse 18, 10785 Berlin (☎ 01888-24000).

Ministry of Economic Co-operation & Development (BM für Wirtschaftliche Zusammenarbeit und Entwicklung), Europahaus, Stresemannstrasse 94, 10963 Berlin (☎ 030-185350)

Ministry for Economics & Technology (BM für Wirtschaft und Technologie), Scharnhorststrasse 34-37, 10115 Berlin (☎ 030-2014 5208).

Ministry of Education & Research (BM für Bildung und Forschung), Hanoverschestrasse 28-30, 10115 Berlin (☎ 01888-570).

Ministry for the Environment, Nature Conservation & Nuclear Safety (BM für Umwelt, Naturschutz und Reaktorsicherheit), Referat Öffentlichkeitsarbeit, 11055 Berlin (☎ 030-83050).

Ministry for the Family, Senior Citizens, Women & Youth (BM für Familie, Senioren, Frauen und Jugend), Alexanderstrasse 3, 10178 Berlin (☎ 030-18555).

Ministry of Finance (BM der Finanzen), Wilhelmstrasse 97, 10117 Berlin (☎ 030-186820).

Ministry for Health (BM für Gesundheit), Friedrichstrasse 108, 10117 Berlin (☎ 030-184410).

Ministry for Labour & Social Security (BM für Arbeit und Soziales), Wilhelmstrasse 49, 10117 Berlin, PA, 11017 Berlin (☎ 030-1852 72236).

Ministry of the Interior (BM des Innern), Alt-Moabit 101 D, 10559 Berlin (☎ 030-186810).

Ministry of Justice (BM der Justiz), Moehrenstrasse 37, 10117 Berlin (☎ 030-185800).

Ministry for Transport, Building & City Development (BM für Verkehr, Bau- und Stadtentwicklung), Invalidenstrasse 44, 10115 Berlin (☎ 030-183000).

Parliament (Deutsche Bundestag), Platz der Republik 1, 11011 Berlin (☎ 030-2270).

German National Tourist Offices

Amsterdam: Duits Verkeersbureau, Postbus 12051, 1101 Amsterdam, Netherlands (☎ 020-311 3929, 🖥 www.duitsverkeersbureau.nl).

Beijing: c/o Delegate of German Industry and Commerce Beijing, Landmark Tower 2, #0811, 8 North Dongsanhuan Road, Chaoyang District, Beijing 100004, China (☎ 010-659 0092 6215, ✉ gntobj. xu@ahkbj.org.cn).

Brussels: Gulledelle 92 Val d'Or, 1200 Brussels, Belgium (☎ 02-245 9700, ✉ gntobru@d-z-t.com).

Budapest: Lüvöház utca 30, H-1024 Budapest, Hungary (☎ 01-3457 633, ✉ dztbud@ahkungarn.hu).

Chicago: Box 59594, Chicago, IL 60659-9594, USA (☎ 773-539 6303, ✉ info@gntoch.com).

Copenhagen: Vesterbrogade 6 D III, 1620 Copenhagen, Denmark (☎ 033-436800, ✉ gntocph@d-z-t.com).

Frankfurt-am-Main: Beethovenstrasse 69, 60325 Frankfurt-am-Main (☎ 069-9746 4287, 🖥 www.germany-tourism.de).

Helsinki: c/o Deutsch-Finnische Handelskammer, PL 859, 00101 Helsinki, Finland (☎ 09-680 1779, ✉ dztinfo@dfhk.fi).

Hong Kong: German National Tourist Office, 3601 Tower One, Lippo Centre, 89 Queensway, Hong Kong (☎ 252-65481, ✉ info@ahk. org.hk).

Jaffa: c/o Lufthansa Airlines, 37 Sheerit Israel Street, 68165 Jaffa, Israel (☎ 03-513 5306, ✉ dzt@barak.net.il).

Ljubljana: c/o im.puls d.o.o., Levstikova ul.22, SL-1000 Ljubljana, Slovenia (☎ 01-251 1111, ✉ haberl@siol.net).

London: Box 2695, London W1A 3TN, UK (☎ 020-7317 0908, ✉ gntolon@d-z-t.com).

Los Angeles: 1334 Parkview Avenue, Suite 300, Manhattan Beach, CA 90266, USA (☎ 310-545 1350, ✉ info@gnto.lax.com).

Madrid: San Agustin 2, Plaza de las Cortes, E-28014 Madrid, Spain (☎ 091-4293551, ✉ infoalemania@d-z-t.com).

Milan: CP 10009, I-20110 Milan, Italy (☎ 02-8474 4444, ✉ gntomil@ d-z-t.com).

Moscow: c/o Lufthansa German Airlines, Olimpinski Prospekt 18/1, Moscow 129110, Russia (☎ 0495-9319836, ✉ dztmow@germany-club.ru).

New York: 122 East 42nd Street, New York, NY 10168-0072, USA (☎ 212-661 7200, 🖥 www.cometogermany.com).

Oslo: St Olavs Plassen, PB 6723, 0130 Oslo, Norway (☎ 022-853480, ✉ info@dztosl.com).

Paris: 21 Rue Leblanc, 75015 Paris, France (☎ 01 40 20 07 46, ✉ gntopar@d-z-t.com).

Prague: c/o Travel Plus SRO, Na Prikope 24, Prague 11000, Czech Republic (☎ 02-244 22952, ✉ info@dzt.cz).

São Paulo: Câmara de Comércio e Indústria Brasil-Alemanha, Rua Verbo Divino, 1488-3.andar, São Paulo, São Paulo 04719-904, Brazil (☎ 011-5181 2310, ✉ dzt.brasil@ahkbrasil.com).

Stockholm: Box 10147, 10055 Stockholm, Sweden (☎ 08-665 1881, ✉ gntosto@d-z-t.com).

Sydney: c/o German Australian Chamber of Industry & Commerce, Box 1461, Sydney, NSW 2001, Australia (☎ 02-8296 0488, ✉ gnto@germany.org.au).

Tokyo: 7-5-56 Akasaka, Minato-ku, Tokyo 107-0052, Japan (☎ 03-3586 0380, ✉ gntotyo@d-z-t.com).

Toronto: 480 University Avenue, Suite 1500, Toronto, Ontario M5G IV2, Canada (☎ 416-968 1685, ✉ info@gnto.ca).

Vienna: Schubertring 12, 1010 Wien, Austria (☎ 01-51327, ✉ deutschland.reisen@d-z-t.com).

Warsaw: VIA POLSKA Sp. z.o.o., Skryt. Poczt. 767, Warszawa 01950, Poland (☎ 022-636 6110, ✉ waw@d-z-t.pl).

Zürich: Talstrasse 62, 8001 Zurich, Switzerland (☎ 044-213 2200/11, ✉ gntozrh@d-z-t.com).

Miscellaneous

Allgemeiner Deutscher Automobilclub (ADAC), Am Westpark 8, 81373 Munich (☎ 089-76760, 🖥 www.adac.de).

American Chamber of Commerce, Rossmarkt 12, 60311 Frankfurt-am-Main (☎ 069-929 1040, 🖥 www.amcham.de).

Association of German Chambers of Industry & Commerce (Deutscher Industrie-und Handelstag), Breitestrasse 29, 10178 Berlin (☎ 030-203080, 🖥 www.diht.de).

British Chamber of Commerce in Germany, Französischerstrasse 48, 10117 Berlin (☎ 030-206 7080, 🖥 www.bccg.de).

British Council, Hackescher Markt 1, 10178 Berlin (☎ 030-311 0990, 🖥 www.british council.de).

British Trade Office, British Consulate-General, Yorckstrasse 19, Dusseldorf (☎ 021-9448, ✉ central.coordination.unit.dusseldorf@fco.gov.uk).

Central Placements Agency (ZAV), Villemomblerstrasse 76, 53123 Bonn (☎ 0228-7130, 🖥 www.arbeitsamt.de/ZAV).

Federal Insurance Agency (Bundesversicherungsanstalt für Angestellte), 10704 Berlin (☎ 030-8651, 🖳 www.bfa.de).

German Academic Exchange Service (DAAD), 34 Belgrave Square, London SW1X 8BQ, UK (☎ 020-7235 1736, info@daad.org.uk) and 871 United Nations Plaza, New York, NY 10017, USA (☎ 212-758 3223, ✉ daadny@daad.org). The HQ of the German Academic Exchange Service (Deutscher Akademischer Austauschdienst) is Kennedyallee 50, 53175 Bonn, or Postfach 20 04 04, 53134 Bonn for postal correspondence (☎ 0228-88207, 🖳 www.daad.de – available in English).

German Arts Council (Deutscher Kulturrat e.V), Bundes-geschäftsstelle, Chausseestrasse 103, 10115 Berlin (☎ 030-2472 8014, 🖳 www.kulturrat.de).

German-British Chamber of Industry & Commerce, Mecklenburg House, 16 Buckingham Gate, London SW1E 6LB, UK (☎ 020-7976 4100, 🖳 www.germanbritishchamber.co.uk).

German Federal Labour Office (Bundesagentur für Arbeit), Regensburgerstrasse 104, 90478 Nuremberg (☎ 0911-1790, 🖳 www. arbeitsagentur.de).

German Sports Federation (Deutscher Sportbund), Otto Fleck-Schneise 12, 60528 Frankfurt-am-Main (☎ 069-67000, 🖳 www.dsb. de).

Goethe Institut Inter Nationes, Helene-Weber-Allee 1, 80637 München or Postfach 19 04 19, 80604 München (☎ 089-159 2107, 🖳 www.goethe.de).

Institute for Foreign Relations (Institut für Auslands-beziehungen e.V.), Charlottenplatz 17, 70173 Stuttgart (☎ 0711-222507, 🖳 www. ifa.de).

National Association of German Business Consultants (Bundesverband Deutscher Unternehmensberater), Zitelmannstrasse 22, 53113 Bonn (☎ 0228-9160, 🖳 www.bdu.de.).

National Chamber of Tax Consultants (Bundessteuerberater-kammer), Neue Promenade 4, 10178 Berlin (☎ 030-2400 870, 🖳 www.bstbk.de).

APPENDIX B: FURTHER READING

In the lists on the following pages, the publication title is followed by the author's name and the publisher's name (in brackets). Note that some titles may be out of print, although you may still be able to find a copy in a bookshop or library. Books prefixed with an asterisk (*) are recommended by the author.

The lists below contain only a selection of the hundreds of titles about Germany. In addition to the (mostly) general guides listed, there are numerous guides covering individual regions and cities. The publication title is followed by the author's name and the publisher's name (in brackets). Some titles may be out of print but may still be obtainable from book shops and libraries. Books prefixed with an asterisk are recommended by the author.

General Tourist Guides

AA Explorer Germany (AA Publishing)

*Baedeker's Germany (Baedeker)

*Berlin, Gordon McLachlan (Odyssey)

*Daytrips Germany: 60 One Day Adventures by Rail or by Car in Bavaria, the Rhineland, the North and the East, Earl Steinbeck (Hastings House)

Fodor's Germany (Fodor's)

Fodor's Berlin's 25 Best with Map, Christopher Rice & Melanie Rice (Fodor's)

*Frommer's Germany, Darwin Porter & Danforth Prince (Frommers)

Frommer's Germany's Best-Loved Driving Tours, British Auto Association (Frommer's)

Frommer's Munich and the Bavarian Alps, Darwin Porter & Danforth Prince (Frommers)

Germany at its Best, Robert S. Kane (Passport)

Germany, Joanna Egert-Romanowskiej & Malgorzata Omilanowska (Eyewitness Travel Guides)

Germany for Dummies, Donald Olson (For Dummies)

*Germany Pocket Adventures, Henk Bekker (Hunter Publishing)

*Insight Guide: Germany (Langenscheidt)

*Karen Brown's Germany's Exceptional Places to Stay & Itineries, Karen Brown (Karen Brown Guides)

*Let's Go Germany (St. Martin's Press)

**Lonely Planet: Germany, Andrea Schulte-Peevers & Others (Lonely Planet)

*Michelin Green Guide to Germany, Amy S. Eckert & Owen Cannon (Michelin)

*Michelin Guide Deutschland (Michelin)

*Michelin Red Hotel and Restaurant Guide: Germany (Michelin)

Moon Metro Berlin (Avalon Travel Publishing)

*Munich and Bavaria, Andrea Schulte-Peevers, Jeremy Gray and Catherine Le Nevez (Lonely Planet Regional Guides)

Rick Steve's Germany & Austria, Rick Steves (Avalon Travel Publishing)

*The Rough Guide to Berlin, Jack Holland & John Gawthrop (Rough Guides)

*The Rough Guide to Germany, Gordon McLachlan (Rough Guides)

History & Politics

*A Concise History of Germany, Mary Fulbrook (CUP)

*After the Wall, Marc Fisher (Simon & Schuster)

A History of Modern Germany 1800-2000, Martin Kitchen (Blackwell Publishing)

*The Beer Drinker's Guide to Munich, Larry Hawthorne (Freizeit Publishers)

Berlin: The Downfall 1945, Anthony Beaver (Penguin Books)

Defeat in the West, Milton Shulman (Cassell Military)

Elections, Mass Politics and Social Change in Modern Germany: New Perspectives, Larry Eugene Jones (Cambridge University Press)

*Germans or Foreigners: Attitudes Towards Ethnic Minorities in Post-Reunification Germany, Richard Alba (Palgrave Macmillan)

*The Germans: When Lies Were Decreed As Truth . . . and a Nation Allowed Itself to be Deceived, Harry Conway (Shengold)

*Germany and the Germans, John Ardagh (Penguin)

Germany: A New History, Hagen Schulze (Harvard University Press)

*Germany in the Twentieth Century, David Childs (Batsford)

Germany in Transit: Nation and Migration, 1955-2005, Deniz Gürktürk (University of Cambridge Press)

Germany Inc., Werner Meyer-Larsen (John Wiley)

Germany Profiled, Barry Turner (Palgrave Macmillan)

Germany Since 1945, Pol O'Dochartaigh (Palgrave Macmillan)

Germany: The Third Reich 1933-45, Geoff Layton (Hodder Murray)

Jews in Germany, Nachum T. Gidal (Konemann)

*Journey to the White Rose in Germany, Ruth Bernadette Melon (Dog Ear Publishing)

Modern Germany: Society, Economy and Politics in the 20th Century, V.R. Berghahn (Cambridge University Press)

The Origins of Modern Germany, Geoffrey Barraclough (WW Norton & Company)

Party Politics in Germany: A Comparative Politics Approach, Charles Lees (Palgrave Macmillan)

Politics & Culture in Modern Germany, Gordon Craig (UWP)

Recasting East Germany, Chris Flockton & Eva Kolinsky (Frank Cass)

The Regions of Germany: A Reference Guide to History and Culture, Dieter K. Buse (Greenwood Press)

*The Rise and Fall of the Third Reich, William L. Shirer (Fawcett Crest)

A Traveller's History of Germany, Robert Cole (Interlink)

*Understanding Contemporary Germany, Stuart P. Parkes (Routeledge)

Miscellaneous

*America in the Eyes of the Germans: An Essay on Anti-Americanism, Dan Diner & Alison Brown (Markus Wiener)

Being Jewish in the New Germany, Jeffrey M. Peck (Rutgers University Press)

Culinary Voyage Through Germany, Hannelore Kohl (Abbeville)

Customs and Etiquette in Germany, Waltraud Coles & Uwe Koriek (Bravo)

Doing Business with Germany, Jonathan Reuvid (GMB Publishing)

Festivals of the World: Germany, Richard Lord (Gareth Stevens)

Garden Lover's Guide to Germany, Charles Quest Ritson (Princeton)

The German Way, Hyde Flippo (McGraw-Hill)

Germany by Bike, Nadine Slavinski (Mountaineers books)

Germany: in Pictures, Jeffrey Zuehlke (Lerner Publishing)

*Germany's Romantic Road, Gordon McLachlan (Cicerone)

Germany Today: A Student's Dictionary, Charlie Jeffrey & Ruth Whittle (Arnold)

*Germany: Unraveling an Enigma, Greg Nees (Intercultural Press)

*The Germans, Norbert Elias (Columbia University)

*Hitler's Sites: A City by City Guidebook, Steven Lehrer (Mcfarland & Company)

*Langenscheidt's Pocket Menu Reader Germany (Langenscheidt)

*The Longing for Myth in Germany: Religion and Aesthetic Culture from Romanticism to Nietzsche, George Williamson (University of Chicago Press)

Simple Guide to Customs and Etiquette in Germany, Waltraud Coles (Global)

Management and Organizstion in Germany, Thomas Armbruster (Ashgate Publishing)

*Prost! The Story of German Beer, Horst D. Dornbusch (Siris Books)

*These Strange German Ways, Susan Stern (Atlantik-Brücke)

A Traveller's Wine Guide to Germany, Kerry Brady Stewart (Interlink)

*Twelve Years: An American Boyhood in East Germany, Joel Agee (University of Chicago Press)

*Understanding American and German Business Cultures, Patrick Schmidt (Meridian World Press)

Universities in Germany, Werner Becker & Others (Prestel Verlag)

*Walking in the Bavarian Alps, Paddy Dillon (Cicerone)

*Walking in the Black Forest, Fleur & Colin Speakman (Cicerone)

*The Wines of Germany, Stephen Brook (Mitchell Beazley)

*Xenophobe's Guide to the Germans, Stefan Zeidenitz & Ben Barkov (Oval Books)

Appendix c: Useful Websites

German Websites

Berlin (⌨ www.berlin.de). The website of the German capital containing copious information about all aspects of life in the city.

Berlin Mietspiegel (⌨ www.stadtentwicklung.berlin.de/ wohnen/ mietspiegel). Provides information on rents in Berlin.

Bund (⌨ www.bund.de. A portal which provides access to numerous official websites. If you want to find out anything about what the government does and what it wants you to do, this is a good place to start looking.

Campus (⌨ www.campus.de). Information for foreigners thinking of studying in Germany.

Deutschebibliothek (⌨ www.ddb.de). Website of the German National Library.

Deutschebildungsserver (⌨ www.bildungsserver.de). Everything about German education.

Deutsche Welle (⌨ www.dw-world.de). Website of the German equivalent of the BBC World Service.

Ebookers (⌨ www.ebookers.de). Last-minute travel and hotel bookings.

Film (⌨ www.film.de). News from the world of the cinema in Germany and abroad.

Flugplan (⌨ www.flugplan.de). Flight timetables to just about everywhere.

Focus Money (⌨ www.focus-money.de). Financial information.

Frankfurter Allgemeine Zeitung (⌨ www.faz.de). The online version of Germany's premier newspaper.

Frankfurter Rundschau (⌨ www.frankfurterrundschau.de). The online version of Germany's principal liberal newspaper, the equivalent of *The Guardian* in the UK.

Germany Info (⌨ www.germany-info.org). Comprehensive information about many aspects of Germany in English.

Kultur Portal Deutschland (💻 www.kulturportal-deutschland.de). A portal which provides access to an array of German cultural information.

Munich (💻 www.munich.de). Information on rents in Munich.

Paperball (💻 www.paperball.fireball.de). Search engine which covers the German press.

Privatschulberatung (💻 www.privatschulberatung.de). Information about private schools in Germany.

Shopping24 (💻 www.shopping24.de). Web shopping portal for everything from flights to flowers.

Sport (💻 www.sport.de). Portal to comprehensive sports coverage but with the emphasis on football and Formula 1 motor racing.

The Voyage (💻 www.the-voyage.com). Website which provides information on German-British youth exchanges.

Weihnachten Info (💻 www.weihnachten-info.de). Information on Germany's many Christmas markets.

Wohnen (💻 www.immobilienscout24.de). Lots of links related to accommodation.

Wowi (💻 www.wowi.de). Website intended for landlords and investors in rental property but containing much of interest to tenants, particularly clear and straightforward coverage of changes in the law in this area.

General Websites

British Expatriates (💻 www.britishexpat.com). Designed to keep British expatriates in touch with events in and information about the UK.

Direct Moving (💻 www.directmoving.com). General moving information, tips, and numerous links.

Escape Artist (💻 www.escapeartist.com). One of the most comprehensive expatriate sites, including resources, links and directories covering most expatriate destinations. You can also subscribe to the free monthly online expatriate magazine, *Escape from America*.

Expat Exchange (🖳 www.expatexchange.com). Reportedly the largest online 'community' for English-speaking expatriates, including articles on relocation and a question and answer facility.

Expat World (🖳 www.expatworld.net). Information for American and British expatriates, including a subscription newsletter.

Expat Expert (🖳 www.expatexpert.com). Run by expatriate expert Robin Pascoe, providing advice and support.

Family Life Abroad (🖳 www.familylifeabroad.com). A wealth of information and articles on coping with family life abroad.

Just Landed (🖳 www.justlanded.com). Useful relocation information for 26 countries.

MASTA (🖳 www.masta.org). An advisory service for travel abroad including useful factsheets and personalised health briefs available by telephone (UK ☎ 0906-822 4100).

Save Wealth Travel (🖳 www.savewealth.com/travel/warnings). Travel information and warnings.

The Travel Doctor (🖳 www.tmvc.com.au). Contains a country by country vaccination guide.

Toytown Germany (🖳 www.toytowngermany.com). Extremely popular website for English-speaking expats living in Germany.

UK Trade Partners (🖳 www.uktradeinvest.gov.uk). A UK government-sponsored site whose main aim is to provide trade and investment information on just about every country in the world. Even if you aren't planning to do business abroad, the information is comprehensive and up to date.

World Health Organization (🖳 www.who.int). Health information.

Worldwise Directory (🖳 www.suzylamplugh.org/worldwise). This website, run by the Suzy Lamplugh charity for personal safety, provides a useful directory of countries with practical information and special emphasis on safety, particularly for women.

The World Press (🖳 www.theworldpress.com). Links to media sites in practically every country.

World Travel Guide (🖳 www.wtgonline.com). A general website for world travellers and expatriates.

APPENDIX D: WEIGHTS & MEASURES

Germany uses the metric system of measurement. Those who are more familiar with the imperial system of measurement will find the tables on the following pages useful. Some comparisons shown are only approximate but close enough for most everyday uses. In addition to the variety of measurement systems used, clothes sizes often vary considerably with the manufacturer (as we all know only too well). Try all clothes on before buying and don't be afraid to return something if it doesn't fit.

Women's Clothes

Continental	34	36	38	40	42	44	46	48	50	52
UK	8	10	12	14	16	18	20	22	24	26
US	6	8	10	12	14	16	18	20	22	24

Pullovers

	Women's						Men's					
Continental	40	42	44	46	48	50	44	46	48	50	52	54
UK	34	36	38	40	42	44	34	36	38	40	42	44
US	34	36	38	40	42	44	sm	med	lar	xl		

Men's Shirts

Continental	36	37	38	39	40	41	42	43	44	46
UK/US	14	14	15	15	16	16	17	17	18	-

Men's Underwear

Continental	5	6	7	8	9	10
UK	34	36	38	40	42	44
US	sm	med		lar	xl	

Note: sm = small, med = medium, lar = large, xl = extra large

Children's Clothes

Continental	92	104	116	128	140	152
UK	16/18	20/22	24/26	28/30	32/34	36/38
US	2	4	6	8	10	12

Children's Shoes

Continental	18	19	20	21	22	23	24	25	26	27	28	29	30	31	32
UK/US	2	3	4	4	5	6	7	7	8	9	10	11	11	12	13

Continental	33	34	35	36	37	38
UK/US	1	2	2	3	4	5

Shoes (Women's and Men's)

Continental	35	36	37	37	38	39	40	41	42	42	43	44
UK	2	3	3	4	4	5	6	7	7	8	9	9
US	4	5	5	6	6	7	8	9	9	10	10	11

Weight

Imperial	Metric	Metric	Imperial
1oz	28.35g	1g	0.035oz
1lb*	454g	100g	3.5oz
1cwt	50.8kg	250g	9oz
1 ton	1,016kg	500g	18oz
2,205lb	1 tonne	1kg	2.2lb

Length

Imperial	Metric	Metric	Imperial
1in	2.54cm	1cm	0.39in
1ft	30.48cm	1m	3ft 3.25in
1yd	91.44cm	1km	0.62mi
1mi	1.6km	8km	5mi

Capacity

Imperial	Metric	Metric	Imperial
1 UK pint	0.57 litre	1 litre	1.75 UK pints
1 US pint	0.47 litre	1 litre	2.13 US pints
1 UK gallon	4.54 litres	1 litre	0.22 UK gallon
1 US gallon	3.78 litres	1 litre	0.26 US gallon

Note: An American 'cup' = around 250ml or 0.25 litre.

Area

Imperial	Metric	Metric	Imperial
1 sq. in	0.45 sq. cm	1 sq. cm	0.15 sq. in
1 sq. ft	0.09 sq. m	1 sq. m	10.76 sq. ft
1 sq. yd	0.84 sq. m	1 sq. m	1.2 sq. yds
1 acre	0.4 hectares	1 hectare	2.47 acres
1 sq. mile	2.56 sq. km	1 sq. km	0.39 sq. mile

Temperature

Celsius	Fahrenheit	
0	32	(freezing point of water)
5	41	
10	50	
15	59	
20	68	
25	77	
30	86	
35	95	
40	104	
50	122	

Notes: The boiling point of water is 100C / 212F.

Normal body temperature (if you're alive and well) is 37C / 98.4F.

Temperature Conversion

Celsius to Fahrenheit: multiply by 9, divide by 5 and add 32. (For a quick and approximate conversion, double the Celsius temperature and add 30.)

Fahrenheit to Celsius: subtract 32, multiply by 5 and divide by 9. (For a quick and approximate conversion, subtract 30 from the Fahrenheit temperature and divide by 2.)

Oven Temperatures

Gas	Electric	
	F	C
-	225–250	110–120
1	275	140
2	300	150
3	325	160
4	350	180
5	375	190
6	400	200
7	425	220
8	450	230
9	475	240

Air Pressure

PSI	Bar
10	0.5
20	1.4
30	2
40	2.8

Appendix E: MAP

The map opposite shows the 16 German states and their capitals (indicated by black dots) and other major towns (white dots). Note that the cities of Berlin, Bremen and Hamburg are states in their own right. The states are listed below, with the German name in brackets where it differs from the English name.

Baden-Württemberg

Bavaria (Bayern)

Berlin

Brandenburg

Bremen

Hamburg

Hesse (Hessen)

Lower Saxony (Niedersachsen)

Mecklenburg-Western Pomerania (Mecklenburg-Vorpommern)

North-Rhine Westphalia (Nordrhein-Westfalen)

Rhineland-Palatinate (Rhineland-Pfalz)

Saarland

Saxony (Sachsen)

Saxony-Anhalt (Sachsen-Anhalt)

Schleswig-Holstein

Thuringia (Thüringen)

DENMARK

North
Sea

Baltic
Sea

Kiel

SCHLESWIG-
HOLSTEIN

Rostock

MECKLENBURG-
WESTERN POMERANIA

Hamburg

Schwerin

Bremen

HOLLAND

LOWER   SAXONY

POLAND

Hanover

BERLIN
Potsdam

BRANDENBURG

Magdeburg

NORTH-RHINE
WESTPHALIA

Weser

SAXONY-
ANHALT

Rhine

Dusseldorf

Leipzig

Elbe

Cologne

Dresden

BONN

HESSE

Fulda

Erfurt

SAXONY

BELGIUM

RHINELAND-
PALATINATE

Werra

THURINGIA

Frankfurt

Wiesbaden

Mainz

LUXEMBOURG

Main

CZECH
REPUBLIC

SAARLAND

Heidelberg

Nurenberg

Saarbrücken

FRANCE

Rhine

Stuttgart

BAVARIA

Danube

BADEN-
WÜRTTEMBERG

Munich

AUSTRIA

SWITZERLAND

State capitals

ITALY

INDEX

M

N

O

T

U/V

W

Z

SURVIVAL BOOKS

Survival Books was established in 1987 and by the mid-'90s was the leading publisher of books for people planning to live, work, buy property or retire abroad.

From the outset, our philosophy has been to provide the most comprehensive and up-to-date information available. Our titles routinely contain up to twice as much information as rival books and are updated frequently. All our books contain colour photographs and some are printed in two colours or full colour throughout. They also contain original cartoons, illustrations and maps.

Survival Books are written by people with first-hand experience of the countries and the people they describe, and therefore provide invaluable insights that cannot be obtained from official publications or websites, and information that is more reliable and objective than that provided by the majority of unofficial sites.

Survival Books are designed to be easy – and interesting – to read. They contain a comprehensive list of contents and index and extensive appendices, including useful addresses, further reading, useful websites and glossaries to help you obtain additional information as well as metric conversion tables and other useful reference material.

Our primary goal is to provide you with the essential information necessary for a trouble-free life or property purchase and to save you time, trouble and money.

We believe our books are the best – they are certainly the best-selling. But don't take our word for it – read what reviewers and readers have said about Survival Books at the front of this book.

To see our current list of titles, visit our website: **www.survivalbooks.net**

CULTURE WISE SERIES
The Essential Guides to Culture, Customs & Business Etiquette

Our *Culture Wise* series of guides is essential reading for anyone who want to understand how a country really 'works'. Whether you're planning to stay for a few days or a lifetime, these guides will help you quickly find you feet and settle into your new surroundings.

Culture Wise guides reduce the anxiety factor in adapting to a foreign culture; explain how to behave in everyday situations in order to avoid cultural and social gaffes; help you get along with your neighbours, make friends and establish lasting business relationships; and enhance your understanding of a country and its people.

People often underestimate the extent of the cultural isolation they can face abroad, particularly in a country with a different language. At first glance, many countries seem an 'easy' option, often with millions of visitors from all corners of the globe and well-established expatriate communities. But, sooner or later, newcomers find that most countries are indeed 'foreign' and many come unstuck as a result.

Culture Wise guides will enable you to quickly adapt to the local way of life and feel at home, and – just as importantly – avoid the worst effects of culture shock.

Culture Wise – the wise way to travel

To see our current list of titles, visit our website: **www.survivalbooks.net**

LIVING AND WORKING SERIES

Our *Living and Working* guides are essential reading for anyone planning to spend a period abroad, whether it's an extended holiday or permanent migration, and are packed with priceless information designed to help you avoid costly mistakes and save you both time and money.

Living and Working guides are the most comprehensive and up-to-date source of practical information available about everyday life abroad. They aren't, however, simply a catalogue of dry facts and figures, but are written in a highly readable style - entertaining, practical and occasionally humorous.

Our aim is to provide you with the comprehensive practical information necessary for a trouble free life. You may have visited a country as a tourist, but living and working there is a different matter altogether; adjusting to a different environment and culture and making a home in any foreign country can be a traumatic and stressful experience. You need to adapt to new customs and traditions, discover the local way of doing things (such as finding a home, paying bills and obtaining insurance) and learn all over again how to overcome the everyday obstacles of life.

All these subjects and many, many more are covered in depth in our *Living and Working* guides – don't leave home without them!

To see our current list of titles, visit our website: **www.survivalbooks.net**

BUYING A HOME SERIES

Buying a home abroad is not only a major financial transaction but also a potentially life-changing experience; it's therefore essential to get it right. Our *Buying a Home* guides are required reading for anyone planning to purchase property abroad and are packed with vital information to guide you through the property jungle and help you avoid disasters that can turn a dream home into a nightmare.

The purpose of our *Buying a Home* guides is to enable you to choose the most favourable location and the most appropriate property for your requirements, and to reduce your risk of making an expensive mistake by making informed decisions and calculated judgements rather than uneducated and hopeful guesses. Most importantly, they will help you save money and will repay your investment many times over.

Buying a Home guides are the most comprehensive and up-to-date source of information available about buying property abroad – whether you're seeking a detached house or an apartment, a holiday or a permanent home (or an investment property), these books will prove invaluable.

To see our current list of titles, visit our website: **www.survivalbooks.net**

OTHER SURVIVAL BOOKS

A New Life Abroad: The most comprehensive book available for anyone planning to live, work or retire abroad, containing surveys of over 50 countries.

The Best Places to Buy a Home in France/Spain: Unique guides to where to buy property in France and Spain, containing regional profiles and market reports.

Buying, Selling and Letting Property: The best source of information about buying, selling and letting property in the UK.

Earning Money From Your Home: Essential guides to earning income from property in France and Spain, including short- and long-term letting.

Foreigners in France/Spain: Triumphs & Disasters: Real-life experiences of people who have emigrated to France and Spain, recounted in their own words.

Investing in Property Abroad: Essential reading for anyone planning to buy property abroad, containing surveys of over 30 countries.

Making a Living: Comprehensive guides to self-employment and starting a business in France and Spain.

Renovating & Maintaining Your French Home: The ultimate guide to renovating and maintaining your dream home in France.

Retiring in France/Spain: Everything a prospective retiree needs to know about the two most popular international retirement destinations.

Running Gîtes and B&Bs in France: An essential book for anyone planning to invest in a gîte or bed & breakfast business in France.

Rural Living in France: An invaluable book for anyone seeking the 'good life' in France, containing a wealth of practical information about all aspects of country life.

Shooting Caterpillars in Spain: The hilarious and compelling story of two innocents abroad in the depths of Andalusia in the late '80s.

Wild Thyme in Ibiza: A fragrant account of how a three-month visit to the enchanted island of Ibiza in the mid-'60s turned into a 20-year sojourn.